THE ROUTLEDGE COMPANION TO HISTORICAL STUDIES

'In an impressive solo performance Alun Munslow succeeds in the difficult task of presenting a personal case for a re-thought history, while at the same time providing an invaluable work of reference.'

Beverley Southgate, *University of Hertfordshire, UK*

'Thirty years after the publication of Raymond Williams's *Keywords*, Alun Munslow's *Companion* has fulfilled a similar task for history. Although its entries are arranged alphabetically any resemblance to a putatively disinterested dictionary or encyclopaedia ends there. Like Williams's earlier text, this is a committed work. It calls on the reader to engage in a series of informed and rigorous reflections upon some of the key concepts and categories – the vocabulary – that currently constitute the most vibrant areas of historical thinking; an essential text that no student or teacher should be without.'

Keith Jenkins, *University of Chichester, UK*

The Routledge Companion to Historical Studies serves as a much needed critical introduction to the key issues, historians, philosophers and theories which have prompted the rethinking of history and its practice that has gathered pace since the 1990s.

Key concepts that address both how historians work and organise the past, such as class, empiricism, agency/structure, epistemology and hermeneutics, are examined through the ideas of leading historians and philosophers such as Vico, Croce, Collingwood, Elton, Kant, Nietzsche, Derrida and White. For this new edition many entries have been substantially updated and offer an essential analysis of the state of history thinking and practice today. Alun Munslow has added twenty-nine new entries including Carl Becker, Frank R. Ankersmit, Richard Rorty, Jean-François Lyotard, Jean Baudrillard, gender, justified belief, the aesthetic turn, race, film, biography, cultural history, critical theory and experimental history.

With a revised introduction setting out the state of the discipline of history today, as well as an extended and updated bibliography, *The Routledge Companion to Historical Studies* is the essential reference work for all students of history.

Alun Munslow is a well-known commentator on the nature of historical thought and practice, and founding and UK editor of *Rethinking History: The Journal of Theory and Practice* (Routledge). He is Visiting Professor of History and Historical Theory at the University of Chichester, and Professor Emeritus of History and Historical Theory at Staffordshire University. The author of a number of books on the nature of history, his most recent include *Experiments in Rethinking History* with Robert A. Rosenstone (Routledge, 2004) and *The Nature of History Reader* with Keith Jenkins (Routledge, 2004).

THE ROUTLEDGE COMPANION TO HISTORICAL STUDIES

Second edition

Alun Munslow

LONDON AND NEW YORK

First published 2000
by Routledge
2–4 Park Square, Milton Park, Abingdon, Oxon 0X14 4RN

Simultaneously published in the USA and Canada
by Routledge
270 Madison Ave, New York NY 10016

Second edition published 2006

Routledge is an imprint of the Taylor and Francis Group

Typeset in Times by The Running Head Limited, Cambridge
Printed and bound in Great Britain by Antony Rowe Ltd,
Chippenham, Wiltshire

British Library Cataloguing in Publication Data
A catalogue record for this book is available from the British Library

Library of Congress Cataloging in Publication Data
Munslow, Alun, 1947–
The Routledge companion to historical studies / Alun Munslow.—2nd ed.
p.   cm.
Included bibliographical references and index.
1. Historiography—History—20th century—Dictionaries.
2. History—Philosophy—Dictionaries. I. Title.
D13.M86 2005–06–21 907′.2—dc22

200515706

ISBN10: 0–415–38576–8   ISBN13: 9–78–0–415–38576–3 (hbk)
ISBN10: 0–415–38577–6   ISBN13: 9–78–0–415–38577–0 (pbk)

Dedicated to my parents
Beatrice Munslow
(15.9.1922–13.3.1999)
and
Samuel Wallace Munslow
(18.11.1924–3.11.1997)

CONTENTS

INTRODUCTION TO THE SECOND EDITION

In writing this new and considerably extended edition of *The Routledge Companion to Historical Studies* I have reflected further on why any historian should spend their time writing about history rather than just doing it. And the reason is, I believe, that no historian can 'do history' without recognising their own role in it. In my case, I consider history to be only in a limited way engaged with the past. As a written cultural practice it is clearly always about the present and its needs but, and maybe even more importantly, also the historian's wishful thinking. Maybe this is a function of growing older, but the more I reflect on history the greater is my confidence that my own diminishing future lies in trying to understand what will become of history as the future of the past. History is, therefore, always unstable, plastic, unsure and precarious. It is at all times being revised because it is made according to the requirements of the historian's own situation. In this sense the truth of the past (defined as what 'the past' means) can only ever be historical, that is, situated in the present and with an eye to the future. What this implies is disturbing to many historians: that knowing 'what happened' cannot of itself define the concept of historical truth. While 'knowing what happened' (in simple empirical terms) remains *a* basic of 'doing history' our 'thinking about' history forces us to abandon the comforting but fundamentally misleading notion that empiricism is *the* sole basis of history. Believing this has led us to the rather odd notion that the logic of history is (at its most fundamental level) an act of 'discovery'. This is wrong. History is, rather, a representation and, like all aesthetic representations, a creation.

This book – defined as an epistemologically sceptical vocabulary if you like – is about half as large again as the first edition, with twenty-nine new entries that I think address the growing concerns of historians generally with ethics and aesthetics, various 'post-ist' developments and their exponents, and specific forms of history that have become increasingly significant since the turn of the century. As before it can only remain a personal reflection on the nature and functioning of history. The bibliography is appropriately enhanced and updated, as is my 'Author's introduction'.

LIST OF ENTRIES

E

Elton, Geoffrey
Empiricism
Emplotment
Enlightenment, the
Episteme
Epistemology
Ethical turn
Event
Evidence
Experimental history

F

Facts
Film and history
Form and content
Foucault, Michel

G

Gender
Genre

H

Hegel, G.W.F.
Hermeneutics
Historical explanation
Historical imagination
Historicism
Historiography

I

Inference
Intellectual history
Intentionality

J

Jenkins, Keith
Justified belief

K

Kant, Immanuel

T

Teleology
Trope/figuration
Truth

V

Vico, Giambattista

W

White, Hayden
Women's history

AUTHOR'S INTRODUCTION
Rethinking history

In one important respect at least, this is no different from any other book written about the nature of history in that it is authored from a particular perspective. That perspective is the result of my experience and understanding of the post-empiricist challenge to history. As a history student in the late 1960s I was immersed in the then vogue for the social sciences, as social history became the constructionist successor to reconstructionist political and economic history. Then, in my final year as a postgraduate student, in 1973, the American historian Hayden White published his book *Metahistory*. Although its rethinking of the impact of the literary composition of history was not recognised until the early 1980s it is now viewed as signalling history's linguistic turn. But that decade also witnessed the emergence of cultural and women's history resulting from developments in European philosophy as well as cultural and linguistic theory, and practical politics. Although I was hardly aware of it at that time, the basic model of history that had been established and popularised as the direct result of the Enlightenment and its empiricist and positivist social science thinking, and of which social history had been but the latest manifestation, was being radically challenged.

With these developments in mind I have tried to provide a substantial critical introduction to the keywords, concepts and issues central to the rethinking of history that has taken place since the early 1970s (hence the reason that this new edition is substantially expanded). In my experience the major practical obstacle to understanding the contemporary challenge(s) to the standard model of historical study is the need for students of history to acquaint themselves with intellectual developments in other humanities disciplines and the ideas of thinkers outside the conventional boundaries of historical thinking and practice. To understand the challenge to history today requires knowledge not only of the accepted basics of conventional historical explanation and method, but also of the ideas of key theorists and practitioners of history, as well as awareness of ideas in cultural and critical theory, literature, linguistics and philosophy. This *Companion* is intended to introduce and contribute to this rethinking about history.

While this rethinking in 'doing history' has been most obvious in the development of cultural, gender and women's history, it has entailed a far more fundamental reassessment of how we come to know things about the past. The result has been to ask serious questions about the discipline's empirical foundations, the nature and functioning of evidence, the role of the historian and his/her use of social theory, the significance of narrative and genre as forms or modes of explanation, and the more radical post-empiricist idea that history is as much an invention of the past as a discovery of it. This has also raised other questions about objectivity and truth in historical study, the methodology required to guarantee them, and the impact of the form of representation in which its conclusions are described.

This rethinking of history focuses on two competing claims. The modernist claim is that 'proper' history's boundaries are those of the limits of its procedures for objectively understanding the evidence and creating truthful interpretations, and the postmodernist counter-claim is that the frontiers of history can be expanded by moving beyond the empirical to fully explore the argument that it is the culturally situated historian who, in his/her composition of the history text, is producing an invented narrative form of knowledge. It is the implications of these claims that this book addresses.

The *Companion*

The form chosen for this intervention in the debates over the thinking and practice of history today is that of a series of definitions ordered alphabetically. To ease usage all cross-references are written in **bold** when they are first deployed. Thus, in the entry on the 'linguistic turn', you will find references to Richard **Rorty**, **historical explanation**, **objectivity** and **truth**, all of which are entries in their own right. In addition, suggested other adjacent references are noted in brackets in CAPITALS. Moreover, a full bibliography of recommended readings is appended to each entry. A substantial index is also provided. By the fact of their selection and their definitions the entries are intended to demonstrate my assumptions and conclusions about the disputed nature of history today. My judgements reflect how I perceive the post-empiricist challenge to conventional thinking about the past. In the entry on 'evidence', for example, I acknowledge how the 'rules of evidence' are conventionally regarded as necessarily based on the assumption that **empiricism** constitutes history's basic procedure. My position, however, offers an alternative perspective. As an epistemological sceptic of a post-empiricist kind, I am prompted to ask if the 'rules of evidence' ought not to be viewed as a choice rather than a given around which there cannot be disagreement. In other words, empiricism is an option, not a prerequisite to history. This is not to say that we should dispense with accurate reference to the past, but it is to suggest that history can be conceived in many different forms. I have also provided an introductory chapter, called 'History today: critical perspectives', in which I try to set out the state of the discipline as it appears to me at the present time. This commentary chapter, which is also cross-referenced, may be read before, during or after consulting any of the entries. While it is not, of course, necessary to read this chapter at all, it does offer the overall rationale for the *Companion* and explains more fully my particular perspective on how to rethink history in light of the post-empiricist challenge and the contemporary efforts to neutralise its fundamental critique of our professional engagement with the past.

HISTORY TODAY
Critical perspectives

The empirical foundation: realist history

Modernism, as the product of the seventeenth- and eighteenth-century **Enlightenment**, produced the dominance of certain ways of thinking about how we create knowledge. Postmodernism in the late twentieth century, in a variety of recent manifestations such as **experimental history**, the **aesthetic turn**, the **ethical turn, post-structuralism, post-feminism, post-Marxism**, occasionally in the study of **gender** and issues surrounding **representation**, has directly questioned those ways of thinking. The two central modernist avenues to knowledge are sceptical **empiricism** and **positivism**, both of which directly influenced the creation of history as a discipline. Empiricism, defined as the observation of the **evidence** of our senses and the **inference** of its meaning, is the prerequisite to positivism defined as the derivation of the laws that govern the sensible world (the world known through the senses and which, in effect, can be mimicked on paper – the **mimesis** effect). Modernist or 'proper' history bases its claims to legitimacy as a discipline by discovering the meaning to the pattern of past reality: a meaning that is enduring and can be described or represented faithfully by the suitably distanced historian. The historian is equipped, therefore, to faithfully recover that which is gone. The historian's cultural significance resides in his/her ability to know the meaning of the past. Without this, so modernist history thinking claims, we are condemned to live in a perpetual present, an everlasting now without a sense of who we are and having abandoned the lives of those people who came before us. It is this claim of needing to know the past as it actually was, in order to know ourselves, which has been challenged through the post-empiricist revolution in history thinking. The challenge to modernist history has been to deprivilege its thinking as *the* way to knowing about our changing selves over time, and that our empirically derived knowledge of the past is an indispensable feature of our lives.

For modernist – unlike postmodernist – history, the written representation of empiricism's discoveries is an issue less significant than the verification and comparison of the evidence that will produce a **justified belief** about what happened and what it most likely means. In other words reality or the content of the past determines the form of history in the shape of the historical **narrative** (see FORM AND CONTENT; FILM AND HISTORY). This determinist and reductive empiricist priority of content over form was clearly expressed throughout the Enlightenment. Take the example of the Scottish philosopher and historian (of the common-sense school) Adam Ferguson (1723–1816) and his influential entry on History in the second edition to the *Encyclopaedia Britannica* (1780). Ferguson's view of history was emblematic of his age. He

3

viewed history as the account of **facts** arranged in the true order in which they actually took place, together with their **causation** and effects. This definition stated what was, for Ferguson, the 'natural' desire to know the past and, by maintaining the distance between the observer and the observed, to impartially and objectively represent such domesticated knowledge in the language of the **discourse** of history (see OBJECTIV-ITY; CLIOMETRICS).

Ferguson, in his modernist desire to exercise control over that which is 'out there', was, like his friend the sceptical empiricist philosopher David Hume, self-reflexive enough to realise that he had to organise his knowledge conceptually before (re-)presenting it as history (see CONCEPTS IN HISTORY; REPRESENTATION; MIMESIS). This process of conceptually organising the past I shall henceforth refer to as 'the-past-as-history'. As I think Ferguson realised, 'the past' and 'history' are not the same. Ferguson understood that there was a paradox or inconsistency/contradiction in mod-ernist thinking and it was the existence of the objective and yet engaged historian. This discrepancy, that historians write history but can be objective (see HISTORI-OGRAPHY), is unavoidable in modernist thought because one of the key features of Enlightenment-inspired modernism is the eighteenth-century bourgeois **liberal human-ism** that places the rational, purposive and undivided thinking self at the centre of all things – the intentional and centred subject, 'Man', 'the self', 'I' (see INTENTIONAL-ITY). The 'I' was also taken to be, as convenience dictated, 'reality' or 'the evidence'.

The autonomy inscribed in this ideology of the 'I' or 'the evidence' gave birth to many dualisms that still ground much Western analytical thinking, in addition to the inconsistency of the separation of the self/subject from the other/object, but also the conscious from the unconscious, fact from fiction, **truth** from invention, world from word, signifier from signified, real from unreal, and presence from non-presence. In the eighteenth century the philosophy of liberal humanism, as the ideology of mer-cantile and eventually market industrial capitalism, self-interestedly promoted the notion of the white, masculine and preferably middle-class, eurocentric, freedom-loving, self-conscious, knowing subject who could exercise sovereignty over himself, his environment, his future and his past (the masculine self, for example, exercising authority over the feminine other, or the imperial over the colonised) (see WOMEN'S HISTORY; GENDER; POST-FEMINISM; POSTCOLONIAL HISTORY). Central to the ideology of the 'I' is its belief in its own universality. The inconsistency is that the centred knowing subject, as the originator of and authority for knowledge, can still be capable of separating him ('I') or itself ('evidence') from the process of knowledge creation. The aim of this bourgeois ideological manoeuvre was to establish credentials for the argument that this is *the* natural, unalterable and universal process for knowing while it was actually fixing as immutable certain preferred or assumed social, economic and cultural conditions for that knowing.

For Ferguson **historical explanation**, although it must begin with direct reference to the known **event**, the need for conceptualisation as well as its description, required his-tory to be subject to the control of the historian. Ferguson recognised that as a result each historian would, in all likelihood, describe the past differently. But while, as he said, one historian may choose to build it around the names of statesmen and warriors, another around scholars and men of letters, this was still a matter of content rather than form. Avoiding the implications of the modernist inconsistency was easily done in fact, by insisting that factualism and its written representation were synonymous. Sceptical though he was about his evidence and its ability to reveal reality to him, Ferguson believed the language of historical facts was quite adequate to convey meaning through the pen of the knowing subject. He believed that if his historical narrative fell short of an absolute reflection of reality it had more to do with the shortcomings of the evidence and the historian's inference than his/her powers of representation. Empirical procedures thus avoided the relativist implications of the modernist inconsistency (see RELATIVISM). The implication of this has been singularly important: namely that objectivity and truthful knowledge of reality can be achieved by the honest historian, as revealed in the parallel or continuity/conformity between his/her explanation and the shape of the narrative (see MIMESIS). The match between explanation and the language of description should be as high as possible. The tighter that connection, the better the history.

As with all modernist disciplines, therefore, history possesses a **metaphysics** that comprises a coherent structure of inquiry into being and reality through the knowing subject (in this case the historian). One of the most awkward problems with the discipline of history, especially for new students, is, as we shall see, that it is not fixed or permanent in the sense that there is no universal and constant agreement about what it is and how it works. This can be seen in the way successive generations of historians have remade the discipline in ways that reflect their personal assumptions about how they prefer to engage with the past. There have been, for example, several versions of history that have been called the **new history** (some given the title as an official designation, others loosely referred to as new [approaches to] history). Indeed, in a very real sense every time a history is written it is never quite the same as the last one. This is obvious in the sense that there is usually a new interpretation of the same set of facts/data. This is because different historians have employed diverse conceptual filters, different arguments and definitions, and have, therefore, processed them in altered ways. Sometimes it is the same historian who has changed his/her approach. By way of illustration I started out as a hard-core social science historian thirty years ago, but I am certainly not one now. Hence, for me, the discipline is quite different – not just my interpretations or my database. It is different not because my powers of inference have strengthened or weakened, but because I hold to and endorse a radically changed set of assumptions and concepts about how I think knowledge of the past can be derived. So it is probably worthwhile remembering that history is never just about the past, it is always about itself in the present. History is very much a contemporary activity that always looks to its own future as well as responding to needs in the present. A one-time new history was, for example, postcolonial history, as was post-feminist history, or post-Marxist history. In a very significant sense, the future of the past is just as important as the past itself. The reason should be fairly obvious. It is not simply because the only access we have to the past is through the (changing) discipline of history, it is because all we have is history.

Because of the problematic nature of the discipline most historians would probably only agree on the general point that the architecture of history's metaphysics is that its content (the study, through the evidence, of change over time) dictates a way or, more realistically, several different ways of thinking about past reality and existence, that which philosophers refer to as its **ontology** (or ontologies). In turn, how historians conceptualise or categorise their knowledge of it is referred to as its **epistemology**. Putting it plainly, postmodern historians have a different epistemology than do their modernist colleagues. Indeed, because the term epistemology has itself been appropriated (by modernists) to describe how modernist historians think, postmodern historians have been forced to reject the term itself. The issues that have arisen concerning the conflict between the two approaches to history, and the resulting conflict over techniques deployed to go about acquiring historical knowledge which constitute the methodology or procedures of historical explanation, have been a major concern of **intellectual history** – the history of how historians have studied the connection between the past and history. Ontologically, then, modernist history holds that we can know, through the universal-centred knowing subject, the reality of the-past-as-history. This translates in turn into the epistemology of empiricism, positivism and inference. This is modernist history's epistemological turn.

Ferguson chose to believe that empiricism and positivism, as the key features of the metaphysics of 'proper' history, were founded on a particular set of assumptions. Upholding its truth-acquiring self-belief, 'proper (i.e. modernist) history' depends on four assumptions: first, that there is a past reality that is intrinsically knowable by the knowing subject through the discovery of its structural principles; second, that historical truth is found in the referential correspondence of the historians' facts to that structural reality, as derived through the conceptual procedure of inference; third, that language is up to the job of written representation; and fourth, that from these prior beliefs one absolutely basic law of human behaviour becomes evident: by knowing things about the real past we can reasonably conclude, as liberal humanists, that individuals act rationally and possess purposive agent intentionality (see AGENCY/STRUCTURE). These four assumptions directly dictate the procedures of modernist historical explanation. These procedures can be seen in the methodology and cliometrics of hypothesis testing, the **colligation** and verification of the evidence and the eventual determination of meaning through the establishment of causation. The conclusions inferred from this process of empiricism tempered by conceptualisation can then be offered in the form of truthful and historical descriptions (see JUSTIFIED BELIEF).

This thinking derives from that of the German philosopher Immanuel **Kant** (1724–1804), who argued that only when the knowing subject strikes the right balance between concept and fact will he/she know the truth about reality. Accordingly, modernist historical procedures are founded specifically on the process that philosophers refer to as abductive inference. Abduction is the imaginative derivation of meaning from a limited range of evidence. This process has three necessary steps: first, the outline of hypothetical but potentially explanatory concepts; second, the colligation or organisation of the facts through each concept in turn; finally, the verification of the most plausible/probable explanation by yet further reference to evidence and concept. The aim of this process is to find the pattern in what may seem at first blush to be disordered events. This process thus effects a convincing and meaningful explanation. This seeking out of probable connections is literally reasoning after the event. We should be quite clear here: the metaphysics of modernist history consists of an ontology of subject-centred knowable reality, accompanied by a dedicated epistemology and methodology of explanation that requires the separation of the discovery of meaning from writing it up as history (see HISTORIOGRAPHY).

The empiricist method of historical explanation, being explanation after the event, requires that historians distinguish between **a priori** and **a posteriori** forms of explanation. A posteriori explanations derive knowledge from the evidence through the three-step abductive inference process. Additionally, a posteriori thinking invokes Kant's belief that, because reality is independent of historians and their representations of it, history can know the truth of reality without reference to a known or desired outcome (see TELEOLOGY). Such teleological explanations are to be avoided, not because they necessarily preclude the truthful explanation of the intentions of people in the past, but because such explanations have tended to be open to the charge of wish-fulfilment on the part of those historians who are trying to discover the past's and hence history's inner directedness. To avoid this, the 'proper' modernist historian views historical knowledge as being created by factual inference and ordered and classified by the rational mind of the knowing subject rather than through a priori or propositional logic, the truth of which may be determined either by a known outcome – that is, driven teleologically – or more unusually without reference to factual reality at all (see CLIOMETRICS).

It should be clear by now that modernist historical methodology is an evidence-based empirical and a posteriori study, the aim of which is to generate a truthful and objective historical explanation founded upon the discovery of the relationship between causation and its effects. It suggests that its means of operation is a practical, pragmatic and constrained positivism in the application of only the best-attested theories of behaviour, or **covering laws**, which allow historians to explain individual human actions essentially as one would events in the natural world by acknowledging their regularity of occurrence (see POSITIVISM). Individual events are often explained as examples of a commonly occurring category (of events); that is, there is a pattern to be discovered in apparently disordered events. Not surprisingly, given the strength of the appeal of liberal humanism, the most common cause of patterned behaviour in modernist human experience is agent intentionality as explained according to the (liberal humanist) ontology of rational action.

In the last quarter of the twentieth century, self-reflexive modernist thinking, or call it postmodern rethinking if you prefer, suggests there is no longer a consensus about the ontological nature of existence and, therefore, the epistemology of history. History's procedures for the derivation of meaning are no longer universally accepted. Not all historians share the same measurement as to what it is that constitutes history (Hunt 1998). It is this uncertainty that has defined what are the three main approaches to history today, **reconstructionist history**, **constructionist history** and **deconstructionist history** (Munslow 2003b; 1997a). More recently these approaches have been argued to be the three major examples of **genre** in history. Reconstructionists, like the British historians

Geoffrey **Elton** and Arthur Marwick, and the Americans Jack Hexter and Gertrude Himmelfarb, are thin on the ground these days because they profess to believe that a genuine knowledge of empirical reality is achievable (Elton 1967, 1991; Hexter 1972; Himmelfarb 1989; Marwick 2001). Knowledge of empirical past reality is obtained, so they argue, through a restrained abductive inference that is soberly referential, shrewdly anti-theoretical (because concepts usually beg questions of the evidence), and non-judgemental. Its empirical procedures deliberately detach questions of knowledge (epistemology) from being (ontology), keeping knowing and being separate – the modernist inconsistency of which the American early twentieth-century historian Carl **Becker** was suspicious (see NEW HISTORY). This foundational thinking makes the centred knowing subject the only route to objective historical knowledge. The intentions of people long dead can be known by this method (and it must be perceived as a (the?) method rather than an ontologically situated epistemology) because people in the past were just like us – rational, purposive and knowing creatures. Without any discernible embarrassment reconstructionism accepts, as a gift from nature, a liberal humanist rationality translated into the epistemological gap, which it is claimed does and must exist between the knowing subject and the object of knowledge.

One of the more obvious, if not cheap, ploys of postmodernist historians has been to attack the easy target of reconstructionist history. The fact that not many historians today admit to being active or consenting reconstructionists has blunted the postmodernist message. While historians still seek the evidence to a knowable past, most claim not to be doing it in the manner of a knowing subject intent on discovering *the* meaning of an event. Few historians fall into the trap of viewing the past and history as one and the same. Instead the majority assert that they are practical or critical realists who know the implications of the modernist inconsistency, and they are also aware of the constraints imposed by history's textualism in its documentary raw materials, as well as their own manufactured writings. However, the mainstream contend that neither the modernist contradiction nor history's textualist basis mean it is impossible to do 'proper history' that, these days, must be a version or subspecies of constructionist history (see *ANNALES*). By definition, no modernist historians would regard themselves, therefore, as supporters of the **New Historicism** that constantly places the concepts of truth and objectivity under a question mark. Developing in literary theory in the past quarter century, the New Historicism views history as just another textual practice that is not privileged as a way of knowing. Indeed, every effort to 'discover' or reveal 'the truth' merely hints at the essential incompatibility of content and form and the demarcation between the two dissolves. The vast majority of historians prefer to believe that, though they are actively engaged in constructing the past, that activity in no way contradicts the basic principles of the discipline of history as a truth-acquiring activity.

Constructionist history (incarnated in the early part of the last century as the first 'New History' to be deliberately called that) comes with a vast range of subjects and a medley of complex theoretical models. The constructed nature of history is evidenced by its varieties. An increasingly popular historical invention is **oral history**. Until recently on the periphery of 'proper', that is archival and documentary-based history, oral history is an interesting case of the evolution of the discipline. Coming in a range of types or forms it varies from the heavily empirical to semiotic (linguistic) studies, via the analysis of memory, folklore, etc. Though firmly located as a form within the genre of constructionism, it is regarded as a special example of a new kind of social history that engages with the wider population outside the closed regimes of academic history as well as those groups often marginalised 'within history'. Still essentially regarded as an empirical-analytical and positivist activity, in the hands of more adventurous narrative-linguistic historians oral history is widening its epistemological boundaries and it clearly has strong connections with life writing and **biography**. It also raises fundamental issues concerning the relationship between the content of the past and the form we give to it as history (see FORM AND CONTENT).

The relevance of constructionist or mainstream history lies in its truth value, which is demonstrated by its conceptually informed empiricism and the correspondence theory of knowledge (Thompson, E.P. 1963, 1978; Appleby *et al.* 1994; Callinicos 1995; Kirk 1995; Windschuttle 1995; Bunzl 1997; Evans 1997a; Iggers 1997; McCullagh 1998, 2004; Snooks 1998; Warren 1998; Zagorin 1999; Tosh 2001; Perry 2002; Davies, S. 2003; MacRaild and Taylor 2004; Thompson, W., 2004). The constructionist historian, unlike his/her reconstructionist cousin, does not just cut and paste evidence with a minimum of conceptual glue. In his late 1970s attack on what he saw as the pernicious effects of what was a **structuralism** out of control in the work of French Marxist Louis Althusser, the British social historian E.P. Thompson summarised and set the standard for Anglo-American constructionist historians with a modified, liberal humanist-inspired, and materialist correspondence theory of history. In defending his (self-proclaimed humanist) version of Marxist history as a continuous dialogue between theory and empiricism as *the* way to recover the real (rather than the empirically impoverished structuralism of Althusser), Thompson renewed his vows to the belief in the knowing subject and rational action theory (see POST-MARXISM).

The post-empiricist challenge to Thompsonian constructionism has subsequently and primarily rested on questioning the intellectual assumption of referentiality and representationalism. What is claimed to be novel in this challenge can, in fact, be read in the work of a number of historians and philosophers of history stretching back to the Neapolitan philosopher Giambattista **Vico** (1668–1744) and re-emerging in the work of the Italian historian and historiographer Benedetto **Croce** (1866–1952), the British philosopher-archaeologist-historian R.G. **Collingwood** (1889–1943) and the British historian of the Soviet Union and successful part-time philosopher of history E.H. **Carr** (1892–1982). Each in their own way questioned the representationalist correspondence theory of knowledge that supports all four assumptions of proper historians. These critics confronted the claim that documentary **sources** are knowable because, in spite of their patent textuality and rhetorically compositional character, they possess a transparency of meaning (Bunzl 1997; Poster 1997; Munslow 1997b, 2003b; McCullagh 2004). Both reconstructionists and constructionists read the documents, therefore, for the reality they reflect, intending to re-present their meaning in a linguistically unambiguous historical text. What I have called the deconstructionist rendering of history disputes the possibility of this written representational correspondence between the word and the world. In other words, deconstructionist historians are rethinking modernist history's priority of content over form that results from the distinction of the ontological and the epistemological, but, and this is most important, they are not offering this reversal as an alternative, better and more truthful process. When modernist historians ask how else can we know the reality of the past – that is, its truth – except through the priority of its content, deconstructionist historians respond that it is not a matter of 'how else' because there is no single privileged route to it.

This reorientation has produced the so-called **linguistic turn** that has moved historical explanation to a discussion about the part played by language in producing and shaping historical meaning: what the American philosopher Richard **Rorty** (1931–) calls 'making true' (Rorty 1991: 4; Rorty 1992 [1967]). The issue is about the extent to which truth, objectivity and justified descriptions are feasible once we reverse the priority of empirical content (the past) over its form (the-past-as-history). Just how can we grasp the meaning of events through the representational form of the historical narrative? This raises what Hayden **White** (1928–) referred to in his 1973 book *Metahistory* as the poetics of history and what is increasingly referred to as yet another kind of new history. By the poetics of history White means an alternative to the conventional constructionist or practical realist theories or concepts of history customarily deployed to squeeze out the truth of the past. White is, for example, particularly antagonistic to Marxian history's assumption that in the evidence it has discovered *the* truth of the past that it can then successfully reveal as *the* narrative of historical materialism (White 1995). Arguably White was central to the inauguration of a new historical thinking and practice, one that is much more sensitive to its narrative and linguistic structure and creation.

The alarming result of rethinking the priority of content over form, of the past over history, is the collapse of what have hitherto been regarded as the partitions between history, fiction, perspective and ideology. The linguistic or narrativist turn has revitalised the relativist and/or anti-representational implications of the modernist inconsistency/contradiction. By placing form before content it means that what are also highly significant in creating a sense of the past are the ways in which historians organise, configure and prefigure it. The important issue becomes *how* we constitute those informing concepts, classifications, theories, arguments and categories that we use to order and explain historical evidence and generate meaning from it. Doing history in the post-empiricist age requires turning to the epistemological or explanatory power of our narratives, which in turn means re-examining the ontological–epistemological relationship.

However, such is the state of flux in historical studies that there have been a number of different reactions against the postmodern reversal of many epistemological assumptions. Increasing numbers of constructionist historians – especially in the field of **cultural history** – are saying they are tired of hearing how little historians can be sure of about the past and that the hitherto common and accepted belief in representationalism heralds a dangerous abandonment of realism. Among others – what we might call 'new empiricists' – there is an effort to domesticate the postmodern doubts usually summarised as epistemological scepticism. It has been claimed by these new empiricists that recognition of 'the role of narrative' in writing history is not really a bar to grasping the meaning of the past. There is a kind of 'post-linguistic turning' back to the primacy of empiricism. Knowable past reality thus continues to be accessible and we should be grateful to the small band of epistemological sceptics whose brief and now happily diminishing role reminded empiricists of the importance of language. However, it may just be that epistemological scepticism has actually done more than keep empiricists honest. Might it turn out to have changed our conception of the discipline at its most fundamental level?

The postmodern reversal: the real end of history or the end of realist history?

Recent variants of constructionist history, like the New Cultural History, the latest variant(s) of the New History and post-feminism, gender and post-Marxist history, have grown not only as the result of the deliberate acts of the historian behaving like a highly self-conscious **author**, purposefully borrowing ideas and concepts from other disciplines (like anthropology, sociology and philosophy), but also as a result of the wider intellectual movement of post-structuralism that emerged from literary theory in the 1970s (Hunt 1989; Munslow 2003b). This has become the vanguard of the post-empiricist/postmodern rethinking of history by accepting the full implications of seeing *both* the past *and* the-past-as-history as knowable only through the model of narrative discourse. Rethinking history as a discourse through which meaning is created rather than discovered stresses the cultural processes of knowledge creation and organisation, rather than simply seeing knowledge as some kind of discoverable given that is capable of a truth-insightful naturalistic representation (see NEW HISTORICISM). This is an alternative view that sees history as a truth-making rather than a truth-finding discourse. As such, history is conceived of as producing subjectivity. Such a rethinking of history, as critics like Keith **Jenkins** (b. 1943), Frank **Ankersmit** (b. 1945) and more radically Jean **Baudrillard** (b. 1929) and Jean-François **Lyotard** (b. 1928) argue, confronts the determining knowing subject with the situation that it is not he/she (in the shape of the liberal humanist) who is the privileged origin of meaning, but that other equally or even more important forces are at work (Jenkins 1995, 1997, 1999b, 2003 [1991]; Ankersmit 1994). In effect it is not the past or the evidence that originates history defined as a reality-duplicating process; instead all we have is a non-privileged cultural discourse I call the-past-as-history. We cannot 'get back' to a situation before the-past-as-history to view the naturally occurring past. The question is, then, what is the nature of the discursive and culturally determined character of the-past-as-history? It is revealed, I suggest, in the implications of the postmodern reversal of content and form.

This reversal, which holds that rather than the existence of a knowable past reality there is nothing but the-past-as-history, is derived from the work of European cultural historians and philosophers of history like Benedetto Croce, Jacques **Derrida** (1930–2004) and Michel **Foucault** (D.D. Roberts 1995). Jacques Derrida, heavily indebted to the German founding father of the idealist strand of **continental philosophy**, the philosopher Friedrich **Nietzsche** (1844–1900), rejects Anglo-Western analytical philosophy's preoccupation with the knowing subject, and its translation, as he describes it, in the power of presence in its explanations. According to Derrida this presence reveals itself in the precedence given to speech (content) over writing (form). This misleads us into believing that (the presence of) the speaker is evidence for the fixed origin of, among other things, author and agent intentionality and meaning, and that there must be a given or fixed connection between the signifier (the word) and the signified (the world) so we can legitimately believe in empirically derived essential meanings/truth of the referent. What I have called deconstructionist history does not stop at challenging the correspondence theory of knowledge and its corollary the representational theory of perception, and therefore, but following Derrida, the ontological belief that knowledge emerges from the intentional, centred individual and objective knowing subject.

The deconstructionist rethinking of the conditions and procedures for generating historical explanations is under obligation to the tradition of continental philosophy and a revised **hermeneutics** (the study of the nature of interpretation), which questions that the truth of external reality is waiting to be 'discovered' and is not the result of the human mind or its facilities for perception. Much of Derrida's deconstructive criticism hinges, therefore, not just on rejecting the idea that our understanding of reality is not dependent on its description, but also on the whole range of assumptions and preconceptions upon which modernist history is built: rational propositional logic, the correspondence theory of knowledge, empiricism, the contextualisation of evidence, representationalism, the truthful statement, inference and social theory constructionism.

One reason for the unpopularity of deconstructionist history hitherto (apart from the fact that it doubts that objective truth will emerge through the empirical process of prising open what is assumed to be a knowable past) has been the necessity to grasp some (fairly basic, it has to be said) philosophy. In order to make an informed judgement on post-empiricist history, historians need to become acquainted with the consequences of continental philosophy's divergence from the analytical tradition. This really began with the rethinking by G.W.F. **Hegel** (1770–1831) of Kant's epistemology or theory of knowledge. In opposing Kant, Hegel noted the historical situatedness, or what Nietzsche would later call the perspectivism of knowledge, specifically that the self, as the knowing subject, is not natural or universal, is not a given, but is a construction of time, place, discourse and ideology. This suggests that while an observer may not choose to doubt the existence of reality (and it takes little talent to be a referential being), its true meaning cannot be known or represented absolutely or, in fact, anywhere near the level of certainty that empiricism imagines flows from the contact between the word and the world.

Indeed, it cannot be other if we accept that the autonomous subject (that believes this) is itself a creation of a particular ideology and/or set of cultural practices (that demands this belief). It follows that, ontologically speaking, Kant's transcendent reason must be subject to a greater or lesser degree of relativism – to time, location, ideas, material circumstance, teleology, personal ambition, gender, **race**, language use and so forth. So knowledge of what the past means becomes, at the very least, relative not only to the evidence or to the reasonable correspondence of word and world but also to its composition as a narrative that exists within the larger discourse of the cultural practice I have called the-past-as-history. For Hegel the self-conscious knowing subject and the object of his/her attention must be ontologically related because they exist within the same cultural ground, discourse or practice. The modernist contradiction and much of the intellectual trappings of modernist thinking are – happily – swept away if we choose to view the knowing subject as no longer privileged, as itself determined rather than determining, and if we accept that knowing (as a self-conscious act) plays a crucial part in our understanding of being (Mensch 1997).

This Hegelian and Nietzschean idealism divided into several related domains of criticism in the twentieth century, notably a revised hermeneutics and a voguish post-structuralism. Hermeneutics defined as the process of textual interpretation was offered in a revised form, for example, by German philosopher Martin Heidegger, who suggested that we grasp the meaning of texts by virtue of our being in the world. Rethinking the ontological–epistemological relationship is particularly evident in the post-structuralist work of Derrida and Foucault as well as in a variety of **critical theory** thinkers starting with Max Horkheimer (1895–1971) and the Frankfurt School. As a direct consequence of their doubts over the knowing subject, both Derrida and Foucault rejected the possibility of a mirror-like picturing of external reality by the interpreter and the fixing of what Derrida described as the transcendental signified or ultimate meaning. They conclude that history, like all forms of culturally generated knowledge, is primarily about the uses of power and ideology, as well as the failure of representation. Whatever history is, it is not a culturally neutral depiction of past reality. Once historians come to terms with the full implications of this, history becomes the-past-as-history. History starts out as an empty signifier but does not remain so for very long. It is filled with the meanings and definitions we want. It is not a naturally occurring given.

The debates between representationalist and anti-representationalist philosophers that began in the early twentieth century with the likes of Ludwig Wittgenstein (in his later phase), Martin Heidegger and John Dewey, and developed more recently with Donald Davidson, W.V. Quine, David Dummett, Wilfred Sellars and Richard Rorty, have never had much impact on practising historians. Apart from the empiricist suspicion that dabbling in speculative philosophy is ultimately dangerous to the health, it is the metaphysics of its four assumptions that demands it must be in touch with the truth defined as correspondence to reality. Although this full-strength epistemological absolutism is cut by sceptical empiricism, there is still no modernist alternative to truth defined as correspondence to reality.

Deconstructionists, however, do not demand such metaphysics. Truth is not just an empirical phenomenon. They would say you only have to look at mainstream constructionist history to see that. Not sharing either modernist ontology (the knowing subject) or epistemology (that places content before form), deconstructionist or post-empiricist historians do not think the fissure between truth and its demonstration is resolvable by empiricism alone. Instead they resort to ethical decision-making; that is, historical meaning flows from what it is good or socially responsible to believe *about* the evidence of the past, rather than discover its *true* moral content. To discover the meaning of the Holocaust or to correct the prejudice of masculinist modernist epistemology is dependent not just on facts, but on the belief that certain things are wrong in a moral sense. The data does not 'tell you' it is wrong to kill millions of people. Referentiality is an integral part of the ethical and cultural landscape, to be sure, and those who derive and deploy the data do so with moral claims in mind. Reconstructionist, constructionist and deconstructionist genres of history are ethical as much as epistemological positions (see ETHICAL TURN). Beyond the simple factual or truth-conditional statement, historical truth is always ethically situated, culturally dependent and rhetorically created. Historical truth should, perhaps, be defined pragmatically as a term of commendation rather than as signifying an epistemology that can access the intrinsic meaning of the world that once was (Rorty 1991: 21–34; *Rethinking History: The Journal of Theory and Practice* 1998, Special Issue, 2(3)).

Before the advent of the postmodernist intellectual movements of hermeneutics, post-structuralism and post-empirical deconstructionism, there was, therefore, little reflection on truth beyond its correspondence definition. It fell primarily to Hayden White to point out that history cannot fathom the intrinsic nature of the past through reference alone because it is a rendered knowledge that creates its own reality through its composition and construction as a contemporary or historicist text (see HISTORICISM). The past may thus directly influence history, but it does not determine it. Post-structuralism, which rejects the modernist idea of the existence of deep structures that organise the world, and that make knowledge of the real possible, specifically addresses how we use language, how language uses us and, most significantly, language's inadequacy as a mirror of reality (Rorty 1979) (see MIMESIS). For writing the-past-as-history, post-structuralism raises, therefore, the issue of how figuration and rhetoric directly determine the power of the narrative to create meaning.

The cultural, gendered and ideological positionings of language, as focused through the self of the historian (traditionally the white, male, eurocentric and bourgeois-centred knowing subject) are constraints that inference and the referential truth-conditional statement cannot sidestep. History, like all cultural discourses, is an inherently and intensely relativist activity. The cold water of the post-empiricist reversal may be seen in how deconstructionists, and increasingly constructionists, reject the belief that history, through its claim to representational authority, must correspond to *the* objectively knowable past. This is not, as some scare-mongering realists still like to suggest, to deny the factualism of the past (Warren 1998; Zagorin 1999). Denying factualism, it is said, results in the monstrosity of Holocaust denial and produces propaganda history. Well, it may well do that when empiricists do elect to tell lies. But, fortunately, that has nothing to do with epistemic scepticism.

The deconstructionist historical consciousness is concerned instead with the relativism that exists in the process of creating the meanings of the-past-as-history because history, despite its referentialism, is a cultural practice, a discourse subject to other discourses. Deconstructionist history is not anti-factual or anti-referential but is intent on exploring how the meaning(s) of facts are constituted through their organisation in a coherent narrative. Consequently it welcomes the ever more widespread acknowledgement of the (rather mundane?) observation that it has never been the past that has produced varieties of history like those of **class**, or cultural history, or women's history. Instead it should be openly acknowledged that it is historians who author those histories as (very often) ethical ways of balancing or countering the prejudices of the modernist male and individualist history of which they disapprove – as ways of commending the truth of the-past-as-history as a moral as much as an epistemological or, for that matter, an empirical act.

Because it expresses the idea of the end of realist history rather than the real end of history, it is the question of narrative that is at the heart of the reversal. The deconstructive or Nietzschean-inspired incredulity about the epistemological basis of realist history has meant understanding the narrative form of historical writing and the array of **metanarrative** questions this entails. Do we live our lives as narratives, do historians retell *the* narrative of past events, or do historians invent *a* narrative in order to impose a conceptual (sense of) order on the sublime character of what once was and is now irrevocably gone (Danto 1965; Mink 1978; White 1987; Ankersmit 1994; Jenkins 2003 [1991])? Other metanarrative issues do, of course, focus on the fiction–reality polarity. The insecurity of the modernist notion that all historical texts must not only reference external reality but also be knowable as such prompts the question of whether historians should *primarily* address the cultural and language-use forms in which history is written and conceived. Should historians rethink their evidence and sources, not as the privileged centre of knowledge, but as *one* site of knowledge among *many*? The traces of the past cannot give exclusive historical knowledge, only an impression of pastness.

In other words, why not challenge the epistemological straitjacket of the priority of empirical content over narrative form? As both Nietzsche and later Derrida argued, the best reason for this post-empirical reversal is that knowledge of the real is understood through its metaphoric character (Bruner 1990, 1992; D.D. Roberts 1995; Mensch 1997). The assumption that our knowledge of the real past flows from the reciprocity of the concept and the empirical is nothing more than what the French cultural commentator Roland **Barthes** (1915–80) memorably called the reality effect of figurative language (Barthes 1957, 1967, 1977, 1988) (see REALITY/REALISTIC EFFECT; TROPE/FIGURATION). Because it is a second-hand narrative knowledge, Barthes concluded (in contradiction to the conclusion of Ferguson and all subsequent sceptical empiricists) that history is epistemologically little different in its imaginary narration from novels or plays. The consequence is that history, precisely because of its preconfigured narrative form, can never be more than a referential illusion (Bann 1984). This is famously and spectacularly seen in the way in which the vast bulk of historical narratives – even self-reflexive constructionist history – almost invariably omit the historian as author, the 'I', in favour of the 'real' source of historical knowledge, the evidence. This procedure, claims Barthes, is intended to sustain the distinction of knower and known (built on the modernist inconsistency) in order to retain history's claim to empiricist objectivity and its truth-knowing status.

At this point deconstructionist historians submit that sceptical-empiricism cannot escape the pre-figurative character of narrative. The historical narrative is never able to evade its prefiguration because of the rhetorical use of language, the deployment of rational action theory as a historical argument or any other kind of political, ethical, gendered, post-colonial, feminist, post-feminist or whatever other personal preference of the historian. Deconstructionists insist that it is not enough for historians to note history's constraints as a cultural discourse while at the same time invoking, as an escape clause, the belief that its empirical and inferential procedures will preclude untruthful interpretations. Deconstructionists hold that history's priorities should be ontological, anti-epistemological and rhetorical. Rethinking the nature of history in this way not only reverses history's metaphysical status but, which seems dreadful to most hard-hat empiricists, will not allow that history has in any genuine way been radicalised when all they have done is maybe tweak its methods, open up a new archive or import yet another bright theoretical idea from anthropology or sociology.

Post-empiricist history recognises, therefore, that history is a literary performance. It is first and foremost a deliberate and calculated written act on the part of the historian, rather than a neutral reflection or correspondence. Modernist history's claim to a mirror-like referentiality in its narratives (*the* narrative of the historian (form) reflects *the* narrative in the past (content)), and because of this its capacity to discover the truth cannot be sustained. History is an authored impression of pastness. In creating and acknowledging such an impressionistic process, and in recognising the parallel existence of the historian, history itself becomes the other, the 'alterior' (a mix of alternative and other). It cannot be identical to reality for it is an absence of, or an alternative to, reality. It can no longer conform simply to empirical definitions of truth. Historical truth is henceforth beyond the simply referential.

Historical truth, defined as that which people commend as being good within a defined community at a particular time, is a view much associated with the American philosopher Richard Rorty. Denying he is a relativist, Rorty insists he is an anti-representationalist whose aim is to highlight the historicist nature of knowledge in the humanities and social sciences. When Rorty claims that historical knowledge and the assumptions that underpin it are historicist, he means that every historical epoch or **episteme** possesses its own peculiar (rather than manifesting transcendent) measures through which it resolves what was, and is, truthful knowledge. The definition of historical truth for me is that, while a historical statement possesses referentiality, its meaning is the product of its linguistic composition as well as the discursive structure of the epoch in which it was produced. The concept of the episteme is central to post-empiricist criticism in that it alerts us not only that all historical periods organise the acquisition and utilisation of knowledge according to differing criteria and for distinct purposes, but, as Michel Foucault suggests, that the criteria for knowledge creation invariably revolve around the social distribution of power. Historians do tend to use 'the facts' to create their own meanings. If they did not then would history be much less revisionist (re-visionist) than it is?

The episteme signifies the connections that exist between all the separate discourses (for example those of science, medicine, philosophy, literature or history) that together generate those ontological and epistemological assumptions that mediate the power structures upon which they are built. The nature of the episteme reveals itself through the figurative and narrative structure of human thought. It is the troping process, or the way in which, say, the meaning of the Nazi-engineered Holocaust is created through the human capacity to recognise and articulate difference, which gives each episteme its peculiar cultural and epistemological signature. Like the historical agents whose lives they reconstruct/construct/deconstruct, no historian can escape from his/her own

epoch. As a result all written history is inflected by the textualised epistem
well that conditions the historian's existence (ontology) and production of the-past-
as-history (epistemology and methodology). It is being captured in time, space, culture
and language that precludes genuine knowing and, most importantly, true meaning.
Can any amount of referentiality avoid that?

As both Foucault and the leading philosopher of the linguistic turn Hayden White
suggest, historians are epochal as well as textual creatures and as such will prefigure
the historical field accordingly. Historians will, therefore, be influenced by the ontological and epistemological assumptions of the present. These assumptions, like the
four that are foundational to modernist history, are established and made manifest as
the historian brings his/her narrative, conceptual and ethical explanatory strategies
to bear on the content of the past. This is done through the activity of the **historical
imagination** in the initial process of troping or using figurative language to distinguish
meaning. The historical imagination next composes the historical narrative through the
deliberate sequencing of events to effect an explanation; what modernists would think
of as finding the pattern, but what for deconstructionists is the imaginative process of
emplotment. In the judgement of those persuaded by Vico, Nietzsche, Foucault and
White, how we emplot the-past-as-history is, unavoidably, a mediation of the episteme
in which we exist. The history we write is, therefore, always and unavoidably an engagement with our own age.

It is the function of the historical imagination not just to establish connections
between the documents, but also join the past, the present and the future. The historical
imagination, working through the troping process of analogy and difference, creates (as
opposed to discovers) causal links in the form of metaphorical descriptions. Metaphor,
as Donald Davidson and Richard Rorty suggest, is as much a cognitive and epistemological process as is empirical referentiality (Rorty 1991: 163). Indeed it is perhaps
more so, as those historians who choose to believe that the observation of the document stimulates knowledge misunderstand empiricism – specifically that the document
must have conveyed that knowledge. This is a simple but devastating error. What you
see is not what you get. Following Vico, Nietzsche and Foucault, Hayden White suggests how each age secures and applies its evidence-based knowledge by it being fixed in
a culturally provided figurative language. White's major contribution to post-empiricist
thinking is his suggestion that historians interpret the cultural history of any period by
reference to its dominant tropic prefiguration, while bearing in mind the epistemic signature of their own epoch (Munslow 1992). It is this self-consciousness on the part of
the historian that makes the-past-as-history self-reflexive and revisionist.

With this in mind Foucault suggested that historians should consult the historical
archive in order to establish the precise nature of that aggregate of discourses (particularly, in Foucault's case, the disciplines of history and medicine) that established
and developed what passed for knowledge within different historical epistemes or eras.
Foucault has advised historians to investigate the linguistic and narrative bases that,
when taken together, create rather than correspond to, or represent, the world of real
things. In other words historians should relinquish the quest for *the* original meaning
of events in favour of locating the culturally determined discursive practices, both then

and now, that provide the form in which linguistically based knowledge has been created. Hence the notion that meaning in history cannot be only factual but must be discursive. Not accepting this allows room for the specious argument that knowing that an event occurred in a certain way equates with 'the truth' of that event.

It certainly seemed reasonable to the British historian R.G. Collingwood that the inference of meaning in history is ultimately a projection of what is first imagined as a figurative relationship. Empiricism alone, Collingwood suggests, cannot provide the necessary connections. But Collingwood, ultimately a realist, drew back from what in later years has become the post-empiricist and Foucauldian tropic or poetic end result to his line of thought. Collingwood argued that metaphor is the mechanism that enables the historian to create the correct mental picture of things as they actually occurred. Collingwood, however, missed the point understood later by Foucault and White, that history is about the textualised rendition and exploration of cultural power. This failure to rethink history, or think the unthinkable, that facts and truth do not necessarily correspond, has led mainstream historians to share the conclusion of the philosopher of history William B. Gallie, when he defined history as getting at *the* story based on the evidence (Gallie 1964).

The big question, so forcefully put by Hayden White, is does the-past-as-history correspond with *the* story that exists in the evidence? How can *a* historian's narrative discover *the* real narrative (the modernist homology of the empirical and the descriptive)? White, while believing in the past at the factual level and in our capacity to represent it with some accuracy, maintains that, nevertheless, historians do not discover *the* story. Instead we invent emplotments to explain the facts (some to 'find the truth') because we prefigure the past as a history of a particular kind. The stories we impose on the past are imposed for reasons that are contemporary cultural, linguistic, conceptual, discursive, ideological – for reasons that are epistemic. Historians always have an end in mind. The nature of our present existence demands it (even if it is that particular cultural demand that they get *the* truth). History, for White, is always written teleologically through its prefiguration. In other words, choices are made about how the-past-as-history is composed and configured, because of wished-for ends; for some it may be the need to discover the truth (however they define that), while for others it is the wish to establish and promote a variety of intellectual, gender, ethical, cultural, economic or social programmes.

By assuming a different set of conditions to those of modernism, deconstructionist historians insist that the metaphysics of history will be different. If we do exist in a condition of being and knowing that is postmodern, encompassing an ontological uncertainty about knowable reality, then a decentred subject, who is a subject of his/her material, cultural, ideological and linguistic situations, will no longer invest much time or effort in the natural referential correspondence of the historians' facts to reality through inference. He/she will, moreover, not accept language as being up to the job of direct representation, and may well find him/herself agreeing that the liberal humanist assumption of purposive agent intentionality is little more than a male, middle-class, heterosexual, ideological fiction that has served its time. Our engagement with the past has now entered a new period, one where all the old verities must be challenged.

Conclusion

Deconstructive or post-empiricist history is most clearly manifest in its anti-modernist assumption that 'proper' history is overdue for a rethinking of its metaphysical status. Writing the-past-as-history is not only about epistemology – it is an ontological issue. The historian is an author in a particular state of existence, not an impersonal observer outside time and place. What is the point of pretending it is not me creating the-past-as-history? Relatedly, and perhaps most importantly, because I have a moral sense that some things are wrong and others right, an important element of post-empiricist history is that I do not expect my evidence to direct me to objectivised knowledge, that the facts will contain *the* ethically correct answer. Of course, the issue of the historian's ethical choice is not resolved by simply acknowledging this situation. I would suggest that, given the unavoidability of their moral making, historians recognise that history is as ethical as any historicist, constructed and cultural narrative can or cannot be – in other words, ethics and representing the-past-as-history exist in the same universe of narrative making. Now, I don't know whether historians offer a value added to the world of ethical living or not, but if they do, I believe it is the result of their demonstrable sincerity and prudence in thinking *about* history as an aesthetic form of representation, rather than just doing it honestly – in other words, specifically re-situating the empirical-analytical epistemological model with its commitment to meaning through what happened and knowable agent intentionality. In order to acknowledge the relationship between the construction of the history narrative and ethics, I recommend that historians first deconstruct the discipline, recognise its post-epistemological character, and thereby be more ready to recognise that their historical representations are as much about what they have faith in, as they are anything else. To put this plainly, the writing of history may be seen as a series of narrativised political and value judgements that enthuse and saturate the most credible present- and future-orientated historical writing. Because we cannot avoid history being an ethical activity we must acknowledge the honest moral choices we make as we construct it as a representational narrative about the past. We should not assume that ethics exist in the past and that from that locale such ethics can be mined. So, I suggest, it is the *writing* of history that allows us to make choices on political standards and ideals. Of course, not understanding this leaves historians in danger of assuming that they can learn from the moral stories assumed to exist in the past. But what is crucially important is the professional requirement that as moral commentators historians are always subject to the criticism of their readers (see ETHICAL TURN).

Post-empiricist history is an authored story constructed out of evidence, argumentation, language, culture and my own ethical choices. My history is historicist and epistemic, which makes it a contemporary emancipatory cultural practice that does not depend on the desperate, distressed and distracted modernist insistence that empirical reality will equate with truth. Moral argument does just as well when I want to believe things about the past. It is not necessary, in other words, that in order to know or believe things about the past I must solely depend on its documentary traces as the only vessels for truth or meaning (which I presume I will always want in some form or another). Instead, historical study can escape the suffocation induced by seeing evidence as the be-all and end-all of history by being open to non-conventional modes of historical representation. History can be experimental in its form and wider in what it chooses to call historical knowledge (see EXPERIMENTAL HISTORY). We can learn, as Hayden White suggests, by exploring the content of the form.

For me the-past-as-history is a cultural history that is an overtly critical discourse. It is anti-representational in that it questions a sceptical empiricism paraded as the only game in town. My history collapses knowledge and representation, and representation and being, and enjoys the permeable relationship of past factualism and the present. It critiques conventional concepts of materialist-inspired cause, effect and inference, emphasising instead the ideas of the historian, his/her ideology and perception, and how language and description create meanings. To recognise that we are textualised creatures widens and deepens the range of the historical project – it has already – moving historians into new areas of identity construction, embodiment, cultural appropriation, liminality, and the 'other', but above all into thinking about how we construct the-past-as-history out of our ontological and epistemological principles.

Much in our thinking about history has thus changed in the past quarter-century. Few historians today are unaware of the invented nature of their work. Few would try to deny that they are creatures locked in the cages of time and language, or that they can or want to shake off ideological preferences, or that they do not have gender, race, sexual, class and cultural predispositions and affiliations. Most historians today are also aware that they construct narratives under the impress of language, tropes, preferred arguments and emplotments that are plausible because they resonate epistemically. But the bulk of the historical mainstream are still reluctant to let go of the modernist wreckage and accept that we cannot know the true meaning of the past. They continue, therefore, to endorse the idea that we can have a direct and essentially unmediated access to past reality through referentiality alone. In the turn from epistemology to language I would suggest, however, that historians no longer need to read documents as Adam Ferguson did, solely and exclusively as referents, and do not need to assume there is knowable truth locked within them. Though it is referential in the strict sense that it refers back to what we feel justified in believing once happened, history might be better understood in the future as what it plainly is, primarily a mind- and language-dependent representation – a narrative-making activity – and its cultural importance and utility should be judged in those terms.

A

AESTHETIC TURN

While it is probably true that the empirical-analytical conception of history is the model of history adopted by most historians, the big issue in the past forty years or so has been the status of history as an aesthetic, specifically a literary construction of the author-historian – in effect a representation of the past. Historians are still fond of thinking of 'Big Questions' in history being about fresh interpretations based on new evidence accompanied by dramatic arguments, fresh concepts and novel theories. But, thanks to the unceasing and rigorous analysis of narrativist (and, depending on how you define their work, anti-narrativist and anti-representationalist) philosophers and theorists of history primarily (following in the wake of Giambattista **Vico**, Friedrich **Nietzsche** and Benedetto **Croce**) Louis O. Mink, Paul Ricoeur, Hayden White, Fredric Jameson, Frank **Ankersmit** (who may be regarded as the modern intellectual progenitor of the aesthetic turn), Richard **Rorty**, Hans Kellner and Keith **Jenkins**, it has become very clear that the biggest question in history is the disciplinary one of whether history is a **narrative** representation of/about the past, as much as it is anything else (see LINGUISTIC TURN; NARRATIVE; REPRESENTATION; NEW HISTORY; Jean BAUDRILLARD). That 'anything else' is either an extensive reconstruction that is fundamentally evidence- and sources-based or, more sophisticatedly, a construction that has an explanation that both best fits the evidence and is appropriately supported and scaffolded by the most suitable conceptual apparatus(es) as its guiding principle(s) (see CONCEPTS IN HISTORY; CONSTRUCTIONIST HISTORY; RECONSTRUCTIONIST HISTORY).

Sometimes also referred to (confusingly) as the linguistic turn and/or the **New History**, the nature and significance of aesthetic approaches to history contrasts with mimetic representation (see MIMESIS). The latter – through the power of representation – claims to re-present the past as it really was. The aesthetic move or turn assumes that there is always a space between any representation and what is being represented. The aesthetic turn insists that this space is the key to understanding the nature of historical analysis. We need to consider what history is, as much as what it is of. As Frank Ankersmit has argued, historians should be aware of the essential aesthetic nature of history not to replace rational thought or empiricism but to widen the possibilities of the study of the past. The central thing to be decided by every historian is how they (you and I) respond to the critical epistemological question of whether the meaning of the past is primarily determined by its content (the past itself) or its form (written, visual, oral, digitised, pop-up book, graphic novel or even performance), or some indeterminable combination of the two (see FORM AND CONTENT). If you think it is its content then the aesthetics of its form(al) construction are not epistemologically significant. You will believe that the fact that history has to be written does not get in the way, as the realist philosopher of history C.B. McCullagh maintains, of 'providing credible, intelligible and fair history' (McCullagh 2004: 194). If, however, you harbour uncertainties, as I do, about history as some kind of facsimile of the past because it is a written or some other kind of construction, then exploring its aesthetic character becomes an imperative.

The usual definition of aestheticism – in literature – is that it is a principle that views beauty as an end in itself and that the arts in general ought not to become the subject or promoter of a particular moral view of the world. This definition does not really help historians in determining what is history as an aesthetic act in that historical explanation is unavoidably **ontological** and subjectively rooted in ideological beliefs about how the world now and in the past works. Because history is always located, fettered, positioned and perspectival, trying to keep history out of politics is probably a meaningless exercise. Few historians of a constructionist ilk are aesthetes who would take the notion of 'art for art's sake' and translate it into 'history for history's sake'. Such a purist position might be closer to the aims of reconstructionist historians who (like Peter Gay below) tend to believe that knowing what happened is some kind of insulation against ideology (see RECONSTRUCTIONIST HISTORY). Much more useful in understanding the recent turn toward viewing history as an artistic act is the notion of aesthetics as the rational analysis of the character of history as a rhetorical and narrative-making process and as an account of how 'past things' and 'present words' are made to connect.

Historical narratives are compound literary constructions the aim of which is to tell a story based on the available evidence of what happened and which, eventually, the historian believes they are justified in saying is the true (or the most likely) story (see JUSTIFIED BELIEF). But, because all histories are literally/literarily made – that is, they are assembled as a string of selected and linked events and recounted in the shape of a narration/discourse – there is an ineluctable element of 'narrative technique' and, for Frank Ankersmit, an underpinning general theory of representation as well as many

'true statements' and also adherence to the historian's preferred ethical rules and standards (Ankersmit 1983; 2001: 95). This, for Ankersmit, is the complex and what he calls the 'aesthetic' basis of all history writing. In other words, our theory of representation precedes cognition (true statements about that which is to be represented) and our value (ethical rules) assumptions. The key principle of the aesthetic turn is to recognise that in giving a narrative form to the past the act of history writing is unavoidably 'de-forming' it. It is 'turning' it into something else – that which we call history. Though this is a banal observation the consequences are far from insignificant for what we think history is, the purposes to which it can be put, who or what writes it, the investment we make in its truth-acquiring characteristics and, ultimately, which histories we should invest most time in reading when we want to decide on the moral precepts and standards we wish to adopt. To reiterate, the main principle of the aesthetic turn is that history as a narrative representation can only be compared with other narrative representations, and not with the past itself. All else about history flows from this (see EVENT; FACTS; INTELLECTUAL HISTORY; ETHICAL TURN).

There has long been recognition of the historian's art and its consequences for knowing things about the past. The best-known riposte to the aesthetic turn was offered, even before the philosopher of history Peter Gay or anyone else acknowledged it as 'a turn', in his *Style in History* (1974), a study of the written histories of Gibbon, Ranke, Macaulay and Burckhardt. In this he recognises what he views initially as the reciprocal connection between content or matter and form or style. After a long and fascinating disquisition he maintains that the historan's 'literary devices are not separate from historical truth, but the precise means of conveying it. It is this aim that principally dictates his [*sic*] stylistic choices' (p. 216). In other words, in creating a narrative the historian is being told how that narrative will connect events together.

Gay's conception of style is complex and not just limited to damning the use of rhetorical trimmings. He recognises the use of figurative language (see TROPE/FIGURA-TION) and the compressions of time that historians unavoidably have to create in turning 100 years into a book of 80,000 words, but he views them – as most historians still do – as 'devices' that should only serve the reportorial function of the historian. Hence it becomes possible to argue that history is not a construction but a discovery and that issues of representation simply melt away.

At a fundamental level this denies the epistemological consequences of the actuality of writing history. It fails to acknowledge the genuine ontological interventions of the historian by assuming not just that there is the possibility of a history for history's sake but that historians are duty-bound to believe it and work according to its principle. History for Gay remains a mode of realist communication rather than a storytelling exercise. History is the narration of past events in which, ideally, no traces of the historian/writer appear but, when they do, they must be regarded as supplementary and subordinate to the larger demands of 'what happened'. Excluded from history should be all autobiographical linguistic forms and references to the situation of the author-historian (note that earlier in this entry I referred to myself as I am doing again now – an act that would be regarded as an unnecessary and dangerous subjective intervention by Gay). As the literary critic Émile Benveniste (1902–76) argued, the act of speech is the locus of meaning. The historian is never a dispassionate reporter but is always an interlocutor even though he/she tries to maintain their non-identity. In effect historians and the language they use are always an 'absent presence'.

The aesthetic turn is a primary and highly significant development in grasping the full nature of history. It directs us to acknowledge that history is part of the trajectory from the past world to its present representation but, and even more significantly, that history loops back to become an element in the trajectory that produced it. Through a realisation that history, whatever its referential aims and purposes, is always a narratological and hence an aesthetic activity and that it can only be compared with other iterations of itself (as narrative representations can only be compared with each other – in what for many appears to be a disquieting self-referentiality), the analysis of narratives raises all the central issues about what is history, not least its linguistically authored character and what precisely, as an aesthetic act, it signifies and what it tells us it knows.

Further reading

Ankersmit, F.R., 2005a, 2005b, 2001, 1998a, 1994, 1983; Ankersmit, F.R. and Kellner, H., 1995; Benveniste, E., 1971; Danto, A., 1998, 1997, 1981, 1968b; Gallie, W.B., 1964; Gay, P., 1988 [1974]; Genette, G., 1990 [1983]; Goodman, N., 1968; Hammermeister, K., 2002; Hunt, L., 1989; Jameson, F., 1976; Jenkins, K., 2003; Jordanova, L., 2000; Kellner, H., 1989; Lorenz, C., 1998, 1994; McCullagh, C.B., 2004; Megill, A., 1985; Mink, L., 1978, 1970; Munslow, A., 2003b; Ricoeur, Paul 1994 [1978], 1984, 1984, 1985; Roberts, D.D., 1995; Rorty, R., 1989.

AGENCY/STRUCTURE

Among the best-known of the many dualities and oppositions in the organised study of the past is agency *and* structure. To more fully grasp the significance of the duality we also need to address the relationship as one of agency *or* structure. But to understand agency and structure as fully as we can we must recognise that both exist *within* each other – they may be viewed as integrated. In other words, all agents work within structures and all structures have agents and they interact through time. In essence, agency and structure provide the key battleground for historians as they answer (in their different ways as they pursue their own narratives for the past) the 'how' of history. Indeed, they have come to represent two distinct approaches to, or ways of thinking about and doing, history – 'how' to do history. These can be referred to as either an individualist or a structural approach to historical change (see CLIOMETRICS; COVERING LAWS).

As they are orientations devised by historians these approaches do not necessarily exist in the past itself (some historians will claim that they do, others that they do not); they have the status of concepts construed by historians about what they feel justified in believing causes change over time (see CAUSATION). Some historians prefer to emphasise the role of the individual in the past, others place individuals within larger more powerful structures, and yet others try to see the two interacting in a variety of more or less complex ways. Perhaps the most famous analysis of agency and structure (though he didn't put it in those terms) was when Karl Marx argued that human beings (he actually said 'men') make their own history, but not just as they please, rather under circumstances encountered from the past. In other words, human beings make themselves within forces over which they have little direct control. In Marx's case it was the evolving mode and means of capitalist economic production.

As the early twentieth-century Marxist philosopher Antonio Gramsci acknowledged in his work on the role of the intellectual in historical and social change, the connection between agency and structure is probably not quite as obvious or as easily determined as Marx liked to believe. Just try to figure it out in your own life. What affects your power to choose one course of action over another? How much choice do you *really* have? Are your decisions constrained primarily by your place in the capitalist production process or by what else you think controls your life? What is probably clear today, even in wealthy Western society, is that no one has unfettered choice, that there are always constraints upon our freedom to do as we want. In other words, forces beyond our control always inhibit our

agency/power of action and dominant ideas (a kind of intellectual hegemony) that so often seem to operate at the level of 'common sense' also confine our freedom of action (though we can work out a counter-hegemony if we wish to make the effort). The French sociologist Pierre Bourdieu tried to integrate agency and structure with his concept of *habitus*, in which he argued that agents exist in a social space constructed out of power relations and reinforced by social practices that are usually (economic) **class**-based.

Another issue is that our chosen path of conduct (our social practices/decisions) is not always rational and so we often cannot work out why our decisions cannot be followed through to the conclusion for which we hoped, reaching the objective we aimed for. However, agency also means the ability of human beings to adapt to or plan ahead for changing circumstances, which are often manifested as a variety of structures of power as well as unexpected happenings/**events**. Agency also is taken to mean the ability of people to influence, if not ever actually control, the situation in which they find themselves.

If all this is then applied to historical actors in the past it should be clear how many problems arise for historians when trying to interpret the actions and decisions of such people in the past. The key issue is usually the perennial one of **causation**. It is difficult enough to determine the causal relationship between events and, as R.G. **Collingwood** and Benedetto **Croce** and later history theorists like Mark Bevir and Frank **Ankersmit** have discovered, it is extremely difficult to accurately ascribe cause in human choice even if some historians, and Collingwood in particular, placed such a strong emphasis on human agency (see INTENTIONALITY). So, although it is complex, establishing causes between events is usually regarded as less problematic than figuring out what made people act the way they did. It does, however, often become infuriatingly difficult when the search turns toward finding causes between events that must at some point encompass human agency. Just how important in a strictly causal sense, for example, was Alexander Berkman to the development of the American anarchist movement at the end of the nineteenth and start of the twentieth century? Or did President Truman's decision to drop the atomic bomb on Japan really – as is often claimed – bring the war in the Far East to a much more rapid end, thus possibly saving the lives of thousands of US servicemen and -women?

Agency also raises another central matter for all historians about whether it is 'good practice' to apply metaphors, explanations and ultimately interpretations of a past culture not derived from the discernible and evidenced thoughts that could have purposefully directed the actions of agents. Should historians use concepts not known to the historical agents themselves? Thus while it might make sense to a modern audience to talk of English imperialism as a cause of the American Revolution, it was not a term known to historical agents in 1776. So to produce a detailed historical explanation of the American Revolution based on the concept of English imperialism raises very serious issues about how historians construct the relationship between agency and structure. It seems that most historians are aware of this problem but to do away with 'the invented concept of structure' would make history at best sterile and at worst probably just tediously antiquarian.

So just what do historians understand by the concept of structure? An individualist historian will have a view on the essential nature of being and existence that assumes agency to be the power of individual human beings to take action and effect change at all levels (social, political, economic, cultural, etc.). By contrast a historian who adopts structural ontology is one who emphasises the existence of processes and institutions that are external to and ultimately determining of human choice. Indeed human beings may end up, as the historical theorist Christopher Lloyd notes, when viewed from this perspective, as 'passive carriers of collectively generated social forces' (Lloyd 1993: 42). Historical change (economic, social, cultural, political or whatever) would be interpreted in this light as originating with the human social totality and it is merely the function of people to give effect to it. The French Marxist Louis Althusser argued, for example, that individuals are 'interpellated' ideologically into situations of intellectual subservience by material forces – most usually in the form of social institutions like the Church, media and educational structures – that they cannot control. Agency thus ceases to exist as subjects ('freely') accept their subjection. The humanist Marxist historian E.P. Thompson among others fiercely rejected this kind of thinking when he denied 'the poverty of (structural) theory'.

For most people (in post-**Enlightenment**, Western, capitalist and supposedly 'democratic', multi-cultural, **gender**-blind societies), lack of ultimate choice seems an unlikely situation and somewhat unpalatable. It appears more desirable to believe that people have substantial self-conscious decision-making power and that ultimately individual action (or to be more precise millions of self-conscious individual actions) in pursuit of self-improvement as well as collective social responsibility precedes structures and their power. But such a picture is as ideological as any other and probably no more 'real' than is its polar opposite, and for a historian to deploy either (or any other) in their engagement with the past is to construct history as a projection from the present backwards. The real 'problem' here is that it cannot really be done any other way (so should it probably not be seen as a 'problem' at all?). Historians cannot dump their ontological and epistemological beliefs at the door of the archive and because of that it might not be worthwhile seeing agency and structure and their relationships as anything other than a historian's preference for organising the past in order to turn it into a culturally utilitarian practice much as the earliest twentieth-century exponents from the *Annales* school did.

Structure (or structural) history was a term used by *Annales* historians to designate that kind of history (which they applauded and defended) that has a substantive theoretical/conceptual aspect – a deeply analytical history that addressed the complex and not always obvious underlying (social, economic, cultural, political) forces which constrain human choice and intention. The use of a description like 'deeply analytical' should not, of course, be taken to equate with 'objective' history (see OBJECTIVITY). The founders of the discipline of sociology, Auguste Comte and Emile Durkheim, heavily influenced the founders of the school and inevitably their ideas and epistemological position pushed its social science version of historical study in a generally anti-Marxist direction.

Clearly, these two approaches to history – agency and/or structure – have ideological overtones, generally conforming to the political right and left (as with everything in life it is never quite so straightforward but it will do to make the point). However, to post-structuralists it is not necessarily a choice of one or the other because both are historical constructs that require deconstruction before we can fully appreciate their utility or value (see POST-STRUCTURALISM). As has been indicated, prior to debates about agency and/or structure are the epistemological, ontological and conceptual assumptions that precede their formulation and then, following on from these levels, the implications that arise for historical practice – the follow-on methodological procedures entailed by each concept and their and/or relationship(s). A post-structuralist like Michel **Foucault** would, for example, regard agency as a power-effect within the broader notion of the death of the subject. Regarding 'man' (the subject) as a modernist (specifically a capitalist and entrepreneurial) humanist invention, deliberately placed at the hub of the cultural, social and economic world, is an idea that will be expunged in time. Clearly, the postmodernist notion of loss of internal identity (the self) is incompatible with modernist notions

of agency (the idea of a fixed identity and capacity for purposeful choice) (see POST-MODERNISM). Structures would be seen equally as inventions but specifically inventions for the expression and transmission of power (economic, cultural, political, racial, historical, national, sexual, etc.) which would, of course, be disguised through the creation and 'management' of, among other things, agency (see RACE; GENDER; CLASS).

The strength of agency and/or structure is testified to in the way even so-called 'postist' or 'discourse and culture' historians still debate them as categories of analysis (see DISCOURSE), usually as they attempt to rationalise them away. Postist historians assume that history is not a simple reflection of the reality of the past because that reality can only be apprehended through the body of concepts and theories human beings use. So, essentially, the concepts of agency and structure are built into the language of a discursive system. In the end both agency (action) and structure (power) are, therefore, discursively constructed and mediated. That is, they are categories invented by and in the language universe (sometimes called the 'social imaginary') that all of us inhabit (see EPISTEME).

Further reading

Althusser, L., 1971; Ankersmit, F.R., 2001; Barthes, R., 1977; Bevir, M., 1999; Bourdieu, P., 1972; Cabrera, M.A., 2004; Collingwood, R.G., 1994 [1946]; Dayton, C.H., 2004; Dreyfus, H.L. and Rabinow, P., 1983; Fairburn, M., 1999; Fulbrook, M., 2002; Gramsci, A., 1972; Hekman, S., 1995; *History and Theory* themed issue 2001; Lloyd, C., 1993; Taylor, C., 1985; Thompson, E.P., 1978.

ANKERSMIT, FRANK R. (1945–)

Frank Ankersmit's contribution to the philosophy and theory of history viewed as a **narrative**-making activity is to be found in a substantial body of literature produced since the early 1980s (in both English and Dutch) beginning with his first key text *Narrative Logic: A Semantic Analysis of the Historian's Language* (1983). This was followed with a collection of his major journal articles *History and Tropology: The Rise and Fall of Metaphor* (1994) (which includes his indispensable 'The use of language in the writing of history' and 'Historiography and postmodernism'), collaboration with Hans Kellner on *A New Philosophy of History* (1995), two books on the nature of **representation**, *Historical Representation* (2001) and *Political Representation* (2002), and most recently his *Sublime Historical Experience* (2005).

The theme throughout his extensive writings and one he takes initially from Hayden **White's** narrativism but then develops in his own semantic way is his explanation of what happens when historians move from the level of the single statement of **justified belief** about what happened (what happened = events under a description) 'up' or 'into' that of the narrative substance of the text itself. For Ankersmit the historical text is in part made up of factual statements that are the product of archival research and which are accreted/accumulated. This is what gives history its quality and appearance of factualism (see REALITY/REALISTIC EFFECT; Roland BARTHES). But it does not stop there. Inevitably the historian has to infer and 'weigh up', and then determine the relative importance of a selection from the vast range of factual statements, and which ones to use in their interpretation. The historian is now doing something quite different – she or he is constructing a narrative *about* the past that is then offered to the reader as a proposed picture *for* (not *of*) the past. But this narrative picture is not a mosaic or jigsaw of the factual statements. It has become a completely different order or level of intellectual undertaking.

Understanding this is crucial to grasping how the historical narrative is constructed. While single statements of belief can usually be justified according to the existence of a leftover of the past (see EVENT; EVIDENCE;

SOURCES; TRUTH; RECONSTRUCTIONIST HISTORY; OBJECTIVITY), proposed pictures *about* the past cannot be so verified. The reason is that *the past* possesses no such pictures through which later ones can be justified comparatively. It is certainly true that such history pictures can be compared with other history pictures, but that comparison does not get us out of the situation that propositions are speculative and cannot be regarded as 'the real thing'. This leads Ankersmit to conclude that only modernist historians stop at the level of the statement of justified belief, while those who think through the implications of the narrative/textual level are postmodernists.

This leads on to Ankersmit's further important point that the empirical (so-called synthetic truth) can never be the only (and, therefore, the primary) foundation for history (historical knowledge/interpretation). The reason is that to create meaning historians invariably produce statements that are at once synthetic (empirical) and analytic (which is truth independent of factual empirical reality). This boils down to the simple point that there are no facts without theory, or language, or argument, or **form and content**, or **trope/ figuration**, or **inference**, or text, or ideology, or **emplotment**, and the notion that we can reconstruct the past as it most likely was without the intervention of theory is nonsense (see Geoffrey ELTON; CONSTRUCTIONIST HISTORY). We cannot have a meaning for the past that is only empirical or derived entirely or primarily from the empirical. This effectively denies the essence of the epistemological position which assumes that reality is unmediatedly available in the history text and that nothing of significance occurs on the trajectory between 'the past' and 'history'.

As you may already have worked out, Ankersmit's position demands both the recognition and the examination of the **aesthetic turn** – specifically that we can only know the represented through its **representation** and, in addition, only our descriptions can be true or false (see LINGUISTIC TURN). Hence it is that historians (and indeed all human beings in any situation that demands a description) offer propositions as to what is the state of reality. There is no access to the truth of reality without these elements of proposition and description. The empirical insistence that the word and the world match (more or less and well enough) in Ankersmit's judgement will not do. To accept that it 'will do' is to endorse the very doubtful notion that historians stand outside 'history' and the past dictates itself to them, that for example there is an essence in a certain set of events that is 'humanist Marxist' or 'feminist' or 'postcolonial', or indeed that the past gives us 'the Renaissance', 'The French Revolution', 'The Hungry Forties', or 'The Jazz Age'. There is no actual 'humanist Marxism' or 'Jazz Age' in the past – only in our descriptions of it (see above – synthetic plus analytical statements = history).

As should by now be obvious, for Frank Ankersmit (as for Hayden White, Richard **Rorty** and Keith **Jenkins**, as well as the author of this book) the realist belief that there is a distinction between past reality and language makes no sense. Language cannot *reflect* nature for the simple reason that all we have access to is language (and concept, theory, propositions, etc.). This means that we cannot simply scrape language off the reality of the past (as if it were some kind of camouflage paint) to access its true nature/real nature/ meaning. We can only engage with past and present by describing it and proposing facts about it in language. Every historian, like everyone else who uses language, is directly implicated in creating those discourses (narrative substances) called history(ies). What historians need to do, therefore, is figure out how their preferred and created history discourse either achieves or does not achieve what they might define as truthful knowledge. As Ankersmit has argued, historians need to understand that what they assume to be the natural way to view history (as the representational empirical narrative) is fundamentally flawed, but that does not mean that we have to abandon history altogether.

As Ankersmit argues, it means recognising the epistemological choices historians have in thinking about what they do when they decide to write about (that is, create a narrative substance about), for example, 'the war in Iraq' or, if they prefer, the 'liberation of Iraq', 'the American War of Independence' or, if they prefer, 'the American Revolution'. The usual conceptualisation of the period in US history between 1900 and 1920 is that of the 'Progressive Era'. This is an analytical/conceptual and linguistic construction and it does not exist outside itself. The Progressive Era – as a historian's conceptualisation – did not exist (even if people at the time may have used the description – the same logic applies to them as it does to historians). It is what historians construct through the colligation of their array of statements about aspects of those twenty years of the past. The Progressive Era is only 'true' analytically/conceptually. This is because there is no Progressive Era narrative substance 'back there', for statements about it to correspond to, before the Progressive Era is created as a proper noun for its own set of statements. That the Progressive Era is taken to refer to actuality is through usage and collective agreement – the only truth about the Progressive Era is that created as a consensus among historians to accept it as a viable proposition. Another example is 'The Long Nineteenth Century' that literally extends periodisation. Hence, maybe (probably?), some day 'The Cold War' will be rejected as a narrative substance and be replaced by another 'analytical truth' of history.

This returns us to the distinction between 'the past' and 'history'. Neither 'the past' nor its evidence creates 'history' – only historians do that. They do it when they construct a narrative the logic of which, in turn, becomes the default logic of history. History is, as Ankersmit perceptively explains, a substitute representation for the past. This means, of course, rejecting the conventional definition of epistemology that connects word and world. We should now be better able to see that a representation (or presentation for that matter) can only through some form of artifice connect word to world. In other words, history is just another linguistic object in the world (see TROPE). Assuming history is a substitute representation for the past (which I think it plainly is), how can we seriously expect it to be literally true at any level beyond the single statement of justified belief? We do not expect this from any other substitute representation that we regularly come into contact with – painting, film, website or theatre/street play (see Jean BAUDRIL-LARD and the notion of simulacra). This also frees (the representation of) history from its literalist chains. Hence we can – we could always – experiment with unconventional history (see EXPERIMENTAL HISTORY). As Ankersmit seems to recognise, history is always 'as if' and 'what can be'.

Further reading
Ankersmit, Frank R., 2005a, 2005b, 2003a, 2003b, 2002, 2001, 2000, 1998a, 1998b, 1994, 1989, 1983; Ankersmit, F.R. and Kellner, H., 1995; Bann, S., 1984; Chartier, R., 1988; Friedlander, S. (ed.), 1992; Jenkins, K., 2003, 1999b, 1997; Jenkins, K. and Munslow, A., 2004; Kellner, H., 1989; Munslow, A., 2003b; Munslow, A. and Rosenstone, R.A., 2004; White, H., 1992; Zagorin, P., 1999.

ANNALES

The ways in which historians approach the past are almost numberless. It is probably little exaggeration to say that for every historian you come across there is a route to the time before now. The reason for this is not difficult to work out. It is that history is a constituted and positioned knowledge about the past and this status is due to three of its most obvious characteristics: first, its vast range of empirical **sources** to choose from (as the basis of its **empiricism**); second, its analytical dimensions (**inference, a priori/a posteriori** thinking, conceptualisation and theorised explanation) and finally, the different epistemological

and ontological assumptions open to practitioners (see EPISTEMOLOGY; ONTOLOGY; REALITY/REALISTIC EFFECT; LINGUISTIC TURN; AESTHETIC TURN; GENRE; CONCEPTS IN HISTORY; TELEOLOGY; NARRATIVE; DECONSTRUCTIONIST HISTORY; POSTMODERNISM; REPRESENTATION; NEW HISTORY; CLIOMETRICS). All this allows enormous scope for the process of manufacturing knowledge about the past. In other words, history is and remains a construction all the way through and, as a result, produces strong feelings both pro and anti its varieties and their proponents.

However, and this is perhaps just as important, there is also a strong tendency among historians to herd. As possessors of paper qualifications that attest to their professional status, like-minded historians are inclined to develop an intellectual impetus (and then often an institutional one) to join together. Collections of compatible historians have always been prone to intellectual herd instincts. Students of history are introduced at an early stage to this development, which is invariably based on a particular subject matter and a collective approach taken to it, e.g. British mid-nineteenth-century social history inflected with a Marxist humanist perspective means they tend to read a particular group of historians. A Weberian status position requires they read a different set. Then they get to compare and contrast them in an essay (or the assumption is that they will). History students are required to read lots of different groups of historians to try to understand how and why their thinking and practice differ.

It is a very important, though an often neglected, circumstance of history as a professional act that much of its work – as a means of knowing about the past – is done through a set of shared assumptions about 'the right way' to do it. Very few debates in history are actually about new sources, but they do tend to be about new ways of organising them, what new theories to apply to them and the most appropriate way(s) to conceive of the discipline itself as a result. It is this that evidences the three predominant epistemological approaches to history today: **reconstructionist**, **constructionist** and **deconstructionist**. Each views the relationship between the historian and the past in radically different ways. Thus, if a historian imagines 'the-past-as-history' as a culturally informed and historicist (see HISTORICISM) discursive practice that can only signify the reality of the past (represent it and do that poorly), she or he will tend to be deconstructionist in her or his approach to history. If, on the other hand, the historian views 'history' as the 'without prejudice' discovery of the most likely meaning of the past through the process of empiricism and inference then she or he will tend to be reconstructionist in perspective. It would be a large generalisation, but not that inaccurate as such things go, to say that the vast majority of historians today lie somewhere between those two 'extreme alternatives'. And it is in this vast, complex, often prolix and murky area of empiricism and analysis that the most famous 'school of history' emerged in the early part of the last century, and which continues up to the present: the French *Annales* School. In many ways this school defines the concept of constructionist history though it has practised it in its own ways over the years. While the *Annales* is significant for the development of history as a discipline, its origin lies in the way in which one of its co-founders (Marc Bloch) mused upon what remains the central question, 'what is the use of history?' (Bloch 1963 [1954]: 3). His musings were influenced by the philosopher of history Henry Berr (who was among the first of many philosophers of history whose careers have been blighted by their refusal to simply 'do history'). Berr's own journal preceded the *Annales* and provided a launch pad for it.

The views of an arch-reconstructionist historian, Sir Geoffrey **Elton**, the English Tudor historian, on so-called social science or constructionist history and the *Annales* and its journal in particular, are typical of the (reconstructionist) approach and perspective. He said,

> The social sciences tend to arrive at their results by setting up a theoretical model which they then profess to validate or disprove by an 'experimental' application of factual detail. The belief . . . became dominant with the appearance of the French School based on the journal *Annales*. That school deliberately resorted to various theoretical models developed by such social sciences as economics, sociology and social anthropology. The result, we are assured, was to revolutionize the history of France, especially by replacing interest in the evanescent event by the extraction of long-term structure – a neat concept because it left so much uncontrolled speculation in the hands of the historian. . . . And yet it is wrong, and yet it threatens the virtue of history.
>
> (Elton 1991: 10)

This 'virtue of history' view is balanced by that of Georg Iggers, who in the 1990s claimed that the French *Annales* School of historians

> occupy a unique place in the historiography of the twentieth century. In the course of more than eight decades they have profoundly changed conceptions of what constitutes and who makes history. They have offered a very different conception of historical time from that held by most historians in the nineteenth and twentieth centuries. *Annales* historians have insisted that they do not represent a 'school' . . . but rather a spirit marked by openness to new methods and approaches to historical research. To a very large extent they are right.
>
> (Iggers 1997: 51)

While one might disagree with Iggers on the profundity of the *Annales* challenge to history, according to the American historians

Appleby, Hunt and Jacob, for example, the *Annales* was relatively insignificant in the United States. However, its social science methods and approach to a 'total history' (producing a synthesis of all that went on in the past) influenced the American home-grown **New History**, which initially emerged in the first two decades of the last century (Appleby *et al.* 1994: 86). Unlike most 'schools' of history the *Annales* began with the deliberate founding of a journal that acted as its ambassador and megaphone. This was the *Annales d'histoire économique et sociale* (*Annals of economic and social history*) founded in 1929 by Lucien Febvre and Marc Bloch. What connected the two historians was dissatisfaction with the sterility and con-ceptual narrowness, especially as Febvre saw it, of much contemporary French (essentially political) history and particularly the narrow empiricist fact fixation of leading French historians like C.W. Langlois and Charles Seignobos. Both Febvre and Bloch were influ-enced by the **positivism** of Emile Durkheim and Auguste Comte and social and economic historians like Françoise Simiand. Together they produced a heady mix of interdiscipli-nary history, which for Febvre was to explore the *mentalité* of an age via its literary culture and by deploying psychology (a move rein-vigorated in the 1980s and 1990s). Bloch was enamoured of the social and made his major contribution in the study of feudal society. Succeeding Febvre and Bloch came the non-Marxist constructionist or social science history of Fernand Braudel. Braudel's con-tribution was to take on to another level the declaration of intent made in the first issue of *Annales* – to break down barriers between disciplines that dealt with the past while maintaining and enhancing a broad explora-tion of the past.

Braudel's great disciplinary combination was that of geography and demography which is most readily seen in his most famous work *The Mediterranean and the Mediterra-nean World in the Age of Philip II* (two vols 1949, published in English 1972–3). In this text Braudel experimented with his concep-tion of different historical time spans in an effort to explain the past. These were the long duration of geographic/climatic/envi-ronmental change (*la longue durée*), the middle span of social and economic change (*la moyenne durée/conjunctures*) and the short span of the human life and especially politi-cal events (*la courte durée/événements*) (see EVENT). Like many history experiments, few people repeated it even while some like Michel **Foucault** may have appreciated the effort. It was enough, however, to place a little strain on the epistemological supports of more conventional approaches. In the end, nevertheless, Braudel was still tied to classic formulations for understanding how history works (as opposed to the past), by continu-ing to investigate and (despite his hesitation) often endorse the **agency and structure** duality and through its appeals to hypothesis-testing and, as appropriate, **covering laws** liberally saturated with quantification and **cliometrics**. The best-known example of this was E. Le Roy Ladurie's *Peasants of Languedoc* (1966). It also became a part of the French intellec-tual establishment losing something of its avant-garde character.

The continued vibrancy of the Annaliste perspective on 'the-past-as-history' is evi-denced in its ability to adapt to and explore the trends and vicissitudes of history fash-ion. From the 1960s and to the present the emergence of **cultural history** and its narrative-linguistic incarnation and challenge simply became more grist to its continuously turning mill. But there remains a strong sense of 'history' as a constant creation – fashion-ing new histories for each new age. Rather than simply publish the latest interpretation or the most recent application of theory, *Annales* engages constantly with history as a question mark.

Further reading

Appleby, J. *et al.*, 1994; Bloch, M., 1963 [1954]; Braudel, F., 1972–3 [1949], 1980; Burke, P., 1990; Carrard, P., 1992; Elton, G.,

1991; Hunt, L., 1986; Huppert, G., 1997; Iggers, G., 1997; Ladurie, E. Le Roy, 1981, 1978, 1974 [1966]; Le Goff, J. and Nora, P., 1985; Stoianovich, T., 1976.

A PRIORI/A POSTERIORI

The distinction between a priori and a posteriori thinking derives from the debate over what can be known by pure reason alone. A proposition, object or a concept (see CONCEPTS IN HISTORY) is known as a priori if its content is determined true or false without reference to experience (see TRUTH). Such a judgement is based on deductive inferential reasoning (see INFERENCE) from abstract general premises (what philosophers call deductive-nomological knowledge). Philosophically speaking, apriorism maintains that our minds can acquire knowledge separately of experience through logic, intuition, ingrained ideas or mental capacities. The term a priori is distinguished from a posteriori, which is the acquisition of knowledge by means of the senses and inductive/abductive inference from **evidence** (see SOURCES). Such knowledge does not entail the necessary, universal and truthful outcomes of apriorism. A posteriori thinking, therefore, produces judgements that have an empirical origin (see EMPIRICISM). The a priori is assumed to be independent of the experience that the a posteriori presupposes.

Immanuel **Kant** argued that a priori thinking established truths through the mental categories that organise experience. This was the central aim of his *Critique of Pure Reason*, namely the establishment of the intuitions and concepts through which we understand the world: time, space, cause, number, substance, etc. Kant's basic argument is that the concepts and categories we use must be attached to our experience, and in applying the concepts we can make objective statements (see OBJECTIVITY). This Kantian or rationalist position is important to historians because of its **epistemology**; that is, the acceptance that

some knowledge of the evidence a posteriori is a necessary prerequisite to establishing the concepts involved in an a priori proposition. As Kant said, the attempt to extract from an arbitrary idea the existence of an object corresponding to it is an unnatural procedure. Historians since the **Enlightenment** have taken this to mean that empiricism precedes rationality, hence the foundational claim that historical knowledge begins with inductive/abductive inference though it be processed by the rational mind. Thus it is that most historians argue from the (essentially anti-rationalist) position that all knowledge is ultimately obtained from experience and so, by definition, historical knowledge is derived a posteriori.

The truth of an a priori proposition can, therefore, be conceived and understood by reason alone, but the unpredictable truth of an a posteriori proposition can only be found by reference to a matter of fact. For example, the sum $47 + 45 = 92$ is known a priori, whereas the statement 'the American labour propagandist Henry D. Lloyd was married to Jenny Bross' is known a posteriori. The truth of the addition sum is known logically (deduction) whereas the truth of the statement can only be justified empirically by the observation and verification of evidence. When historians say they rely primarily on a posteriori propositions for truthful knowledge they reference history's raw materials (people, events, actions and social processes). It is in the nature of these raw materials to demand inference that is inductive/abductive rather than deductive.

Like most people, historians tend to stretch the Kantian notion of the a priori into a world-view. They find that the implicit meaning of certain empirical observations becomes part of their own psychological a priori. My redefinition is very much in line with Friedrich **Nietzsche**'s position that a priori categories considered as foundational concepts do not have absolute or universal validity because they are ultimately the products of personal, cultural and ideological perspective. Historians come to possess what some see as the rational apriorism of, for example, **class**, **race**, **gender**, nationalism or whatever. These empirically based and 'rationally justified' conceptual filters form the mental grid through which methodologies are constructed and interpretations are made.

This mental or propositional grid thus 'explains' the appearances found in the evidence. Reconstructionist historians (see RECONSTRUCTIONIST HISTORY) do tend to deny that this grid of metaphysical (see METAPHYSICS) categories prefigures their methods by arguing that empiricism is the natural method of history and their interpretations are confirmed through judicious hypothesis-testing. Although they will admit that a priori or necessary truths exist, they deny that such truths can give us the full picture of what really happened in the past. The reason for this is that the past is presumed to be contingent and while rational agent **intentionality** is of central importance in historical explanation, actions and events are not primarily determined by human logic or, for that matter, any other single cause (see CAUSATION). What to some may look like a priori categories (like the assumption of rational agent intentionality) reconstructionists consider to be justified and truthful a posteriori interpretative statements founded on research in the archive (see JUSTIFIED BELIEF).

Clearly, experience of the archive is relevant in moulding the psychological a priori. According to reconstructionist and constructionist historical thinking (see CONSTRUCTIONIST HISTORY), historians need the evidence to acquire the appropriate concepts. For example, when considering the nineteenth-century 'Condition of England' question most historians deploy a hierarchy of concepts like 'class', 'the city', 'pauperism' and 'crime'. Under the concept of class might be subsumed other concepts like alienation. The evidence suggests, however (i.e. the process of inference), that certain concepts like 'poverty' are inappropriate, as the consensus among British social historians holds that 'poverty' was a concept not known to agents

at the time and, therefore, could not have affected their actions. 'Poverty' does not exist in the evidence. The rationale for this sophisticated empiricism is provided by the British nineteenth-century liberal and empiricist philosopher John Stuart Mill's claim that the only historical truths are empirical and founded on observation and perception (i.e. known a posteriori).

What we have then is the synthesised a priori widely found in history thinking. As the products of a self-reflexive **modernism**, historians do not deny that reason has a role in what they do. But they are careful to say that reason is dependent on the evidence of experience. History thinking requires observation of the evidence followed by limited generalisation that then loops back to empirical justification and that, after a number of loops, produces objective knowing. The problem with this is, of course, that historians have to accept that this process offers no proof, only exemplification and plausibility. In this they accept the British empiricist philosopher John Locke's belief that there are areas of knowledge that are, at best, only likely to be true – and history is one of them.

In none of the foregoing have I made mention of either the role of the **historical imagination** or the importance of language and culture in establishing truthful a priori or a posteriori knowledge. It is through our imagination that we come to terms both with our psychological a priori, the scepticism that a sophisticated empiricism demands, and with the presentism of the here and now. What I am suggesting is that there are linguistic determinants and cultural processes that serve to collapse the distinction of knower and known, and influence the way we bring together our concepts and the evidence (see CONCEPTS IN HISTORY).

The history thus produced testifies to the historian's a priori belief that the evidence was necessarily connected in some way. As I have argued, this is central to the mechanism whereby historians come to hold certain core convictions about the past. It is possible to consider the structure of **narrative** as a priori and that historians order their perceptions of the evidence through narrative's pre-packed figurative codes. This encodation is worked into the historical narrative according to the nature of our metaphoric prefiguration – allocating meaning to events through similarity and resemblance, contiguity and difference, cause and effect. It is only a brief step from this troping process (see TROPE/FIGURATION) to making moral judgements in and about history and taking up ideological positions about what constitutes dominance and subordinance in society. Even if all the individual sentence statements in a historical narrative are deemed to be true a priori or a posteriori, the narrative structure imagined and brought into existence by the historian is a performative and organisational act that sequences and patterns knowledge without being knowledge itself. Figuration and narrative interpretation, as the basis of historical telling, mediates both a priori and a posteriori knowledge.

Further reading

Bonjour, L., 1985; Danto, A., 1965; Kant, I., 1933 [1781]; Moser, P.K., 1987; Priest, S., 1990; Putnam, H., 1983; Quine, W.V., 1963.

AUTHOR

How far is the-past-as-history an act of discovery by the historian? Since René Descartes, Immanuel **Kant**, John Locke, the **Enlightenment** and the advent of **liberal humanism**, Western society has reaped the benefits of its investment in **epistemology** (its theory of knowledge) with historical knowledge being found in the data (see EVIDENCE; SOURCES) as guided by the general inferential rules (see INFERENCE) as understood and applied by the knowing subject (in this case the historian). The Enlightenment favoured and promoted the Cartesian subject – the rational knowing subject, the self, the self-fashioning 'man', the subject as the centre of knowledge, unfettered,

unified, stable, intending, timeless, causal, the controller of culture, the creator and source of meaning, and the autonomous author (of texts). This figure was predicated on the independent existence of mental categories of knowing that reflected reality, and a transparent language *through* which all forms of reality including the historical could be perceived, represented and made familiar. The model for history that this mind-set contrived held sway until the twentieth-century structuralist revolution (see STRUCTURALISM). Such a model assumed, common-sensically, that history tells the **truth** as understood by the discrete empirical subject, the historian (see EMPIRICISM; MIMESIS). Jacques **Derrida** described the subject as the transcendental signified. In the case of the historian, his/her methods are taken to demonstrate objectively his/her hypothesis, thus creating truthful interpretations that provide the wellspring of the history text's definitive meaning and explanation. The past gives us the evidence and the historian deploys reason and inference to make sense of it. The historian is not where the past begins, but where it ends.

In this conventional model the 'historian-as-autonomous-author-of-history-texts' supplies the epistemology through which he/she knows the past and makes it meaningful. The inevitable subjectivity that accompanies authorship is not a problem for the modernist historian because it can be overcome through the strict application of empirical method, which makes for truthful interpretations. The historical **genre** of **biography**, for example, is expected to conform to the principles of the method, but standards are different for degraded types of history like the historical novel or the autobiography. But most historians will admit (albeit reluctantly in some cases) that it is not actually possible to compare and contrast the interpretation of the historian (as statements of fact) with the real past as it happened. This remains the case despite the detailed use of the referential paraphernalia that is meant to suggest otherwise. The effect of what can, upon occasion, be massive empiricist overkill in the footnotes is to obliterate the problem of limited inference and indirect knowledge that permits only of weak **historical explanation**. Nevertheless, empiricist common sense urges the historian to get on with his/her immersion in the archive as the only way to **objectivity**. It is with this tactic that empiricism avoids confronting its liberal humanist **ontology** (its state of being), as well as its epistemological and methodological assumptions.

Empiricist assumptions and referential paraphernalia apart, it is possible that the historian is far more like an author than the proper history of the conventional model is usually willing to admit. The historian-as-author is someone who will manifestly identify with the object of study and who may make conscious interventionist choices about the past, effectively resisting empiricism's objectivist lures. What I am suggesting is that it may be necessary to take another look at the historian-as-author's powers of signification. This should encourage a closer focus on what it really means to talk of the historian as an interpreter, and this should lead to rethinking the nature of his/her subjectivity and his/her connection with the past through his/her history writing.

The shift in recent years away from the model of the historian-as-observer to historian-as-participant (who 'reads' texts within various contexts and then writes about them) has been accompanied by what is for many historians a worrying scepticism in colleagues about that which constitutes historical truth and how we can tell it in an intertextual world. This, it turns out, is far more than a crisis of methodology. Developments in the wake of structuralism, **postmodernism** and **continental philosophy** have challenged the Enlightenment ideal of the steadfast knowing subject and the goal of unclouded **representation** (see Jean BAUDRILLARD). Until the postmodern critique this ground was the firm foundation for the multiple pillars of Western philosophy: objectivism, representation, truth, factualism, reference, real-

ism, the subject–object binary, all of which were ideally located in the figure of the disinterested modernist historian (a.k.a. the knowing subject) (see OBJECTIVITY; TRUTH; FACTS; REALITY/REALISTIC EFFECT). According to at least one leading commentator, the first principle of the postmodern moment is a refocusing on history – about questions of representation and stories told (and untold) with a Will to Power that unavoidably places the knowing and objective subject (a.k.a. the historian) under a question mark (Marshall 1992: 10, 25).

While this challenge is being mounted historians remain mildly embarrassed. The reason is that we know that the grubby practicalities of our work make history, though perceived as a legitimate epistemology, fall far short of the Enlightenment ideal. Historians cannot avoid the fact that they are writing *about* the past. It is hard, therefore, to defend the notion that the past flows *through* us like low-voltage electric current that is not in any way obstructed or short-circuited by its medium. History, as the only access we have to the past, is a second-order epistemology. It has no direct contact with reality. Primary evidence so called is still entirely removed from its referents (all evidence refers to other evidence). I suppose the irony is that in a *real* sense history is dependent for its meaning upon the skills of the historian-as-author and the authoring process for the creation of the reality-effect through its form (see FORM AND CONTENT; FILM AND HISTORY). There is, therefore, an unexpungeable subjectivity in the creation of historical knowledge because the historian is the organiser of the-past-as-history. The evidence of the past is selected, rejected, shaped and formed through inference, theory, trope, argument, style, **narrative**, moral situation, the extant **historiography** (present and past traditions of inquiry and interpretation) and empathy with the object of study (see INFERENCE; TROPE/FIGURATION). Objective historical knowledge demands a platform above and outside history. But historians know that such a platform does not exist. It is the historian who authors the connection between event, narrative, understanding, meaning and interpretation.

The historian is thus heavily dependent upon his/her organisational and authorial skills with the data – most particularly his/her narrative capacities. Because truth does not emerge from any known historical methodology, we are thrown back onto the individual historian's attempt to persuade the reader through his/her narrative construction as well as the judicious use of the evidence. The historical narrative is thereby an act of **historical imagination**, of will, of design, of desire, of form and of content, although many still insist they are demonstrating (a residual modernist belief in) objective knowing. This tension between form and content may well be irresolvable. The Enlightenment assertion that every rational and knowing subject possesses the power to command and reconstruct reality (from the archive) is faced with the collapse of meaning and representation as proclaimed by Michel **Foucault** and Roland **Barthes** in their joint avowal of the death of the subject/author.

It might be helpful to consider the paradox that underpins history as a discipline specifically in connection with the functioning of the historian. Let us revisit the modernist model of history. History is a corpus of thought and material made coherent by its methodology, its shared topics of interest (its objects of study) and its practitioners (the historians). In this model there is a lack of parity between method, that which is known (object) and the knower (historian/knowing subject). The object of study comes first, the method second and the historian last. The paradox (the modernist paradox) surfaces quickly in this model because the end product – historical knowledge (the interpretative narrative of the-past-as-history) – is always associated with the historian. The historian is named and becomes the referent for the interpretation because it is he/she who has *discovered* the truthful interpretation. The

model insists that the historian, in discovering the past, is above and beyond history, is somehow divorced from the whole process. The past unfolds itself. But the historian is, as we know, authorial and is the creator of the text in which he/she reveals the truthful interpretation, explains it, argues for it and displays the evidence he/she has chosen that supports his/her argument. Here is the paradox. The historian has a double consciousness: he/she is both separate and involved, is the witness to the past, yet also must be a participant in it because he/she authors it as written history as a discourse on the past (see STRUCTURALISM; NEW HISTORICISM).

The paradox is never resolved but is coped with by viewing the historian not as an author (creative, interventionist) but as a 'historian' (separate, outside the text, beyond the past; who discovers the truthful interpretation). In 'The discourse of history' (1967) Roland Barthes points to history's investment in the correspondence theory of knowledge and the factualism and objectivism which this produces and which necessitate the elision of the historian as an authorial voice. When Foucault described the death of the author he could have been speaking about the way in which the modernist historian removes him/herself from the project, not as a knowing subject but as the fabricator of knowledge. In this way the historian is complicit in the pretence of allowing 'the past' to use him/her as its vessel or mouthpiece – so the past speaks for itself. It is this confederacy that disguises the paradox of history.

Modernist history thereby denied the characterisation of the historian-as-author long before postmodernism. But the aim was not to decentre the historian-as-author as a knowing subject in order to reveal his/her cultural situatedness, or how language constructs his/her identity, or the lack of control he/she has over the meanings of the text, but rather to demonstrate his/her separation from the present (ideology, society, politics, text) – to make him/her *ahistorical*. This *ahistoricality* is evident in the distinctive caste of historical narrative. It is the-past-as-history, not the historian-as-author, that narrates events. In history there is no 'you', 'me', or 'I'. The past exists in the form of an auto-narrative. This is the modernist aim to blot out history as an authored **discourse**. Why is this done? It is done to perform the (liberal humanist ideological?) function of containing and repressing the connection between the subject and language. In this way the historical narrative is caught in the snare (as has been pointed out on numerous occasions) of the nineteenth-century realist novel whereby the reader is expected to consume the truthful narrative as a coherent reflection of reality. In the same way the historian smoothes out the contradictions in the past usually by acknowledging them (a.k.a. the **historical explanation**), and then offering a resolution (a.k.a. the historical interpretation).

Constructed by the realist historical narrative, the reader is called or hailed by the historical narrative – ideologically interpellated as French cultural critic Louis Althusser describes it – in such a way that he/she recognises him/herself as another knowing subject. He/she thus accepts as natural the existence of the liberal humanist knowing subject. He/she shares what is taken to be a natural situation of knowing. Historical knowing is not, however, natural. Liberal humanist knowing is not the only way. But it is in its appeal to empiricism that history obscures its liberal humanist constructedness. Unfortunately, if the knowing subject (as the subject of ideology and his/her cultural situatedness) is crumbling, fragmented, dispersed, constantly constructed and reconstructed by discourse and in a language that is out of control, that subject cannot fulfil the traditional conception of proper empirical history, and it may end up simply making the paradox in history more stark – a method and object that together are assumed to give access to reality, and the historian-as-author who creates the-past-as-history; what Michel de Certeau has called its closed discourse (de Certeau 1988 [1975]: 21).

If the reader elects to view the historical narrative not as a reflection of the past, but as a construct of an author who is subject to many cultural and linguistic tides – that is, refuses interpellation – then the historical narrative becomes open to a deconstruction (see DECONSTRUCTIONIST HISTORY) (of that which is already constructed), and the process of its production can be examined. The deconstructive aim is first to find the unity of the work, its drive toward explanatory closure and how it goes about dispelling ignorance. Next, the deconstructive reader will try to locate the contradictions in the text and the literary devices that reveal where the text escapes its realist captivity and its meaning becomes plural or fictive. The deconstructive assumption is that the text is always too slippery for the historian-as-author to control. So the deconstructive reader asks, among other things, what is its ascendant trope, what are its underlying arguments (inference and causal analysis), what is the nature of its ideological positioning (moral and ethical appeals), is there a dominant **emplotment**, who or what constitutes the 'hero' and how is the evidence of the hero's life marshalled within the available emplotment or contemporary mythic motifs, and what does the selection of **sources** reveal about the explanation and the aims of the historian-as-author (see BIOGRAPHY/ LIFE WRITING; NEW HISTORY; ETHICAL TURN)?

To deconstruct the history text requires breaking another confederacy, the unstated modernist complicity between the historian and the reader whereby the historian is offering truth to the reader. By viewing the historian as an author who is not only the constructor of the-past-as-history, but who is also him/herself constructed in language, it is possible to see that it is not the past that speaks through the historian, but the text, language and culture. From a postmodern perspective (see POSTMODERNISM) we are never outside the universe of discourse. We can never escape to a place that is extra-discursive. If we could then we would be able to affirm the basis upon which the knowing subject is built – the modernist conviction that individual consciousness is the fount of knowledge, meaning and understanding. Our postmodern condition demands, however, that as we recognise the historian-as-author, at the same time we decentre him/her as a transcendental signified.

The obvious question then is if the historian is aware of all this how does he/she do history? Does he/she author something we can call postmodern history? Well, it may be that the historian-as-author who is no longer weighed down by the modernist sense of the-past-as-history will opt for experimentation, will intervene in or impose him/herself on history. Precisely how these history experiments can be undertaken is the point of the experiment so I cannot prejudge. But, if pressed, I would suggest experimenting with authorial intrusion, exploring the death of the author (decentring the subject in some way), mixing the fictional and factualist forms, offering alternative versions of the 'same' story, and so on. This idea of experimentation in history is not a particularly new idea, of course. Linda Hutcheon described it over fifteen years ago as 'historiographic metafiction' (Hutcheon 1988: 87–101). Historians can exercise a choice; they can elect to write about the past as if they had discovered it as it actually happened, but the historian-as-author is equally free to adopt any post-empiricist position he/she chooses.

He/she may favour disrupting the text so that the reader is given the opportunity to take what they want from the narrative. The reader is no longer forced to accept it as an enclosed, finished, modernist job lot. The point is that, even when the historical narrative claims to leave the question open, the material has been presented in a fashion that presumes there is no other way to do it. Rather than this take-it-or-leave-it attitude that results from empiricism, realism, factualism (i.e. no choice), the reader may be invited to fill in the spaces left by the playful historian-as-author. Would it be too arch for me to suggest that the historian-as-author might list all the references known to them on a particular historical object, write a thousand-word interpretation, then suggest the reader go and read the sources and make up their own mind (history as bibliography)? This assumes that the deconstructive reader will 'play' their part. If they do not, of course, it rather negates the point of the game. No doubt the modernist practical realist historian will say that if the historian plays like this then he/she is not doing history.

Well, it is likely that it would not be modernist, truth-fulfilling history. It would be history that minimally asks who is writing it and why, who is reading it and why, and how many kinds of stories can be told about the same event(s). The historian-as-author would thus be inviting the reader to engage in creating the-past-as-history rather than having it disclosed to them (i.e. exhibited, imparted, divulged, published). As a comfort to the modernist historian I feel obliged to say that none of this means throwing out the moral baby with the empiricist bath water. Creating or authoring the past does not mean fictionalising events, people or processes and being amoral or nihilistic to boot. But what it does mean is decontrolling the project by not offering history as if it were the result of an act of objective discovery, and thereby closing down the options for the reader to participate in, and make up his/her own mind.

There is no ready-made reading list for the idea of the historian-as-author. You will have to consult a variety of texts dealing with the self, the subject, the author and the postmodern critique of history. My recommendations are below.

Further reading

Althusser, L., 1971; Barthes, R., 1977, 1974; Burke, S., 1992; Chatman, S., 1978; de Certeau, M., 1988 [1975]; Derrida, J., 1978; Dreyfus, H.L. and Rabinow, P., 1983; Genette, G. 1990 [1983]; Hutcheon, L., 1988; Marshall, B.K., 1992; Porter, R., 1997; Smith, P., 1988.

B

BARTHES, ROLAND (1915–80)

Roland Barthes was one of the leading French literary theorists and cultural critics of the mid-twentieth century. His reputation generally rests on his work in semiotics and the popularisation among the wider academic community of the principles of **structuralism**. His interest to historians, however, centres on his examination of the relationship between language, literature and the historical narrative. Barthes commented on the *naïveté* of the distinction made between history and (history) writing (*écriture*). Because the historical narrative conforms to a set of literary/narrative codes that give it its form, he argued that it is not readily separated from its content or its historicity, that is, its frame(s) of reference (conceptual, ideological, social, cultural) (see FORM AND CONTENT; MIMESIS). In his text *Writing Degree Zero* (1967) he argued that much wasted effort was put by historians into imagining a style of writing that was assumed and intended to be devoid of all language constraints, and that presumed that the word and the world can be viewed as separate domains. For Barthes literature is language and form its product. Content does not generate form. When form and content are, however, deliberately (and erroneously) conflated, history appears to be the natural product of the evidence. The object of this empiricist (see EMPIRICISM) exercise, claims Barthes, is to deny that myth and ideology exist in written history.

By distinguishing between *histoire* in which events apparently narrate themselves, and *discourse* which is self-consciously authorial, in his essay 'The discourse of history' (1967)

Barthes objects to history's reliance on the correspondence theory of knowledge that generates historical facts, producing along the way the 'reality effect' of 'objective' history. As Stephen Bann has said, the rhetorical analysis of historical narrative 'cannot grant to history, a priori, the mythic status which differentiates it from fiction' (Bann 1981: 5).

Barthes' analysis of narrative in 'The discourse' denies history the status of a distinct **epistemology**. History, he notes, is usually

> justified by the principles of 'rational' exposition [but] ... does this form of narration really differ, in some specific trait, in some indubitably distinctive feature, from imaginary narration, as we find it in the epic, the novel, and the drama?
> (Barthes in Bann 1981: 7)

Barthes reminds historians that their work resides in the translation of the past into a narrative of historical interpretation, and that their common deployment of the minutiae of events, the deliberate control exercised over temporality (compressing, rewinding and fast-forwarding time in the narrative), and the elision of the historian-as-**author** (denying the performative aspect of writing history), all work to produce the perception of realism as though there were a direct hold on the referent from where, as he says,

> history seems to be telling itself all on its own. This feature ... corresponds in effect to the type of historical discourse labelled as 'objective' (in which the historian never intervenes). ... On the level of discourse, objectivity ... thus appears as a particular

form of . . . referential illusion, since in this case the historian is claiming to allow the referent to speak all on its own.

(Barthes in Bann 1981: 11)

Barthes points out that this projected correspondence between ordinary language, the evidence and historical **truth** is also found in realist novels that similarly appear objective because they too have overpowered the signs of the 'I'. Barthes maintains, therefore, that historians thus deploy the real to play the epistemological trick of disengaging historians from the history production process in order to demonstrate unalloyed access to the reality of the past whereby history signals objectivity. Barthes' point is that the historian intentionally mystifies history by collapsing the signified with the referent to create a signifier–referent correspondence. Barthes summarises this by claiming that in objective history the 'real' is never more than an unformulated signified, hiding behind the all-powerful referent. This constitutes history's 'realistic effect' (Barthes in Bann 1981: 17). This is akin to Michel **Foucault**'s notion that discourses are perspectives that generate truth effects (see AUTHOR; NEW HISTORICISM). This is not anti-referentialism, but rather the identification of referentialism's limits as a form of REPRESENTATION (see Richard **Rorty**).

Further reading
Bann, S., 1983, 1981; Barthes, R., 1988, 1986, 1984 [1967], 1983, 1981 [1967], 1977, 1975, 1974, 1972, 1967, 1957; Burke, S., 1992; Calvet, L.-J., 1994; Culler, J., 1983; Genette, G., 1990 [1983]; Payne, M., 1997; Sontag, S., 1982; White, H., 1984; Wiseman, M.B., 1989.

BAUDRILLARD, JEAN (1929–)

A – perhaps *the* – key feature of our postmodern historical experience is the constant challenge to the referential – the assumption that historians can recapture the reality of the past which, in conventional modernist fashion, is still regarded as their first item of business. The modernist notion of the symbolic (strictly speaking it is a semiotic process of) exchange between the (past) world and the (present) word is always secondary to the main task, which is to connect as closely as possible the sign to its (given and recoverable) signification. The most likely meaning of, say, the opening up of the American West is back there and can be recovered if the historian is savvy enough (coolly inferential), and knows their way around the right archives (see INFERENCE; EVIDENCE; SOURCES). This simplistic notion has been confronted, especially over the past forty years or so, by our cultural awareness of the collapse of **representation**, specifically the arbitrary nature of the relationship between signifier and signified and the signs thereby produced. That most historians continue to work by ignoring the consequences of this is, of course, an issue associated less with the force of the **postmodern** critique of representation than with professional intransigence and power structures (deeply embedded vested intellectual interests) within the academy. While historians accept that there can be legitimate debate about the precise nature of the signification of the past – usually called a debate over interpretation – there is little acceptance 'of two minds' or undecided signification. Though historians always say there is no definitive answer to any historical question (there will always be fresh evidence and better inferences), they are at all times determined to 'find' meaning; they cannot be ambivalent or admit that, *given the nature of representation*, there can be no **truth** in terms of 'knowing what the past really or most likely means'. In other words, history must, though symbolically, always 'reflect the past world'.

It is in this context that Jean Baudrillard has been a primary figure since the late 1960s. Starting out as a Marxist sociologist whose interests lay in the nature of modern consumer society (*The Object System*, 1968, *The Consumer Society*, 1970), he argued, especially after 1968, that there was a need for a new kind of sociological critique that recognised how the consuming masses could resist capitalist power. His tools were increasingly taken from Roland **Barthes**, semiology (the science of signs), the theory of symbolism and a critique of the nature of reality (under capitalism). By the 1970s Baudrillard had begun to argue that our understanding of reality was a phase in the economic and cultural development of Western society based on exchange value but, in addition, that the system was itself becoming unfixed and 'the reality' of consumption, exchange and value was being replaced by the 'hyper-reality' of its symbolism (see *The Mirror of Production*, 1973, published in English 1975).

In other words, 'the real', which we could only 'know' through its first representational iteration or 'simulation', is (then) successively 'known' through the progression of simulacra (images, representations, likenesses) (see Frank ANKERSMIT). Baudrillard embarked from the 1980s onwards on an intellectual scheme that (so he believed) effectively replaced the Marxist/materialist stage theory model of social change, with this postmodern model of simulation – copies of the once real that assume their own independent status. Loosely following the stage model of Michel **Foucault** and the **episteme**, but still connected to a materialist stage theory, Baudrillard claims that there are three orders of simulacra in the modern era. The first is the pre-industrial age counterfeit that refers directly to the original, the second is brought on by industrialisation and the simulacrum is constituted as a series of replicas that each possess the same value, and then there is the postmodern, associated with the cyber universe of simulated (hyper-) reality that is more real than the real because it has now lost its original reference entirely. Hence in postmodern society we exist in a universe of codes (e.g. of and in 'capitalism') and arbitrary signs and 'simulations' of power replace the 'real' (exercise of power). The only response we can have to this exercise of simulated power is to derive our own simulation in which we imagine a countersign.

To grasp the implications for the thinking and practice of history under such a Baudrillardian postmodern condition, one needs to understand the link between hyper-reality and the crisis of representation that underpins the **aesthetic turn**. Baudrillard's hyper-real is not a deformation (or denial) of the once real as such, but the difference between the real and the representation is effectively rubbed away through cultural usage. Using Baudrillard's logic we might track the simulacra of history. Though each history claims to refer to the once real, each iteration moves it further away from it (the 'real past'). At first the sign is presumed to be the reflection of a basic reality because of the use of referential(ism) language, which is akin to Roland Barthes' **reality/realistic effect**. Then we might recognise the second simulation as what historians refer to in their texts/lectures as 'the **historiography**' where the interpretation, ideology, social theory/**concepts**, preferred argumentation of other historians become basic to the simulation (of the-past-as-history). Next we might come to the simulation of commentary on the nature of the historical enterprise itself (books like this one that examine the complicity of the **author**-historian in the production of the past?). Next, and maybe the last stage in this little model (a model that is *about* organising reality and its representation), the history bears no affiliation to any reality – it is just a pure simulacrum. It is invariably just the 'image', which carries with it 'a meaning'. Images could be of iconic historical figures, or monuments, or Remembrance Days, or National Holidays, or re-enactments, or 'model historical villages', or TV programmes, or digital games. It all adds up to a simulation of 'the past'. This is most often seen in national curricula for studying the past. The point is that none of this is intended to be 'unreal', but to be more real than the real – hence hyper-real (more than real). History is turned into an aesthetic but one that, only because of its cultural and academic professional pretensions, appears to retain its commitment to being coolly distanced, objective, non-authorial, epistemological and real (see AESTHETIC TURN). But history has now fallen into the world of representation, art, the History Channel, recreation (re-creation?), fashionable theorisation, play and urgent and ever more desperate capitalist consumption. History is the new rock and roll and has lost its sense of being able to do anything but entertain, divert and yet still cling to the now bizarre notion that it 'can tell the truth'.

In such a (postmodern) world the old ideas that clung so persistently to epistemological versions of historical knowledge are thrown off, discarded. History as *the* **metanarrative** is no longer viable (just another simulacrum). The notion of history as access to the once real is now both a deceit and a conceit. From the perspective of Baudrillard in his *The Illusion of the End* (1994) the 'end of history' is inevitable and welcome. The epistemological idea of being 'in touch' with past reality (which brought with it the realist baggage of linearity from past to present to future) is now pointless in a world of simulations. 'The past' unavoidably becomes simulated eventually as an ironic 'not the past' but (perhaps more usefully and often more entertainingly?) as a poem, a play and/or an action. Eventually it manifests itself as debates on the future of the past. What do we want to turn the past into in the future? Sooner or later we end up asking, like Keith **Jenkins** and Beverley Southgate, why bother with history? What do we gain from history if it is just another simulacrum? Would we not be better off without 'the past' and its chains of simulations? If reality is gone then one of its key fixtures and fittings – history – is now entirely superfluous. Or, contrary to this, we could argue that we must retain history, though it is a simulacrum, to work with, explain and balance every other simulacrum, to become not a metanarrative but metasimulacrum? We need history as a social imaginary to help us explain how we combine the (once) real and our theorising and explanations of it.

Further reading
Ashley, D., 1997; Baudrillard, J., 1998, 1995, 1994, 1983, 1976, 1975, 1973, 1970, 1968; Connor, S., 1989; Drolet, M., 2004; Gane, M., 1991a, 1991b; Jenkins, K., 1999b; Jenkins, K. and Munslow, A., 2004; Jenkins, K. *et al.*, forthcoming 2007; Kellner, D., 1989c; Lechte, J., 1994; Southgate, B., 2000.

BECKER, CARL L. (1873–1945)

Generally speaking, historians are meant to be sceptical. Normally this means being sceptical about the **sources**. The watchwords are 'Don't be taken in by what they seem to say to you'. Always compare, contrast and verify before deploying them. But scepticism is also useful when addressing how to approach the-past-as-history – in other words, scepticism about how to construct your history. Early on in his career, the mid-west US intellectual historian Carl Becker demonstrated this kind of scepticism in his 1910 article for the *Atlantic Monthly*, which he called 'Detachment and the writing of history'. But Becker is generally remembered for his founding membership of that group of early twentieth-century American constructionist historians who clustered around the **New History**, and his 1931 Presidential Address to the American Historical Association (AHA) entitled 'Everyman His Own Historian' (see CONSTRUCTIONIST HISTORY).

Like others in the early years of the American constructionist New History grouping, such as Charles Beard and their mentors including Frederick Jackson Turner and James Harvey Robinson, Becker apparently dared to acknowledge the unavoidable **relativism** in the discipline of history. Arguably, however, he did so with the express aim of salvaging empirical-analytical history with its yearning for neutral realism. While many commentators like Ernst Breisach still insist on Becker's 'pragmatism', which is a bit of a weasel word for his supposed relativism, this is, I would suggest, an inaccurate rendition of his intellectual position. As with the (in)famous (and now very old chestnut) **E.H. Carr–G. Elton** debate on relativism, there is much less to Becker's relativist attitude toward history as a representational form than meets the eye (see REPRESENTATION).

The key source for this largely spurious but rumbling debate on Becker's epistemological position is the latter part of his 1931 AHA Presidential Address. In this lecture Becker defined the essence of history as the memory of things said and done and concluded 'that every normal person, Mr Everyman, knows some history'. Becker was arguing that history is something that lives in the present and in the anticipation of the future. The picture that Mr Everyman has of the past is not only a picture of things said and done in the past, but it is always associated with a picture of things to be said and done in the future. As he said, 'to be prepared for what is coming to us it is necessary, not only to recall certain past events, but to anticipate (note I do not say predict) the future'. He thereby insisted that 'in a very real sense it is impossible to divorce history from life'. Echoing Benedetto **Croce**, he argued that history is alive, is contemporaneous and is a 'living part of our present world of semblance'. He concluded that Mr Everyman fashions out of history his individual experience and adapts it 'to his practical or emotional needs, and adorns it as well as may be to suit his æsthetic tastes'.

Now, at first blush this sounds like Becker was saying that history is hardly a discipline at all (if Everyman can do it?) and is dangerously presentist or, at worst (and as a consequence), it must be highly relativist. But Becker is not saying that at all. He insists there is a limit to this Everyman approach to the past, not least that unlike the historian, Everyman is not interested in learning 'the whole **truth**' and does not want to arrive 'at ultimate causes'. Indeed, history done the Everyman way (remembering that which is useful) can be functional for navigating everyday life but inadequate for doing proper history.

Although Becker acknowledges that historians are Everyman too, constrained by time and space, weaving things remembered, that we are the 'wise men of the tribe' being bards and storytellers who have been entrusted to keep the 'useful myths', this is not an act of creation but has the purpose of guarding the 'actual and the remembered series of **event**s' so our society can judge 'what it has done' as well as what it hopes to do. That Becker does not view history as a science but as a narrative storytelling form written in the present, and thus a product of its time, hardly demands the bad press he has been given by successive generations of reconstructionist historians (see RECONSTRUCTIONIST HISTORY). Of course, given their assumptions, reconstructionist historians would, naturally, say this. Though they tend to omit this from their criticism, Becker is keen to make it clear that the story of the past as written by historians is 'in aim always a true story'. But, you may think sensibly, he recognises that history is always a story that deploys

> all the devices of literary art (statement and generalization, narration and description, comparison and comment and analogy) to present the succession of events in the life of man, and from the succession of events thus presented to derive a satisfactory meaning. The history written by historians, like the history informally fashioned by Mr. Everyman, is thus a convenient blend of truth and fancy, of what we commonly distinguish as 'fact' and 'interpretation'.
>
> (1931 AHA Presidential Address)

Becker then brilliantly dissects the constructionist heart of the history enterprise with his comment that the historian's 'first duty is to be sure of his facts, let their meaning be what it may'. Nevertheless, as he says, 'in every age history is taken to be a story of actual events from which a significant meaning may be derived; and in every age the illusion is that the present version is valid because the related facts are true, whereas former versions are invalid because based upon inaccurate or inadequate facts' (see FACTS; OBJECTIVITY; TRUTH).

Becker's analysis of factualism and history as a narrative undertaking is as rational, reasonable and fresh now as it was more than seventy years ago. Laying out the facts is not like dumping a barrow of bricks. Unlike a brick, which retains its form wherever placed, the form and substance of historical facts, 'having a negotiable existence only in literary discourse, vary with the words employed to convey them'. Lest this drift into some kind of irretrievable relativism, however, he insists that since history is not part of the external material world, but is *an imaginative reconstruction* of vanished events, its form and substance are inseparable. History is still a reconstruction while he acknowledges that as a literary form the substance of history is always an idea *constructed* by the historian. So it is that the special meaning, which the facts are made to convey, emerges from 'the substance-form, which the historian employs to recreate imaginatively a series of events not present to perception'. Becker is thus trying to retain the notion of history as a reconstructive activity while acknowledging its constructive character.

Becker also insists on the utilitarian function of history – that the research that historians do must be transmuted into common knowledge. History in books 'does no work in the world', as he says. History must be practical. History must have a social purpose. Becker claims that because of this every age inevitably produces its own New History in order to understand the past and anticipate the future. This does not generate a malicious history that takes people in, but is an effort at understanding in the light of contemporary needs and hopes. Rather than a fall into an abject relativism, this seems a strong defence of history as an unavoidably contemporary and hugely practical cultural activity.

The echoes of the debate on Becker are still with us today as evidenced in the views of Joyce Appleby, Lynn Hunt and Margaret Jacob in their 1994 book *Telling the Truth about History*. They argue that the sway of postmodernism among late twentieth-century historians would have been much less if the discipline of history had not already been primed, as it were, by historians like Becker (and his partner in crime Charles Beard). Appleby, Hunt and Jacob maintain that crucial to the change 'was the entering wedge of relativism and scepticism . . . As early as the 1930s' with Becker's (and Beard's) 'clarion call of historical relativism by insisting that everyman . . . would write his own history [sic]'. For Appleby, Hunt and Jacob this meant that Everyman had his own version of history and that history functioned as a cultural myth rather than an objective account of the past. This they say is a position not far from that of Friedrich **Nietzsche**. For Appleby, Hunt and Jacob, while they claim to be sophisticated practical realists they are intent on defending the 'objective reconstruction of the past' (Appleby *et al.* 1994: 216). What seems to upset them in particular is the inference they draw from Becker's position (as they read it) that the historian can pick and choose among the facts 'guided by his ideological presuppositions' (ibid.).

Unhappily for Appleby, Hunt and Jacob, this is probably a more 'practical' and 'realistic' appraisal of what historians do, as clearly demonstrated by their own ideological liberal belief in the pluralist and yet individualist, democratic American civic ideal (which, for what it is worth, I would personally endorse – but because I acknowledge it is my ideological preference, just like theirs, rather than think of it as a historical, factual and knowable given). To argue that a proper understanding of 'American history' can only but demonstrate the achievement of its democratic culture seems – ironically – a position of hope over experience given what seem to be the regular outbreaks of anti-liberalism in America's past. Becker's final comment in his AHA address seems fitting. He said that however accurately historians establish the 'facts' of history, they and our interpretations of them and, down the line, our interpretation of our own interpretations, will be perceived in a different perspective as humanity 'moves into the unknown future'.

Life seems to be replete with paradox, and the main one that hangs over Becker's legacy is the confusion of those historians who still think he is defending a dangerous relativism. But only a die-hard and insistent naïve realist could believe this. What seems more likely, at least to me, is that Becker has a far more 'realistic' understanding of the complex and difficult nature of the historical enterprise than that for which he is normally given credit. Although Peter Novick over-eggs the pudding with his view that Becker's (and Beard's) 'assault on objectivist epistemology . . . opened up a long-overdue consideration of what historical scholarship could and should do' (Novick 1988: 277), what Becker did was to acknowledge the evanescent nature of historical interpretation and the myth-making properties of even the most heavily factualised history, while warning the profession not to believe everything it said about the past and, perhaps most of all, what it says about itself. But this falls far short of the charges of metaphysical relativism that are still regularly levelled against him. Frankly, Becker never pushed his case hard enough to earn that criticism. Indeed, the historians who should be worried about what Becker was saying are those who do have severe concerns about the knowability of the past at the most fundamental level – worried should the majority of historians ever figure out what Becker probably meant, and come to agree with him. Becker's position is, perhaps, the best antidote to historical relativism you could find.

Further reading
Appleby, J. *et al.*, 1994; Becker, C., 1931, 1945; Breisach, E., 2003, 1993; Kammen, M., 1973; Novick, P., 1988; Snyder, P.L., 1958; Zagorin, P., 1999.

BIOGRAPHY AND LIFE WRITING

In his influential little book *What is History?* the English historian E.H. **Carr** put the question 'is the object of the historian's inquiry the behaviour of individuals or the action of social forces?' (Carr 1961: 44) (see AGENCY AND STRUCTURE; INTENTIONALITY). Carr's position was pretty clear on this. What he called the 'Bad King John theory of history' was a throwback from 'the primitive stages of historical consciousness' (ibid.: 45). Such an attitude, he said,

> clearly does not fit the more complex society of our times; and the birth in the nineteenth century of the new science of sociology was a response to this growing complexity. Yet the old tradition dies hard. At the beginning of this century [the twentieth] 'history is the biography of great men' was still a reputable dictum.
>
> (Ibid.)

Now Carr was a historian who leaned towards the Marxist left and, hence, he may be fairly regarded as a constructionist historian (see CONSTRUCTIONIST HISTORY) and thus existing within the fold of the empirical-analytical epistemology of history. He wanted to place the individual within the group (he also defined group as a **class**, tribe, or nation). He went on to say it was tempting to distinguish between biography, which treats historical agents as individuals, and history, which treats them as part of a whole, and to argue as a consequence that good biography makes bad history. But, he concluded, this would be wrong. He went on to argue that there is much biography that is also good history.

But there are also biographies that are plainly best thought of as literature because that discipline is methodologically and conceptually limited to viewing historical change as primarily the result of individual behaviour and even personal eccentricity. The subject of the biography too often swamped biographers, even those professional historians who engaged in the activity, as they tended to neglect the bigger structural and contextual issues of economics, science, politics, etc. Carr offers the conclusion that is still generally believed by most historians almost fifty years after he made his judgement that he prefers to reserve the word 'history' for 'the process of inquiry into the past of man [*sic*] in society' (ibid.: 48). So, to be proper historians biographers need, well, to be more like historians – disciplined, methodological, objectively empirical and, unlike biographers, with no inclination toward engaging the author closely with the subject, and maybe sensing the needs of the reader for a moral tale?

This leads us to an initial key point. Historians – even those predisposed to biography as a legitimate historical form – appear to see it as straddling the two disciplines of history and literature and this contaminates and diminishes the former. The reason is, as you will probably have worked out, that most historians do not perceive the individual simply as the motor of change over time – it is far more likely to be the agent *and* structure. And this is where many of the interpretational brush fires of history break out – because no one individual historian's preferred relationship between the two is the same as another's. But there is a further – and far more significant – issue about biography and its latest amplification and theorisation as 'life writing' which is worthy of consideration.

This is the impact of the spectre of epistemological scepticism. It concerns the historian's ability to reconstruct a past, whether it is a past life or other process of change over time. Scepticism about this possibility questions impartial knowledge of any kind when dealing with the past, especially when the historian is conscious of her or his narrative-linguistic construction of history as a historicist cultural discourse (see NARRATIVE; LINGUISTIC TURN; EMPLOTMENT; DISCOURSE; HISTORICISM). Because of this, biography and life writing more broadly

have been under a dual attack – from a modernist avowal that biography is, at best, a 'history-lite' because it tends to concentrate too much on agency alone, and from a postmodernist insistence that no life is anything other than a literary construction with invented beginnings, middles and ends, imposed emplotments, and the unavoidable 'ficticity' of all history writing. This has been complemented by the **aesthetic turn** in recognising the process of **representation** as being of prior importance in any understanding of that being represented.

But, paradoxically, this latter attack has been turned most recently toward a greater appreciation of the postmodernist possibilities in biography as a way of 'doing history' and of illuminating the nature of history itself. The closer intimacy between writer and subject and the acknowledgement that all life is a construction rather than a discoverable given has produced many different forms of historio-bio-graphical experimental work. Perhaps because of its being on the epistemological cusp between history and literature, biography has been an increasingly exciting site of history experimentalism (see EPISTEMOLOGY; EXPERIMENTAL HISTORY).

Among the best-known examples that address the problem of fitting a life to the modernist history planes of cause, event and effect is the 1999 experimental biography of President Ronald Reagan, *Dutch*, by Edmund Morris. Here the author assumed that only an invented life could do justice to the 'untellable' nature of the 'reality'. Recent work in women's life writing has also blended well with the desire to rewrite **gender** as history. This has produced in the past thirty years the development of a substantial cache of **women's history** and also critical responses to the constitution of gender as a history concept invoking a range of critics such as Michel **Foucault**, Jacques Lacan and, in opposition to him, Julia Kristeva, Luce Irigaray and Hélène Cixous. In specific terms that historians might be more familiar with, are Natalie Zemon

Davis, Carolyn Steedman and Liz Stanley, who have tried to incorporate gender awareness with other historical conceptualisations like **class**, while Gayatri Spivak has attempted to do the same with **race** and Judith Butler with **discourse** and performance. Hence gender history/biography has become a locus for the deconstruction of the discipline more broadly.

Most historians probably still think of biography, however, in the context of R.G. **Collingwood** and his argument in favour of the historian empathising with and rethinking the thoughts of the historical agent. But isn't this dangerous? There is the continuing mistrust that getting into the heads of people in the past, while it seems very sensible at one level, also runs the risk of creating a form of history that seems too structured, too pat, too organised, too limited, too narrow. But, if the postmodern critique of 'history' defined as a modernist discipline has any value, it is to pacify these worries by proposing that history as a form of knowledge is not epistemological (based on the idea of the knowing and unified subject), but ontological – the effect of our being in the world (see ONTOLOGY). Combining this with the aesthetic turning toward the questioning of correspondence notions of representation may explain the resurgence of biography as a history genre, but one that is dangerous to the discipline cast as a modernist mechanism for knowing. If distance cannot be put between the historian and his/her history then this can be most readily explored in the construction of individual lives.

One of the most famous examples of the engaged and self-consciously emplotted biography is that of Friedrich **Nietzsche**'s life of Richard Wagner, 'Richard Wagner in Bayreuth', which is enraged as much as it is engaged – so much so that the line between biography and autobiography has become permeable (Magnus and Higgins 1996). But the point that should always be remembered is that the inventory that historians can call upon to write biography is as wide

as the choices they make about the nature of their narrative construction. Like all histories, biographies are designed, and there is as much fiction, narrative voice (who speaks) and author focalisation (who sees) in them as in any history. The bad press that biography has tended to receive from professional historians is probably, in the end, the result of the potential for confusing speaking with seeing. In other words, the historian who sees might also be too readily conflated with the voice telling the story. In addition the overly self-conscious historian-biographer may get completely carried away and bring into the whole process the reader (narratee).

Just as the 'new biography' proclaimed by Virginia Woolf in 1927 suggested that biographers must pay attention to factually reporting the lives and achievements of their subjects, they must also, henceforth, explore personality (though there are costs, she felt, in trying to marry the 'granite' and 'rainbow' of facts and personality). The **New History** in a sense must also do this kind of thing – reporting, explaining and evaluating past action but doing it in recognition of the constraints and opportunities of history construed as a historicist, aesthetic, linguistic, cultural and discursive representation. History can still retain its concern, as Susan Tridgell has noted most recently, for a **truth**, but only as a 'nuanced, moderate realism' (Tridgell 2004: 165). This, I would argue, suggests a narrative truth rather than any other putative kind written in full consciousness of the ironic parody of pastness that history must eventually become.

Despite the debates about biography as a historical **genre** and the uses to which it is put, it continues to occupy shelves in huge numbers in bookstores. The reason probably has little to do with the debates over the epistemological and ontological constructedness of the genre, but more likely stems from the popular belief that historical biographies illuminate 'the bigger picture' of historical change by 'filling in' the details of the past, and elevating the role of the individual in creating change over time. This seems a reasonable conclusion to reach for most purchasers, though it is also a disappointing recognition of the modernist entrapment and definition of biography as just an ersatz form of 'proper history'.

Further reading

Ankersmit, F.R., 2000; Ashton, O.R., 1991; Bevir, M., 1999; *Biography* quarterly journal 1978–; Blanning, T.C.W. and Cannadine, D., 1996; Davis, N.Z., 1995; Edel, L., 1957; Hook, S., 1943; Jolly, M., 2001; Magnus, B. and Higgins, K.M., 1996; Marcus, L., 1994; Morris, E., 1999; Munslow, A., 2003a, 2001, 1992; Passerini, L., 2000; Rosenstone, R. A., 1988, 1975; Shortland, M. and Yeo, R., 1996; Steedman, C., 1986; Tridgell, S., 2004; Woolf, V., 1958.

C

CARR, E.H. (1892–1982)

Edward Hallett Carr was recognised as a distinguished historian of Russian and Soviet history. However, he is often, if not better, remembered for his ideas on the character of history in his book *What is History?*, first published in 1961. These were regarded initially, and still are in some quarters, as dangerously relativist. The divisions over history as an **epistemology** (theory of knowledge) are nowhere better demonstrated than in the conflicting opinions held on Carr's views on history, or the way his legacy can readily be appropriated by all sides, proper and postmodern (see POSTMODERNISM). Until Keith **Jenkins**'s reappraisal of Carr's philosophy of history, Carr had been seen, almost universally among historians, as standing for a distinctively relativist, if not indeed a sceptical, conception of the functioning of the historian (Jenkins 1995).

Explaining Carr's 'radicalism', the philosopher of history Michael Stanford has argued that Carr 'insisted that the historian couldn't divorce himself from the outlook and interests of his age [*sic*]' (Stanford 1994: 86). Stanford also quotes Carr's own claim that the historian 'is part of history' with a particular 'angle of vision over the past' (ibid.). As Stanford points out, Carr's 'first answer . . . to the question "What is History?"' is that it is a dialogue between the historian and his/her **facts**, generating an unending debate between the present and the past. The British historian John Tosh also weighs in with his judgement that Carr's arrogant thinking, by placing the historian at the centre of the history project,

merely strengthens the hands of the epistemological sceptics (Tosh 2001: 126).

These examples do not seem to me worrying for historians because they do not represent a case of epistemological radicalism (see EXPERIMENTAL HISTORY). My concerns about Stanford and Tosh's doubts are, of course, the product of my intellectual situatedness as a writer about the past. Today, with our sense of the frailties and failures of representationalism, referentialism and inductive **inference**, more and more history writing is based on the assumption that we can know nothing genuinely truthful about the reality of the past beyond the single sentence-length statement (see REPRESENTATION). It is quite wrong (probably the result of an outbreak of epistemological moral panic), in my view, to suggest that Carr views history as the fabrication of the historian. Rather, what has happened is that our contemporary conditions of existence have created a much deeper uncertainty about the nature of knowledge creation and its (mis-)uses in the humanities.

It follows, a growing number of historians believe, that we do not 'discover' (the 'truthful?' 'actual?' 'real?' 'certain?') patterns in apparently contingent events because, instead, we unavoidably impose our own hierarchies of significance on them (this is what we believe/want to see/read in the past) (see EVENT). I do not think many historians today are naïve realists. Few accept that there is only one given meaning in the **evidence**. While we may all agree at the event level that something happened at a particular past time and place, its significance (its meaning as we narrate it), most historians believe, can only be provided by them (see NARRATIVE). The meaning is not immanent in the event itself. Moreover, the challenge to the distinction of fact and fiction as we configure our historical narratives, and further acknowledgements of the cognitive power of rhetoric, style and trope (metaphors are arguments and explanations), not only provide a formal challenge to traditional empiricism, but force us to acknowledge that as historians we are making moral choices as we describe past reality (see TROPE/FIGURATION; ETHICAL TURN).

Does all this add up to a more fundamental criticism of historical knowing than imagined in *What is History?* by Carr? I think so. If this is what historical **relativism** means today, I believe it provides a much larger agenda for the contemporary historian than Carr's acknowledgement that the historian is in a dialogue with the facts, or that **sources** only become evidence when used by the historian. As Jenkins has pointed out, Carr ultimately accepts the epistemological model of historical explanation as the definitive mode for generating historical understanding and meaning (Jenkins 1995: 1–6, 43–63). This fundamentally devalues the currency of what Carr has to say, as it does that of all **reconstructionist** empiricists who follow his lead. This judgement is not, as you would imagine, shared by them. For illustration, in misunderstanding the nature of 'semiotics – the postmodern?' as he querulously describes it, the historian of Latin America Alan Knight has claimed that Carr remains significant today precisely because of his warning a generation ago to historians to 'interrogate documents and to display a due scepticism as regards their writer's motives' (Knight 1997: 747). To maintain, as Knight does, that Carr is in some way pre-empting the postmodern challenge to historical knowing is unhelpful to those who wish to establish Carr's position in *What is History?*

Carr, for example, tried to fix the status of evidence with his objections to what he understood to be the logic of R.G. **Collingwood's** sceptical position. Collingwood's logic could, claims Carr, lead to the dangerous idea that this/here is no certainty or intrinsicality in historical meaning – this/here are only (what I would call) the discourses of historians – a situation that Carr refers to as 'total scepticism' – a situation where history ends up as 'something spun out of the human brain' and which leads to the dangerous conclusion that this/here can be no 'objective historical truth' (Carr 1987 [1961]: 26) (see DISCOURSE; OBJECTIVITY; TRUTH). Carr explicitly rejects Friedrich **Nietzsche**'s notion that (historical?) truth is effectively defined by fitness for purpose. The basis for Carr's opinion was his belief in the power of empiricism to deliver the truth, whether it fits or not (ibid.: 27). Historians ultimately serve the evidence, not vice versa. This guiding precept thus excludes the possibility that 'one interpretation is as good as another' even when we cannot (as we cannot in writing history) guarantee 'objective or truthful interpretation'.

For all his epistemological conservatism, Carr wished to reinforce the notion that he was a radical. As he said in the preface to the 1987 second edition of *What is History?*, 'in recent years I have increasingly come to see myself, and to be seen, as an intellectual dissident' (ibid.: 6). But his contribution actually lies in the way in which he failed to be an epistemological radical. In the manner of his return to the Cartesian and foundationalist fold lies the importance of *What is History?*. The book's distinction is its rejection of epistemological scepticism.

The *idée fixe* of mainstream historians today is that history is an inferential and interpretative process that can achieve truth through objectivism – that is, getting the story straight (from the evidence). The unresolved paradox in this is the legacy of *What is History?*. I assume a good number of historians still recommend Carr to their students as the starting point of methodological and philosophical sophistication in order to vouchsafe the ultimate priority of factualism and objectivism over the dialogic historian. This is why *What is History?*, for the majority of historians, is something of a bulwark against post-constructive and post-empirical history. For others it remains a walk on the epistemological wild side.

Further reading
Carr, E.H., 1987 [1961], 1958–64, 1950–3; Cox, M., 2000; Jenkins, K., 1995; Jones, C., 1998; Knight, A., 1997; Stanford, M., 1994; Tosh, J., 2001.

CAUSATION

This is one of the most important metaphysical issues that historians come across (see METAPHYSICS). Its importance is, oddly, reflected by the fact that most professional historians tend to avoid talking about the nature of causation. Generally speaking, causal relations exist between events (see EVENT): if event A occurs then event B occurs, and it can be reasonably demonstrated that event A explains the subsequent (temporally sequential) occurrence of event B. The central question for most historians is how to explain the determining nature of the relationship. The fact that the debate on the nature of causality remains potent among philosophers of history (if not among its practitioners) is evidenced by Benedetto **Croce**'s and R.G. **Collingwood**'s questioning as to whether causality is really a part of what it is that historians do. Both Croce and Collingwood suggested that all history is the history of thought, and while this does not mean that causation is wholly redundant in history, it does imply that the really important object is to find the thought behind the action (see INTENTIONALITY; INTELLECTUAL HISTORY; REPRESENTATION). This means that the event itself is secondary to a prior form of knowledge that is ideational, that is of, relating to or produced by ideas in the mind of the historian and the agent (Collingwood 1994 [1946]: 214–15) (see A PRIORI/A POSTERIORI). Re-enacting

thoughts behind actions and events is thus one way to address causation. Another is that of the **covering laws** as proposed by Carl Hempel whereby historians subsume actions/events under general laws that explain particular groups of actions/events. Causation has thus divided the philosophers into at least two camps: idealists and positivists. The debate still exists today in the work of idealist philosophers of history like William H. Dray and Alan Donagan, and positivists Patrick Gardiner and more recently Clayton Roberts.

In determining causal relations the historian is caught in the perennial bind of what appears to be and what is. The Scottish sceptical empiricist philosopher David Hume argued that in judging the nature of a causal relationship all we have to go on are our perceptions of the pattern(s) of connection (see EMPIRICISM). We cannot know, through observation, the *real* nature of determining forces. By consulting the evidence and under the influence of appropriate social theory, historians do, however, believe that this problem can be overcome, thus making understanding causal connections the central feature of **historical explanation**. As such, historical explanation demands that historians discover the *real* causes of the events and processes found in the past through inference.

What has become the conventional view of causal analysis was summarised by the British historian E.H. **Carr**, who argued that the relation of the historian to causes is the same as that to **facts**:

> The causes determine his interpretation of the historical process, and his interpretation determines his selection and marshalling of the causes. The hierarchy of causes, the relative significance of one cause or set of causes or of another, is the essence of interpretation.
>
> (Carr 1987 [1961]: 103)

Hence, as Carr claims, the study of history is a (circular) study of causes (and facts). Carr's recommendation to the historian when faced with events and the need to explain them is first to assign several possible causes, then establish a hierarchy that implies a pattern of relationships between the facts as events. Once the historian distinguishes underlying as well as more immediate causes he/she is well on the path to an interpretation that can then be cast as a historical **narrative**.

Carr alerts us to the problem that all historians face, which is understanding the role of necessity in cause and effect. For the main part historians reject the philosopher David Hume's scepticism about not being able to know real causes, preferring to seek out those forces that necessitate subsequent events. This is sometimes (and confusingly) referred to as sufficient causality. Such a posture is demanded by the empiricist and realist thrust of most conventional **reconstructionist history** and **constructionist history** (see GENRE). The empiricist theory of causation recognises its enormously complex nature, but it is founded four-square on the presumed existence of objectively derived and knowable 'facts', only through which can we find causes. Take the question of what caused the assassination of Abraham Lincoln. A full explanation of why it occurred involves the historian recognising that Lincoln wanted to visit Ford's Theatre to relax with his wife (agent intentionality?); that, given Lincoln's anti-slavery stance, some Americans would hold a grudge (human nature, a covering law or historical determination of some kind?); and that handguns can kill people (the mechanistic physics of nature?). Any of these 'facts' could be regarded as the primary cause of Lincoln's assassination. Or any from another list.

A cause is sufficient, therefore, if the effect always follows that cause (being shot at point-blank range is sufficient to kill you). Sufficient cause is usually distinguished from necessary cause. A cause is necessary if its effect would otherwise have been absent (the assassin had not been in the theatre). Most historical explanations thus depend on sorting out what are necessary and what are sufficient causes, and what hierarchy exists among what may

turn out to be chains of causes. Also what of the counterfactual situation – what if Lincoln had not had an anti-slavery stance? The complexity of causation is further evidenced by the reversal of Friedrich **Nietzsche**, that to grasp the nature of causality (or rather to reject it altogether) the effect is primary in the search for cause. In a larger sense the future always determines the past because it determines our apprehension of the present – the future is the place where we locate our goal-making desires and the past is the material for their realisation. This orientation suggests why history is written like fiction. It is because historical narrative has the power to complicate cause and effect. Causes do not have to be offered sequentially, indeed they are often described in the historian's narrative as a problem in need of a solution – behind the effect a prior fact lurks that 'explains the situation'. So it is that in history causes are often given as effects in search of an interpretational explanation (see TELEOLOGY).

In the physical or natural sciences deductive inference has generally held sway. In science, causation is a matter of observation of regular occurrences, hypothesis-framing, and then empirical testing (experimentation) with the express aim of generating covering laws. **Truth** emerges through the correspondence theory of knowledge. In the literary or human sciences we are less able to see behind the appearances of (historical and usually textualised) phenomena. Tailor-made for most conventional historians, however, is the realist-inspired explanation of causality provided by the philosopher C. Behan McCullagh. Working from the assumption that the aim of causal theory is to distinguish those aspects of causes that explain what are causes and what are not, McCullagh confirms the definition offered in the first paragraph of this entry, but adds the gloss that a cause 'is an event which produces a conjunction of something that has a tendency to produce an effect of the kind which occurred in certain circumstances, and [in] the presence of . . . triggering circumstances' – probabilities plus a combination of necessary and sufficient causes (McCullagh 1998: 179).

But the decisions involved in such a realist process of causal analysis are almost entirely based on the assumptions held by the historian. His/her presentist and teleological assumptions concern the forces he/she believes influence people, processes and events like **agency/structure**, intentionality, motivational psychology and various determinisms such as geography, **gender**, ideology, ethics, materiality, culture and **race**. The teleological assumptions held by the historian (the future conceived in the present determines the past) influence the form in which causal questions are put. Because of his/her prior consideration of the historical field, the questions he/she frames about causality take a particular shape. In asking why this happened or whether, if something else had happened, the same effect would be found, the historian is not only predetermining meaning (to a greater or lesser) extent by the form in which he/she casts the problem, but he/she is also working teleologically within his/her own selection and arrangement of the **evidence**.

Causal analysis is undertaken, therefore, according to a set of pre-formed ideas about what is most likely to be the meaning of one set of events occurring after another. The decision to fix meaning through a particular causal connection will be based, in large part, on the historian's preference for a particular interpretative outcome rather than for *the* one found objectively in the evidence. Facts, fairly obviously, do not just turn up and certainly do not carry within themselves predetermined meanings. In the end much depends on the type of historian you are and what answers you give to questions like 'How did the world work in the past?' (or, for that matter, does in the present), 'What are your ontological beliefs?' and 'What methodology do you intend to apply to give effect to them?' Do you believe in agent **intentionality**, or the materialist theory of history, or the power of complex social structures to flatten out historical change (see AGENCY/STRUCTURE)?

Just what mechanism do you believe shapes change over time either generally or in specific instances?

The nature of causation can be usefully explored, therefore, by looking at it from the other end of the process – from how and why we deploy our theories of causality. As we know, the assumptions and desires of the historian are eventually cast in a narrative form of explanation. How does the construction of our narrative influence our causal explanation? Only the crudest of reconstructionist historians (see RECONSTRUCTIONIST HISTORY) believe that if their interpretational historical narrative is written with direct reference to the evidence, then its structure or pattern will correspond to the causal structure of the past. Slightly more sophisticated reconstructionists and probably all constructionist historians (see CONSTRUCTIONIST HISTORY) realise that causation, when translated into narrative, is a far more complex process than the simple notion of the narrative defined as 'this happened, then that'. Narrative does not require or entail that *the* cause be followed by *the* effect. From the politically liberal perspective of those who believe in agent intentionality, narrative represents people's decisions as choices, and events as particular responses rather than effects. Narrative is explanatory for politically directed liberal historians because they reject a deterministic causality that they believe to be associated with ideological positions of which they disapprove. The reverse also applies, of course.

We should be clear that the complexity of causation cannot be easily divorced from questions of narrative explanation, not least because narrative itself has an ambiguous status among historians. Some philosophers of history, like William Gallie, believe that narrative is *the* essence of history because there is a strong epistemological connection between evidence and explanation via causality as translated into the narrative form (see FILM AND HISTORY; FORM AND CONTENT). Other historians like John Tosh speak for the constructionist mainstream in finding narrative to be a relatively weak method for explaining the past if it is simply a causal description of 'this happened, then that' (Tosh 2001: 96).

The ambiguity of narrative seems, therefore, to have something to do with the individual historian's attitude to the authority of empiricism as a way of knowing and its ability to establish and explain causal connections (see EPISTEMOLOGY). Historians like Hayden **White** claim that the narrative, as an explanation of causal connectivity, is imposed precisely because it is prefigured by the historian. White criticises as naïve any rustic empiricist evidence–causation–narrative symmetry. As he says, the idea that the causes 'for events (necessary if not sufficient) or reasons (conscious or unconscious) for events' taking place as they in fact did [and which] are set forth in the narrative in the form of the story it tells' fails to recognise the variety of narratives that can be told and that themselves prefigure the type of causal connections to be made (White 1987: 41). White endorses the argument that the historian brings to the evidence beliefs in all manner of things that affect their thinking about how history 'works' as an epistemology. It is White's particular contribution to the argument to point out that, because history is a literary artefact, historians make causal links as part of their overall constitution and prefiguration of the historical field through the exercise of their **historical imagination** and employment of trope, **emplotment**, argument, ideological preference and philosophical orientation (see TROPE/FIGURATION).

All this suggests that causation is a central but, like so much else in history these days, an open question. The strong advocate of constructionist social science history Christopher Lloyd argues that any ambivalence about causation among historians may be the fault of philosophers because of their lack of agreement about the nature of causal explanation (Lloyd 1993: 50–1). From Lloyd's perspective, causal explanation is necessarily bound up with hypothesis-testing and model-making, and without that historians cannot offer convincing explanations. As Lloyd puts it, the need for historians today is to establish causal connections between complex social structures, and that demands the construction 'of the problems and objects for enquiry [which] takes place within theories [that are] responsive to empirical findings that they help to uncover and interpret' (ibid.: 51). Like Patrick Gardiner, Lloyd seems to be saying that empiricism alone is never enough; it has to be theoretically informed and, by implication, the form in which the causal analysis is cast is of secondary significance.

But there is little doubt that in recent years the interest in history has moved increasingly from absorption with causation and social science explanation, to the form in which historians deploy their stories. The search for the Holy Grail of Real Causes is now discredited as an example of (what it always was?) bad metaphysics (Gardiner 1961 [1951]: 110). It seems clear that it is the contribution of Hayden White that has prompted this shift in focus to the analysis of history as a discourse, rather than simply as a trade in empirical data organised via the free market of social theory. History is seen more and more as being constituted through the poetic, ideological and ethical decisions of the historian, but most importantly there is the growing acceptance that the empirical foundation is not a sheet anchor that guarantees contact with the real past (see NEW HISTORICISM; AESTHETIC TURN; LINGUISTIC TURN; Frank R. ANKERSMIT). Historians now often begin their work thinking about the kind of narrative they wish to generate as much as the evidentially secure and true statements they endeavour to make.

Michel **Foucault**, for example, offers his own version of causality and its role in the creation of historical knowledge. He argues that as a linguistically determined perspective, historical knowledge cannot distinguish between what philosophers of history think and what practitioners do. It is only when history is busy examining its philosophy, and where its knowledge comes from (and how it is used), that we can confront anew issues like causation and the nature of change over time. Through his deployment of the **episteme**, the term he uses to refer to how a culture co-ordinates knowledge within a historical period, he has radically challenged the conventional notion of causality. His paradigm of four epistemes holds that historical epochs do not grow organically out of each other, but instead unexpectedly emerge homologously to fill in the epistemological spaces suddenly vacated by other conditions of knowledge creation. Foucauldian causality does not exist in the modernist (see MODERNISM) sense of evolving historically, but rather issues forth structurally as a discursive formation (see DISCOURSE).

It is important in thinking about causality to grasp the significance of the present debate on the nature of history: that the challenge to the empiricist paradigm assumes that our descriptions of historical events are at best only representations because there is no direct way to acquire first-hand historical knowledge (see REPRESENTATION). Moreover, historians should admit the consequences of the overlapping character of historical event and historical interpretation, in that the historical text is an inter-text touched and chastened by the social and political structures of the age that produced it (see HISTORICISM). This seems to suggest that causality will always remain uncertain. Uncertain because of the way it can only point to what *appears* to be, because of its inferentially construed nature, and because of the vast array of assumptions and prefigurations the historian brings to bear. These qualifications undermine the reconstructionist and constructionist foundational commitment to an accurately discernible reality 'out there', and the belief that we can adequately justify causal explanation through empirical testing.

Further reading

Carr, E.H., 1987 [1961]; Collingwood, R.G., 1994 [1946]; Croce, B., 1970 [1927], 1968 [1917], 1964 [1913], 1923; Donagan, A., 1959; Dowe, P., 1992; Dray, W.H., 1957; Gardiner, P., 1961 [1951], 1959; Hempel, C.G., 1965, 1942; Lloyd, C., 1993; McCullagh, C.B., 1998; Munslow, A., 2003b, 1997a; Roberts, C., 1996; Tosh, J., 2001; White, H., 1996, 1987.

CLASS

Class is a substantive concept (see CONCEPTS IN HISTORY) that historians deploy to organise the-past-as-history. Two basic questions must be asked of class as they are asked of all the concepts that historians use. First the epistemological (see EPISTEMOLOGY): as a way of knowing why does a particular historian prefer one concept to another to explain the-past-as-history? Second the ontological (see ONTOLOGY): how influential on the choice is the historian's present state of existence (see HISTORICISM)? It seems to me that the concepts we use are as much the result of a conscious choice about the form of the history we wish to write (a choice that may be ideological, and in the case of class usually it is) and the particular position on the anti-realist/realist spectrum that the individual historian occupies, as they are derived from the evidence (see FORM AND CONTENT).

According to the leftist cultural materialist historian and literary critic Raymond Williams, class as a modern historical term emerged in English history in the period 1770 to 1840, growing out of the social experiences of the industrial revolution and urbanisation: effectively redefining class from the earlier sense of estates, ranks or orders to one of an emergent social system based on changed material structures. As Williams's exercise demonstrates, distinguishing the senses in which the term class was used in that period is regarded as an important function of the historian with, it is argued, the utility of the concept dependent upon the **source(s)**. But – I suggest – does it not also depend upon the historian's attitude toward the nature of representationalism and reality, as well as his/her personal and ideological predispositions (see REPRESENTATION)? Just as Williams may perceive class through his own epistemological and ontological assumptions, so an American historian reading Alexander Hamilton's Federalist essay number 35 might elect to infer in a particular way the relationship of class to an anti-Federalist position based upon his/her understanding of linguistic usage in the late 1780s (see INFERENCE). Equally, his/her personal preferences for a particular representational relationship between class and federalism cannot be overlooked. The historian may find the meaning sought in the concept he/she invents.

The work of the historian is bounded by many constraints. But two are particularly important here: inferentialism (the notion that reality generates concepts) and representationalism (that the concepts thus generated represent reality). These boundaries, while permitting the defence of empiricism, also allow that concepts presuppose language use and social practice(s). Without this acknowledgement how else can we explain the huge variety of uses and meanings squeezed out of the concept of class? Every use of class illustrates the links between **evidence**, the historian's position on representation and reality, and their conceptual organisation of content through form (see REPRESENTATION). For example, in the **historiography** of class the reductionism so beloved of economistic Marxists has been modified often and vigorously by, for instance, Lenin's reformulation through the vanguard of the proletariat, by Antonio Gramsci's recasting in the shape of hegemony and the organic intellectual, by E.P. Thompson's emphasis upon the younger (and less reductionist) Marx, by Gareth Stedman Jones's anti-representationalist recognition of the languages of class, through to Patrick Joyce's narratives of class. As for the often unstated assumptions of amateur historians conducting oral history interviews, well, who knows (see ORAL HIS-

TORY)? Few historians doubt that certain well-attested events occurred, but the particular class model invoked by a historian is much more the consequence of their attitude toward the knowability of reality and their belief in their capacity to represent it.

Patrick Joyce, for instance, in his analysis of class in England, points to the evidence of how class was constituted as part of a **discourse** rather than as a single unalloyed fact. He claims that the Reform Bill of 1832 became justified as the 'representation' of the burgeoning middle class who viewed him- or herself 'as an objective social fact (a facticity it has ever since retained, such is the power of this nineteenth century discourse over us)' (Joyce 1995: 323). So powerful did this facticity become in the hands of certain historians that Joyce maintains that the lineage of the middle class has been imagined to go back to the Middle Ages. In other words, how historians use their concepts directly structures their disposition of history. Joyce's intellectually marginalised position among British nineteenth-century social historians stems from his anti-representationalist *and* anti-inferentialist assumptions that class is not intrinsic to the past, but is largely the historian's **narrative** imposition upon a pre-existing social discourse. Following the work of Gareth Stedman Jones and others, Joyce views the middle class as the discursive construction of nineteenth-century political liberals rather than the brute experience of class relations as generated by the harsh realities of the industrial city.

I would suggest that historians who deploy class (or for that matter any foundational or realist concept) constantly demonstrate what pragmatic and anti-realist philosophers like John Dewey, Charles S. Peirce, W.V. Quine, Wilfred Sellars and, more recently, the anti-representationalist Richard **Rorty** have argued, that the logical empiricist distinction between what is granted to the evidence by the mind of the historian is a social convenience rather than an epistemological necessity. Concepts like class, because of their centrality to much historical explanation, have to be confronted epistemologically by asking if historians can rely on either representationalism or inference to derive truth value. In spite of being thought of otherwise, concepts like class are not representations of reality, and neither are they indisputable inferences – they are only guides to further thinking within the discourse of history.

The response of the practical realist defenders of concepts like class is to suggest to the deconstructionist historian (see DECONSTRUCTIONIST HISTORY) that all concepts, words, standards and values in history unavoidably coexist and react with the other material structures and social experiences of the past. Historical understanding is far more complex than the assumption of anti-representationalism and anti-realism will allow. This debate is unlikely to be resolved given the gulf in the assumptions of the linguistic-turners and those practical realist historians who believe in conceptually knowable and objective social experience – or as one of America's leading historians of class Harvey J. Kaye might insist, thinking historically by seeing the reality.

Listed below under 'Further reading' are useful introductions to the nature of class as a historical concept that (usually and perhaps unintentionally on the part of the author) also tell us much about attitudes toward reality and representation.

Further reading
Alexander, S., 1984; Balibar, E. and Wallerstein, I., 1991; Belchem, J. and Kirk, N., 1997; Brody, D., 1979; Dworkin, D.L., 1997; Jones, G.S., 1983; Joyce, P., 2002, 1998, 1995, 1994; Kaye, H.J., 1995; Kiernan, V.G., 1988; Kirk, N., 1995, 1987; Marable, M., 1995; Rothenburg, P.S., 1998; Thompson, E.P., 1963.

CLIOMETRICS

Cliometrics is a term that came into common usage from the 1960s onwards in the context of the rise of econometric (economic measurement) or the New Economic History (see NEW HISTORY). The term cliometrics is a neologism fabricated by connecting Clio, the Greek goddess or Muse of history, to mathematical and/or statistical measurement (hence clio-metrics). One of the most straightforward definitions of cliometric history is that provided by the historian who was, arguably, the leading late twentieth-century exponent, Robert W. Fogel, in his book *Without Consent or Contract: The Rise and Fall of American Slavery* (1989). He said cliometrics is 'the application of the behavioural models and statistical methods of the social sciences to the study of history' (p. 423). Simple and to the point, this methodological development literally led to the 're-counting' of what really happened in the past in order to stiffen the discipline's most basic **epistemological** principles – not least the testing of propositions through comparison via the study of the **sources** and amenable kinds of historical **evidence**.

The broad aim for historians is to justify their statements about, and descriptions of, what happened in the past. **Inferences** are drawn as to what it all means and usually historians recognise that **events** and processes are rarely simply matters of chance. It is routinely observed that certain events are somehow connected with each other. The regularity of an association suggests **causation**. That the vast majority of working-class Irish Catholic immigrants in the city of Boston, USA in the 1890s apparently voted for the Democratic Party mayoral candidates, while Protestant third-generation members of the middle classes voted Republican, suggests that certain voting preferences clearly existed, but it might also tell us something about the political assimilation of immigrants. The problem is, of course, that regularity does not of itself confirm cause and effect. What appear at first blush to be regularities in human behaviour may turn out to be spurious because of their strictly limited context or skewed evidence, or simply because they are an example of the ecological fallacy (the fallacy that because two variables occur in the same context they are causally connected, e.g. a high correlation between rainfall and divorce rates does not mean that wet weather brings on marital discord). Quite often what seems to have a cause and effect relationship in the short term simply dissolves over a longer period or when new data are injected. Moreover, law-like regularities or **covering laws** are not at all like the laws we find in science – the significant feature of which is unvarying repetition and, therefore, predictability. But this does not stop many historians using law-like generalisations as they try to infer meaning.

Indeed, the rise of the social sciences from the late nineteenth century (sociology, economics, politics) and the development of the *Annales* generated a huge demand among historians for ways to sharpen up, as the mid- to late twentieth-century American political historian Lee Benson suggested, their 'impressions' (he was specifically referring to the realm of American politics in the 1830s and 1840s) about what happened and what it meant. There was quickly also a parallel demand to harden the **objectivity** and **truth** of historical analysis as well as to reduce the significance of **agency** before **structure.** Critics of cliometric approaches – of which there were and still are many – have claimed that statistical technique dehumanises people, ignores the qualitative, is too deterministic, crudely apes science and simplifies the complexity of human decision-making. Despite such criticisms of statistical analysis, many historians are ready to admit that the use of mathematics and statistical analysis has substantial methodological benefits. However, there is very little attention paid to the epistemological assumptions behind it. Essentially, cliometrics presupposes a severe and relentless **constructionist** orientation to the past and though it aims at empirical and statistical accuracy it is, of course, no less (or no more?) ideological than any other form of history – as the rather odd *Which Road to the Past?* (1984), which was the product of

collaboration between the arch cliometrician Robert W. Fogel and **reconstructionist** Geoffrey **Elton**, reveals.

The modern(ist) use of statistical sources and evidence by historians really began with the rise of German economic and social history in the last thirty years of the nineteenth century, and was pursued up to and through the work of the French and British economic and social historians to a flowering in the mid-twentieth century in the work of, for example, B.R. Mitchell, Phyllis Deane, E.A. Wrigley, J.R. Vincent and Peter Laslett, as well as quantitative methods popularisers like Roderick Floud in the 1970s and beyond. Social science and quantitative history are now an integral part of the history landscape with their own institutional structure (catered for by specialist publishers, dedicated journals and, for example, every two years a major European Social Science History Conference attended by thousands of like-minded historians).

However, the chief boost for cliometrics was undoubtedly provided in the United States in the 1950s with the emergence of the New Econometric/Economic, New Political and (as the latest kind of) New Social Historians. One of the first landmarks was the paper on the profitability of slavery by Alfred H. Conrad and John R. Meyer published in 1958, followed from the 1960s by a widely published group of (invariably American) cliometricians in the economic, political and social genres that included William O. Aydelotte, Robert Fogel, Lee Benson, Peter Temin, Allan G. Bogue, Walter Dean Burnham, Joel Silbey, Stephen Thernstrom, Stanley Engerman, Roger L. Ransom, Herbert Gutman, Richard Sutch, Paul David, Donald McCloskey, Robert P. Swierenga, J. Morgan Kousser and many others. Certain topics remained constant throughout this thirty-year period: measuring slavery, aspects of US economic change such as the counterfactual (hypothetical) arguments about the economic impact of the railroads (if the railroads had not been built, what difference would it have made to US economic growth?), voting behaviour, social stratification, transportation, immigration, demography, etc. All were areas where large amounts of statistical data were available and ready to be processed.

Cliometrics received a technological boost in the 1960s and up to the present with the advent and wider use of computers and computational software packages and its dissemination in the periodical literature and in the training of social science historians. Indeed, your author completed his PhD in the 1970s, producing a cliometric study of the urban political assimilation of European immigrants in America between 1870 and 1920. It was a study packed full of social science model making, hypothesis-testing, proxy variables, significance levels, coefficients of elasticity and regression equations with their coefficients of determination (useful in establishing the degree to which a certain variable is related to other variables). In spite of my determined use of the *Call/360 Statistical Package (STATPACK) Version Two*, published by the IBM Corporation (1969, 1970, second edition, February 1970) my once shiny PhD now languishes, supporting a shaky bookcase. But there are better-known examples of the 1960s and 1970s statistical turn, which are to be found in a 1970s proliferation of journal articles explaining the appeal and utility of the cliometric methodology. Formidable titles include, for example, A.J. Lichtman's 'Correlation, regression and the ecological fallacy: a critique' (1974), J. Morgan Kousser's 'Ecological regression and the analysis of past politics' (1973), E. and M. Black's 'The Wallace vote in Alabama: a multiple regression analysis' (1973) and E.T. Jones's 'Using ecological regression' (1974). And there are probably hundreds if not thousands of similar examples in the literature of the time produced in North America and Western Europe. Statistically informed histories retain their vigour up to the present. Taken from the most recent issue I have to hand of the *Economic History Review* is, for example, Joyce Burnette's 'The wages and employment of female day-labourers in English agriculture, 1740–1850' (Burnette 2004). In this article the author deploys an array of sophisticated statistical techniques that include scatterplots (of nominal female summer wages and relative female employment), regression analyses (wages) and trends (in nominal wages, summer wage ratios, real summer and winter wages).

One interesting methodological consequence of the rise of cliometrics was the emergence of counterfactualism – 'what if' history. In a sense all history thinking is counterfactual in that the historian sets up a proposition – a thought experiment along the lines of 'what if we assume . . . ' – and then either knocks it down or knocks it into shape, bringing it closer to 'this is what did happen'. The aim is, as always, to find out the truth of the matter. Indeed, the debate between Fogel and Elton in their joint venture *Which Road to the Past?* (1984) reveals the continued power of that aim. While they could not reconcile their constructionist and reconstructionist differences (over whether history was or was not a social science) they agreed on the need to pursue 'truth'. Cliometrics clearly distinguishes itself from the empirical reconstruction of the past revelling in its appeal to deductive-nomological explanations based on what is assumed to be rational action (behaviourist) theory. For cliometricians, because they have a propensity to rely on the observable, the intentional and the rational, there is always an assumption of fixity in human behaviour (see AGENCY/STRUCTURE; COVERING LAWS; EPISTEMOLOGY; HISTORICAL EXPLANATION).

History thus 're-counted', or 'history by numbers', is not going to become unfashionable in the near future, certainly as long as enough historians have the urge to measure and calculate past economic, social, political and cultural phenomena. To the extent that to quantify or not has been an issue that divides historians it is largely because of personal preference and whether or not you want to learn the mathematics. Much the same argument might be made about those historians, for example, who refuse the lure of the narrative-linguistic approach as such changes can be problematic given the re-skilling demanded by such choices, not to mention the epistemological and ontological debates that have to be engaged with. For myself, as a historian who 'switched' epistemologies in mid-career, from social science cliometric approaches to the discursive and deconstructive, I think what should always be remembered about Clio is that she really is epistemologically open, and we historians are free to choose the kind and nature of our engagement with the past.

The digitised technological revolution of the 1990s – computing and the Internet – has undoubtedly further advanced quantitative history. In addition to the obvious benefits of computers for the retrieval, storage and manipulation of data, primary sources, archives, databases and datasets are now more readily available via the World Wide Web (plus abstracts, indexes, electronic history journals, discussion lists, genealogical sites, etc.) and in college and university libraries (the ubiquity of the CD-ROM is testament to this).

Cliometrics is a term used less often these days, passed over in favour of more specific genre definitions such as econometric, behaviourist, 'serial' or social science, or quantitative history. The reason is in part because it is an ugly and inelegant description of a scientificist approach that, in the wake of the **linguistic**, **aesthetic** and **ethical turn**s, seems out of place and vaguely *déclassé*. But, as with every trend in history (and there are always plenty of them), it either fades away or becomes so entrenched that it ceases to be recognised as something special at all. This latter development is the case with cliometrics – reincarnated now as a set of specialist methodologies within the overall epistemological history model. There is little doubt as to its continued appeal for many social, political and economic historians.

Further reading
Aydelotte, W.O., 1971; Aydelotte, W.O. *et al.*, 1972; Benson, L., 1961; Black, E. and M., 1973; Bogue, A.G., 1968; Burnette, J., 2004; Burnham, W.D., 1965; Conrad, A.H. and Meyer, J.R., 1958; David, P.A., 1967; David, Paul A. *et al.*, 1976; Engerman, S., 1967; Fairburn, M., 1999; Floud, R., 1973; Fogel, R.W., 1989, 1975a, 1975b, 1966; Fogel, R.W. and Elton, G.R., 1984; Fogel, R. and Engerman, S.L., 1974, 1971; Gutman, H., 1975; Harvey, C. and Press, J., 1996; Jones, E.T., 1974; Kousser, J.M., 1980, 1973; Laslett, P., 1972; Lewis, M.J. and Lloyd-Jones, R., 1996; Lichtman, A.J., 1974; McCloskey, D.N., 1987; Mitchell, B.R. and Deane, P., 1962; Rabb, T.K., 1983; Ransom, R.L. and Sutch, R., 1977; Silbey, J., 1985; Stein, S., 1999; Swierenga, R.P., 1968; Temin, P., 1973; Thernstrom, S., 1973; Tosh, J., 2001; Vincent, J.R., 1967; Wrigley, E.A., 1966.

COLLIGATION

Many historians have a view of inductive **inference** that holds that any concepts (see CONCEPTS IN HISTORY) used to navigate the past are determined by observed **facts**. Most historians possess, therefore, an empiricist explanation for the formation of their concepts (see EMPIRICISM). When historians conceptualise a structure or pattern to the **event**s in the past it is generally assumed, if correct inferential methods have been deployed, to be an objective discovery (see OBJECTIVITY; EMPLOTMENT). The question, however, is whether these are *real* structures or patterns, or whether they are deformed as they are filtered through the mind of the historian. Indeed, are they ultimately just imposed by the historian? Colligation describes this process of discovering–imposing new explanatory patterns on the past.

The philosopher of history W.H. Walsh brought the idea of colligation to the attention of historians, based on the Kantian-inspired thinking of the British nineteenth-century philosopher-scientist William Whewell (1794–

1866) (see Immanuel KANT). Following Whewell, Walsh argued that colligation was what was distinctive in historical methodology. He claimed it was the basic means to explain an event by tracking its primary connections to other events within their shared historical context. So the nineteenth-century Irish migration to Argentina can be explained as part of the earlier Catholic links between Ireland, Spain and her South American colonies. The connecting link lies in the complexities of the Irish Diaspora. It is assumed by Walsh that what create these links are purposive actions by individuals at the time (see INTENTIONALITY), and we as historians understand by examining, in this instance, the diasporic context (Walsh 1984 [1967]).

Colligation as a mechanism of **historical explanation** raises several issues. Not least is the role of the historian's concepts in the process of induction and the creation of **constructionist history**. There is, as many students over the years have noted with resigned regret, a constant process of revisioning going on in history. This revisioning occurs according to newly discovered facts and to new ways of presenting, organising and representing them (as well as re-presenting all the old ones!). It may be helpful here to think of historical explanation as the narration of observed effects in terms of a proposed hypothetical cause (see TELEOLOGY). Every so often a fresh conceptual or hypothetical organisation of the facts takes place in order to represent (and re-present) their **causation** afresh. The new conceptualisation (of causation) then connects the facts together in a new narrative description. To make history, the refreshed colligation process has to link events plausibly, touching as many evidential bases as possible. This is usually summarised as inference to the best explanation (McCullagh 1998).

Although inference to the best explanation is an imprecise way of producing history, historians are generally sure about what constitutes the best explanation because they hold to a crucial 'common-sense' belief.

Historians do not worry too much about the theory-ladenness of their words and concepts. Except when concepts are being deliberately redefined, common sense dictates that concepts are empirically well understood. Most historical facts are described presupposing a shared and generally accepted **truth** about them. Thus 'containment' as a term describing American foreign policy is used as a common-sense empiricist concept the definition of which all historians agree upon. Unfortunately, this is never the case. All uses of words and concepts are fluid, and observed facts are no guarantor of meaning. The line between reality and invention is constantly crossed. Nevertheless, the colligation of facts by means of a concept as explanation remains a pivot of historical explanation. Colligation requires the historian to seek out *the* pattern in the past – determinedly with knitted brow – colligating hitherto disjointed and incongruous past events into meaningful historical sentences.

Further reading
McCullagh, C.B., 1998; Roberts, C., 1996; Walsh, W.H., 1984 [1967]; Whewell, W., 1967a [3 vols 1837], 1967b [2 vols 1840].

COLLINGWOOD, R.G. (1889–1943)

R.G. Collingwood was one of the most influential twentieth-century philosophers of history. He believed history was a justifiable and objective **epistemology** (way of knowing and organising knowledge). History was not, however, totally indebted to the rationalist legacy of the **Enlightenment**, nor did it ultimately depend upon the scientific or covering-law model (see COVERING LAWS; INTELLECTUAL HISTORY). But most significantly he placed the historian at the heart of the historical enterprise (see A PRIORI/A POSTERIORI; CONTINENTAL PHILOSOPHY; Benedetto CROCE; HERMENEUTICS; INFERENCE; OBJECTIVITY; POSITIVISM; BIOGRAPHY AND

LIFE WRITING; Giambattista VICO; Hayden WHITE). For Collingwood the key question in history was, how did people in the past derive the meaning of their lives? His answer was to equate meaning with agent **intentionality**. From this assumption, that to seek the meaning of the past we must infer its purpose, he launched his two big ideas: first, that the interrogative historian must empathise with past experience by rethinking past thoughts in the present, and second, that the means for this was his/her particular vision of the **historical imagination**. Collingwood accepted what might today be regarded as a postmodern idea (see POSTMODERNISM): that the historian must be self-reflexive enough to grasp his/her own wants, wishes and purposes as well as those of the historical agent.

Although Collingwood's historical method presupposes a narrow historicist (see HISTORICISM) philosophy that centres upon the actions and intentionality of individual historical agents, to explain such intentionality historians must begin with self-knowledge. By this Collingwood meant knowledge about human nature and the human mind: how human beings universally act and think. This suggests that the primary concerns of the historian are above the simple level of the empirical (see EMPIRICISM). For Collingwood the right way 'of investigating mind is by the methods of history' and 'history is what the science of human nature professed to be' (Collingwood 1994 [1946]: 209). What this meant, for what he called the plain method of history, was that the historian should look at both the outside and inside of **events**. The historian cannot look for **causation** in isolation from the thoughts that gave rise to the agent's actions that precipitated events. The only way to do this is through empathy: by rethinking past thoughts in the historian's own mind within the fullest possible knowledge of period and context. Only then can the historian accurately decode the words that expressed those thoughts. Because all history 'is the history of thought' Collingwood concludes that when the historian knows the facts he/she knows why they happened – the facts have their purpose embedded in them (ibid.: 215).

Taken at face value this *verstehen* approach (internal understanding rather than objective observation) is asking rather a lot of the historian – to rethink and re-experience thoughts and actions in the past. Not only was it asking a lot, for historians like E.H. **Carr** it was a step too far in the direction of an idealism (and continental philosophy) that jeopardised objectivity. How can the historian be self-conscious and historicist? In this case aware of, but divorced from, the present. To be fair, what Collingwood is actually doing, I think, is suggesting that historians should try to get inside the heads of people in the past to contemplate what they probably thought, and discover which thoughts prompted their actions (inasmuch as they can be judged by the available evidence). In doing this Collingwood rejected what he called scissors-and-paste history whereby historians just collate the testimonies of sources (Collingwood 1994 [1946]: 257–61). Collingwood is thus offering historians a methodology that is dependent upon a particular vision of the powers of the historian's imagination: the power to rethink and re-experience *imaginatively*.

As I have explained it Collingwood did not favour any picture of history that placed a primary emphasis on examining only the outside of the event: empiricism to the exclusion of the thought of the agent. Essential to entering the thoughts in the mind of the agent is to grasp the way in which they imagined their present and future. The interrogative historian thus engages or meshes imaginations with the historical agent, and is then better equipped to think as they did with their own anticipations in mind (see TELEOLOGY). Collingwood, although no idealist, was always conscious of the idealist risks of his method. So, while he insisted that the guiding principle of all historical activity was the self-justifying historical imagination, its form was always to be constrained by its content (see FORM AND CONTENT) (Collingwood 1994 [1946]: 249). Keeping the historian's imagination on a short leash was assured by three simple rules: the imagined past must be localised in space and time; it must be consistent with itself; and it must be bound by the evidence. Having said this, Collingwood's empiricist leash was always strained by his emphasis on the role of the historian in the here and now. It was the historian, after all, who provided an 'innate idea with detailed content' that could only be assured by using the present as the model for the past. As he said, every present 'has a past of its own, and any imaginative reconstruction of the past aims at reconstructing the past of this present, the present in which the act of imagination is going on, as here and now perceived' (ibid.: 247). By this method the historian is tethered to the reality of the past while acknowledging the effects of the here and now.

There are clearly problems with this vision of how the historian works, especially that thinking in the present can somehow not affect what the content of the past means (a point Collingwood acknowledged in his 1940 *An Essay on Metaphysics*), or the difficulties with the fashioning of an imaginative insight of purposive action into a **narrative**, or how rethinking the past can resolve the problems associated with language use and chains of significatory meaning. Nevertheless, the fact that he was loyal to a narrow conception of empirically verifiable and objectively knowable human action, intentionality and causation, while emphasising the role of the historian, has made his perspective lastingly influential for all but the most sectarian of reconstructionist or radical of deconstructionist historians (see DECONSTRUCTIONIST HISTORY; EMPIRICISM; GENRE).

Further reading
Ankersmit, F.R., 1994; Carr, E.H., 1987 [1961]; Collingwood, R.G., 1994 [1946], 1940; Cox, M., 2000; Donagan, A., 1962; Dray, W.H., 1995, 1989, 1980; Gardiner, P., 1961 [1951]; Jenkins, K., 1995; Jenkins, K. and Munslow, A., 2004; Jones, C., 1998; Mink, L., 1969.

CONCEPTS IN HISTORY

Thinking about the use of concepts in history points to the ontological (concerned with our general state of being/existence; see ONTOLOGY) and epistemological (concerned with the theory of knowledge; see EPISTEMOLOGY) distinctions between the three main kinds of historian: common-sense or reconstructionist realists (see RECONSTRUCTIONIST HISTORY); mainstream constructionists (see CONSTRUCTIONIST HISTORY); and postist or anti-representationalist sceptics (see DECONSTRUCTIONIST HISTORY; POSTMODERNISM; RELATIVISM; AESTHETIC TURN; LINGUISTIC TURN). For the first two groups history is generally adequate to the task of explaining the past because it is by the method of relating **empiricism** (the **evidence** of experience) and concept (its analytic organisation) that reliable and justified historical knowledge can be represented and demonstrated (see JUSTIFIED BELIEF). For postist anti-representationalist sceptics this is problematic because they view historical knowledge as a linguistic and cultural creation and history, therefore, as a secondary epistemology (see EMPLOTMENT; NARRATIVE; REPRESENTATION; Frank R. ANKERSMIT). They would tend to chime with the postist views of British social historian Patrick Joyce, that history is indistinguishable from its textual representations and the conceptual and ideological forces that construct them (Joyce 1991a: 208). The question is, 'Why do historians choose to adopt certain concepts and why do so many believe they offer access to the **truth** of the past?'

To philosophers concepts are the essential constituents of thought, the categories through which we apprehend reality (see Immanuel KANT), summoned up to explain the nature of being and knowing. They can be applied to mental images, graphic representations, the senses, objects, **event**s and words, as well as order our rational processes. Mention concepts to most historians, however, and they will likely think of the guiding principles that emerge out of the past to make sense of its incoherent nature. Among the most obvious examples are **race**, **gender**, **class**, nationalism and imperialism (see POST-COLONIAL HISTORY). Given what is a restricted notion of concept (restricted to the epistemological realm of knowing) the questions most often asked about the conceptual choices made by historians are those of an epistemological kind: Why is this historian adopting concepts that produce a feminist/gendered epistemology while another deploys concepts that generate race, nationalist, imperialist or class epistemologies (see POST-FEMINISM)? But in asking such questions there is a tendency to forget the broader philosophical definition, which suggests that conceptualisation in history stretches beyond the organisation of content. It moves into the ontological realm of the creation of form as well (see FORM AND CONTENT; EXPERIMENTAL HISTORY; FILM AND HISTORY).

If indeed concepts are the instruments through which we give the past its form (the-past-as-history), then it is important that we acknowledge our dependence upon the conditions of knowledge in which we work. By conditions of knowledge I mean the epistemic state of affairs in the disciplines adjacent to history and upon which historians regularly call for their ideas, theories of society, philosophies of history and concepts (see HISTORICAL IMAGINATION; HISTORICISM; NEW HISTORICISM; EPISTEME; MODERNISM; POSITIVISM). Historians have no fixed object. Historians study a process, not an object: change over time. For the post-empiricist historian this absence at the centre of history is necessarily filled by the present conceptual state of the historian's mind as mediated by his/her present ontologi-cal situation. The question postists then ask is to what extent the historian believes he/she can escape his/her ontological situation (his/her present existence) to locate the truth of the past through his/her conceptualisation derived from the evidence.

Unlike philosophers, who validate their concepts through logic and a priori mechanisms, historians have to infer (see INFERENCE) the truth of their propositions and statements in the crucible of the evidence **a posteriori**, or after the fact (see A PRIORI/A POSTERIORI). In seeing themselves as yo-yoing between evidence and explanation historians run the risk of creating a rather naïve science, where the investigation and verification of facts can all too easily become the be-all and end-all of the process. When this happens it is usually because the propositional and here-and-now nature of the conceptualisation exercise has been forgotten. Historians who claim that their concepts arise from the evidence, then, forget that they borrow concepts from disciplines in the here and now. The point is made by the European cultural historian Carl E. Schorske (1998: 220–1). According to Schorske not only are our raw materials second-hand – the rags and remnants of evidence – but so also are the concepts we use to process them, bought in from other disciplines. Like all second-hand dealers we historians do our best to make the trade look good by polishing pre-owned concepts so that they will appear attractive and marketable.

This points to the most significant consequence of this second-hand trade, the tendency to use concepts as a way of giving evidence a plausible meaning, to invest historical interpretations with a persuasive conviction. What I mean by this is that historians very rarely try to prove the truth of the concepts they have borrowed, assuming instead that they must be appropriate because they come from the specialist discipline that deals with the area of evidence they happen to be addressing and, what is more, they appear to 'fit' the **facts**. If a historian is seeking to explain the connection between slavery and the political structures of the United States in the first half of the nineteenth century, he/she may well feel satisfied in borrowing selectively from the wide variety of race or class models readily available off the sociology or politics shelves. It is quite easy in all this to lose sight of two things: the teleological or future-anticipating nature of our second-hand concepts (presumably there is a reason for buying in someone else's vision of the future to apply to the past?), and that they, and propositions, are not analogous to objects or facts (in spite of the good 'fit') (see TELEOLOGY).

The sophisticated constructionist historian does have some inkling of these problems of course, realising that concepts are not mental bridges that link the word (the written or speech act) and the world (references to reality). Instead of being the mental representations of events/actions/processes in the past, concepts stretch to *how* we imagine the form in which we cast history. Generally speaking, most historians feel they have no choice but to work on the prior principle of concepts embodying referents (the word, the object and its meaning) because otherwise they would not be doing history but philosophy instead or, what might be even worse, the philosophy of history (see REALITY/REALISTIC EFFECT). Reconstructionist historians are much less exercised by these worries, maintaining that concepts are accurate enough descriptions of reality when they are properly thought out. To ensure the quality of history, therefore, the only concepts that can be used are those that exist independently and immanently in the real past and that thereby constitute its discoverable causal principles (see CAUSATION). For the reconstructionist historian there are no irresolvable ontological or epistemological questions here.

This thinking is the foundation for the reconstructionist claim that historical knowledge is capable of being objectively discovered through the rationally justifiable process of inference from the evidence (see OBJECTIVITY). This inferential process demonstrates the natural existence of the concepts inspired by the evidence, so there is very little problem with conceptual **relativism**. Contrary to the post-empiricist sceptic's (anti-realist) view, proper historians do not make the past. Historians only create descriptions that the real past may fit (or may not as the case may be). Without a real past there is nothing from which to derive concepts, and nothing to which to re-apply them. It is then up to the historian's skill with the evidence to establish their accuracy and explanatory power. Reconstructionist historians equate the past with reality, and treat it accordingly.

The post-empiricist (or conceptual relativist) does not view history in the same way as the empiricist, that is, as past reality (see EMPIRICISM). The problem of knowing the past is not, as the empiricist historian assumes, the same as the problem of knowing reality. While most post-empiricist historians accept that the past existed at the basic level of the single descriptive statement, and that we can presuppose reality in our everyday lives because we have immediately verifiable sense experience of it (and postists in their daily lives ignore the arguments of extreme scepticism against *really* knowing through experience), we cannot make the same assumption for the past (see JUSTIFIED BELIEF; REPRESENTATION). History is not like that; it is not ontologically objective and, therefore, independent of our formalised representation or conceptualisation of it (i.e. content knowable, and form given) (see OBJECTIVITY). Every application of a social theory, or a concept in the pursuit of history, is a destabilisation of the past. Every conceptualisation and every appeal to laws of human behaviour is an intervention. The post-empiricist assumption is that, in effect, the past existed but not independently of the historian's mind, which is unavoidably implicated in fashioning that which seemed to have happened. Historians are not ontologically detached bystanders but are, through our organising concepts, active participants in making knowledge of the past – not what it once was, but what it now is.

Further reading

Callinicos, A., 1995; Gardenfors, P., 1997; Jenkins, K. and Munslow, A., 2004; Joyce, P., 1991a; Munslow, A. and Rosenstone, R.A., 2004; Neisser, U., 1981; Peacocke, C., 1992; Schorske, C.E., 1998; Searle, J.R., 1995; Smith, E.E. and Medin, D.L., 1981; Weitz, M., 1988.

CONSTRUCTIONIST HISTORY

Constructionist history describes a range of approaches to the past by historians from the sophisticated practical realist to the post-empiricist methodological and epistemological spectrum (see EPISTEMOLOGY; METAPHYSICS). Although it designates a wide variety of orientations to the study of the past, as a generalisation all constructionist types of history share the belief that history results from a conceptual dialogue between the historian and the past. Not even the most unreconstructed of reconstructionist historians (see RECONSTRUCTIONIST HISTORY; GENRE) denies that he/she must be active in seeking meaning in the past. As the British historian-philosopher R.G. **Collingwood** put it, no historian just scissors-and-pastes **evidence** and **sources** (Collingwood 1994 [1946]: 33, 257–82). Central to constructionist history, as an act of intervention by the historian, is the way its **truth** is cast as history via the process of conceptualising the evidence (see CONCEPTS IN HISTORY).

For most practical realist historians the judicious application of social, political or economic concepts (e.g. **race**, **gender**, nationalism, **class**) is a prerequisite to understanding the structures that shaped the lives, the decisions and the actions of people in the past. Historians generally do not view this intervention as producing history that could be regarded as wholly or even primarily fabricated. The kind of interventionism suggested by this vision is inspired by a sophisticated and self-conscious, yet fundamentally empiricist (see EMPIRICISM), methodology (see COLLIGATION). Regardless of the assumptions they make about the nature of the past, realists view concepts, categories and tools of analysis (native to history or borrowed from other disciplines) as the servants of the evidence.

A somewhat more sceptical view of history as a construct holds that it can only offer a highly mediated and indirect access to the past because, as R.G. Collingwood suggested, it deals only with its traces. His position assumes that our knowledge of the past is the result of the historian's imaginative and constructive engagement with the evidence (see HISTORICAL IMAGINATION; AUTHOR). Although Collingwood doubted that empiricism can provide a distanced platform for knowing, his scepticism was moderated by the belief that, while we exist in the here and now, our powers of inference are flawed and our language is uncertain, historical methodology will ultimately offer us reasonable grounds for knowing (see INFERENCE; NARRATIVE; MIMESIS) (Collingwood 1994 [1946]: 319).

Both Collingwoodian sceptics and practical realists, therefore, ultimately remain firmly realist – their historical constructionism is directed to reconstructing the past as it most probably was. For various kinds of non-realist, however, the term 'constructionist' as a modifier of 'history' is redundant. History is, from the post-empiricist perspective, clearly the construction of the historian and the language that they use, or that uses them in the narratives they create (see NARRATIVE). Every application of a social theory, or a concept in the pursuit of history, is a destabilisation of the past. Every conceptualisation and every appeal to laws of human behaviour is an imposition or an arrangement of the past by the historian. From the perspective of language as a localised, unfixed and polyvalent medium of communication, history is only ever constructed, and its meanings are situational and historicised (see LINGUISTIC TURN). It follows that we access the past through concepts that are created in language and that can only do their work of **historical explanation** through our narratives.

Constructionism can refer to social theory-invoking general laws of historical explanation, as in the French *Annalistes*' attempt at total explanations, or to the sociologically inspired work of individual historians like Robert Darnton. It can also be taken to mean the modernisation theories of W.W. Rostow and C.E. Black, or the Marxist and neo-Marxist materialist school represented in the work of Eugene Genovese, Christopher Hill, Herbert Gutman, Eric Hobsbawm and E.P. Thompson. It can designate the anthropological or sociological history of Clifford Geertz and Anthony Giddens. Constructionist history emerged from the empiricist mainstream in the nineteenth century thanks to Marx, Comte and Weber. This was not because they or historians in general doubted the modernist belief in the existence of factual knowledge as discovered in the evidence, but because of the naïve empiricist claim that it was feasible to have justified historical interpretations based on observable evidence alone, with the historian standing outside history, outside ideology, outside pre-existing cultural narratives and outside organising concepts.

Further developments in **continental philosophy** in the twentieth century resulted in the so-called **linguistic turn** away from empiricist epistemology toward the recognition of the role of language and discourse in creating historical understanding (see AESTHETIC TURN). What became seen as the dangerous incursion of postmodernist thought into the mainstream of history was noted by the British historian Lawrence Stone in a 1979 article, 'The revival of narrative', in which he detected the end of one form of constructionist or social theory history, with a return to an earlier kind of narrative history (see POST-MODERNISM). In a later article, 'History and post-modernism', Stone argued that history was, by the early 1990s, in danger of losing sight of its foundationalist narrative empiricism because of the argument that there is no reality outside language. Here Stone located the latest form of constructionism – the linguistic turn to a rhetorical constructionism based on the notion that language constitutes meaning in the social world, and the object of historical study is always created by the historian (Stone 1979, 1991; Fay *et al.* 1998).

The implication is clear, that our access to the past is always textualised – the text as source, as the historian's written interpretation and as meaning and knowledge. Stone rejected the consequence of, as he saw it, this form of extreme rhetorical constructionism, that history is only about the relationships existing between texts, with real life being squeezed out. More sanguine has been the view of the French historian Roger Chartier, who has argued that all historical texts are best viewed as the result of a construction on the part of the historian forming *a* representation of the past, not its reality (see REPRESENTATION). For Hayden **White** also, history is unavoidably a literary construction created out of tropes, figuration (see TROPE/FIGURATION), emplotments (see EMPLOTMENT) and ideology. Constructionist history, therefore, may be best considered as a self-conscious description of the variety of ways available to understand the past, ways that recognise the epistemological, methodological and narrativist impositions made by professional historians.

Further reading
Bann, S., 1984; Bunzl, M., 1997; Callinicos, A., 1995; Chartier, R., 1997; Collingwood, R.G., 1994 [1946]; Fay, B. *et al.*, 1998; Geertz, C., 1983, 1973; Giddens, A., 1976; Goldstein, L., 1976; LaCapra, D. and Kaplan, S.L., 1982; Munslow, A., 2003b, 1997a; Scott, J.W., 1989, 1988; Stone, L., 1992, 1991, 1979.

CONTINENTAL PHILOSOPHY

The fact that historians are now, as never before, actively rethinking the temper, theory, purposes and conditions of historical knowledge is evidence of the direct challenge to analytical philosophy – the tradition upon which the Anglo-American processes of historical analysis and **hermeneutics** are built – of continental philosophy. To understand the nature of the challenge we need to be mindful of what it is that is being challenged (see INTELLECTUAL HISTORY).

The principles underpinning two millennia of Western historical inquiry have culminated in the traditions of analytical philosophy, namely all that flows from the Platonic/realist understanding of meaning, **truth** and knowledge. In the Platonist universe genuine knowledge of the object 'out there' is waiting to be 'discovered' and is not the product of the mechanism(s) deployed for the inquiry (language, psychology of perception, etc.). This means that reality (the world) is independent of **discourse** (the word), and genuine knowledge must be ahistorical – perspectively neutral. From these basics a variety of **Enlightenment**-inspired interlinked foundational concepts (see CONCEPTS IN HISTORY) have developed that have, in large part, informed historical thinking and methodology: propositional logic and coherent argumentation, the correspondence theory of truth, **empiricism**, the contextualisation of **evidence**, referentiality, representationalism (see REPRESENTATION; Frank R. ANKERSMIT), factualism (see FACTS), truth conditions for historical descriptions, **inference** and social theory constructionism. These principles are normally couched as dualities – the separations of knower and known, observer and observed, history and fiction, history and historian, and truth and value.

So what is the nature of the critique of continental philosophy? While the questions of truth and knowing are as elemental to it as they are to analytical philosophy, the continental tradition begins to differ in its thinking

with G.W.F. **Hegel**'s reconceptualisation of Immanuel **Kant**'s theory of knowledge. Unlike Kant, Hegel accepted the historical situatedness of reason and knowledge (Kant's categories are in themselves historical creations). Knowledge, reason and truth cannot escape the gravitational pull of the world. The perspectivism that emerges with Hegel is confirmed given that the individual knowing subject also exists within a proscribed time and place (see the ENLIGHTENMENT). The fact that the individual knowing subject is the product of his/her conditions of existence means that, although reality exists, it cannot be wholly independent of his/her representations of it. So with Hegel we move from the ahistorical to the conditional, from the individual (as the source of knowledge) to cultural processes. Modifying Kant's transcendent rationality means that knowledge must be, to a greater or lesser extent, subjective and/or contingent.

This means that the historian (like everyone else who is trying to gain 'genuine knowledge') is a part of the reality being examined. For Hegel this suggests that the subject (possessing consciousness) and the object (external reality) are ontologically connected – part of a chain of being (see ONTOLOGY). Because our categories of analysis and methodologies, like ourselves, are culture-bound there is no way to break free of **class**, **race**, **gender**, ideology, etc. For Friedrich **Nietzsche** neither the world of 'what is' nor 'what seems' can offer a measure by which to judge the truth claims of genuine knowledge. Eventually, Nietzsche argued, certain knowledges are regarded as truthful just because their genealogy is so remote. This suggests that truth is perspectival and time- and place-dependent – a cultural practice that generates a **reality/realistic effect**, rather than a separate and genuinely knowable reality.

The nineteenth-century basis to continental philosophy provided by Hegel and Nietzsche has branched in the twentieth century into several related spheres associated with a number of key thinkers: phenomenology (Edmund Husserl (1859–1938), Martin Heidegger (1889–1976) and Jean-Paul Sartre (1905–80)); **hermeneutics** (Hans Georg Gadamer (1900–) and Paul Ricoeur (1913–)); **post-structuralism** (Michel **Foucault** (1926–84), Roland **Barthes** (1915–80), Jean-François **Lyotard** (1924–) and Jacques **Derrida** (1930–2004)); and **critical theory** (Jürgen Habermas (1929–), Theodor Adorno (1903–69), Max Horkheimer (1895–1971) and Louis Althusser (1918–90)). Phenomenology, as a theory of knowledge, and directed by its founder Edmund Husserl, takes up the notion of perspective and ways of knowing as problems of perception and consciousness (what we only genuinely know is our a priori consciousness: see A PRIORI/A POSTERIORI). Hermeneutics, as the art of textual and (post-Wilhelm Dilthey) cultural interpretation, is indebted especially to Martin Heidegger, who, for example, examined the subjective aspect of knowing through his attempt to understand the nature of the being of the interpreter of texts (*Dasein*). Heidegger's phenomenology is hermeneutic in that being is not viewed as an a priori/transcendental access to reality, for our being is prefigurative. We are pre-programmed to understand the meaning of texts by our being in the world (interpretation thus reveals our being beyond the texts). Heidegger's pupil, Gadamer, also explored the period, place and conceptual boundaries of the subject's 'horizon' of knowledge, and that truth arises in the dialogue between knower and known, and the document and the interpreter (each possessing different horizons) that occurs at a particular time and in a certain place.

Rethinking these connections is most clearly demonstrated in the work of the post-structuralists Michel Foucault and Jacques Derrida, with their joint (Nietzschean-inspired) questioning of the fixity of truth conditions, the transparency of representation (see Jean BAUDRILLARD) and the transcendental signified – all producing forms of knowledge that are tied to power, ideology, space and time, rather than corresponding to a knowable and discourse-independent reality. Critical theory is largely indebted to the so-called Frankfurt School of German philosophy and sociology founded by (among others) Max Horkheimer in 1923, and his belief that social theory can be only relatively independent of context. This means that social critics, sociologists, philosophers and historians must evaluate the origins of their explanations (be self-reflexive) rather than accept them as the products of independent and value-free methodologies of knowledge discovery.

For historians the impact of continental philosophy has been most obvious in the postmodern (see POSTMODERNISM) challenge to history's foundational tenets, although the term 'postmodern history' is probably misleading. As my comments indicate, the philosophical origin of much that is described as postmodern actually began in the nineteenth century with Hegel, and especially with Nietzsche's critique of the Enlightenment conceptualisation of language and being. Much that we call postmodern history is, in effect, continental philosophy's critique of its own modernist (post-Hegelian) founding principles. There is nothing, for example, novel or postmodern in Nietzsche's deconstruction of causality (the effect is primary in the search for cause) (see CAUSATION).

The properties or features that we associate with postmodern history, but which are the product of continental philosophy, include many new questions and a willingness to accept fresh orientations to the study of the past. These include a questioning of epistemological certainty (see EPISTEMOLOGY), placing a question mark over inference, assuming an anti-representationalist position, being open to teleological explanation (the past viewed as future flight) (see TELEOLOGY; NEW HISTORICISM), accepting that there is no knowable reality (there are only discourses), viewing history as truth-effect rather than truth, presuming we do not *discover* patterns in contingent events but instead impose them because that is how we want to emplot (see EMPLOTMENT) or organise the past. In addition it means rethinking the facile distinction of fact and fiction, welcoming the ideological self-reflexivity of the **author**-historian by rejecting grand **narrative**/totalising or foundationalist concepts of explanation (e.g. class did not exist in the past until historians borrowed it from sociologists as a concept), reconceiving historical truth as existing at the local here-and-now level, noting that narrative closure is not essential to writing the past, granting there are no historical facts (apart from simple consensual statements), and acknowledging that metaphors are deployed as historical explanations (see HISTORICAL EXPLANATION; JUSTIFIED BELIEF). Finally, it means confirming that history is always about moral choices (not assuming that there *must* be a given meaning in the evidence, and what it *must* suggest according to a transcendent ethic), and exploring the possibilities in the relationship of **form and content** in historical explanation (see ETHICAL TURN). This is a list that could be extended depending on what you choose to borrow from the continental philosophy tradition.

Further reading

Appleby, J. *et al.*, 1996; Baynes, K. *et al.*, 1987; Bernstein, R., 1983; Dews, P., 1987; Kearney, R. and Rainwater, M., 1996; Lechte, J., 1994; Roberts, D.D., 1995; Stromberg, R.N., 1994.

COVERING LAWS

As a form of **historical explanation** the covering-law model assumes history to be an empirical (see EMPIRICISM) undertaking, the **facts**, **event**s and processes of which can be explained according to the conditions that govern their probable, regular or law-like occurrence. So, although individual events cannot be explained as individual events, they can be taken as examples of a particular category of occurrences determined according to conditioning explanatory laws (see HISTORICAL EXPLANATION). The philosopher of history and science Carl Hempel suggested that historians invoke covering laws all the time to account for human behaviour (Hempel 1942). Conventionally taken to be opposed to this law-seeking constructionist (see CONSTRUCTIONIST HISTORY) approach to historical explanation is that of the sophisticated hermeneutic (see HERMENEUTICS) or interpretative tradition represented by the British philosopher and historian R.G. **Collingwood** (and subsequently by others including William H. Dray, Alan Donagan and G.H. von Wright) as well as in the work of a variety of reconstructionist (see RECONSTRUCTIONIST HISTORY) historians and philosophers (like G.R. **Elton**, Arthur Marwick, Jack Hexter, Gertrude Himmelfarb, Neville Kirk, C. Behan McCullagh, Michael Stanford, Chris Lorenz and Perez Zagorin).

However, according to the anti-realist philosopher of history Frank **Ankersmit**, there is less to this division than meets the eye, because both orientations are essentially inferential and constructionist, and their respective practitioners believe that history can explain what really happened in the past (see INFERENCE). Hempel's short article on 'The function of general laws in history' published in 1942 loosed a wave of positivist-inspired (see POSITIVISM) constructionist **empiricism** which suggested that history could work according to general laws, which themselves could be determined by the deduction of the meaning of the event (the *explanandum*) from statements consisting of the general law and antecedent conditions (the *explanans*). Hempel understood, however, that historians do not work in such a strictly deductive manner, instead producing what he called 'explanation sketches' that, after the cultivation of the **evidence**, would yield – in all probability – the relevant laws of human behaviour from which the likely causes and meaning of events and processes could be inferred (see CAUSATION; COLLIGA-

TION; SOURCES). This covering-law model was, in effect, a watered-down version of what philosophers call deductive-nomological thinking, whereby events can be explained by a set of initial conditions plus the application of a general law, so the event described *must* follow given the premises undergirding it.

As Ankersmit points out, conservative reconstructionist historians have generally rejected the full-strength Hempelian covering-law model (with the same assurance as they have rejected the sceptical idealism of Collingwood). They regard it as quite unnecessary to their analysis of the sources or their constitution of unique historical facts and events, because it is unavoidably deductive and, therefore, an inappropriate form of historical thinking. The issue between constructionist advocates of such a model (like Karl Popper, Patrick Gardiner, Ernest Nagel and Clayton Roberts) and extreme reconstructionist doubters (see above list) is whether the subject matter of history – accounting for agent **intentionality** – is amenable to such explanation (see BIOGRAPHY AND LIFE WRITING).

Ankersmit argues that the attempt has been made to locate a dilute form of the covering-law model based on inductive **inference**, as a compromise between the extremist models of sceptical empiricist reconstructionism and history-as-science (a compromise promoted by Clayton Roberts). The compromise derives from the wish, prevalent among mainstream constructionist historians (see CONSTRUCTIONIST HISTORY), to defend as objective and truth-conditional (see TRUTH) their preferred methodology that is – unsurprisingly – founded on the inductive inference (i.e. derivation) of agent intentionality (see OBJECTIVITY; AGENCY/STRUCTURE). It follows that laws or theories of behaviour are only at best suggestive of likely causes for events – explanations to the best fit. Indeed, it can be argued that historians happily enjoy a theory-free existence in the sense that no covering law and no large-scale theory can explain what historians are actually interested

in – the immediately needful, and rational (or occasionally irrational for 'good' reasons) intentions of people in the past. Neither are historians concerned with projections about the future (see TELEOLOGY). Most are pleased to indulge in exploring large-scale social and institutional structures while accepting that such imaginative speculations do not permit the absolute prediction of individual intentionality or action. For Ankersmit this suggests that both approaches have moved toward a convergence in their joint attempts to domesticate the past and promote the idea that the historian's referential language can mirror it faithfully (see MIMESIS). Premised like this, the majority of historians continue to believe that history is an interpretative yet factualist act of agent-intentional discovery and, it follows, that the discipline is a distinctive truth-seeking **epistemology**.

It is at this point that the deconstructionist historian (see DECONSTRUCTIONIST HISTORY) will submit that neither approach can effectively resolve the central problem of **form and content**, namely that, while history may wish/claim to be about getting closer to the real truth of the past (its content), it is actually never able to escape from the language or concepts (see CONCEPTS IN HISTORY) used to describe it (the form of the past that is the-past-as-history). As Ankersmit suggests, the covering-law model cannot both encompass a knowable agent intentionality and fully control the historian's language as a mirror of reality, that is, bridge the gap between knowing and telling, and history and **historiography** (see Hayden WHITE; LINGUISTIC TURN; Richard RORTY; AESTHETIC TURN; REPRESENTATION). The same criticism would, of course, also be levelled at mainstream Collingwoodian-type interpretative history.

Further reading
Ankersmit, F.R., 2005b, 2003a, 2001, 1994; Donagan, A., 1962; Dray, W.H., 1957; Hempel, C.G., 1942; Lorenz, C., 1998; Murphey, M.G., 1986; Nagel, E., 1961;

Popper, K., 1962 [1945]; Roberts, C., 1996; Snooks, G.D., 1998; Stanford, M., 1994; von Wright, G.H., 1971; Zagorin, P., 1999.

CRITICAL THEORY

This is one of those terms that is associated with a specific intellectual development but which has subsequently been appropriated to mean almost anything vaguely associated with or derivative from its original meaning. Critical theory is usually and for convenience associated with the University of Frankfurt's Institute for Social Research established in 1923. However, some characteristics of it can be found in a variety of earlier thinkers, for example in the work of Immanuel **Kant**, G.W.F. **Hegel**, Friedrich **Nietzsche**, Karl Marx (1818–83), Ferdinand de Saussure (1857–1913), Antonio Gramsci (1891–1937) and Georg Lukács (1885–1971). Although defining it is harder than nailing jelly to a wall, critical theory does have some key features.

First, it establishes a clear relationship between theory and practice; whatever form it takes (especially before the 1960s) it is a solid defence of 'theory' as a means not only to gain knowledge but also to change society and to do both from a general Marxian perspective. Second, it is (paradoxically given the above and only since the 1960s) often informed by a sceptical epistemological relativism usually in the shape of a structuralist Marxism (see EPISTEMOLOGY; STRUCTURALISM). Third, in its realist mode it addresses issues around self/identity/subjectivity (see AUTHOR). Fourth, it examines how cultural institutions (like the media, organised religion, science, politics and education/scholarship/academic disciplines like history) play a role in organising self/identity/subjectivity and how/why some groups are ideologically and in other ways marginalised and how this can be corrected through civic/political/intellectual action/practice (see Michel FOUCAULT; Jacques DERRIDA).

Fifth, critical theory explores how **Enlightenment** reason has become a form of oppression (science is not value-free and, for example, rational rather than irrational people make totalitarianism work).

Any short selection of the key critical-theory thinkers demonstrates the variety of their critical theory(ies) credentials. Take, for example, Louis Althusser's structural Marxism and the functioning of ideological state apparatuses, Jacques Lacan's post-Saussurean linguistically self-conscious psychoanalysis, Martin Heidegger's work on time and existence, Roland **Barthes**' Marxist post-structuralist semiotics and history's 'reality effect' (see POSITIVISM; REALITY/ REALISTIC EFFECT), Julia Kristeva's, Luce Irigaray's and Hélène Cixous' feminism, Jacques Derrida's post-structuralist analysis of '*différance*', Jürgen Habermas's defence of modernity against **postmodernism** and Pierre Bourdieu's post-structuralist sociology and studies of cultural consumption and production (habitus) as well as the variety of its forms. But this listing does not include the first generation and founding fathers of critical theory – Max Horkheimer, Theodor Adorno, Herbert Marcuse and fellow traveller Walter Benjamin.

Associated with the Frankfurt School these were a set of primarily Marxist philosophical and sociological theorists whose ideas were brought together under the impress of its key leader, and from 1930 its director Max Horkheimer (1895–1973). The Institute closed in 1934 after the Nazi rise to power but was re-opened as the New School for Social Research in New York when Horkheimer and other émigré intellectuals like Herbert Marcuse and Theodor Adorno arrived. The reasons for the relocation centred on the Marxist orientation of the critical theorists as well as the race policies of the new Nazi regime. The New School relocated back to Frankfurt after the Second World War.

While he was head of the 'Frankfurt School' Horkheimer expounded the 'critical theory' of the Institute, giving a clear leadership to an interdisciplinary programme of social study (that included history, philosophy and the social sciences). In 1937 he wrote the article 'Traditional and Critical Theory' in which he set about what became a sustained deconstruction of the grounds of modernist history and reason (from an essentially Marxist perspective). In the early 1940s he and his colleague Theodor Adorno co-wrote *Dialectic of Enlightenment*, which turned out to be one of the most significant contributions to the critical-theory oeuvre. In this book Horkheimer and Adorno mapped modernity in terms of *Aufklärung* (enlightenment through rationality) but offered a substantial critique of the baleful influence of the (Enlightenment idea of the) autonomous knowing subject/agent/individual. They drew a clear connection between rational self-sufficiency and the rise of totalitarian regimes and other social and 'managerial' formations. Much later, in 1973, reflecting on the Nazi Holocaust, Adorno wrote *Negative Dialectics*. Gloomily he concluded that progress was an illusion – essentially repeating the pessimistic conclusion of *Dialectic of Enlightenment* that reason could result in totalitarianism but the hope existed (maybe) that critical theorists might just be able to come to the rescue. The defender of modernity Jürgen Habermas later rejected this pessimism, redirecting critical theory toward communicative action. Adorno's friend Walter Benjamin (1892–1940), though often invoked as a proto-postmodernist because of his apparent dissolution of high and low art forms and his view of history as multi-voiced (see the text *Illuminations*), perhaps ultimately comes down on the side of the modernists with his rejection of what became known as the **aesthetic** and **linguistic turns**.

From the 1960s critical theory is almost exclusively concerned with a range of related intellectual developments in the social sciences, arts and humanities but specifically in literary theory, **continental philosophy**, cultural studies, the often obtuse theoretical debates within Marxism, **structuralism**, **post-structuralism**,

theories of **representation**, deconstruction and aesthetics (see AESTHETIC TURN; NEW HISTORICISM; INTELLECTUAL HISTORY; NARRATIVE; JACQUES DERRIDA; DISCOURSE; DECONSTRUCTIONIST HISTORY). If this second life of critical theory has any point at all for historians, it is that as an umbrella term it signifies a variety of scholarly approaches to reading and writing texts, the overall effect of which is to question history as a **epistemology** or as having a great deal of utility because it works, in effect, to colonise the past and its subjects rather than free them. To the extent that critical theory is self-reflexive and aware that it is ideologically and ethically driven (see ETHICAL TURN), it is significant for historians as a body of thinking which can be invoked as part of their theoretical and practical engagement with the past.

This may take the form, as in the development of British **cultural history** in the past twenty years or so, in which a Marxist model remains predominant in elucidating how the meaning of the past is generated. This is not a form that strayed too far outside the classic determinist base–superstructure model. Such orthodoxy views the production of cultural meaning (including historical meaning) as a severely empirical-analytical-conceptual process that is overtly anti-postmodern, viewing that as yet just another incarnation of capitalism (and rejecting, *tout court*, Jürgen Habermas, Levi 501s, Jean **Baudrillard**, Coca-Cola, Jean-François **Lyotard**, consumption for pleasure, Fredric Jameson, commodity fetishism, irony and the aesthetic turn).

However, critical theory has been important to historical thinking through developments in the interpretation of literature and literary criticism as informed by aspects of continental philosophy. Literary theorists, like historians, have long asked what is the nature of their discipline but, unlike historians who have tended to have a very narrow conception of what is history (essentially a **reconstructionist** or a narrow **constructionist** understanding), literary theorists have been much more open to debates at the epistemological level. This is clearly demonstrated in the proliferation of 'schools' of literary thinking and practice, for example, Marxist, New Criticism, new historicism, deconstruction, Russian formalism, formalism, reader-response, feminism (of many varieties), post-structuralism, postcolonial, structuralism, narratology (of various persuasions) the psychoanalytic, and drifting into adjacent areas such as cultural studies. The distinctions between these schools emerge from substantially different intellectual origins and practices.

The application of both critical and literary theory to history in the past thirty years can be accessed through the work of a vast variety of historians, critics and philosophers like Roland Barthes, Hayden **White**, Michel **Foucault**, Jaques Derrida, Jean Baudrillard, Jean-François Lyotard, Frank **Ankersmit**, Keith **Jenkins**, Dominick LaCapra, Douglas Kellner, Paul Ricoeur, Michel de Certeau, Robert Rosenstone, Elizabeth Deeds Ermarth, Greg Dening, Dipesh Chakrabarty, Iain Chambers, Joan Scott and many, many others. Such an eclectic listing serves to indicate how the application of critical theory has disrupted the traditional demarcation in history between the empirical-analytical and the narrative-linguistic-philosophical. Historians are now far more than ever before aware that there are epistemological and metaphysical issues in translating the past real world of experience into a discursive form of interpretation. The effect has been to force some historians to break the rules of 'traditional' history that have hitherto hidden its intellectual deficiencies, and fashion new disciplinary approaches, speculations and discourses. What we have today, therefore, seems to be what we might call a 'historical-critical' approach to the organisation and explanation/understanding of the past which is characterised epistemologically by its use of literary criticism, especially the theory of narratology, debates around representation and realism and truth and objectivity. Although it may introduce a certain vertigo into his-

torical study, never before has there been an opportunity for historians to test the limits of the discipline experimentally (see EXPERIMENTAL HISTORY) or in unconventional ways. Once we understand that the past is categorically different from the narrative we write about it, we are in new territory epistemologically. Henceforth, working the past into a useful history means recognising that we are undertaking a literary representation and, therefore, we can only do it as we critically theorise it.

Further reading

Adorno, T. and Horkheimer, M., 1972; Althusser, L., 1971; Arato, A. and Gebhardt, E., 1982; Barthes, R., 1988, 1986, 1981 [1967], 1975, 1974, 1972, 1957; Baudrillard, Jean 1983, 1976, 1973; Benjamin, W., 1999, 1973; Bourdieu, P., 1972; Chakrabarty, D., 1992; Chambers, I., 2000; Cixous, Hélène and Clément, C., 1986 [1975]; de Certeau, M., 1988 [1975]; Dening, G., 2002, 1992; Derrida, J., 1976; Ermarth, E.D., 2001, 1992; Foucault, M., 1980, 1977, 1973a, 1973b, 1972, 1970; Geuss, R., 1981; Habermas, J., 1987; Heidegger, M., 1962; *History and Theory* 2002 'Unconventional History' Themed Issue; Horkheimer, M., 1972; Irigaray, L., 1992, 1985; Jenkins, K., 1999b; Jenkins, K. and Munslow, A., 2004; Kellner, D., 1989a, 1989b; Kellner, H., 1989; Lacan, J., 1977; LaCapra, D., 1995, 1989; Lyotard, J.-F., 1988, 1979; Macey, D., 2001; Munslow, A. and Rosenstone, R.A., 2004; Nealon, J.T. and Giroux, S.S., 2003; Norris, C., 1992; Payne, M., 1997; *Rethinking History: The Journal of Theory and Practice* 1997– passim.; Ricoeur, P., 1994 [1978], 1984, 1984, 1985, 1981; Rosenstone, Robert A., 2003, 1996, 1995a, 1995b; Rush, F. (ed.), 2004; Scott, Joan W., 1996a, 1996b, 1988.

CROCE, BENEDETTO (1866–1952)

A one-time Marxist and positivist, the Italian philosopher Benedetto Croce became increasingly attracted to idealism (what he called his philosophy of the spirit), **historicism** and the study of the connections between literature, the aesthetic (art), philosophy and history (see POSITIVISM; INTELLECTUAL HISTORY; AESTHETIC TURN). Croce is an important philosopher of history because of his rejection of the basic tenets of positivism and **metaphysics**; his response to the ideas of Giambattista **Vico**, Immanuel **Kant**, G.W.F. **Hegel**, Friedrich **Nietzsche** and Karl Marx; and his views on history as an art form, and because of his influence on philosophers of history like R.G. **Collingwood**, Martin Heidegger, Hans-Georg Gadamer, Richard **Rorty**, Jacques **Derrida** and Hayden **White**. Croce's ultimate contribution to the study of the-past-as-history was what he called 'absolute historicism' or doing history in a twentieth-century world that is never fully formed, where there are few if any certainties and all that is solid eventually melts into air. Hence it is that historical knowledge cannot be scientific because such knowledge depends on nature being in virtually all respects finished, completed, knowable and explicable.

In trying to compromise the rational and the aesthetic, Croce maintained (in a materialist and realist fashion) that the historical event is the wellhead of philosophy and, under Hegel's influence, the study of history is essential to understanding meaning (see EVENT). But his philosophy of history was also heavily influenced by his idea that the aesthetic, built upon his notion of the (lyrical) intuition, exists prior to **representation** and that to rely solely on common-sense **empiricism** is to tell only half the story (see AESTHETIC TURN). For Croce **facts** come into existence only when they have been imaginatively created by the historian from the thoughts of the historical agent (see the ENLIGHTENMENT; HISTORICAL IMAGINATION; CONCEPTS IN HISTORY). Croce, in his appeal to the idealist connection of being and consciousness, tried then to resolve the problem of historical knowing in a world without dependable empirical foundations.

Croce believed that art, produced through intuition, is a pre-conceptual (non-scientific) **epistemology** (a way of knowing) holding that works of art are pure forms of knowledge precisely because they are non-material and intuitively created. Knowing exists not just in science alone but in the image produced by intuition of which it is the expression. Artists have intuitions and (because they are artists) they have the capacity to express them clearly and so create understanding. The material form (see FORM AND CONTENT) given to the expression – located in the technique of representation – is central to the process of understanding what there is in the real world. The expression (the form) of that which is intuited can have, so Croce chose to believe, a transcendental aspect so it encompasses the universal human spirit. This can be found only in great art, literature and history. His notion of the origin of intuition has a certain parallel with Vico's conception of the first or metaphoric stage human beings create – the fantastic age of gods and myth (*fantasia*).

What does it mean if history is viewed as an art form? It means at least two things: first, that the intuitive a priori creates the-past-as-history through the mind of the historian rather than the correspondence theory of knowledge; and second, that history (and art) represents the unique and the individual. Although Croce believed (in a realist sense) that our historical knowledge of the event was the basis of all understanding, the origin of historical knowledge itself (the meaning of the event constituted as facts and then as truthful interpretations) must emerge from the historian's power to imagine or intuitively think out the meaning of the single object of study. The historian intuits the meaning of the object by predicating its meaning (see A PRIORI/A POSTERIORI; INFERENCE; HISTORICAL IMAGINATION; REALITY/REALISTIC EFFECT; RELATIVISM). As described thus far this is not that different from what most orthodox constructionist historians do (see CONSTRUCTIONIST HISTORY). Their perception and inference from the **evidence** is organised by concepts/theory as expressed in language. While not accepting the full anti-correspondence implications of history as an art form, this can be of some comfort to empiricists everywhere. As the realist philosopher of history Patrick Gardiner says, in summary of Croce's position and borrowing heavily from Kant, intuitions without concepts are blind (Gardiner 1961 [1951]: 42). Gardiner is not intending, of course, to vindicate Croce's idealism, but rather to justify his own positivism by stressing Croce's realist side.

But where Croce differs from the constructionist historical mainstream is when he talks about what makes history an independent programme of knowledge. This is the historian's power to envision and contemplate the thing done, at the expense of placing the unique factual event under a general explanation (generalisation), system of thought, social theory or abstract covering law (see COVERING LAWS). Indeed, Croce has a severe idealist-inspired doubt about the very concept of **causation** (see COLLIGATION). Linking facts together by seeking the causal connections between them seems wrong to Croce because it means that historians must be working from a false principle, that we have the empiricist capacity to discover the First Cause when all we actually have is an infinite regression of causes. From the perspective of a realist Croce appears to be demanding here that without an absolute knowledge of why something happened we couldn't be sure it did happen. While a fuller reading of Croce would dispel that impression the question remains, how can the historian obtain any degree of certainty? For Croce the only hope of gaining historical **truth** is to rethink, as R.G. **Collingwood** later also insisted, the thoughts that gave rise to it.

This idealist (sceptical anti-science) view of history is reinforced by Croce's insistence that history is the **narrative** representation of the facts via linguistically embedded concepts as construed and conceived by the historian. This not only suggests a break with categorising and generalising about events as a scientist would, but also means doubting the referentiality of the correspondence theory of knowledge. This confirms for Croce the need for historians to intuit (infer?) the meaning of the past by mentally reliving it. For Croce rethinking the unique event seems to bear out the peculiar nature of historical thinking that characterises history *sui generis* (unique to itself).

Croce places himself in the situation of trying to maintain history as a legitimate discipline, defined by its access to past reality, while at the same time arguing for the central role of the historian in creating historical knowledge. Although Croce begins with history, his idealism places the historian at the centre of the process of doing history. This leads to Croce's most famous opinion that all history is contemporary because, as he says, the past vibrates in the here and now, within the evaluative historian's mind. As the American philosopher of history David Roberts says, Croce's vision of history offers a way of coming to terms with both knowing and doing in a post-metaphysical (see METAPHYSICS) world (D.D. Roberts 1995: 82).

This conception of history has made Croce unpopular with the mainstream of orthodox realist historians, who prefer to believe in knowable reality because they are sensibly sceptical about what the evidence can tell them. In spite of Croce's wish to find out the truth of the past, critics like positivist Patrick Gardiner are largely dismissive of Croce, along with fellow idealists like Michael Oakeshott and R.G. Collingwood, because of their contention that history must begin with the thoughts of historians (Gardiner 1961 [1951]: 31). The reconstructionist historian Geoffrey **Elton** views Croce (and Collingwood, who is also irredeemably lost) as the very worst of historians – he (they) were utterly wrong, he said, to place the historian at the centre of the historical reconstruction (Elton 1991: 43) (see RECONSTRUCTION-

IST HISTORY). The British reconstruction-ist social historian Arthur Marwick has delighted in suggesting that Croce (whom he lumps in with Hegel) meant little to him as a historian because of the **relativism** that was Croce's legacy (Marwick 1989 [1970]: 8, 79). While these realists/representationalists have little time for Croce's variety of history, his pursuit of historical truth through the intuitive historian remains some kind of balance to the hard-hat empiricism of reconstruction-ist history and the 'probable' history of constructionism (see CONSTRUCTIONIST HISTORY; GENRE).

Further reading

Brown, M.E., 1966; Collingwood, R.G., 1994 [1946]; Croce, B., 1970 [1927], 1968 [1917], 1964 [1913], 1923; Elton, G., 1991; Gardiner, P., 1961 [1951]; Marwick, A., 1989 [1970]; Moss, M.E., 1987; Roberts, D.D., 1995, 1987; Struckmeyer, O.K., 1978; Wellek, R., 1981.

CULTURAL HISTORY

Before we can define cultural history we must define culture. I take culture to encompass three main features of lived experience as understood in the West; the first and second are the aesthetic/intellectual, and the social (see the ENLIGHTENMENT; MODERNISM; POSTCOLONIAL HISTORY; POST-MARXISM; AESTHETIC TURN; REPRESENTATION). First, by the aesthetic/intellectual dimension I mean cultural development in respect of thinking about and producing the scientific and academic disciplines of history, art, literature, political ideas and philosophy. Included here are the intellectual processes and practices whereby society reflects upon its past self, the present and the future, and how it invests its intellectual and social life with meaning (see EPISTEMOLOGY; ONTOLOGY). By the social features of culture I mean those cultural practices that are understood through

lived experience. As historians we should not forget that such historical understanding is organised by the concepts (see CONCEPTS IN HISTORY) that our intellect provides to make sense of our experience – in this example we may utilise **class**, **race** and **gender** (see WOMEN'S HISTORY). The upshot is that we choose to view intellectual and social life over-determining each other. The third feature in my definition of culture is the **representation** of these first two elements – how we re-present or mediate our intellectual and social life, and create meaning. This is the textual or signifying dimension to culture. This feature is, I would suggest, dependent upon the other two in respect of how society understands, problematises and organises cultural practice(s) as cultural representation (see FORM AND CONTENT; FILM AND HISTORY; REPRESENTATION).

It is the exploration of these three defining and inter-related features of culture that is both the subject matter of cultural history and which influences our thinking about its form. Questions of form cannot be ignored because cultural history is itself a cultural practice differentiated by its modes of representation. The varieties of cultural history evidence the extent to which they are the products of the professional and discipline consensus of historians, as well as actual historical circumstance. Just as history itself emerged as an eighteenth- and nineteenth-century modernist project, with the intention of domesticating and giving useful meaning to the past, so the long crisis of modernity since the end of the eighteenth century (the intellectual crisis of **ontology** (being) and **epistemology** (knowing)) produced history's various forms as responses to the **event**s (intellectual, social, political and material) of that long crisis.

However, almost as soon as the German empiricist historian Leopold von Ranke (1795–1886) had begun to impose his classic objectivist epistemology, with its priority of content over form on the emergent discipline of history, an early social history burgeoned under the influence of the influential Swiss-born historian Jacob Burckhardt (1818–97) (see EMPIRICISM; OBJECTIVITY). In his *The Civilization of the Renaissance in Italy*, first published in 1860, Burckhardt established what, according to the theorist of cultural history Peter Burke, were to become several of the central concerns of later cultural history (Burke 1997). In the book Burckhardt addressed the intellectual, social and representational aspects of the Renaissance cultural history of Italy. He described the role of the individual within an emergent national polity, the role of history as a nationalist force, the growth of the academic disciplines, the role of **biography**, the relationships between men and women, and various aspects of popular culture including costume and fashion, festivals, social etiquette, domestic life and home management, music, education, religion and superstition, and poetry and language, which he saw as a subject of 'daily and pressing importance' (Burckhardt 1990 [1860]: 240).

In the early part of the twentieth century the rise of the masses into political life, the increasing impact of science and technology, the consequences of a hugely unbalanced wealth creation, the arrival of total war and the intellectual promise of the social sciences combined to produce the century's dominant form of historical study – social (and to a lesser extent economic) history (see ORAL HISTORY). Widening historical study in this way did not at first create doubts about the empiricist nature of the exercise. Indeed, while both Burckhardt and his successor as the pre-eminent 'cultural historian' Johan Huizinga (1872–1945) stressed the empathic approach to the study of the past, the advent of the social sciences (and the application of statistics to history – **cliometrics**) seemed to reinforce the historian's capacity for telling the truth about the past as it actually happened (see R.G. COLLINGWOOD; OBJECTIVITY). But it was the total-history approach (covering all aspects of culture) of the *Annales* School in France that transmuted

social history into cultural history – the present highly complex study of the inter-relationships of the three aspects of social life noted above.

The rise of cultural history in the second half of the twentieth century and up to the present has been very much the result of the influence of contemporary events in the United States and Western Europe on the lives of historians. The clashes of race, class and gender, in an age of rapid technological change and imperial and internal de-colonisation, have meant that the historian's own lived experience of social and material life, as well as the post-empiricist intellectual debates of the past twenty years, have constituted the character of today's cultural history (see LINGUISTIC TURN; RELATIVISM; TRUTH; POST-COLONIAL HISTORY). The contemporary material and intellectual crisis of modernity has been, therefore, the context for the emergence of cultural history in its manifestations as historical analysis and cultural practice. All this means is that cultural history today is the prime intellectual site for competing visions of what constitutes history and the study of the past.

Cultural history is now the focal point for many different (sometimes converging, sometimes diverging) developments within historical studies. Because of the nature of cultural history (covering all aspects of past intellectual and social life and their representation), as well as experiencing the impact of the intellectual developments of the post-modern (see POSTMODERNISM) and deconstructionist revolution (see DECON-STRUCTIONIST HISTORY), the cultural historian has to be continuously self-reflexive in his/her thinking about how to do history. The medley of theories, concepts, approaches, philosophical positions, metahistorical perspectives and forms, as well as the new ranges of topics, **evidence**s and **sources** now available have meant an explosion of epistemological and methodological choices for the cultural historian. What epistemological choice to make is often the most difficult. Today, historians can elect to accept or challenge the very idea of history as a licit discipline, by occupying any position on a continuum that stretches from naïve reconstructionist empiricism, via a bewildering variety of social theorising and historical constructionism (see CONSTRUCTIONIST HISTORY), through to (any one of several forms of) post-empiricism. However, while the linkages between history and the discipline of anthropology, but also psychology, archaeology, sociology, philosophy, **critical theory** and literature, have occupied ever-increasing numbers of historians, the common currency of these disciplines – the investigation of cultural change and formation, and the role of the intellectual in its understanding and representation – remains. So whichever epistemological and/or methodological orientation is preferred – whether deconstructionist or 'new empiricist' – the topics of culture continue to be central.

When she wrote almost twenty years ago, Lynn Hunt argued that 'the anthropological model' then reigned supreme in cultural history (Hunt 1989: 11); she was quoting the work of Clifford Geertz with his 'Thick description: toward an interpretive theory of culture', and 'Deep play: notes on the Balinese cockfight', in *The Interpretation of Cultures* and *Local Knowledge: Further Essays in Interpretive Anthropology* as the most visible contributions then made to the field (Geertz 1973: 3–31, 412–54 and 1983). According to Hunt there are also other 'models' for cultural history quoting the 'anti-historical' work of Michel **Foucault**, the cultural materialism of E.P. Thompson and Natalie Zemon Davis in their explorations of *mentalités*, and Hayden **White** and Dominick LaCapra in their deconstruction of historical narrative. However, according to the cultural historian Peter Burke, the undoubted indebtedness of cultural history to anthropology has not yet replaced the mid-nineteenth-century modernist conception of Burckhardt or Huizinga (Burke 1997). For Burke, however, cultural history is less defined by its methods and approaches than by the variety of its con-

tents. Taking a somewhat contrary position, the French cultural historian Roger Chartier argues the annexation by cultural historians of other 'fields of study, techniques, or standards of scientific objectivity' (especially in the evaluation of the *histoire des mentalités*) tends to suggest the continuing social scientific credentials of cultural history, while at the same time he acknowledges the contemporary debates on the objective existence of social structures and the subjectivity of their representations (the illusions of the historian's discourse?) (Chartier 1988: 3–6). These differing views of Hunt, Burke and Chartier typify today's debates on what constitutes the appropriate epistemology, methodology and content of cultural history (Hesse, 2004; Mandler, 2004).

However, the epistemological and/or methodological as well as the evidential and/or topic choices made by cultural historians (form as well as content decisions) mean that all three elemental features constituting the study of past cultural life are usually recognised (to a greater or lesser extent) in all works of cultural history. On a bibliographical note it would be impossible to list here all the significant works of cultural history. What ought to be said, and the cultural historian Peter Burke said it in his book *Varieties of Cultural History* (1997), is that while historians have adapted and adopted many different and sophisticated models and explanatory theories, the heritage of Jacob Burckhardt and Johan Huizinga can still be seen in the topics addressed.

Further reading
Bowman, P., 2005b; Burckhardt, J., 1990 [1860]; Burke, P., 1997, 1993, 1991; Chartier, R., 1988, 1987; Darnton, R., 1986, 1980; Dworkin, D.L., 1997; Geertz, C., 1983, 1973; Ginzburg, C., 1982; Goodman, J., 1997; Harvey, D., 1989; Hesse, C., 2004; Hunt, L., 1989; Mandler, P., 2004; Maza, S., 1996; Munslow, A., 2003b, 1992; Pittock, J. H. and Wear, A., 1991; Poster, M., 1997; Thomas, K., 1978; White, H., 1978, 1974.

D

DECONSTRUCTIONIST HISTORY

A term used to designate the application of several postmodern approaches to the study of the past, particularly those associated with a variety of historians including Michel **Foucault**, Hayden **White**, Keith **Jenkins**, Alun Munslow and Frank R. **Ankersmit**, and cultural theorists like Jacques **Derrida**. One of the basic philosophical assumptions of the Cartesian-inspired **Enlightenment** was that genuine knowledge is possible through the processes of logic and rational thought all made accessible through a neutral, passive and stable system of language that operated beyond the object of description. Such a metaphysical realist position enables us to deduce the realities beneath the misleading world of appearances and sensual data (see META-PHYSICS). But philosophical developments since the eighteenth century have undermined this belief in the nature of knowing and the power of language to represent the real world accurately. While some historians may still have a certain sympathy for foundationalism, in spite of the **linguistic** and **aesthetic turns**, more and more have taken its implications into account in their work.

Frank R. Ankersmit provides, I think, an appropriate short introduction to the issue of deconstructionist history. He begins with the comment that 'postmodernism's aim . . . is to pull the carpet out from under the feet of science and modernism . . . [and] . . . the best illustration of the postmodernist thesis is . . . provided by historical writing' (Ankersmit 1994: 167–8). What Ankersmit goes on to argue is that historical interpretations exist only in relation to each other (there is no orig-

inal meaning that **hermeneutics**, the art of interpretation, can uncover). This means their identity is determined by their relationship to other texts (see JUSTIFIED BELIEF; REP-RESENTATION). Just as significantly, the historical interpretation exists only in language that suggests to Ankersmit, as it does to Hayden White, that the traditional distinction between language and reality loses its meaning. Language cannot be the mirror of nature, for it is directly implicated in the reality depicted (see MIMESIS). Language (written down history) and the past become one. So historians are led to talk about the past as if they were making statements about reality, rather than participating in the construction of that reality through their interpretative historical narratives (see NARRATIVE). To use the language of feminism or **class** is, therefore, to constitute a preferred reality (see POST-FEMINISM; POST-MARXISM). Avoiding this 'mistake' has been a traditional aim of historians. But this aim is now always honoured in the breach. For Ankersmit, this makes the historical narrative an essentially postmodernist (see POSTMODERNISM) undertaking. Thinking about the implications of the conflation of language and reality is at the forefront of deconstructionist history. To understand in more detail what a deconstructionist history entails it is necessary to establish the intellectual derivation of deconstructionism as a sceptical philosophical tendency.

Deconstruction, at its most general level, refers to the interrogation of those discourses (see DISCOURSE; NEW HISTORICISM) through which human beings attempt to engage with the real world. The deconstructionist objective is to establish how such discourses, like the discourse of history, can achieve or fail to achieve the objective of truthful knowing (see TRUTH). Deconstruction as a process of investigative thought should be important to historians, as Ankersmit points out, because it questions our traditional disciplinary investment in the concept of referential language upon which we found our belief that we can more or less accurately and truthfully interpret the world of the past as an entity separate from ourselves. The idea of a representational language that permits both the separation and the correspondence of word and world has long been scrutinised by philosophers ranging from Scottish sceptical empiricist David Hume (1711–76), transcendental idealist Immanuel **Kant**, and perspectivalist Friedrich **Nietzsche** in the eighteenth and nineteenth centuries, Ferdinand de Saussure, Benedetto **Croce** and Martin Heidegger in the earlier part of the twentieth century, to Hans-Georg Gadamer, Paul Ricoeur, Michel **Foucault**, Richard **Rorty**, Hayden White and Jacques Derrida more recently. The debate between Hume and Kant on the nature of knowledge and the distinction between appearance and reality, while it is central to all later philosophical developments, is of particular significance here, because Nietzsche's reading of the debate led him in a direction that was to have enormous implications for the emergence of deconstructionist history.

David Hume believed it was impossible to have any definitive or all-encompassing knowledge of the real world. This is a fundamental scepticism that most historians today would probably endorse in some degree. For Hume all our knowledge is proscribed, and can never be total. Our knowledge is limited by our current experience (for historians this is the range of **sources** from which we create **facts**) and, moreover, this situation cannot be ameliorated by any convincing appeal to deductive reasoning (see A PRIORI/A POSTERIORI). Such reasoning cannot, in and of itself, establish historical knowledge. Not even when taken together can experience and

reason either provide unequivocal knowledge of the real world in terms of telling us what actually happened, or permit us to determine what it really meant (see INFERENCE). Historians cannot, for example, establish causal connections irrefutably. We know the Second World War occurred, and we have evidence of the **event**s that prompted the post-Second World War US foreign policy of containment. But historians cannot establish a certain causal connection between such events. By Hume's reasoning all we have is a sequence – world war and cold war. The nature of cause and effect in this example cannot be established through either observation or deductive logic.

As is well known, Immanuel Kant tried to overcome this problem of sceptical empiricism by producing what has been called a representationalist model of philosophy (Critchley 1996: 27). Kant argued that the human mind possessed innate a priori categories (meaning mental categories like space, time and causality existing independently of experience) that allow us to order our experience. The important consequence of this thinking for historians is that, like everyone else, we are capable of discovering the truth of the world at least to the extent that it appears to us, if not the world as it actually is. Kant's distinction between perception and experience translates today into the distinction of the form of experience from its content (see FORM AND CONTENT). Kant argued that we know the form of our experience a priori, the content always a posteriori (according to the evidence of experience). For Kant, objective knowledge is possible because our subjective categories correspond with reality. To have the fullest possible knowledge of reality, of course, we use both form and content. As post-Kantians we cannot, therefore, accept foundationalist empiricism. Nevertheless, the question of reality versus appearance remains. How can we determine which of our mental categories correspond to reality and which to its appearance?

Friedrich Nietzsche, while accepting that

we have a priori categories, challenged Kant by arguing that such categories cannot have any universalist or transcendental validity, because they do not correspond with reality. Indeed, categories and concepts are only ever interpretations, and they are arbitrarily determined by our cultural situatedness, perspective, ideology and power relationships (personal, **gender**, class, **race**, disciplinary). So far as the deconstructionist historian is concerned, Nietzsche's contribution is important because this directly challenges the nature of the very concepts in which not only philosophy states its problems, but all interpretational disciplines, especially history. Nietzsche refuses absolute meaning in concepts and language. For Nietzsche, truth cannot be known because of the blanket of figurative discourse that is thrown over reality. The metaphoric nature of language means that reality and, therefore, truth, are not directly accessible (see TROPE/FIGURATION). It is only by denying this that philosophers can claim unmediated access to reality and to truth. This is a double whammy for historians. It means there are no disinterested historians because no historical concepts can lay a claim to correspondence, and no historical method can overcome the inherent **relativism** of language use.

Nietzsche's perspectivism – that we interpret rather than know – was paralleled by Ferdinand de Saussure (1857–1913) as the structuralist (see STRUCTURALISM) insight. Saussure's crucial argument was to de-couple the word and the world by pointing out (in Nietzschean fashion) the arbitrary nature of the sign – the culturally determined signifier–signified relationship. Saussure made the assumption that meaning in language emerges through the mechanism of difference (as binary opposition). Language does not mirror nature but is a socially constructed medium that can only confound the common-sense idea of object and its (neutral) description. Saussure broke the natural correspondence or link between representation and referentiality (see NARRATIVE; OBJEC-TIVITY; REPRESENTATION). The Kantian response to this – one usually deployed by 'proper' historians – is that the reader possesses a culturally attuned narrative competence that permits conventional understanding of what the text means based on cultural expectation and context, as well as the usually accepted rules of syntax and grammar.

However, the arbitrary nature of the sign is important for deconstructionist philosophy, because it endorses the rejection of the notion of a foundational and universalist (transcendental) knowing signifier. For Roland **Barthes**, for example, language is subject to a second-order or hidden metalanguage that suggests an infinite regression of meaning. We can never scrape back the layers of meaning to arrive at the original. The implications of this line of argument make most 'proper' historians somewhat queasy. This thinking de-privileges history as a form of knowledge by removing certainty in language and also, therefore, in history's interpretational narratives. Such thinking forms the basis of the critique of Western philosophy of Jacques Derrida. He maintains that philosophers (in particular), but historians as well, have continued to claim epistemological authority only by deliberately ignoring the unstable and resistant character of language. Although there are distinct differences between their approaches, Foucault displayed a similar preoccupation with the link between the word and the world. The failure to find origins meant that the past only exists as written history, and is never finished, never tidied up. As the philosopher-historian David Roberts has it, there is nothing but history (D.D. Roberts 1995).

Derrida pursues this with reference to the tropic, figurative and metaphoric device he finds used in the discourse of philosophy. Influenced by Nietzsche's preoccupation with the obfuscatory effects of figurative language, it occurs to Derrida that all texts are hermeneutically unrecoverable (incapable of interpretation back to their original meaning) (see HERMENEUTICS). One implication of this for the study of the past is that historians ought to become more linguistically and narratologically self-reflexive. We should start, perhaps, by recognising that the effacement of the question of language and narrative (and by implication the erasure of the historian as narrator) means that the conception of history as a natural, legitimate, honest, debunking and truthful narrative shield against liars and the morally depraved is rather more effect than reality. Derrida is not saying that reality is textual, rather that everything is language and reality cannot be nailed down through it. So appearance, reality, language, history and representation (metaphor) merge together.

It is, of course, Hayden White who has most famously insisted on a deconstructive approach to history with his now famous return to the issue of form and content. Returning to this Kantian preoccupation, White insists form is more important to the history production process than is usually accepted. For most 'proper' historians the vast majority of the work they do is in the archive, with the historical narrative still assumed to be a convenient receptacle for the results of painstaking research, work which will, with sufficient care, reveal *the* true story discovered in the sources. The deconstructionist historian objects, arguing that the historical narrative is far more central to the process, at least to the extent of placing form and content on an equal footing. History, instead of being seen solely as a practical method for accessing the truth of the past, ought to be viewed as a literary genre possessing distinctive philosophical objectives (see NEW HISTORY).

Deconstructionist historians do not claim that because there is no one absolute way of regarding the real world, then one way must be as good as another. Rather they are suggesting that one particular view ought not to be privileged over another – in effect the correspondence theory of knowledge over the textual. There is a substantial debate between a deconstructionist perspective and,

for example, a thoroughgoing social science constructionist (see CONSTRUCTIONIST HISTORY) 'real-world' approach like that of Marxist historians. The debate centres on whether or not all frameworks are perspectival. Perhaps we ought not be too surprised at the emergence of the deconstructive vision of history given the epistemologically sceptical heritage of the Enlightenment, and the contemporary profusion of models, hypotheses, figurative styles and idioms, topics, concepts, categories, arguments and materials. The interplay of reconstructionist intent and constructionist consequence suggests that history can never be grounded solely in the past, but unavoidably exists in the present, in the presence of the historian, and is effectively proscribed by the seemingly perennial problem of appearance, reality and representation.

Further reading

Ankersmit, F.R., 2005b, 2003a, 2001, 1994, 1983; Bennington, G., 1994; Caputo, J.D., 1997; Critchley, S., 1996; Culler, J., 1982; Derrida, J., 1978, 1976; Eagleton, T., 1983; Elam, D., 1994; Ellis, J.M., 1989; Foucault, M., 1972; Jenkins, K., 2004, 2003, 2003 [1991], 1999a, 1999b, 1998a, 1997, 1995; Jenkins, K. and Munslow, A., 2004; Jenkins, K. *et al.*, forthcoming 2007; Kearney, R. and Rainwater, M., 1996; Megill, A., 1985; Mouffe, C., 1996; Munslow, A., 2003b, 1997a; Munslow, A. and Rosenstone, R.A., 2004; Norris, C., 1990, 1987, 1982; Putnam, H., 1992; Ricoeur, P., 1984, 1985, 1981; Roberts, D.D., 1995; Sallis, J. (ed.), 1987.

DERRIDA, JACQUES (1930–2004)

Born and raised in Algeria, Derrida trained in Paris in the 1950s as a philosopher, coming under the intellectual influence of the founder of phenomenology, Edmund Husserl (1859–1938). Derrida was also influenced by Friedrich **Nietzsche** and Martin Heidegger

(1889–1976). Derrida first came to prominence with his translation of Husserl's *The Origin of Geometry* (1962), but the works for which he is best known were published in the late 1960s and early 1970s (especially his *Of Grammatology*, 1967; English translation 1976) in which he single-handedly established the philosophy of deconstruction. Deconstruction is benchmarked by Heidegger's challenge to the representative theory of perception and the correspondence theory of knowledge/**truth** also heavily dependent upon Nietzsche's insistence on the indeterminacy of language. Following Heidegger, Derrida challenges the Western philosophical preoccupation with the present in its explanations (rejecting Heidegger's early acceptance of the transcendental signified). Derrida's preoccupation is with the traditional Western hierarchy of speech taking precedence over writing (phonocentrism). According to Derrida this idea mistakenly assumes that the speaker provides a privileged or fixed origin for meaning (see AUTHOR; INTENTIONALITY). Put another way, there is no fixity in the relationship of signifier and signified, so no certain or transparent meaning is achievable.

The doubtful thinking that generates this phonocentrism (that speech is the true voice of ideas (*logos*)) implies that writing is an inferior surrogate for speech. Moreover, in writing, the speaker's designs and meanings, no longer present, are betrayed as language takes over and figuration creates and subverts meaning (see TROPE/FIGURATION). So the ascendancy of the voice (*logocentrism*) becomes firm and unchanging, and for Derrida this constitutes a dubious Western philosophical habit. In Derrida's critique of texts this means that as we read texts – unless we self-consciously deconstruct them – we will be compliant in locating a specious centre of truthful meaning. In practice doing this produces quite misleading 'truths', usually in the shape of everyday oppositions like subject and object, masculine and feminine, real and unreal (see POST-FEMINISM; GENDER; WOMEN'S HISTORY). What we ought to

recognise instead is that our understanding of texts is produced by the difference between signifiers (the meaning of the sign is always there *and* absent – under erasure), so that what texts 'mean' is nothing more than a continuous process of deferral, with the reader playing as important a function in deriving meaning as the author. In effect the knowing subject has disappeared (see the ENLIGHTENMENT; STRUCTURALISM).

For as long as the historical **narrative** is felt to be an accurate transcription of the past (and narrative's unpredictable nature is suppressed, domesticated or ignored), so **empiricism** will remain predominant in the **metaphysics** of history. The real presence of the past will thus continue to exert its primacy in history, as it exists in the narrative. Among the consequences of Derrida's basic assumption that there is no transcendental signifier is the doubt inevitably cast on empiricism, **facts**, **inference**, truth, **objectivity** and knowable historical reality. If there is no absolute point of origin for meaning in the shape of author intentionality or the referentiality of the evidence beyond the text, then texts can only be evaluated for their possibilities of meaning within themselves. We should not be misled here: Derrida does not doubt referentiality *per se*, only knowable original meanings. All the historian has are endlessly deferred and undecidable and undecipherable meanings. One of the advantages of this perspective is that it allows historians to radically play with the form of what they write (see FORM AND CONTENT; EXPERIMENTAL HISTORY; FILM AND HISTORY; POST-MARXISM). For Derrida writing is the condition for the creation of history, and so history becomes an effect of writing. This is depressing news for empiricists, because it means that Derrida's neo-Kantian idealism (abandoning EPISTEMOLOGY?) carries the 'cost' of never being able to reach definitive answers through the **evidence** as to what the past *really* means. There can be no closure in history because we cannot pin down the past for what it actually was.

Further reading
Beardsworth, R., 1996; Bennington, G., 1993; Burke, S., 1992; Derrida, J., 1982, 1979, 1978, 1976; Ellis, J.M., 1989; Gasché, R., 1986; Megill, A., 1985; Norris, C., 1987, 1982; Sallis, J., 1987; Sturrock, J., 1979.

DISCOURSE

Historians generally have not made much of the notion of discourse, although the concept possesses a very broad usage among many humanities-orientated disciplines including **critical theory**, linguistics, sociology, philosophy and social psychology (Mills 1997: 1–3). Those few historians who have addressed the nature of discourse have found it central to what they do (see INTELLECTUAL HISTORY; NEW HISTORICISM; Keith JENKINS; Frank R. ANKERSMIT).

The philosopher of history Michael Stanford defines the term in talking about 'history as discourse' to demarcate it from other types of history like history as knowledge; history as action, or **event**, relic, theory; or history as sequence. Stanford's definition of history as discourse refers to the **narrative** (or nonnarrative) means for the conveyance of that knowledge derived about the past that we call history (Stanford 1994: 79–108). History is a discourse but, lest there be confusion, this does not mean that history is generated by its discursive form rather than its content (see FORM AND CONTENT). In other words history is a discourse of **empiricism**. Historical knowledge is obtained, for Stanford, by the appropriate use of established investigative mechanisms: the critical and comparative study of the **evidence**, double-checking the inferences drawn about it (see SOURCES; INFERENCE), establishing causal connections (see CAUSATION) and withal a clear understanding of the constraints of cultural **relativism** and language use. Historical meaning is thus generated as an interpretation, which in its turn is accurately described (getting the story straight). In other words,

history as discourse does not emerge from the historiographical, the writings of historians (see HISTORIOGRAPHY).

What this means, I think, is that while most historians willingly accept that an understanding of the event cannot be wholly separated from their account of it, the discourse of historians is secondary to research, inference of meaning, and explanation through establishing causal connections (see CAUSATION; COLLIGATION; FACTS; OBJECTIVITY; TRUTH). By this 'logic', history, defined as an empirical discourse, can only be constructed as a complex series of statements about a knowable object. To make sense of such evidential statements (to infer their original authorial meaning) historians require an extensive knowledge of the evidence and the historical context(s) to which the evidence refers (see AUTHOR; INTENTIONALITY). In other words, the historian's inferred meaning will be expected to equate to *the* meaning of *the* author, that is, understanding *the* story as related in the text.

History, defined as an empirical discourse, requires that we acknowledge the role of historical description, but it means not forgetting that history and narrative must remain separate. Traditionally understood, history is a way of producing knowledge according to recognised rules of investigation, while narrative is not cognitive in the same way. However, following the arguments of Emile Benveniste, the French philosopher-historian Michel de Certeau notes the peculiarity in the relationship between history and description, what he calls 'a strange situation, at once critical and fictive' and that the 'gap separating reality from discourse' will never be filled (de Certeau 1988 [1975]: 8–9). For de Certeau, unlike Stanford, historiography constitutes the discourse of historians as we try to represent events in referential texts. As he says, at the end of the history process the discourse of the historian is a fiction witnessed in the story that is told as a performance, as a 'a staging of the past' (ibid.: 9; see also Burke 2005).

De Certeau's grounds for these assertions are now the pretty well-known ones of the cultural relativism of the historian, his/her moral position, the social theory he/she imposes and the nature of the composition process that takes the historian from practice to text (*écriture*) (de Certeau 1988 [1975]: 56–113). Writing is not, therefore, just an objectivist investigative method but is an aesthetic cultural practice involving the author of the evidence, the author of the history and the eventual consumer as reader (and we might also add the manuscript referees, the copy editor and the publishing editor).

The unavoidable modernist paradox is that while historical discourse claims to provide a truthful content (based on the rules of evidence) it has to do it in the form of a knowing narrative (see MODERNISM). But, when historians put finger to keyboard to write, there is what de Certeau calls a 'metaphorical slippage': a shift or transposition from one genre to another, from the genre of the event and the factual to a literary form (de Certeau 1988 [1975]: 93–4). The discourse of the historian de Certeau describes as a 'laminated text', a historiographical discourse constructed 'as a knowledge of the other' usually found in the processes of reference, citation and direct quotation. This lamination also requires the effacement of the 'I' in the interpretative text, the use of the event and fact as hooks on which to hang the configured or emplotted narrative (the kind of story invented by the historian), and the creation thereby of the 'realistic illusion' (collapsing the link between signifier and referent) (ibid.: 94–5) (see Roland BARTHES; EMPLOTMENT; REALITY/REALISTIC EFFECT). It is through these processes that we can gain an understanding of the social/cultural/ideological metalanguage of historical discourse, so we accept the fact that writing history is itself an act that imposes a quite different (another?) set of rules and constraints on our understanding of the past (see POSTCOLONIAL HISTORY; POST-MARXISM). Like other discourses history is authored within a social context that is directly affected by other discourses and practices. It is a relativist undertaking that suggests that history, as a discourse, is not a mirror to the past.

Further reading

Bann, S., 1983; Barthes, R., 1986; Berkhofer, R.F., 1995; Burke, P., 2005; Dant, T., 1991; de Certeau, M., 1988 [1975]; Foucault, M., 1970; Mills, S., 1997; Munslow, A., 1992; Pecheux, M., 1982; Stanford, M., 1994; White, H., 1998, 1992, 1987, 1978; Young, R., 1981.

E

ELTON, GEOFFREY (1921–94)

The Library of Congress catalogue has forty-four entries for Geoffrey Elton, which is testament to the productivity of one of Britain's most famous historians (in large part the result of his popular textbook writing). Born in Germany and arriving in England after studying in Czechoslovakia and escaping from the Nazis, his main contributions fell within the Early Modern period, notably politics and society under the Tudors. An important part of his standing was, however, derived from his forthright defence of **reconstructionist history** (notably political history). Elton endorsed a common-sense conception of the referentiality of the past while sturdily repudiating a priori (see A PRIORI/ A POSTERIORI) deductive **inference** (see CONCEPTS IN HISTORY). Theory of virtually any kind was anathema to Elton, who was among the most outspoken promoters of the modernist 'craftsman' vision of historical study, arguing that history was about reconstructing the choices and actions of people in the past (see INTENTIONALITY; MODERNISM). By objectively serving the **sources** (see EVIDENCE), we can thereby judiciously reconstruct the past to get at its **truth** (see OBJECTIVITY).

Elton promoted this vision in a number of important defences, but notably in three books: *The Practice of History* (1967), his debate with social scientist and cliometrician William Fogel in *Which Road to the Past?* (1983) (see CLIOMETRICS) and *Return to Essentials: Some Reflections on the Present State of Historical Study* (1991). In the last he argued that the most important aspect of the work of the historian was the rational and impartial empirical investigation of the documents of human choices within their context (see EMPIRICISM). By these means history would be both accurate and insulated against social theory and ideological **relativism**.

Importing the historian into the process of writing history was, for Elton, a fundamental mistake, a point he made very clear when he took E.H. **Carr** to task for committing (what Elton misconstrued as) some of these sins in the latter's philosophy of history. Elton used his attack on Carr to vigorously rebut and jettison the big idea of R.G. **Collingwood** that writing history necessitates an empathic re-enactment in the historian's mind of the thoughts of historical agents that gave rise to past actions and **events**. Such a dangerous procedure could pull down the barricades of rationalism that stand guard against the dangers of ideology and presentism (see HISTORICISM). As he said in *Return to Essentials*, and he had feminist historians in mind at the time, this 'corruption' was probably the result not of perniciousness, but rather of 'bigoted idleness' (Elton 1991: 67–8) (see POST-FEMINISM; GENDER; WOMEN'S HISTORY). Despite his tone and personal attacks, Elton did, of course, address a key problem that history faces: is it a cultural artefact or the objective pursuit of truth?

The central weakness in Elton's position emerges in his unwillingness to engage in what he dismissed as scullery philosophy. For Elton, firm as he was in his belief in *the* historical method of inductive inference, history is first, last and always about the study of evidence. It is this that makes history both epistemologically independent and capable of reconstructing the past as it actually happened, and without any imposition from the historian (see HISTORICAL EXPLANATION; HISTORICAL IMAGINATION; HISTORIOGRAPHY). To fall from the historian's professional standards is to abdicate 'the task of telling about the past to the untrained and largely ignorant – to the writers of fiction, avowed or disguised, to the makers of films, to the journalists and speculators of the pen' (Elton 1991: 70) (see FILM AND HISTORY). Elton's message was that historians can represent reality objectively, and to doubt that means accepting that we cannot explain anything at all. In spite of its self-proclaimed openness to sophisticated theorising, the Elton legacy continues to propagate itself in the hothouse of the empiricist history intellectual Establishment in both the United States and the United Kingdom (see JUSTIFIED BELIEF).

Further reading
Elton, G., 1991 [1955], 1991, 1990 [1958], 1986, 1983, 1973, 1972, 1970, 1968, 1967, 1966, 1960, 1953; Jenkins, K., 1995; Jenkins, K. and Munslow, A., 2004; Kenyon, J., 1983; McCullagh, C.B., 2004; Roberts, G., 1998.

EMPIRICISM

Empiricism is knowledge acquisition through the use of the senses as we observe and experience life, or through statements or arguments demonstrated to be true (see JUSTIFIED BELIEF). Developing in parallel with scepticism in the Anglo-American tradition of writing history, empiricism has been the methodological foundation of both **reconstructionist history** and **constructionist history**, with its insistence on the corollary of the objective observation of the reality to be discovered 'out there' (see OBJECTIVITY). Empiricism assumes that what we as historians can know about the past is what it tells us through the available **evidence** and **sources**.

This means that we must observe the evidence of our senses without passion or self-interest, without imposition or question-begging. The past is, therefore, a 'given' and historians discover its meaning through the priority of sense over intellect, content before form (see FORM AND CONTENT). It follows that our capacity for **historical explanation** must remain tightly controlled as we extract the meaning found in the evidence.

This immediately sets off alarm bells for sceptics who ask how it is that all we can ever know is what our senses tell us directly. Surely our ideas have to represent the (assumed?) external past world (see REPRESENTATION; Frank R. ANKERSMIT)? Sceptical empiricism (of the common-sense George Berkeley and David Hume varieties) became locked into this dilemma, attempting to resolve it by claiming that, in fact, all we can know about the (past) real world is what our ideas represent to us. But thought, surely, provides us with the categories with which to evaluate and organise sensory data? It is the special contribution of Immanuel **Kant** to historical understanding that he explored the need for this mental addition to the empirical process.

The problem usually encountered by empiricism, then, is that thought does not simply emerge from experience, but actually provides us with concepts or mental categories that we utilise to organise and make sense of our experience. This inevitably leads to the relativist inquiry, 'How can we truly know the reality "out there" given that our observations may well be only constructions of our mind, intuition, or our existence influencing us? How can we prove anything objectively?' Ludwig Wittgenstein (following Kant) pointed out that since sensory data (our evidence) exists only when we comprehend it in our mind we cannot be certain as to its true nature or, for that matter, be certain that other people comprehend it in the same way as ourselves. This is, presumably, the source of the perennial problem of competing historical interpretations: historians do not 'read' or 'see' the evidence in the same way. Reference to 'what happened' tells us very little about it, and even less about what it could possibly 'mean'.

According to the psychologist and narrativist thinker Jerome Bruner, narrative is one of two likely forms of cognition that allow us to categorise and 'make sense' of 'the real'. One of them is empirically verifiable propositional **truth** through argumentation; the other is narrative-making whereby we relate the real to ourselves through its **emplotment**. The logic of each mechanism is different and the greatest misconception among historians is that the discipline of history works primarily according to the former. This leads to the misconception that history can tell the truth of the past in terms beyond simply referring to what happened. Happily, confusing reference with truth is generally an error committed only by fundamentalist empiricist historians.

Most historians today accept a middle position that rejects extreme empiricism (a.k.a. rationalism), maintaining that we observe but we also mentally process information deploying a priori (see A PRIORI/A POSTERIORI) knowledge and categories of analysis as appropriate and helpful. Empiricism can, of course, take the form of a denial of a priori knowledge. Today most historians do not accept that history can be known through an exact correspondence of 'knowing' (see EPISTEMOLOGY) and 'being' (see ONTOLOGY). Most historians see themselves as 'sophisticated empiricists' who judge the reality of the past by a measure of understanding based upon sense data as filtered through the grid of mental structures pre-existing in their minds. In practice this means that the organising concept precedes consideration of the evidence in the shape of a hypothesis to be confirmed or refuted. Few historians today would defend a crude sceptical empiricist position. It is often claimed that such sophistication has resulted in, for example, a feminist empiricism that holds that history (as knowledge) has to be purged of its (usually unconscious) masculinist biases (see POST-FEMINISM; GENDER; WOMEN'S HISTORY). However, as philosopher-historians like Keith **Jenkins** and Frank **Ankersmit** point out, empiricism does not necessarily resolve the word–world translation problem; that is, the evidence of the past is always pre-packaged within stories or **narrative**s so knowable reality is ultimately about the deconstruction of those stories (see DECONSTRUCTIONIST HISTORY). Strictly speaking, of course, empiricism is about sensory input in the here and now, whereas history, being a second-hand trade, is not. There is, therefore, a case to be made for history not being primarily an empirical discipline at all (see AESTHETIC TURN; EMPLOTMENT; LINGUISTIC TURN; ETHICAL TURN; GENRE).

Further reading

Appleby, J. *et al.*, 1994; Berlin, I., 1997; Bonjour, L., 1985; Bruner, J., 1992, 1990; Dowe, P., 1992; Elton, G., 1991 [1955]; Genette, G., 1990 [1983]; Jenkins, K., 2003 [1991]; Munslow, A., 2003b; Nelson, L.H., 1990; Priest, S., 1990; Sellars, W., 1997 [1956]; Topolski, J., 1991; Zagorin, P., 1999; Zammito, J.H., 1998.

EMPLOTMENT

Building on Immanuel **Kant**'s notion of emplotment as a category of knowing, and specifically on the work of literary critic Northrop Frye, Hayden **White** claims that history is the literary artefact that results from the historian's shaping and imposing of a **narrative** on the past. This suggests that historical knowledge and understanding are not acquired exclusively as an empiricist research enterprise, but are rather generated by the nature of representation and the aesthetic decisions of the historian (see EMPIRICISM; REPRESENTATION; NEW HISTORY; AESTHETIC TURN). When viewed from this perspective, our knowledge of the past becomes, to an important degree, the product of the form of the cultural practice we call history (see FORM AND CONTENT). White maintains, therefore, that any model of the historical consciousness ought to recognise the complex arrangement of prefiguration (tropes) and associated levels of explanation of which emplotment is one, along with argument/social theory, and ideological preferencing, in addition to the scrutiny of the **sources** and the **evidence** (see TROPE/FIGURATION; CONSTRUCTIONIST HISTORY). While the precise nature of their connection is not clear, White argues that it is the tropes that possess the power to determine and configure the other levels of **historical explanation**.

When we place **event**s in a particular order ('this happened, then that, because . . .') we are emplotting their sequence. We shape the historical narrative by invoking evidence and causality, blending them together to constitute a plausible and truthful explanation (see CAUSATION; COLLIGATION; TRUTH). In doing this we usually fail to acknowledge the functioning of our (Western) culture's main forms of emplotment – romance, tragedy, comedy and satire. That failure permits us to argue that we have discovered *the* referential connection between the narrative and the evidence. Referentiality supposedly allows us to find *the* story of the events. For White, however, stories are not lived but told, and so reference to what happened *by itself* cannot get us very far in 'discovering' *the* story (i.e. its meaning). As he says, historical situations are not *inherently* tragic, comic or romantic, and 'All the historian needs to do to transform a tragic into a comic situation is to shift his point of view or change the scope of his perceptions' (White 1978: 85). This is a step too far for most empiricists, especially as White goes on to suggest that it is down to the historian to match a favoured plot structure with a chosen set of historical events upon which he/she wishes to confer a particular meaning. This seems to be emptying the past out of history. What empiricists forget, of course, is that the past has to be put into history in the first place through its emplotment.

The type of emplotment that the historian chooses is determined by the power of the hero of the plot over her, his or its environment. A romance, for example, would be identified by the power of the historical agent/hero as ultimately superior to circumstances, questing with ultimate success, seeking and achieving redemption or transcendence. Satire is the opposite in that the agent/hero is a subject of their context, destined to a history of adversity and rejection. In tragic emplotments the hero strives to beat the odds and fails, eventually being thwarted by fate or their own fatal personality flaws. The end result is usually death (actual or metaphoric). In a comedic emplotment there is progress and the hope of at least a temporary victory over circumstance through the operation of reconciliation. At the closure of comedic narratives festivities tend to celebrate the connection and consensus achieved with others by the hero (White 1973b: 7–11).

It would be wrong to see what is a radical modification of the correspondence theory of knowledge – with narrative (form) having priority over the evidence (content) – as allowing historians an absolute freedom to choose any trope–emplotment–argument–ideological arrangement they want, and which they can then impose by fiat on the evidence. Evidence does exist, and the **facts** built on it are constructed as individual referential statements of **justified belief**. Clearly events did or did not happen, and single descriptive statements may be regarded as accurate or inaccurate in degrees. But, lest we forget, facts are themselves only ever events under description, and they only become meaning-full when we emplot them as part of our constructed narrative. The truth of historical research, as expressed in single referential statements, may be demonstrated only inasmuch as they correspond to other statements with the same referent saying the same things about it. This correspondence of internal consistency does not mean that the historian's imposed narrative interpretation is necessarily truthful (or false) in relation to reality (see REPRESENTATION; Frank A. ANKERSMIT; AESTHETIC TURN).

Narrative interpretations can only signify the past. They cannot correspond to it. White is not alone in arguing that history is as much about writing as about archival research. Philosophers of history Louis Mink and William B. Gallie have both observed that the historian's narrative does not depend solely on factualism to work, but also depends on a narrative containing a pattern of events, arguments and ethical positions that the reader can understand (see ETHICAL TURN) and with which they can empathise (Mink 1978; Gallie 1964).

So when historians try to explain the facts of any set of events the issue becomes: 'How are the facts to be described giving priority to one way of explaining them over another?' Establishing that priority is part of the emplotment procedure and it usually demands ideological, social theory and/or cultural decisions (see CONCEPTS IN HISTORY). In the majority of cases events can be emplotted in a number of different ways in order to furnish those events with different meanings. The input of the historian, therefore, resides both in his/her archival work and in his/her ability to develop the figurative character of his/her fabricated narrative as a mode of explanation. The facts, once created out of the evidence, must be constituted again as part of a narrative structure. It is a structure, however, written in anticipation of a preferred outcome (see TELEOLOGY). There are always purposes for history but rarely other than the mundane. In spite of the severe complexity of its construction, there is often far less to the purpose of history than meets the eye.

Further reading

Berkhofer, R.F., 1995; Callinicos, A., 1995; Carr, D., 1986a; Frye, N., 1957; Gallie, W.B., 1964; Mink, L., 1978; Munslow, A., 2003b, 1992; Ricoeur, P., 1984 , 1985; Vann, R.T., 1998; White, H., 1992, 1978, 1973b.

ENLIGHTENMENT, THE

This is a widespread intellectual, cultural and technological/scientific movement usually regarded as the origin of the Modern Era (see EPISTEME; MODERNISM). Beginning in the early seventeenth century in England (with Francis Bacon, John Locke and Thomas Hobbes) and France (with René Descartes), and ending at the close of the eighteenth in France and Germany (with Voltaire, Denis Diderot, Immanuel **Kant** and G.H. Lessing), but found throughout Europe, thought was characterised, in a time of great technological and scientific change, by an acceptance of new ideas like **positivism**, experimentation in science and the close observation of natural phenomena with reason and rationality promoting explanation through the knowing subject (see LIBERAL HUMANISM). Other new ideas emerged concerning government through contract rather than force (based on the emerging doctrine of liberalism, with its central tenets of popular sovereignty and equality of opportunity), and a new conception of the marketplace as a rational economic mechanism. The Enlightenment must also be acknowledged for its influence over the **form and content** of history. As a historical period characterised by the acquisition and organisation of knowledge in particular ways, its epistemological legacy had a direct bearing on how we, in subsequent periods, have understood the historical project itself (see EPISTEMOLOGY; ONTOLOGY; INTELLECTUAL HISTORY; CRITICAL THEORY).

The Enlightenment, as a description, is usually taken to signify the contrast with the superstitious irrationality that is presumed to have been the cultural and intellectual signature of the Middle Ages. The period is often regarded as the seed plot of several of the basic principles (see METANARRATIVE) of modernism, namely reason is the motor and measure of historical change; humanity (man) is capable of progress; all men (if not women) are by their faculty for reason created equal and should, therefore, enjoy equality before the law while exercising tolerance to minorities (reason ruling passion); the sovereignty of 'We, the people'; and the protection of individual rights against the tyranny of undue force. It is sometimes claimed that the ideals that engineered the French and American Revolutions represent these principles in civic practice. The American Declaration of Independence and the US Constitution are often viewed as key documents of the Enlightenment because they are held to embody these principles. The political consequence of the Enlightenment is evidenced in the growth of the doctrine of liberalism (rational political choice), with its chief economic consequence in the free market (rational economic choice).

Its impact on history is in the very creation of it as a discipline founded on the belief that it could, and should, become the record of progress and human perfectibility (for an opposite judgement see CRITICAL THEORY). Perhaps inevitably, Enlightenment rationalist thought eventually turned in on itself, questioning its own central tenets. While this self-assessment has been most notable in our own present (or postmodern age: see POSTMODERNISM), the reaction(s) to the Enlightenment project became a central feature of the nineteenth and early twentieth centuries. In the nineteenth century a number of thinkers began to question the assumptions that underpinned the Enlightenment as the disastrous effects of free-market industrialisation and nationalism became clearer – both processes and movements unleashed as a consequence of the Enlightenment frame of mind. The notion of automatic progress was attacked by Karl Marx as merely the ideological construction of the emergent bourgeoisie, while Friedrich **Nietzsche** rejected wholesale the belief that the real world could ever be adequately represented in an unmediated mirror-like fashion (see MIMESIS). The corollary was to doubt objectivity and science-inspired rationality. Modernism – the offspring of the Enlightenment – was radically transmuted at the close of the nineteenth century into an often violent anti-modernism, especially in the literary and artistic worlds, producing surrealism and Dadaism in art, shifts in literature from author to text to reader, and the confronting and challenge to history conceptualised as the distanced and objective reconstruction of the past (see CONSTRUCTIONIST HISTORY; DECONSTRUCTIONIST HISTORY; RECONSTRUCTIONIST HISTORY; EXPERIMENTAL HISTORY; GENRE).

Further reading
Appleby, J. *et al.*, 1996; Gay, P., 1966–9; Hyland. P., 2003; Jacob, M.C., 2001; Kors, A.C., 2002; Kramnick, I., 1995; Mensch, J.R., 1997; O'Brien, K., 1997; Porter, R., 1990; Williams, D., 1999.

EPISTEME

Michel **Foucault** uses the term to designate how a culture acquires and organises knowledge in a given historical period (see EMPIRICISM; EPISTEMOLOGY; ONTOLOGY). The episteme connects all the separate discourses (see DISCOURSE; NEW HISTORICISM) (religious, scientific, historical, medical, etc.) into a more or less coherent structure of thought founded on a set of shared assumptions about how such knowledge is obtained and deployed. These shared assumptions are elaborated and fixed through the troping process (see TROPE/FIGURATION), which takes place at the deep level of the human consciousness, and which is basic to the emplotments (see EMPLOTMENT) that historians generate. Foucault maintains that knowledge is generated through the human faculty or sense of difference and/or resemblance that all human beings possess. In *The Archaeology of Knowledge* (1972) Foucault offers the following definition:

> something like a world-view, a slice of history common to all branches of knowledge, which imposes on each one the same

norms and postulates, a general stage of reason, a certain structure of thought that the men of a particular period cannot escape – a great body of legislation written once and for all by some anonymous hand.

(Foucault 1972: 191)

The notion of the episteme is not new, having been previously elaborated by the Neapolitan philosopher Giambattista **Vico** in the eighteenth century. In fact Foucault's definition makes it sound very similar to the concept of the *Zeitgeist* or spirit of the age. He constructs his notion of the episteme on the same premise that fired Vico – that we can have any degree of certainty only about that which we have ourselves created. Knowledge and history emerge from our own social constructions – in this instance Foucault is offering to us the epistemic basis of historical experience. Knowledge has thus been organised within each of the four distinctive historical epistemes that Foucault maintains existed from the sixteenth to the twentieth centuries: Renaissance, Classical, Modern/Anthropological and Postmodern.

Foucault assumes that the four epistemes did not grow organically out of each other. Instead they spontaneously appeared in parallel, filling in the spaces suddenly vacated by competing varieties of knowledge creation. In this fashion we see an archipelago of branches of knowledge constituting epistemes rather than a peninsula linked by bridges of causality – as seen in other forms of knowledge like **class**, industrialisation processes, frontier experiences, catastrophic famines, scientific discoveries, individuals bent on world domination, information revolutions or whatever else is taken to link historical epochs. In the language of **structuralism** Foucauldian history does not evolve, but is best understood as a discursive structure.

The first episteme, from the Middle Ages to the late sixteenth century (the Renaissance), characterises knowledge according to the dominant cultural/linguistic or narrative protocol of resemblance or similitude.

In the second episteme, from the seventeenth century to the eighteenth (the Classical), knowledge was generated according to the linguistic protocol of the representation of differentness. The epistemological breaks between epistemes thus provided the space for the third episteme (the Modern or Anthropological), from the end of the eighteenth century through to the early twentieth, and which was preoccupied with Man ('I', the 'self') as the subject and object of reality. This preoccupation is, for Foucault, best understood through the invention of the knowing subject and the discipline of history. History's modernist definition requires the understanding of social change by tracing origins and development as cast in the trope of differential succession by the knowing subject (a.k.a. the historian).

In this fashion Foucault perceives the Modern episteme as creating a basic epistemological paradox for humanity: man as the product of his lived social experience, and also the constitutor of knowledge. This invention created the predominant nineteenth- and twentieth-century conception of history as a realist epistemology, a conception that is seen now for what it is, as a vestigial remain of a previous epoch preserved by **reconstructionist history**. It is the intellectual space in which this crisis of modernist history exists that suggests to many historians the existence of the fourth episteme. For the post-empiricist historian the assumptions and/or attitudes that characterise each age are located in language (metaphors of similarity or difference), and they are displayed in the narratives (see NARRATIVE) that prefigure access to the 'reality' supposedly found in the **sources** and **evidence**.

Further reading
Bernauer, J. and Keenan, T., 1988; Forum 1993; Foucault, M., 1972; Munslow, A., 1992; Noiriel, G., 1994; White, H., 1974, 1973a.

EPISTEMOLOGY

Epistemology is the branch of philosophy that addresses the nature, theory and foundations of knowledge, its conditions, limits and possibilities. Historians, as the creatures of the modernist (Cartesian or **Enlightenment**) revolution, have tended to stick with a particular vision of what history is, derived from a certain kind of analytical philosophy (this is often un-thought out as most historians are not actively engaged by philosophy of any sort). When it is articulated it usually takes the following form: historical knowledge is ultimately discovered through the (highly complex and) rationally justifiable process of the evidence-based inductive method (see CAUSATION; COLLIGATION; CONCEPTS IN HISTORY; EMPIRICISM; EVENT; FACTS; INFERENCE; INTENTIONALITY; TRUTH; INTELLECTUAL HISTORY HISTORICAL EXPLANATION; HISTORICAL IMAGINATION; OBJECTIVITY).

As practical realists, most historians would also accept that, while this process will help to distinguish knowledge from unjustified belief, it cannot, through either a priori thinking or model-making or a posteriori empiricism (see A PRIORI/A POSTERIORI), offer an error-free and unambiguous correspondence between the evidence and the given meaning it is assumed to possess. The reasons for this are, of course, well understood, namely, we have no direct contact with the past, and historical explanation depends on the interpretation of the evidence that must be selected (subjectivity enters the process at this point if not much earlier), or it may be that the evidence we have is misleading, or then again our inferences may be faulty, or we may misconceive the appropriate social theory (see COVERING LAWS; POSITIVISM) that we think is suggested by the evidence, or we cannot establish all the necessary truth conditions that will make even our singular statements fully reliable (see JUSTIFIED BELIEF).

For most historians a compromise is advisable – but it is necessarily one that leans toward a realist position, that historical statements, if we stick to tried and tested methods of historical scholarship, will pretty much match our mind-independent observation of the evidence – so we derive knowledge through criteria that are usually cast in terms of arguments to the best explanation. To justify our historical knowledge means bringing our object (historical event, process, action) within a circle of explanatory propositions. This is normal inductive inference, and it will permit, so realist historians anticipate, the constitution of truthful statements about the past (in the sense of discovering the most likely meaning in the evidence of the past). Empiricism (evidence of experience) and logic (reason) together will iron out most of the problems encountered by most historians, most of the time.

For post-empiricist historians epistemology is about the extent to which, and precisely how, historical knowledge is prefigured and composed (for example, a feminist epistemology is knowledge for whom?) (see POST-FEMINISM). For epistemologically sceptical historians (not necessarily the same as anti-realist historians) it is not only (or even?) a matter of asking if there is anything in historical method that can generate reliable and/or truthful historical statements. It is also necessary to ask what happens when our statements are incorporated into the bigger historical narrative, which itself may be the product of, and relative to, a set of even larger-scale cultural practices and intertextualities. It is a question not just about the possibility of inference up to this level, but about what there is in the Western (analytical-empirical) tradition in the first place that can guarantee reliable (and ungendered?) interpretations.

Much **continental philosophy** insists that Western analytical philosophy grants no privileged access to justifiable historical knowledge, and this has prompted increasing numbers of historians to address its implications in terms of whether or not history can make a legitimate claim to being a distinct epistemology. Such a position represents a paradigm shift away from (Western) analytical philosophy in both its empiricist and logic forms. The rejections of empiricism, inference, truth conditions, natural language, representation, proof and logic all indicate a shift to anti-realism/post-empiricism, with its associated collapse of the distinctions of **ontology** (being) and epistemology (knowing), the priority of content over form (see FORM AND CONTENT), the conflation of observer and observed, and the authorial integration of historian and history (see AUTHOR; REPRESENTATION). Some, like the post-empiricist philosopher Frank R. **Ankersmit**, have declared the end of epistemology (viewing history *pace* Gadamer in ontological terms), while others like Keith **Jenkins** have announced the end of history (as a modernist moment now dead and gone) (Ankersmit 1994, 2005b; Jenkins 1999b). Doubting the epistemological foundations of history means, therefore, that there is also collateral damage to notions of **objectivity** and truth.

Further reading

Ankersmit, F.R., 2005b, 2003a, 2001, 1994; Atkinson, R.F., 1978; Audi, R., 1998; Barthes, R., 1981 [1967]; Bevir, M., 1994; Code, L., 1991; Collingwood, R.G., 1994 [1946]; Cooper, D.E., 1999; Ermarth, E.D., 1992; Foucault, M., 1977, 1972; Hunt, L., 1998; Jenkins, K., 2003, 1999b; Scott, J.W., 1989; Veyne, P., 1984; Zagorin, P., 1990.

ETHICAL TURN

There has been a recent rethinking of the idea that history could or should be an ethical pursuit. This is not a retread of the 'learning lessons from history' argument, but it grows out of the postmodern **aesthetic turn** to questioning the nature of our engagement with the real past. This is characterised by the belief that how we narrate/represent the past determines not just the nature of his-

tory but, most importantly, its ethical utility. In other words, history is as ethical as any other non-privileged historicist, constructed, cultural narrative can or cannot be – that is, ethics and representing 'the-past-as-history' exist in the purposeful universe of narrative-making. It is a moot question as to whether historians offer a value added to the world of ethical living, but if they do, it is likely to be as a result of their demonstrable sincerity and prudence in thinking *about* history as an aesthetic form of **representation** that is secondary to ethics which the Lithuanian-born French-naturalised moral philosopher Emmanuel Lévinas (1905–95) called a first philosophy.

Assuming this is the case – ethics as/is prior to history – it means resituating and redefining the empirical-analytical epistemological model (see EPISTEMOLOGY) with its commitment to linear time and meaning through what happened and knowable agent **intentionality**. Put plainly, the writing of history may be seen as a rational set of narrativised political and value judgements arrived at for the purpose of coping with our postmodern condition. Hence we can legitimately have many forms of ethics that inform history writing, thinking and practice, for example, a feminist ethics, bio-ethics, class ethics, etc. Given this, the 'most sincere' and the 'best' political principles and ethics are those that enthuse and saturate the most credible historical writing. So, if we want history to be an ethical activity, historians must acknowledge the moral choices they make as they construct the past as a representational narrative, rather than assume that ethics exist *in* the past and out of which they can somehow be 'discovered' and mined. The ethical turn means that it is how we choose to write history that allows us to take up certain political options and uphold preferred moral standards and moral ideals. Moral lessons do not emerge 'from history'; they are built into it as we construct it in order to cope with our own present, as well as a handy way of deconstructing the-past-as-history (see DECONSTRUCTIONIST HISTORY).

From the perspective of an epistemic sceptic who has ontological commitments (see EPISTEMOLOGY; ONTOLOGY), what does it mean to suggest that ethics exist before, during and after we make history – before we honestly, sincerely and in 'good faith' reflect upon and constitute the **facts** and emplot them as a form of committed literature (see EMPLOTMENT), and then again in the social consumption of that history? In other words, it means that 'making history' is always ethically separated from 'the past'. So 'ought' precedes 'is' or 'was' in the realm of history and ethics. Following the logic of Immanuel **Kant** we should acknowledge that we all separate 'the real world of facts' from the 'territory of values' because, quite simply, neither can be derived from the other. Now the really important point about this is that once the process of knowing (and especially historical knowing) is no longer seen as the origin of ethics then the **Enlightenment** notion of progress is also placed under a question mark. So when we write/emplot/narrate history it is not predetermined by a belief in the pursuit of *the* ethical end. This does, of course, bring with it doubts about the epistemological metanarrative of **truth**, not in the sense of knowing 'what happened', but in 'making sense' of it, that is, figuring out what it means. This also raises the whole vexed issue of Michel **Foucault**'s 'regimes of truth'.

Past (and present) reality, lest we forget, must reflect or at least be mediated by a human mind – and a mind that looks constantly to its own future as much as to the past. This mediation does not have to be defined in Kantian terms, as Friedrich **Nietzsche** pointed out. Most idealists do not go so far as to say that the mind creates the real world but, in a weaker version, they claim that in explaining the nature of reality we must at all times take into account the way the mind operates. This clearly becomes important when historians wish to make historical value judgements about goodness, legitimacy, right and wrong. Now, given the nature of the holocaustic twentieth century

few people are these days genuinely optimistic about the future and the notion of historical moral progress.

Of course, for constructionist historians seeking a way out of this dilemma (as they usually perceive it to be) of what is a Kantian and Nietzschean universe, they have to believe that they can work out/theorise the underlying structure of empirical appearances and that there must be some ethical truth back there that they can find. It is assumed that their theorised mechanism of investigation, if done properly, can pretty much guarantee the objectivity of their constructed narratives and it is this that provides the foundation not just for 'good history' but for the 'good of history' – that is, history that is ethical because it is truthful. But surely this is seriously naïve? Is there anything in 'doing empirical history' that can have any connection with ethics? Clearly not, especially if one accepts that we view 'the real' through our beliefs about the nature of existence in the Enlightenment-inspired and modernist twentieth and early twenty-first centuries. The German cultural critic Walter Benjamin (1892–1940) in the 1930s argued that all events in the past are plastic in terms of what they can mean. He made a sceptical judgement about **modernism** that, because no modernist event has any stability of meaning, all documents of so-called progress and civilisation are at the same time documents of retreat and barbarism. This is not simply because of the plurality of cognitive perspectives available to every historian. All that would mean is that history as an in-depth knowledge of what happened could be no more ethical than the historian who writes it (which, of course, might be true). What Benjamin meant, rather, was that our modernist condition of existence was itself such that there is no given meaning in empirical reality. Hence, no matter how detailed our empirical knowledge of events (reference, reference, reference), neither the Nazi Holocaust of the 1930s/40s nor the American Trail of Tears native American holocaust a hundred years before can teach us moral lessons today.

This is because we cannot assume that both of these modernist events were aberrations or anomalies brought on by men and women making immoral decisions from which we can learn. If modernist events are at once barbaric and civilised, we cannot possibly learn from the past because to do so demands stability of meaning.

So, in a universe of unstable meanings, how can we, as historians, navigate our way through it? If we assume that our histories are figuratively inspired models of explanation then the idealism of post-Nietzschean philosophers like the German Hans Vaihinger (1852–1933) may be helpful. Vaihinger's reading of Kant and Nietzsche (in his book *Philosophy of 'As If'*, published in 1911) led him to the conclusion that, while our perceptions are real, everything else consists of a jumble that we subjectively make sense of through pragmatically justified fictions and useful fabrications. Vaihinger accepted Kant's judgement that knowledge cannot reach back to things-in-themselves (as bits of reality) and that the chaos of existence (so familiar and disconcerting to Nietzsche) could be coped with only by creating fictional explanations of the factual world 'as if' there were good reasons for believing that our fictions reflected reality. The 'as if' is thus – maybe – a locus for ethics and for understanding how historians as historians can be ethical creatures.

Instead of thinking of history epistemologically as a **reconstruction** of past social, cultural, economic, scientific or whatever conditions and from the effects of which we can 'learn lessons' and 'make ethical moves', we rethink it as an ontological process that is future-orientated. In this way, perhaps, we can understand the connection between history and ethics as the potential narrative connections we make. Conventionally, so far as the status of knowing is concerned, empiricism will deny 'as-if-ism' just as it rejects the Kantian belief that the object conforms to the mind, as well as the perspectivism or subjectivism of Nietzsche. Thus, for the empiricist, thought and representation must correspond

to reality as closely as possible and must exist outside the 'here and now'. Hence Kant's transcendental idealism (subjectivism), that by its very logic denies humanity a doorway to the material world, must be rejected. To reconstructionists, granting a transcendental and anticipatory basis for knowing seems to be offering too constructionist a role with respect to explaining experience – if, indeed, it is not simply anti-realist.

Of course, for those who have substantial doubts about the knowability or the 'true meaning' of the past this turns into a history that can only be viewed deconstructively, and possibly experimentally (see EXPERIMENTAL HISTORY). Deconstructionist history assumes that our anticipatory acts must be fictive enterprises where '**facts**' – defined as those connections made by the historian about the past as a complex mix of the empirical, analytical, narrative, linguistic and ethical to make sense of the jumble of the past – are seen as the creations they patently are, and the factual reality of the past is never more than events under description.

Okay, so now what foundation can we have for our ethics as history practitioners? Well, the short answer seems to be that if there is nothing in 'doing history' or in being a historian that makes one ethical or better equipped to learn from history there is no foundation apart from our own presentist existence. At this juncture we may briefly invoke Lévinas again. Lévinasian ethics centres on the mutuality in the relationship between oneself and 'the other' and the process of 'othering'. Assuming ethics to be the first philosophy and the origin of all other philosophies, behaviours and attitudes, the implication is that the practice of 'the good' even transcends thinking. If 'knowing the truth' is untenable in a **post-structuralist** world – not because of the denial of past reality but in terms of understanding the meaning of 'the other' – then the moral worth of 'the-past-as-history' can only be located in the narratives we construct about it 'as if' they mean something we ultimately find desirable (just look at political party manifestos to see what 'desirable' can mean!). Assuming that ethics precedes truth and that knowing 'things' that happened in the past is no guide to an ethical life, then the historian who wishes to have an answer to what it all might mean can only begin with her/his own attitude toward 'the other'. Indeed, maybe we should look past the past to the present and assume the incommensurability of history and ethics.

However, if we do not wish to live without some linkage between history and ethical meaning (and we do have a choice about that) we must look to how the narrative story is assembled by the historian, and 'the-past-as-history' can be ethical to the extent that the historian controls their rhetoric to make it so. History viewed as a narrative shapes the world certainly as much as it is shaped by it. This produces flux and microclimates of morality and situated ethical niches in history – as it does everywhere.

Arguably, being a cognitive relativist, which means making ethical judgements without 'foundations' for them, is perhaps the best insulation against becoming nihilistic and amoral because if we cannot rely on the empirical for our guide then all we have are what we might call our own 'justice resources'. It is hardly a matter of *if* we want moral closure in our histories, but how best to understand how *we create them*. If we choose to argue it, all histories (even those that do not seek to get beyond the banal level of 'this happened, then that . . .') demand and possess a moral evaluative weight that is located in the historian. If the anti-representationalist position has any force, then how historians relive the lives of past historical agents is important in the lessons they provide for their readers rather than in the nature of the past itself. If we constantly rethink our morality in the here and now, then it is possible that previous generations did so as well, and hence what can we learn from them that has any universal application? In other words, there is no normative or stable language of morals to be found either in 'the past' or in 'history'. And it is this knowledge that makes (or should make) historians increasingly self-conscious about their moral choices when they write about the past and confront 'the other'.

Further reading
2004 'Historians and ethics', *History and Theory* themed issue 43; Ansell-Pearson, K., 1994b; Becker, L., 1992; Benjamin, W., 1973; Carr, D. *et al.*, 2004; Finney, P., 1998; Foucault, M., 1985; Guyer, P., 1992; Jenkins, K., 1999b; Kant. I., 1993 [1786]; Lévinas, E., 1984, 1961 [1969], 1947 [1978]; Lyotard, J.-F., 1988; Marchitello, H., 2001; Nietzsche, F., 1966; Parker, D., 1998; Rabinow, P., 1999; *Rethinking History: The Journal of Theory and Practice* 1998, Special Issue, 2(3); Singer, P., 1991; Todorov, T., 1995.

EVENT

At first sight it may seem unproblematic to define what constitutes an event in historical analysis. An event is commonly assumed to be a singular occurrence or incident: the charge of the Light Brigade, the assassination of Abraham Lincoln, the Cuban Missile Crisis. Usually historians define a single event as a change of situation. Such a definition distinguishes it from the bigger process(es) of which it may form a part: the Cuban Missile Crisis as an event in the Cold War that effected a change, over time, in US foreign policy. For philosophers of history like C. Behan McCullagh the truth conditions of events can be ascertained and described, so it is worthwhile (and necessary) to linger over events so as to determine their significance/triviality. While individual events may teach us relatively little by themselves, fitting them into the overall picture (**narrative** of history) teaches us much (the process of **colligation**). In filling in the detail we can get close to the **truth** of what went on (see METAPHYSICS). The detail provides the boundary we walk between the important and the insignificant in the past and in the present (see Benedetto CROCE).

Without being able to determine the nature of events accurately we lose, it is claimed, the capacity both to judge moral worth and to discover *the* meaning of the past (see ETHICAL TURN). Moreover, without the ability to construe events as real and understandable we are said to be in danger of losing touch with the reality of the past (see RELATIVISM). But historians recognise that the single event also exists in the mind of the historian. The historian takes what he/she assumes to be a real event and to characterise it imagines it at a point somewhere, for example, between the unique and the commonplace or between the ineffable and explicable (see COVERING LAWS; POSITIVISM). Or he/she can conceive of the event as being capable of accurate description, or lying beyond the powers of REPRESENTATION. This would be discomforting to those historians who believe that it is vital we fix the past in (as?) history. If we cannot pin down the reality of the past through the objective event, we cannot escape the present, and we could end up with a history without a tangible object. This would surely mean falling prey to an inability to distinguish **fact** from fiction, being unable to tell history from literature, and eventually sinking in a sea of historical relativism.

Nevertheless, behind all this thinking about events, and the metaphysical reality of the past, is the ontological state of mind of the historian as manifested in his/her prefiguration of the 'this happened, then that' process (see ONTOLOGY). This narrative configuration is important to the characterisation of the historical event not just to demonstrate that it is the real thing, but as the vehicle for telling the reader what it means. For example, for some historians the 1848 Revolution in France was not a single event but a series of interconnected events driven, to a greater or lesser extent, by an emergent yet fearful bourgeoisie and an increasingly disillusioned proletariat. For other historians it was a series of events connected through individual

decisions based upon the historical agents' perceptions of their own history and desired future. This example suggests that all historians make a personal choice, selecting one of a variety of determinisms – in this instance agent psychologism or **class** (see AGENCY/STRUCTURE).

The nature of the historian's ontological (pre-)conception of the event and its significance determines, therefore, the concepts through which the event is structured and the narrative form in which events are composed and connected. The historian thus decides when an event drastically affects continuity and change, although some events appear to choose themselves by being described as 'crucial for', 'highly significant to', 'major', 'integral to', 'notable because', or 'the war had demonstrated' (see CONCEPTS IN HISTORY; EMPLOTMENT; COLLIGATION; AUTHOR; TELEOLOGY). It follows that how events are conceptually conceived, and then arranged as narrative representations, determines the epistemological outcome, that is, what becomes a significant fact (the fall of the French government in March 1848 as part of the French Revolution of 1848?). Events do not become facts, therefore, until the historian tropes them (see TROPE/FIGURATION). That is, the historian places events under a description (more accurately as a narrative proposal). It is the historian who 'realises' events as history. There are, therefore, no necessary epistemological ties between events, only between events and their description in language (Ankersmit 1994: 75–161) (see Frank A. ANKERSMIT).

According to conventional historical thinking the preconception of the historian investigating the event is modified, or even rejected, when the evidence consistently does not conform to the hypothesis/theory – reference shapes history. But this assumes the modernist precedence of the epistemological over the ontological, which is not always a well-supported assumption (see MODERNISM). The argument is regularly put that patterns, structures and, for that matter, emplotments in history are as real as the events they encompass if their truth conditions can be established – but here again demonstrating this is not straightforward. The historian's ontological commitments quite often remain unclarified in historical writing, and this constantly pushes us up against the limits of historical representation. While events are conventionally regarded as the building bricks of history, they are themselves constructed/represented within a set of assumptions about the nature of existence, what governs it and how we can describe it. The meaning or interpretation of events is, perhaps, ultimately determined by what strikes the historian as right or wrong in ethical terms, *and* how this can be narrativised (see ETHICAL TURN). The historian's a priori (see A PRIORI/A POSTERIORI) is at least as significant as the range and veracity of the evidence consulted about the event (see HISTORICAL IMAGINATION). At some point all historians have to come to terms with the narrative construction of the event and the reality/meaning it is supposed to represent.

Further reading

Ankersmit, F.R., 1994; Danto, A., 1968a; Davidson, D., 1980; Friedlander, S., 1992; Jameson, F., 1984; McCullagh, C.B., 1998; Mandelbaum, M., 1977; Oakeshott, M., 1983; Quine, W.V., 1990, 1969; Sobchack, V., 1996.

EVIDENCE

The empirical method presupposes that what historians know about the past begins with the evidence (see EMPIRICISM). What it is that is distinctive about the historian's intellectual training originates with the way in which the **sources** of the past are mined as evidence for the nature of change over time. It is usually claimed that evidence provides the bond between history and the past. Epistemologically the strength of that bond is to be found in the closest possible correspond-ence between **event**s and their description (see EPISTEMOLOGY). Without evidence, therefore, history would be just fiction. This is the issue. Can we write proper, or non-fictional, history if we reconceive the nature of this bond?

It is hard to underestimate the strength of the epistemological attachment to evidence held by historians. Most members of the profession would be likely to agree, for example, that it is only through a forensic study of the evidence that the 'historical perspective' can be used to illuminate the present through historical contrast. Moreover, the skills of both analytical and creative thinking are honed by working on the evidence – gathering and sifting it, discriminating it prior to interpretation, and overcoming its deficiencies by hypothesis-testing and modification (hence it is claimed that training as a historian makes one highly employable – such skills are fundamental to most jobs). It seems to be in the nature of things that historians only indirectly observe the past through the filter of both primary evidence (in the shape of residual traces of the textual, architectural, oral and landscape remains of the past) and secondary evidence (the history produced by historians). But it is enormously difficult to establish the conditions through which a corpus of evidence can support an interpretation of its meaning. Establishing *possible* connections between evidence and its meaning is not enough to justify our **inferences**.

In spite of this, the pursuit of the justified and hence truthful interpretation remains the historian's *raison d'être* (see JUSTIFIED BELIEF; TRUTH). It is normally maintained that this can be achieved through the aim *and* strategy of objectively assessing the evidence without either dangerous over-enthusiasm or deceiving self-interest (see OBJECTIV-ITY). The aim is to discover the meaning of the past, or get as close to it as our best efforts and procedures will allow. Our interpretation must be as closely aligned as possible to the reality disclosed by the evidence. The better this correspondence the closer we are to the truth. For the reconstructionist historian (see RECONSTRUCTIONIST HISTORY) history is nothing if it is not true and tenaciously held fast by the **facts** (see Geoffrey R. ELTON).

Historians invest much time and effort in organising and categorising primary sources according to type, period and place to judge their provenance (by comparison with other sources), and reliability (knowledge of the perspective of the **author**(s) of the source(s)). The aim is to discover the most likely meaning contained within the sources by drawing inferences (see INFERENCE) to the best explanation about the actions of people in the past. Historians conventionally argue that they look at the sources to gain an insight into the decisions made by purposive historical agents acting under specific circumstances of time and place.

The inference of agent **intentionality** is the result of a long process of hypothesis-testing (refining the problem to be 'answered') and a scrupulous internal criticism (interpretation of the text's content). Historians accept that working with partial and misleading evidence (we know it often signifies something other than that which the author may have intended) often makes deriving *the* explanation impossible. *The* meaning is not really given up and, despite our mining and exploration metaphors, as hard-headed sceptical empiricists we do not expect always to quarry *the* meaning from a source. But we do expect our skills in historical method to offer a good chance of discovering the *most likely* explanation – one that comes pretty close to the broad truth of the past – inference to the best explanation. The resulting 'truthful interpretation' (an oxymoron, in effect) applies until new evidence emerges that demands we revise our interpretation. All history is, therefore, provisional according to our (continuing encounter with the) evidence.

But historians today, under the influence of the postmodern post-empiricist impress, are increasingly acknowledging that despite our critical methods we still have to compose

our interpretation in the form (see FORM AND CONTENT; POSTMODERNISM) of a **narrative** – the written expression of our **historical imagination**. The limits to historical knowledge now become suddenly and bleakly apparent. The narrative composition itself represents the organising process, rather than merely the culminating report of findings. Indeed, the intellectual process of organising and 'seeing' connections between events and people in the evidence of the past is a continuous process that goes on as we engage with the evidence. Indeed, the tropic processing of information within the historical imagination could be considered to be anterior to the research stage (see LINGUISTIC TURN; TROPE/FIGURATION; EMPLOTMENT). Our cultural milieux, along with what is presently *en vogue* among the interests of the profession (and what is professionally sanctioned as 'proper research'), usually determine what topics in the past we want to examine and, also, what is valuable in the evidence (**gender** evidence rather than **race** evidence?).

But it is not just a matter of how the historian uses his/her (chosen) evidence (or how his/her culture uses the historian). At the far more profound level of epistemic uncertainty it may be that insisting evidence is *the* foundation to history is a flawed assumption. No matter how extensively and constantly we hedge our epistemological bets about the evidence by reiterating its capacity to mislead the unskilled, we invariably fall back on our belief in the power of inference to the best explanation as if the incantation will work magic. Instead of realising the shortcomings of our skills and the failings of the inferential method by asking where does meaning emerge between the single factual statement and the monographic interpretation, we persist with the idea that the more evidence we have, and the more we refine the questions we address to it, the closer we must be getting to the truth. This dogged refusal to face up to our flawed methodology is based on the assertion that history, as a crossbred discipline, in fact blends the analytical features of a science (our critical procedures) with the imaginative and figurative qualities of an art (see AESTHETIC TURN).

This widespread view of history as both science and art is founded on several related assumptions. Not least that good historians, by definition, deploy a sophisticated constructionist (see CONSTRUCTIONIST HISTORY) methodology that grows organically out of the evidence. What this means is that evidence is never question-begged by our concepts (see CONCEPTS IN HISTORY). Even more significantly, however, is the implicit assumption that the scientific model that detaches being (see ONTOLOGY) from knowing (see EPISTEMOLOGY) produces and also reinforces factualism, referentiality, objectivity and the disinterested separation of observer and observed (see MODERNISM; the ENLIGHTENMENT). The science model, with its corollaries, requires we believe the evidence is capable of supporting truthful interpretations. But, despite all the problems with evidence, and the epistemic uncertainty that surrounds it and, consequently, all our work, it is claimed the smart historian who knows his/her job will probably succeed (against all the odds) in getting the story straight (see COLLIGATION; EMPLOTMENT).

If we unburden ourselves of this delusion, what does it mean for our use of evidence? Well, among other things, it means accepting the consequences that flow from the location of evidence within an imposed explanatory framework predicated on the historian's views on human behaviour – prefiguring the evidence of an event or process as part of a chosen pattern of historical change and explanation (see TELEOLOGY). Furthermore, as French historian Roger Chartier suggests, all cultural texts, literary or historical, ultimately result from the historian's composition process (Chartier 1988: 42) (see NEW HISTORY). It is through the interpretative and imaginative mind of the historian that all history texts become *a* representation of the

past (see HISTORICAL IMAGINATION; Hayden WHITE; REPRESENTATION). How the historian organises or emplots the evidence creates the-past-as-history for his/her readers. Rather than the bond that cements the past to history through the referential narrative, this places evidence in a secondary position in the history production process (see FORM AND CONTENT).

The challenge mounted through **continental philosophy**, especially by Roland **Barthes**, Jacques **Derrida** and Michel de Certeau, to the straightforward referential bond of the world and its words is one of the main contemporary objections to the traditional understanding of how historians use evidence. So, while no one today seriously advances the idea that we can reconstruct the past by the close scrutiny of evidence viewed as scattered bits of past reality, most historians still maintain the only avenue to the past is through its traces (see RECONSTRUCTIONIST HISTORY). The contention is now regularly put, however, that at best all historical methodology can do (through its treatment of the evidence – inference to the best explanation) is help us create a preferred, socially useful and ideologically plausible reality effect (see REALITY/REALISTIC EFFECT).

The weakness of the historical method means historians are being forced to consider what is, in effect, a frontal attack on the notion of historical truth and objectivity. It suggests we cannot discover the intentionality of the author of the evidence, it means working on the principle of chains of interpretative signification rather than discoverable primal meaning, it disposes with the correspondence theory of knowledge and it rejects the idea of the objective historian being able to weave the analytical and the imaginative as two separate strands to create a pattern of truth. Despite this critique the majority of historians still endorse the idea that historical truth corresponds to past reality *because* of referentiality and induction. This requires historians to seek out *the* story that represents *the* truth to be found in *the* past through *the* factual detail of past events. While most historians accept narrative as the vehicle for the empiricist reconstruction of the past, its essential fictive power is assumed to work in the service of the evidence under all circumstances. It is this foundational belief that is now under its severest test (see EXPERIMENTAL HISTORY).

Further reading
Achinstein, P., 1983; Bloch, M., 1963 [1954]; Chartier, R., 1988; Collingwood, R.G., 1994 [1946]; Dowe, P., 1992; Hoffer, P.C. and Stueck, W.W., 1994; McCullagh, C.B., 1998; Mandelbaum, M., 1977; Munslow, A. and Rosenstone, R.A., 2004; Sosa, E., 1988; Stanford, M., 1986; Tosh, J., 2001.

EXPERIMENTAL HISTORY

The idea of an experimental history, as the 'experimental historian' and historian of film Robert A. Rosenstone ironically says, sounds like an oxymoron. Surely, if there is one thing that is not experimental in the arts and humanities it is the discipline of history? The notion that 'faith unfaithful' keeps one 'falsely true' seems simply bizarre in the context of doing history. The whole point of the exercise is not to produce any contradiction between the reality of the past and the reality/accuracy of the history. The history, if it does not exactly reflect the past, does and must exist in parallel, and there cannot be any contradiction between the two – for if there were what would be the point of history? Brian Fay in his introduction to the themed issue on 'Unconventional History' in the journal *History and Theory* in 2002 argued that one reason for devoting a whole issue to unconventional history was, in part, to learn what conventional history was like. Another – and possibly more convincing – reason was, he said, that unconventional history opens doors onto ways in which historians can understand the past and our understanding of the process of producing history. This entails opening up our thinking to new concepts and fresh forms of **representation** that could extend the possibilities of history. Indeed, the British-American edited *Rethinking History: The Journal of Theory and Practice* was established in the mid-1990s with the express purpose of confronting the epistemological model of history and the ways in which (as a direct result of this model) history has been conventionally practised. Unsurprisingly, perhaps, Robert Rosenstone was one of the co-founders of that journal as well as a contributor to the *History and Theory* themed issue.

The reason that Rosenstone offers in his ironic comment (and may irony itself be an experimental orientation to take when discussing the nature of history?) to explain why historians are suspicious of experimentalism, is that they generally have held to the idea that it is really possible, if not to render the past as it actually was, to be able to reconstruct or construct it again pretty closely to what it was really like. Indeed, this is not simply a desire – it is a requirement. Importantly, what follows from this is not just that they can have a fair stab at understanding what the past most likely meant, but they can be regarded by consumers as honest, fair and reasonable in their accounting for past events. In other words, the work of historians still generally inclines toward getting *the* **facts** straight and *the* story will follow. Unhappily, conventional history (that is empirical-analytical history founded on the epistemological model of knowing) (see EPISTEMOLOGY; ONTOLOGY) is unavoidably encoded if not actually pre-determined by the suppositions, ideologies, preferred forms of argument, **emplotment**, theories and concepts of understanding, and hence is just as contingent as any self-proclaimed experimental history. Maybe, at the end of the day, experimental history is really only a deeply self-conscious conventional history? While professional historians adhere to the principles of empiricism and inference and relegate (the concept of) narrative to the simple notion of a story having a beginning, a middle and an end, this does not automatically bring with it **truth** and **objectivity**.

It is now commonplace among historians to ask (if not to follow up experimentally) how our telling and understanding of the realities of the past are connected. Since the variety of 'turns' in the past thirty years – **linguistic**, **aesthetic** and **ethical** – misgivings concerning the epistemology of the empirical-analytical paradigm and the primacy of its source-based methods have now become commonplace. So much so that epistemological scepticism and the judgement that all history is 'sited' and 'situated' and that we have choice in allocating *a* form to *the* content of the past (see FORM AND CONTENT), suggest that empiricism and inference do not bottom out the historical project. Put plainly, knowing that an event occurred does not mean that we can know what it means and hence produce a 'truthful meaning' (the historian's classic oxymoron?). In doing history, as Frank **Ankersmit** has consistently pointed out, the nature of truth and meaning rests on how we *represent* the evidence. The crude idea that the past can be reconsidered only when new evidence is found or when patently 'better' forms of **inference**/conceptualisation are employed (or ideally both together) is no longer persuasive (was it ever?). We are instead inclined increasingly, as Rosenstone argues, to think about the alternative ways available to us for representing the past – most notably **film** – but we may also add the digitisation of the history, the graphic novel and even pop-up books. Of course, there is plenty of scope for re-forming/re-interpreting/re-writing 'the-past-as-history' on the page (see HISTORICAL IMAGINATION).

If we take our cue from Frank Ankersmit's anti-representationalist argument and Keith **Jenkins**'s judgement that the past and history are not ontologically compatible categories, then all we have is history. The clear implication is that there is no obvious direct association between the **event**s of the past and the truth – defined as true meaning – of our descriptions of them. Despite the requirement that historians be fair and reasonable in the selection, comparison and verification of the sources as well as in their descriptions and hence in the inferences they draw, all that historians can *really* do is to compare histories with histories rather than a history with a series of factoids. Once we crank up from the statement of **justified belief** (the reality of the past or as close as we can get to it in a factual referential sentence) to the narrative (the interpretative level of meaning) then we have to work within the universe of the narrative-linguistic. There is no enchantment in **empiricism** that allows its meaning to be relocated onto the page or, for that matter, the film. Hence it is inadequate to suggest that there is a business-as-usual (and by implication a correct) way of doing history. Once we have broken with this idea then experimentalism opens up before us, as many historians and writers about the past have noted, including Simon Schama, Robert Rosenstone, Greg Dening, Natalie Zemon Davis, Hans Ulrich Gumbrecht, Richard Price, James Goodman, Jonathan Walker, Judith P. Zinsser, Carolyn Steedman, Marjorie Becker and so on (and it is worth noting that few on this list would say they are 'postmodern historians') (see POSTMODERNISM; POST-STRUCTURALISM).

So what is experimental history? It is not simply the mirror image of non-experimental, proper or conventional history because if it were then it would not really be an engagement with the past at all. Experimental historians have no doubts at the level of **metaphysics** about the reality of the past, for example. What they question is the knowability of the supposed pre-given stories that it is usually assumed must exist in the past. As Hayden **White** has long suggested, the historical form is not dictated by the content of the past and epistemologically we need to consider the content of the form. Experimental historians have epistemological choices and what they believe are good reasons for choosing, say, a non-temporal and non-linear narrative, or borrowing the form of journalism, or using pastiche or comic strips, and overtly and deliberately deploying other forms of 'literariness' in their histories. These good reasons centre on several things and have no particular priority to them. First, the inability of conventional historical narration to imagine what might have been. And here of course we have the obvious counter-factual experiments of 'What if' alternate history. In a strict sense historians always imagine what else could have happened in trying to explain what reference tells them did happen – but they rarely make such thinking overt on the page. Why shouldn't the reader know about the inner workings of the historian's artifice – their fictive and emplotment constructions? This is not to be confused with the fictional, though experimenters do sometimes create fictional alternative histories. Second, the historical experimenter makes the deliberate effort to disrupt the reader's expectations that the history writes itself – as witnessed when the historian oversteps the line of empathy for their subjects to one of direct emotional engagement. This is what probably makes **biography and life writing** a dangerous historical form when the **author**-historian gets 'too involved' with their subject. Third, because it can be done – giving a practical effect to our epistemological choices and thereby challenging the straitjacket empirical-analytical mode of thinking about how we know useful things about the past. Fourth, historians can, and perhaps have a duty to, probe the frontiers of what is, actually, a very junior discipline that is only just over a hundred or so years old and, therefore, is not fixed once and for all in what it is and what it can do. Fifth, as a representation *about* the past we have a duty at least occasionally (and it might be as a result of epistemological world-weariness) to kick over the traces. We have, perhaps, an epistemological duty of discontent? If a historian cannot be disobedient then what hope is there for a deeper and clearer understanding of the unspeakably complex nature of truth? Sixth, to explore what a history might be like once

we have dispensed with the desire to 'find' a conclusion that we can legitimately say gives us 'the most likely meaning'. A willingness to admit we cannot break into the sublime unknowability of the past is not a dereliction but may end up being of greater service to the reader. Seventh, take a professional risk. Have faith that there are more ways to skin the historical cat than the conventional written survey text or monograph. The risk here is that senior fellow professionals will not understand that to experiment is not necessarily to fall below 'accepted' professional standards and, more importantly, will not recognise that different forms (especially film) should be judged in their own terms and not by the empirical-analytical model of 'proper history' which, after all, has plenty of (quite possibly terminal) problems of its own.

Experimental history is rarely labelled as such and does not necessarily display all of the above characteristics. The collection called *Experiments in Rethinking History* (2004) edited by Robert A. Rosenstone and your author is a collection of pieces taken from *Rethinking History: The Journal of Theory and Practice* and published to exemplify the variety of forms through which the past can be appropriated. It includes the work of a number of historians who have tried to engage with the past by opening up the relationship between content and form. Jonathan Walker, for example, tells a story using the artifice of a pack of tarot cards. Bryant Simon's experiment began in the South Carolina Division of Archives and History and his chancing upon a letter, which demanded he write a story about a lynching. As an experiment in making narratives it has more power than most histories, and more fear as the historian imagines past their sources. Chris Ward's evocation of the Battle of the Somme uses a variety of literary tricks and innovations to bring the reality of the event much closer to what we might still call history.

To experiment through the overt insertion of the authorial self into history, as experiments require, is not necessarily to be non-compliant professionally, but it is to be rebellious and disobedient in the pursuit of a different understanding of our connection to the past. While the **reality/realistic effect** reigns we somehow feel secure that the historian has only acted as a midwife to the history. History is thereby made comfortable and comforting especially as it tries to dispel myths and misconceptions. Proper history invests heavily in referentiality. Experimental history isn't necessarily like that. Yes, it is deliberately disruptive, troublesome and unruly, yet it must also be carefully and self-consciously fashioned, crafted in the proper sense of the word using technique, literary skill and dexterity. There is a literary term, *mise-en-abyme*, popularised by André Gide, to refer to the duplication within a literary work of the literary work itself. Gide's novel *The Counterfeiters* (1926) is an example in which the central character is writing a book called *The Counterfeiters* which resembles the book in which he is a character. For experimental history the endless regression suggested by this and other texts like John Barth's *Lost in the Funhouse* (1968) has a certain explanatory appeal. If all we have is history then all we have is history. Maybe because of this apparent self-referentiality experimental history still

seems for most historians an *Ultima Thule* – a far away and unknown region. Why explore it, why go there? What can we possibly gain? Worse, how can you measure it for degree and research grant-awarding purposes? Well, the reason – like all the best ones – is the simplest. If, indeed, we think that what we want to understand about the past can emerge only *as we write it* then experiments with narrative are not just useful, they are essential. We do it because it is there – it is history – because we make it.

Further reading

Becker, M., 2004; Davis, Natalie Zemon 1995, 1987a, 1987b; Dening, G., 2004, 1966; Goodman, J., 2004; Gumbrecht, H.U., 1997; *History and Theory* themed issue 41, 2002; Jenkins, K. and Munslow, A., 2004; Kellner, H., 1989; Morris, E., 1999; Munslow, A. and Rosenstone, R.A., 2004; Price, R., 2001; *Rethinking History: The Journal of Theory and Practice* 1997, passim; Roberts, D.D., 1995; Rosenstone, Robert A., 2003, 2002a, 2002b, 1996, 1995a, 1995b, 1988; Schama, S., 1991; Simon, B., 2004; Steedman, C., 2001, 1986; Walker, J., 2004; Ward, C., 2004a, 2004b; Zinsser, J.P., 2004.

F

FACTS

The concept of the historical fact is a complex and contentious one among historians (see Carl BECKER). Even more annoyingly what constitutes the historian's facts, and how they are derived and used, also seems to change between generations of historians. For early twentieth-century French historians Charles Seignobos and Charles Victor Langlois following in the steps of Leopold von Ranke (1795–1886), because history was scientific, empiricist and therefore objective, facts were akin to atoms of information that once collected and collated would definitively reveal the **truth** of the past (see EMPIRICISM; EVIDENCE; OBJECTIVITY). They assumed that the empirical method, rather than the testing of hypotheses, reveals the truth of the past. Subsequent generations of historians have always been in a dialogue with this foundationalist position.

At its most basic, for historical fact(s) to exist there must be a consensus among historians that a particular statement about a historical **event** is true. Facts are taken to be true statements about the past (see JUSTIFIED BELIEF; ORAL HISTORY). So how is it possible to achieve this consensus about what is truthful in what we say about the past? Unfortunately, while there may be consensus about a single event having occurred, there is normally no consensus about what it means. But at an even more basic level the historian is increasingly asking if it is even possible to get at the truth of the past. To establish the truth of historical descriptions demands the assumption that the world of the past is an extension, as philosopher of history C. Behan

McCullagh argues, 'of the present everyday world and conceived of in the same terms' (McCullagh 1984: 4–5). Most historians would regard this assumption as unproblematic and incontestable. But how does accepting that the past once existed mean that it is possible to have direct access to its truthfulness? A growing number of historians no longer regard either their methods or language as having the power to represent the past accurately. The oxymoron of truthful interpretation is increasingly contested.

Conventionally, historians believe that historical truth is a matter of the correspondence between description and discoverable and verifiable facts, with a fact defined as an event, or a process, or a piece of social action upon the occurrence of which historians undisputedly agree, and which, by that token as much as any other, convincingly demonstrates the correspondence of reality and description (the Battle of Waterloo occurred in 1815 – all of the historians and **sources** agree). A historical fact is, therefore, a referential single truth-conditional statement about the actuality of the real world that, by definition, remains unaffected by the act of its description (see JUSTIFIED BELIEF). It is, moreover, usually assumed that the demarcation line between what is fact(ual) and the conceptual process of organising raw data so as to grasp its meaning does not ultimately affect what makes a fact true (see CONCEPTS IN HISTORY).

The historian most often associated with the accurate derivation of historical facts as the central feature of historical study is the German historian Leopold von Ranke), with his belief that history should hold up a mirror to nature recording how things really were (see MIMESIS). For Ranke, and generations of subsequent historians, this is enough to constitute history as a separate and independent **epistemology** or way of knowing. Translated as the classical position it holds that, like experienced craftsmen and -women, the more accurate historians can become in the 'discovery' of facts, then the closer we get to fulfilling Ranke's nineteenth-century dictum *wie es eigentlich gewesen* or knowing history as it actually happened. Deriving the truth is the same as deriving the facts or, if you prefer, truth is reference and reference is truth. The central tenet of this, what would now be regarded as an extremist form of empiricism, is an antipathy to the testing of preconceived theories of explanation.

Extreme empiricists claim to verify their knowledge of the past by insisting that their experience of the real world must be as unaffected by their perception of it as possible – hence they remain objective (see ONTOLOGY). We can gain a useful insight into this position, the conservative heart of empiricism, by reading G.R. **Elton**'s aptly titled 1991 book *Return to Essentials*. Elton insists that the most valuable aspect of the historian's work is the 'rational, independent and impartial investigation' of the documents of the past (Elton 1991: 6, 77–98). Arguing that this reliance on common-sense empiricism does not constitute a theory of knowledge, but is history as it should be properly understood, he goes on to dismiss 'ideological theories . . . imposed upon the reconstruction of the past rather than derived from it' (ibid.:11) (see HISTORICAL EXPLANATION; HISTORICISM; INFERENCE; INTENTIONALITY; POSITIVISM; POSTMODERNISM).

Elton believes that historians must, by definition, pursue the empiricist ideal of passionless disinterest. In rejecting hypothesis-testing we become objective and not judgemental. The way to ensure this is through the usually bone-wearying critical study of the archive (see HERMENEUTICS). Hence we have the axiom 'know the archive, know the past'. Do away with all social theory and philosophy in favour of the forensic treatment of the evidence. However, beyond the immediate level of the factual statement of verifiable relationships, historians unavoidably enter the realm of interpretation. What do we do with the fact(s) when discovered or derived from the evidence? How do we sequence and explain them? In practice this is the same as asking how we colligate or emplot/narrate them (see COLLIGATION; EMPLOTMENT; NARRATIVE). Beyond the usual problems with evidence – that it may be of doubtful authenticity, or unreliable (lies), or simply absent – historians have many other difficulties in constituting facts. What criteria should be used by the impositionalist historian to winnow out that evidence that he/she judges to be irrelevant to the constitution of a fact? How reliable is inference as a method for establishing facts? Should historians all become constructionists 'testing' evidence against a hypothesis to establish a fact? What of the unreliable nature of the signifier–signified–sign equation (see CONSTRUCTIONIST HISTORY)? What of the continuing debate on the linguistic and/or social construction of reality (see LINGUISTIC TURN)?

Today there are a number of different ways to conceive of the origin, nature and functioning of fact(s). The role of language in the construction of reality and facts is important. The American Renaissance historian and philosopher of history Hayden **White** claims that when historians attempt to explain the facts of the French Revolution or decline of the Roman Empire,

What is at issue . . . is not What are the facts? but rather, How are the facts to be described in order to sanction one mode of explaining them rather than another? Some historians will insist that history cannot become a science until it finds the technical terminology. . . . Such is the recommendation of Marxists, Positivists,

Cliometricians, and so on. Others will continue to insist that the integrity of historiography depends on the use of ordinary language. . . . These latter suppose that ordinary language is a safeguard against ideological deformations of the *facts*. What they fail to recognise is that ordinary language itself has its own forms of terminological determinism, represented by the figures of speech without which discourse itself is impossible.

(White 1978: 134)

White is making the post-empiricist point that facts are far more complex than is usually imagined by the hard-line empiricist (see CLIOMETRICS). Faced with the tangle of historical fact(ual) data the historian must unravel them, and then re-weave them into a narrative in order to explain their meaning. It is the view of White that historical facts are always constituted a second time as constituents of a rhetorical or narrative structure that is invariably written for a particular purpose. Historical facts are, therefore, always the constructions of historians. For White, as we invent an emplotment to transform events into historical facts, in its turn the emplotment becomes more than the sum of its parts. As both White and F.R. **Ankersmit** argue, it is the prefigured emplotment in the mind of the historian that initially defines the selection of evidence as well as its description and interpretation. If it is the writing of history that creates understanding, a reality effect may thus be generated as we emplot the past (see Roland BARTHES; REALITY/REALISTIC EFFECT). No matter how pure is our technical recovery/discovery of the past in the contextualising and creation of historical facts, it may be argued that its meaning is always going to be imposed by an ideologically aligned and rhetorically constructionist historian (see DISCOURSE).

This point is well made by the French philosopher Michel **Foucault** in his argument that the language of the document(s) (constituted as a particular discourse) precedes truth, fact creation and interpretation. When we historians interpret the evidence, so he argues, we contribute to a presumed centre of 'truth' by adding our interpretation to the weight of existing interpretations. The meaning of historical facts so created, in effect, mutates as historical interpretations are continually revisited and the meaninglessness of the past has a fresh order imposed upon it through the constant revisioning process of the discipline of history. At the end of the day, perhaps, all the creation of historical fact(s) demonstrates is the complex and irresolvable nature of the relationship between epistemology and interpretation.

Further reading
Ankersmit, F.R., 1994; Elton, G., 1991 [1955]; McCullagh, C.B., 2004, 1998, 1984; Munslow, A., 2003b, 1997a; Munz, P., 1997; Ranke, L. von, 1867–90; Searle, J.R., 1995; Stanford, M., 1994; Stevenson, C.L., 1963; Taylor, B., 1985; Tosh, J., 2001; White, H., 1978.

FILM AND HISTORY

Films are still usually seen as historical evidence (being of the time and useful as evidence for social and cultural historians) and not a legitimate form of history in themselves. The reasons usually offered are that the filmic medium allows for factual inaccuracy, has a tendency to dramatise for effect, may often lack the appropriate insertion of archival film itself (film as primary source) and necessarily prioritises entertainment over truth (Williams 2003: 145–9). Perhaps the other, and often unstated, reason is that the discursive **representation** of the past has always to take the form of a professionally approved referential artefact – usually a history book, graduate dissertation, journal article and/or conference paper. The reason is that these demonstrate that a trustworthy, fair and honest profession is maintaining standards. But what is even more unlikely to be stated is that these physical products reflect the historian's deliberate epistemological choice (see EPISTEMOLOGY). The organisation of the history text as a coherently authored narrative that not only 'does history' but recognises itself 'doing history' is what we might call the substance of the historical expression, and for the empirical-analytical historian (who has made that modernist epistemological choice), only sentence-length statements of **justified belief** shape the substance of the expression because they are regarded as mimetic (see FACTS; EMPIRICISM; MIMESIS). So it is that the past 'referentially tells itself' (even though we all know it is the result of the subjective articulation of the historian) (see AUTHOR). This is the referential deception that lies behind the delegitimisation of film as a form of history. Through their representational nature, sentences, paragraphs, sub-headings and chapters are assumed somehow to reflect and reveal *the* most likely meaning of the past. So when historians incrementally 'get the facts straight' they are presumed to be 'discovering the story'. Filmmakers cannot, of course, do this even if they wanted to. The substance of expression is different. But, if one thinks about history's construction as literary (as opposed to a filmic or any other) form, just how many paragraphs and pages should there be between Thomas Cromwell becoming Lord Privy Seal in 1536 and his death in 1540?

Accepting the referential deception (of an omniscient narrator who simply confines themselves to providing the facts in the right order which can then be reflected on the page and, presumably, in the required number of pages and paragraphs) not only means rejecting the obviously *fictional* (the invention or denial of 'what happened'), but it is also usually taken to mean a rejection of the *fictive* nature of writing. However, as we all know, statements of what happened – justified statements of belief – cannot stand alone. Apart from their constructedness as paragraphs, chapters, etc., they exist alongside theory, argument, concept, strategic ideological practice and the linguistic structure of historical **narrative**. Now, what is important in all this is the epistemological assumption that every history must have the same substance of narrative expression; that is, it must take the shape of a history book, journal article or graduate dissertation. This assumes that the purpose as well as the content of the history book is coincident with its form (see FORM AND CONTENT). The history book thus serves its purpose by being what it is – the substance that *expresses* the story found in the past.

Most historians and narrative realists (like David Carr, Paul Ricoeur, Andrew Norman and William H. Dray) who take books, theses and articles to be the only possible material manifestations or *expressions* for the past do so because to accept alternatives would open up the discipline to epistemological deviationism and corrupted professional practices (the graphic novel cannot possibly be 'proper' history). The assumption is that it is only strictly sanctioned and policed history texts that can be appropriate substances for expressing the historical narrative as guaranteed in the correspondence of the past and history via (its signs and symbols of) referentiality. Hence it is that 'the true meaning of the past' lies with maintaining a 'realist style' of history based on factual statements, paragraphs and chapters stiffened by appropriate conceptualisation and, hence, the book/article/dissertation form of expression. The key epistemological consequence is the understanding that, though the approved form of history fosters historical meaning, the narrative itself does not create it.

Because the book (or journal article/thesis) form is the essence of the traditional empirical-analytical vision of history, forms like film, TV history programmes, the graphic novel, the comic strip, ballet and historical re-enactment are dismissed as inappropriate substances of expression – they cannot constitute 'proper' history because they are not empirically-interpretationally structured (and cannot, therefore, serve their purpose by being what the past is). It still worries many historians that the film (whether it be cast within the genre of a history, docudrama, fictive **biography** or whatever) undermines this foundational epistemological belief in the authorised substance of expression. The fear is that outside the sanctioned history media, 'narrative effects' can be introduced by the historian/director/author such as to destroy the purity of the empirical and analytical connection. Hence it is that the disruption or defamiliarisation of substance can *lead to* or, for that matter, *be a consequence of* errant decisions made by the historian.

But there is a double whammy here because this means that while film obviously communicates spatially (on the screen) its structure/structuring of its story is akin to that in fictional narratives – which clearly should not include history. However, as the leading historian of film Robert A. Rosenstone has long argued, this epistemological position seriously misconstrues the nature of history. Indeed, he has argued that if we want to find what postmodern history might look like then we should go see a few history films. This is a view of the past that does not demand a correspondence theory of historical truth, and certainly doubts that such correspondence can only take place as words on a page scaffolded by detailed references, an engagement with the extant historiography and a heavy-duty bibliography – in other words a certain kind of empirically based and professionally certified discourse. Rosenstone offers a corrective to that view, that basically there is more than one way to 'do history' if by that we wish to figure out a meaning for the past. In other words, historians need to extend the range of criteria by which they judge history – extend it beyond the words-on-a-page 'substance of expression'.

Filmic history is fundamentally different from implicitly epistemological academic substances of expression. In transforming the content of the past into a new form (see FORM AND CONTENT) it is often claimed that major changes are unavoidable

epistemologically. This is true in the sense that each form/medium makes different demands in terms of creating meaning – that filmmaking has a form(al) set of constraints different from those of writing on a page, but in another sense there is less to this epistemic change (the past turned into a filmic history form) than one might think. The reason is very simple. Neither 'written-on-the-page history' nor 'filmic history' are reflections of past reality in any 'meaningful sense'. What the 'filmic turn' reveals is that it and other history substances are all constructions (see CONSTRUCTIONIST HISTORY). Both are fictive through and through. Obviously film often gets a 'bad name' from historians because many film directors monkey about with the 'empirical reality of what happened' because they are constrained by making the film 'entertaining' (which, it has to be noted, is not usually a limitation imposed on most written history) or by their target market (and for which all published histories have a market age/ability group) or by their budget or, just as/more significantly, they are required to represent spatial movement, shape, colour and sound in their visual depiction. So, just like written history, film history is a fictive, **genre**-based, heavily authored, factually selective, ideologically driven, condensed, emplotted, targeted and theorised representation – even though it is meant to be documentary and heavily visually archive-based.

As the anti-representationalist history theorist Frank R. **Ankersmit** maintains, the truths of historical discourse are not situated first, foremost or only in the factual statements, but in the forming of arguments and images, using similes and descriptions – creating narrative substances – the function of which is to allow us to think about and interpret the past. In a reflection similar to this, film and media academic Ewa Mazierska notes that 'examining the historical truth of cinema is inevitably limited to comparing one representation with another' (Mazierska 2000: 213). History on the page is meant by convention not to invent historical agents or events as a film director can do, and this is undoubtedly true if you want it to be conventional. But getting hung up on this (as most historians do) is to completely miss the point. Whether one uses a real or an imagined agent/character/event is irrelevant to understanding the bigger narrative processes going on in producing a history. If the historian-director wishes to stick to 'evidence-supported reality' then that's okay – if they do not then that's equally permissible. Indeed, it is probably salutary because we won't then always equate 'knowing what happened' with 'what it means'. This is not to say that we cannot or shouldn't be certain of our facts if we wish to place a premium on that, but if we choose occasionally not to then we are forced into the unusual position of looking to the-past-as-history for 'what the past means'. Hence, and no matter how factual our representation may claim to be, history is still a representation and it is only through its representation that the represented can be 'known'.

Marc Ferro, in his book *Cinema and History* (1988), posed the question as to whether films can or should try to 'do history'. He says both yes and no. No, because films only reproduce a vision of history generated by others, and then yes if the film aspires to be something more than a reconstruction of the past (see RECONSTRUCTIONIST HISTORY) that is deliberately oppositional, experimental, novel, disconcerting and disobedient and which defamiliarises conventional thinking and practice. Though Mel Gibson's 1995 *Braveheart* has been described as a grossly inaccurate representation of the life of the hero William Wallace and the 1982 film *The Return of Martin Guerre* as quite the reverse because the historian who wrote the book advised on the film, here again the point is still being missed. Film does history differently but not necessarily any worse (or better?). Filmic history has different objectives of which empathy is, for example, high on the list – just as it is for historical **biography** (which also gets a bad press among rustic empiricists). Indeed, inserting 'events that did not happen

according to the available **evidence**' into a historical film serves to make history differently. While factual invention is forbidden in empirical-analytical history (though if we wish to experiment it isn't illicit), film history can be made to serve a different set of epistemological purposes and so the established constraints do not necessarily apply. Indeed changing 'what actually happened' on film is not only available to the director-author-historian but (paradoxically?) it reminds us that historical reconstruction is also a choice. **Truth** is more than reference – for a greater 'truth' we can allegorise and we can invent.

As the critical theorist Walter Benjamin said, the past could be seized only as an image and to articulate the past historically does not mean to recognise it as it really was. Here again we return to the issue of aesthetics and representation (see AESTHETIC TURN; LINGUISTIC TURN). Before simply condemning film as an inappropriate substance of historical expression we need to look again at the nature of written history as a constructed literary artefact (see Hayden WHITE). Rather than spend our time and much angst on how and why films invariably get the facts wrong and the story crooked, we would be better employed in trying to understand history's constructed nature. We should ask how 'proper historians' create authenticity, constitute reality, establish arguments, filter the past ideologically, **emplot/colligate**, **trope**, deploy genre, use narration as a form of reasoning, describe, select evidence, focalise the text, compress and dilate time, engage with the chosen historiography or deploy **agency** over **structure** (or vice versa), and how they explore, for example, the metonymic linking of signs that is the hallmark of realist prose (as opposed to, say, the French metaphoric symbolism of poets like Rimbaud and Mallarmé and the work of Derek Jarman in his 1986 film *Caravaggio*). So while film has its own rules of representation so does written history. But, of course, this does not mean that the one necessarily takes precedence over the other or that both sets cannot be discarded when we want to discard them.

Further reading
2000 'History and film', *Rethinking History: The Journal of Theory and Practice*; Allen, R., 1995; Barta, T., 1998; Benjamin, W., 1999; Carnes, M.C., 1995; Carr, D., 1986a, 1986b; Chatman, S., 1978; Davis, N.Z., 1987b; Dray, W.H., 1970; Ferro, M., 1988; Mazierska, E., 2000; Miskell, P., 2004; Norman, A.P., 1991; Pencak, W., 1995 [1998]; Ricoeur, P., 1984; Rosenstone, R.A., 2002b, 1996, 1995a, 1995b; Sobchack, V., 1996; Sorlin, P., 1991; Toplin, R.B., 1996; White, H., 1996; Williams, R.C., 2003.

FORM AND CONTENT

The term is used to designate the connection between the structural design of the history text (form), and the exterior real-world **events**, actions and processes to which reference is made (content). How the connection is made, whether it be equality between the two terms or dominance/subordinance, determines how we perceive the character of history as an **epistemology**, as a way of knowing. It is inevitable, perhaps, that the relationship of form and content is not an unchanging or immutable one but is, to a greater or lesser degree, constituted by the historian. The individual historian's ontological position on how he/she connects form and content is determined by how he/she sees the extent to which changes in one determine changes in the other (see Immanuel KANT; Friedrich NIETZSCHE; ONTOLOGY).

The reconstructionist historian (see RECONSTRUCTIONIST HISTORY) views the connection as invariably one of the priority of content over form because this allows him/her to endorse the objectivist position that form is strictly about the 'writing up' of the content. The question resolves itself into a matter of format rather than form. What this means is that for such historians form and content are indistinguishable in practice. Such a conflation is required because the whole point of reconstructionist history is to objectively report discoveries made in the archive. From this perspective, history as a form serves the **evidence** as the material reality of the past (see SOURCES). History, as an inductive interpretative **narrative,** is therefore always dominated by its content through the mechanism of **inference**. Historical knowledge derives from the historian's empirical methodology that is then offered as a truthful narrative (see EMPIRICISM; TRUTH). Without this commitment to the content of the past as the determinant of form, so the argument runs, we can have no proper history and we shall slide toward epistemological **relativism** and ontological uncertainty and eventually be able only to write fiction.

The constructionist historian (see CONSTRUCTIONIST HISTORY) is less empirically deterministic given his/her practical realist investment in the constructed nature of his/her a priori (see A PRIORI/ A POSTERIORI) categories through which he/she views the material content of the past. However, constructionist history, as a theoretically informed and empiricist practice, is, like reconstructionist history, also ultimately committed to an inferential and empirical methodology, and as such demands that the historian must, like his/her more empirically conservative reconstructionist colleague, place content prior to form. Most historians accept that their findings, when narrated, do not simply chronicle **events**. The narrative is the interpretative vehicle. Constructionists and reconstructionists alike know that neither of their discourses simply report on the unalloyed state of reality. Moreover, both kinds have to connect with the reader. They have to tap into his/her culture and expectations (see TELEOLOGY). **Arguments**, it is understood, cannot rely on **facts** standing alone. Hence all history texts, in order to be cognitive, are dependent as much on their narrative composition as they are on their sources (see EMPLOTMENT; TROPE/FIGURATION). All historical interpretations are narrated so as to influence, be convincing, and ultimately persuade the reader that they are truthful accounts. Indeed, it may be that storytelling with tropes is mandatory in every account of the past (Reedy 1994: 19).

The historian Peter Gay certainly recognises this when he comments that it is the historian's style that allows him/her to map the content of past. But Gay views style in history as being 'of a very special kind. A few flourishes apart, it must not interfere with the historian's science' (Gay 1988 [1974]: 216). So, even though he argues that form and content are united by style, Gay rejects what he assumes is E.H. **Carr**'s argument that to understand history one begins with the historian not the facts (ibid.: 3, 17). Gay clearly leans toward the reconstructionist orientation with his conclusion that history is 'not a construction but a discovery. The order, the period, are there' (ibid.: 217). Form is still secondary to content in Gay's vision of history.

The deconstructionist historian (see DE-CONSTRUCTIONIST HISTORY; GENRE), however, questions the very idea that content and form are naturally polarised. What is there in the nature of **historical explanation** that demands such a dualism? It is, presumably, the empiricist belief in referentiality and factualism, the idea of a knowable and readily translatable material world. This means that the reconstructionist and constructionist historian does not have to invent a narrative form because the events, actions and processes themselves generate the facts that produce the story form of history – this happened, and then that. If, however, the basic assumption of a knowable and representable past reality is disputed, the polarity and priority of content before form come into question. The obvious question then is what happens to history when we reverse the polarity, with form placed before content? What might be the metaphysical consequences of such an idealist or postmodern reversal (see POST-MODERNISM)? An absolutist placing of form as epistemically prior to content leads to a formalist history whereby historical understanding is known and understood through

the cultivation of artistic and stylistic technique rather than through its subject matter. This procedure could so redefine history that epistemologically (as a way of knowing) it eventually metamorphoses into fiction. But this is likely to be the extreme consequence of a narrativist position that maintains that a genuine knowledge of past reality is unobtainable so that what we call history is only ever a composed narrative written for someone and for some purpose: the-past-as-history.

The extent to which history may claim to represent the content of the past through its narrative form is dependent, therefore, on the degree to which narrative is viewed as an adequate vehicle for historical explanation. Several questions about what constitutes history proceed from the belief that history as it is written is structured as much by its form as by its content. Not only are we forced to ask if empiricism can constitute history as a separate epistemology, but several other questions arise, such as what subordinate function does evidence perform, what is the functioning of social theory in the construction of explanatory frameworks, and just what is the role of the historian?

Historians and philosophers as diverse as Allan Megill, David Harlan, Dominic LaCapra, Frank **Ankersmit**, Hayden **White**, Iain Chambers, Joan W. Scott, Julia Kristeva, Keith **Jenkins** and Paul Ricoeur all, at some point, place 'conventional empiricism' and 'social science theorising' in quotation marks, emphasising instead the importance to historical understanding of the structure of language and the relationship of form and content both in history's **sources** and in its interpretations. Such critics argue that history's content effectively exists only when it is described by the historian. History is a stock of literary goods the significations or meanings of which emerge through (and from?) the narrative structures that are themselves in turn influenced by many social and ideological forces.

Roland **Barthes** and Michel **Foucault**, in

particular, suggest that reconstructionist and constructionist **historical explanations** are inadequate. They argue that if we do not have as a primary consideration how we use language, how language uses us and, for that matter, how language is inadequate, we will inevitably neglect the manner in which figuration directly determines the power of the narrative to explain. In our naïveté we will continue to believe that history, through its representational authority, must correspond to reality (see REPRESENTATION). We will forget that historical truth is often little more than a plausible perspective that appeals to a particular readership because, as the cultural critic Paul de Man pointed out, historical knowledge moves within societal power structures (de Man 1983: 165). For the American philosopher-historian Hayden White history is primarily a literary endeavour inflected with ideology. What we know about the past emerges as much through the architecture of its narrative as from its content. Like Frank Ankersmit, White views language as an active medium that requires historians to resist any pretence to an unmediated knowable past reality. In *Metahistory* (1973) White claims that all history writing is a poetic act. Facts are not discovered but are constituted out of sources according to literary as much as to empirical criteria. So far as White is concerned, the historian has to shape *a* story so as to give *a* meaning to events (see EVENT; FILM; NEW HISTORY), actions and processes that do not intrinsically possess one. These events, actions and processes do not in and of themselves have a story to tell. It is provided by the historian. The past becomes history through the form imposed upon it by the interventionist historian. The only truth in history is that it is the result of a fictive process.

White argues that historians utilise the formal structures of narrative used by writers of realist literature. These are rooted in the tropes. Historians create explanatory narratives through **emplotment** and argument, and their ideological implications. Working from the principle that historical writing is primarily a process of intellectual production, White's thinking about the nature of history begins with its end product – the written artefact – and then working backward infers the nature of the mechanism that gives the historical text its particular form. Because this form is literary, historians are advised by White to extend their methodology to include the examination of literary theory. It is largely because of the influence of White that Carl Schorske has argued that the toolbox of the historian today carries literary theory as well as tools borrowed from anthropology, psychology, sociology, **gender** studies, etc., etc. (Schorske 1998: 230–2).

In White's **historical imagination** the deep well of consciousness (at the level of the tropes) generates the strategies of explanation that determine how historians choose to interpret the content of their narratives. Emplotment, argument and ideology produce what White famously called the content of the form. As White readily admits, events happen, as do actions and processes. They all occurred in the past. But to make sense of them, to 'know about them', historians have to configure them, give them a particular form, by selectively constructing them. So it is that we periodise events, actions and processes, highlight their main features and bring forth a meaning from the chaos of the past. The historian thereby constitutes the content of the past as an object of inquiry (Jenkins 1998a: 70). Prioritising form over content thus directly confronts the empiricist philosophical position by suggesting that history is not a common-sensical craft and certainly not a scientific undertaking. This means that neither expression of history – craft or science – can be redeemed by giving it a practical realist spin. History is, instead, a **discourse**, a manufactured cultural practice. As White suggests, the historical narrative always carries the imprint in its form and, therefore, in its content, of the influence of language and cultural self-interest. History can never escape into disinterestedness.

The implications of rethinking the relationship of form and content are highly significant, therefore, for our understanding of the nature of history. Take the way we use evidence. The reversal that prioritises form over content reminds us that it is we who use the evidence; it does not dictate to us. Historians constantly re-work its meanings like the potter shaping a bowl on the wheel. The clay remains what it is and, in a literal sense, the 'fact of the matter' does not change. But what does alter is the shape we give to the clay as culture makes its demands upon the potter-historian. The central lesson for Foucault is that we can, if we wish, take possession of a new conception of history when we accept that it is informed by the cognitive sway of its narrative form, itself fashioned by linguistic and social perspectives (see Friedrich NIETZSCHE).

It is often pointed out by empiricists like Perez Zagorin, Mark Bevir, Geoffrey R. **Elton** and C. Behan McCullagh that there is a problem in the extent to which White's tropes control the past through its form as history. Surely it must be the historian who controls the tropes? If this is not so, then what we believe about the past is not determined by the traces of the real world. From the post-empiricist perspective it may well be that the past is governed by the dominant tropic influences at work both in the evidence and in the constitution of their own world-views. Following Louis Althusser, White argues that such a self-reflexive process should inform the nature of how historians see the ideological relationship between form and content. In other words, writers of history should review the character of troping *in and of* history (see EPISTEME). It is possible that history may become a much more interesting and livelier project as a result of this extension of the historical enterprise beyond the confines of the supposedly value-free correspondence theory of knowledge (see FILM AND HISTORY).

In the 1990s **deconstructionist history** has attempted to make historians self-conscious (as many as will listen anyway) about how they metaphorically prefigure, construct, emplot, explain and make ethical or political judgements about the past (see ETHICAL TURN). As the American pragmatic philosopher Richard **Rorty** has regularly argued, knowledge comes through some form of representation. This may help us answer the question as to why the histories written by the many different kinds of historian – Marxist, subaltern, gendered, feminist, postcolonial, liberal, conservative – convince only their own readership constituencies (see POSTCOLONIAL HISTORY; POST-FEMINISM; GENDER; POST-MARXISM). It may come down to the fact that if the tropic conventions used by the historian are shared with the reader and agreed by them, then the narrative will appear plausible, cognitive and truthful – whether it be of the genus reconstructionist (the third-person and realist narrative brings the past to life), constructionist (the third-person and realist narrative is a truthful creation) or deconstructionist (the third-person and realist narrative is primarily an invention and not necessarily the way to represent the past at all).

Because language is neither transparent nor innocent, as Foucault and White have tried to demonstrate, the linguistic form of the narrative is implicated in how we understand historical content. But can history be understood in forms other than that of the narrative? By this I do not mean the modernist disruption of the narrative shape that deploys problem or themed history – chapters or titled sections that break up the chronology by dealing with topics taken out of their time-sequence. Nor do I refer to a number of historical objects, concepts and ideas arranged alphabetically (like this book). Such ways of doing the work of historical explanation are still representations as opposed to what I shall call performances (i.e. presentations). Once we start to rethink form and content it should be possible to produce various radical conceptions of history (see EXPERIMENTAL HISTORY; FILM AND HISTORY). Is there anything intrinsically 'wrong' or 'unnatural' about refusing the omniscient narrator-historian in favour of exploring the implications of the historian-as-**author**? Is there an embargo on experiments with stream-of-consciousness history?

But the big question remains. In any experiment with form is the final objective still to seek order in the past, whether it be *the* story or *a* story? The idea of a narrative story suggests an ordered structure (regardless of whether it is claimed to be found or imposed). Empiricists will ask whether, if we abandon the pursuit of the formal, the orderly, the classified, the categorised and the organised, we will not lose the ability or (worse still?) the desire to judge the significant from the insignificant. In such a situation can we still claim to be 'doing history' and how can we possibly tell 'good' from 'bad' history? In this welter of foundationalist worries we should not forget that we historians may rethink our explanatory structures, but we still have to communicate through the some kind of prose(aic) narrative – literally transforming ideas into language. Empiricists would say that this process is not, of course, reliant solely on the correspondence theory of knowledge but is, additionally, dependent on inductive and (its specific form of) abductive inference. When we ascribe **intentionality** or **agency** to people in the past we are only inferring meanings and there are always immense unmapped tracts of uncertainty and indeterminacy. It is at this point, perhaps, that we can most fruitfully exercise our historical imagination. Once we are freed from the boundaries erected by the placing of content before form we are at liberty to challenge every position regularly deployed as collateral support for empiricism. We can confront inference, **causation**, progress, disinterestedness, narrative accuracy, referentiality, realism, truth and **objectivity**.

What makes prioritising form over content even more dangerous is that the choice of emplotment and accompanying argument of explanation imply the forefronting of a possible philosophical position on the part of the historian. It seems that placing form over content must lead to relativism and a history doomed to collapse into **historicism** (writing history from the perspective of the present) and ideology. What White is saying, in fact, is that whether we like it or not we do not have much choice in the matter; the reality that exists in the past can only be knowable through the shape we give to it in the here and now. The question is, as Hayden White asks, why assume history has to be narrativised or story-shaped? Why not try to make history a performance? This might be through a resurgence in experiments with an authorial and interventionist historian, or it might take the form of a non-written narrative, perhaps cinema, television or a computer construction. If prose is chosen why not history as collage, pastiche and/or fiction? History today does not always have to take the form of the empiricist's verism or *trompe l'œil* representation.

Further reading

Ankersmit, F.R., 1994; Ankersmit, F.R. and Kellner, H., 1995; Bann, S., 1984; Berkhofer, R.F., 1995; Bevir, M., 1994; Carr, D., 1986a; Danto, A., 1985; de Man, P., 1983; Gay, P., 1988 [1974]; Harlan, D., 1989; Jenkins, K., 1998a, 1995; LaCapra, D. and Kaplan, S.L., 1982; Lemon, M.C., 1995; McCullagh, C.B., 1998; Mink, L., 1978; Munslow, A., 2003b, 1997a; Munslow, A. and Rosenstone, R.A., 2004; Norman, A.P., 1991; Reedy, W.J., 1994; Rosenstone, R.A., 1995a, 1995b; Schorske, C.E., 1998; Scott, J.W., 1989; Walsh, W.H., 1981; White, H., 1996, 1992, 1987, 1973b; Zagorin, P., 1999.

FOUCAULT, MICHEL (1926–84)

Michel Foucault was the leading philosopher of history to have emerged from the structuralist (SEE STRUCTURALISM; INTELLECTUAL HISTORY; NEW HISTORICISM) and **continental philosophy** revolution of the twentieth century. But, because of his trajectory out of the postmodern (see POSTMODERNISM), his influence within history has been disputed by many conventional or practical realist historians (see CULTURAL HISTORY). Foucault's contribution to the study of the past is to be found in the way he has confronted the Western philosophical and metaphysical (see METAPHYSICS) tradition which assumes that our concepts (see CONCEPTS IN HISTORY) are extra-cultural and extra-linguistic representations of reality – the belief that the word represents the world transparently and largely without deforming it (see REPRESENTATION). Equally, he criticises the **Enlightenment** idea that the knowing subject (thinker, historian, intellectual, philosopher), by rationally deploying concepts, can stand above and beyond the material world of social institutions, customs and power relations (see LIBERAL HUMANISM; MODERNISM). Foucault, in his histories of madness, deviant behaviour and sexuality, demonstrated how modernist thought is moulded by Western patriarchal culture to create the 'other' and how history is complicit in the linkage of knowledge and power (see EPISTEMOLOGY; GENDER; WOMEN'S HISTORY). Both lived experience and history are, for Foucault, best viewed by reference, therefore, to the conventions, practices and discourses (see DISCOURSE; POSTCOLONIAL HISTORY) of social behaviour rather than a given or natural reality that the historian neutrally comes 'to know about'. To replace the notion of representation through conceptualisation, Foucault offered, as we shall see, his own epistemological inventions: archaeology and genealogy.

Foucault was born in Poitiers in 1926 and was a schoolboy friend of Jean-Paul Sartre and Maurice Merleau-Ponty. Foucault immersed himself in Marx, Freud and Friedrich **Nietzsche** while he attended the École Normale Supérieure (1946–50). It was at this time, when he was in his twenties, that he acknowledged his homosexuality and

the idea that biological boundaries, like discipline boundaries, are conventional rather than natural. Disobeying and violating cultural and disciplinary boundaries, in effect, became the motif of his life and work. In 1950 he became a communist, prompted in part by the social conflict in France in the late 1940s, but also as a result of the encouragement of his teacher, the French cultural critic Louis Althusser. This was also the period of the high tide of phenomenology in France (introduced by Edmund Husserl in the late 1920s). Under the influence of the philosopher Georges Dumézil, Foucault came to believe that the norms and practices of society are produced according to the internal economy of discourse. He said 'It was he [Dumézil] who taught me how to describe the transformations of a discourse and its relations to an institution' (Foucault 1972: 98). At this time in his life Foucault lived in the maelstrom of French intellectual life, being further influenced by university teachers and philosophers like Gaston Bachelard, Emile Benveniste, Georges Bataille, Pierre Klossowski and Maurice Blanchot.

Foucault learned from his reading of these intellectuals, as well as of Nietzsche, that life has a strong tendency to disrupt the Enlightenment subject as a subject, in fact to tear the subject from itself and so become something 'other' than a unified self. It becomes dis-associated from itself, decentred. This decentring process emerged especially in his critique of the historian as a knowing subject. Such a traumatic deformation of the subject led him into the study of psychology in the early to mid-1950s and his working briefly with patients in the Hospital of Saint Anne. Recognising the homophobic boundaries within the French Communist Party, Foucault resigned in 1953. Between 1955 and 1959 he taught at the Universities of Uppsala, Warsaw and Hamburg, moving back to France to teach at the University of Clermont-Ferrand in 1960.

Four books in the 1960s established his professional reputation. His 1961 doctoral dissertation became his first major published work, *Madness and Civilization*, which was followed by *The Birth of the Clinic* (1963), *The Order of Things* (1966) and *The Archaeology of Knowledge* (1969). It is within these texts that Foucault conceived and applied his archaeological-genealogical epistemology, producing ideas on the connections between discourses, customary practices, disciplines, historical period, power and knowledge. In the politically climactic year of 1968, after two years in Tunis, Foucault returned to France and took up a philosophy position at the University of Vincennes. Disclaiming by then to be a Marxist, structuralist, phenomenologist or even a philosopher, the following year Foucault was awarded a personal chair in the History of Systems of Thought at the Collège de France. His 1970 inaugural lecture, *The Discourse on Language*, was another milestone. His next project was his study of the will to knowledge and the nature of the control exercised in prisons over those individuals and groups whom society assumes to be abnormal or deviant. His study of this in nineteenth-century France was eventually published as *Discipline and Punish* (1975). His final major area of work was within the field of sexuality with the publication of Volume One of his *History of Sexuality* in 1976. The second and third volumes appeared in the year of his death in 1984 from AIDS-related complications (published in English in 1985 and 1986).

In this corpus of work we find Foucault translate his archaeological-genealogical epistemology into a method that is both synchronic (structural) and diachronic (historical). His archaeological method is a synchronic analysis of the statements or principles within any discourse that unconsciously influence what can and cannot be articulated within it. His archaeology can be seen in his use of the **episteme** or slice of history that characterises the construction of its discourses, cultural practices, knowledges and power arrangements. Genealogy is a diachronic method that reconstructs the origins and evolution of discourses within the flux of *present* experience. Genealogy (after the genealogy of Nietzsche) denies there are foundational origins for anything in the past. Meaning is never foundational but exists only in relationships, as we perceive them from the standpoint and needs of today. There is never an absolutist meaning to be derived either from a transcendental metaphysical fact or principle, or from rational discourse. So the **evidence** appealed to by the traditional historian for access to the **truth** is perceived as polluted because it is always subject to a contemporary methodology or a formative set of rules that deforms the object or referent of the evidence (see HISTORICISM; OBJECTIVITY; SOURCES). For Foucault the conventional historian's disinterested truth-conditional narrative description, which emerges after much labouring in the archive and the strict application of empiricist **inference**, is not a neutral or natural process at all.

What is wrong with this process? First of all Foucault rejects the conventional historical practice of smoothing the past into a seamless narrative that is then taken to constitute an adequate *and* truthful representation of the past (see REPRESENTATION). The modernist process of writing a problem-solving history requires, so Foucault suggests, a contrived bridging of the inherent discontinuities in the past, it demands planing its jagged edges and irregularities, and it results in an act of closure that can only claim to explain the inexplicabilities of the past. There is also a deceitful drive in modernist history to discover *the* essential meaning of events, practices and processes. Not least, there is a will to discover *the* pattern to the past in order to own it (as history and) for what are patently ideological purposes. All this is achieved because the historian is assumed to be *the* knowing subject. Foucault rejects all this. The only order to be found in the content of the past is that provided by the form of the history we write (see FORM AND CONTENT).

History is not the end result of a neutral process of disinterested exploration in the archive by a knowing subject who exists outside time and place. Rather, when we write the past we are doing so as part of a writer–text–reader interactive situation – within the perimeter of what Foucault calls a discursive formation. It is this discursive formation that shapes the meaning we take from the past, not the reverse. History, therefore, has no intrinsicality beyond the historian. Indeed all we have is the-past-as-history. In thinking widely over the nature of modernist history, Foucault questioned, for example, whether there are essential themes in the-past-as-history – or are the historian's topics merely the interests of the present projected onto the screen of the past? But Foucault's most basic charge against conventional history remains the dependence of its practitioners on its empiricist inferential foundations (see EMPIRICISM). The fixation of modernist history with the mechanism of empirically based inference obscures history's true character as a narrative construction shaped by the culturally situated and discursively constituted historian. Once this is recognised, then there is nothing in the past that we must address, and there is nothing we must know that is not dictated by our present needs. The text you are reading probably illustrates that process.

But, if the-past-as-history is always in the present, then it must constantly be being rethought and re-visioned (revisioned). History's revisionism is not just the re-interpretation of its events and processes, but its rethinking by historians acknowledging the changing conditions under which it is written and researched. Historical revisionism is the product of the epistemological conditions within the episteme. The-past-as-history is always about how we can achieve our future ends by changing the way we create the-past-as-history now (see TELEOLOGY). History is written as a part of that business of desiring what we want for the future from the past. To borrow and redefine terms used by the French philosophers Gilles Deleuze and Félix Guattari, history is a future-orientated desiring machine. It is a mechanism by which historians give concrete form to their wants and dreams.

The-past-as-history is, consequently, a relativistic enterprise (see RELATIVISM). This problematises the idea of **causation**. There can be no straightforward causal connections discovered in the past and, perhaps, even less between the past and the present. In its turn this suggests the past cannot be understood in its own terms because to understand causes we must start with what we want the effect to be in the future. To summarise: history is unavoidably relativist, presentist and teleological, and the reason is because it is an engagement between the historian (as writer/**author**), their text (the written past-as-history), and the reader (as a consumer who wishes to 'know' the past in their own way) (Barthes 1974, 1975).

This interactivity of subject positions – writer and reader via the text (in the past as evidence and now as history) – creates meanings. Such interactivity does not permit the discovery of *the* meaning. The historian as author may still try to manipulate the reader by concealing their existence, as in the liberal humanist empiricist and objectivist written act we call the-past-as-history (letting the text speak for itself in relating *the* meaning) or, alternatively, he/she may choose instead to acknowledge his/her situatedness as the historian-as-author. So, here I am, Alun Munslow, the historian-as-author, speaking. What are my being and my agenda and, dear reader, what are yours (see ONTOLOGY)? What does this text tell you about my a priori (see A PRIORI/A POSTERIORI), for example, or tell you about the epistemological decisions I have made about the history production process and, withal, the nature of the episteme in which we both exist but that we mediate and understand differently? Why did I bring out a second edition of this text?

What makes Foucault such a significant historian is his commitment to rethinking but not demeaning or undervaluing the-past-as-history. Everything has its past as well as a history – every action, person, thought, event, place, process, idea and text. But the-past-as-history for each is plastic, unfixed, and not immutable. History is never given, once and for all, or permanent. It is always in flux, always subject to perspective and, occasionally therefore, to parody. Lest there be any doubt, I make the assumption that the traces of the once real past remain available, but the past and its referents are only accessible as a text, set in a discourse, within an episteme, and understood by an implicated historian who writes it up for an engaged reader/author. It is this judgement, as an engaged reader/author, that I wish to take from Foucault's work. The past counts but, like Nietzsche, Foucault accepts that all history's claims must be, to a greater rather than a lesser extent, counterfeit. In his 1971 essay, 'Nietzsche, genealogy, history', he is scornful of the empiricist's attempt to locate the historical truth, arguing instead that because history is formally contrived we are wrong to persist with the fiction that we can stand outside history or our texts. What is worse, this lie is determinedly hidden from history. Foucault agrees with Nietzsche (Nietzsche's genealogy) that history should be 'explicit in its perspective' and should acknowledge that its 'perception is slanted, being a deliberate appraisal, affirmation, or negation', and history (which he recasts as 'effective history') should not efface itself 'before the objects it observes' (Bouchard 1977: 157). This is a postmodern history that rejects the correspondence theory that the 'truth' is 'out there' and dismisses the coarse myths that flood from the conventional model of history: factualism, detached historians, transparent representation, objectivity and the clear distinction between history, ideology and fiction. Perhaps history is the 'other' of the present?

Further reading

Barthes, R., 1975, 1974; Bernauer, J. and Keenan, T., 1988; Bouchard, D.F., 1977; Dean, M., 1994; Deleuze, G. and Guattari, F., 1984 [1972]; Dreyfus, H.L. and Rabinow, P., 1983; Foucault, M., 1985, 1986, 1980, 1979 [1976], 1977 [1975], 1977, 1975, 1973a, 1973b, 1972, 1970; Gutting, G., 1994; Megill, A., 1985; Munslow, A., 1997a; Noiriel, G., 1994; Pencak, W., 1997; Poster, M., 1984; Rabinow, P., 1999.

G

GENDER

Gender history is a type of historical analysis that has developed out of, as well as
alongside, **women's history** in the past forty
to fifty years. In the 1960s and 1970s gender
was often used as a synonym for women's history, but from the 1980s the term developed
as a separate interest among historians and
critics in other disciplines. Gender can be
defined as the study of the cultural (including the historical, social, **class**, intellectual,
economic, political, psychological, literary,
etc.) organisation, functioning, **representation**
and meaning of sex/body difference. As with
other major categories of historical study
(class, **race**, nationalism, imperialism), gender
distinction has been explored as a common
and omnipresent characteristic of society (see
CONCEPTS IN HISTORY; ONTOLOGY).
Gender as a kind/category of analysis, like
other classifying concepts in history, does not
of itself explain anything, but it is an analytical mechanism by which change over time can
be interpreted and represented (see REPRE-
SENTATION; Frank R. ANKERSMIT).

Like all concepts used by historians, its
meaning and functionality have changed over
time as the interests and preferences of historians have developed. Initially in the 1970s it
grew as an adjunct to women's history (itself
a product of the second wave of feminism
that emerged from the 1950s/1960s), addressing as it did patriarchy, male dominance and
why women were hidden from history. Next,
thanks in important part to the work of Juliet
Mitchell and Teresa Brennan, the feminine
and psychoanalysis were brought together
to explain the subjectivity of women through
language. From the 1970s and into the 1980s,
especially through the early efforts of Sally
Alexander and Catherine Hall, women, class
and sexual difference came under the compass of a variety of Marxist historians and
materialist perspectives that tried to enve-
lope the concept within the larger analysis
of economic change. The impact of **post-
structuralist** thought had its impact by the
mid- to late 1980s especially in the work of
Joan Scott (Scott 1986, 1988). By the early
1990s gender had become a substantial topic
among historians and those interested in an
interdisciplinary approach to it. Two edited
texts from that time, Julia Epstein's and Kristina Straub's collection *Body Guards: The
Cultural Politics of Gender Ambiguity* (1991)
and Sue Tolleson Rinehart's *Gender Consciousness and Politics* (1992), indicate the
final arrival of gender consciousness among
historians as well as academics from a range
of adjacent disciplines such as Cultural
Studies, Women's Studies, literature, **biography and life writing**, political science and
anthropology. Gender also made inroads
into philosophy in the early 1990s although
most work was done exploring feminist
epistemology as in Linda Alcoff and Elizabeth Potter's edited *Feminist Epistemologies*
(1993), Ann Garry's and Marilyn Pearsall's
Women, Knowledge and Reality (1996) and
Jean Curthoys's *Feminist Amnesia* (1997).

The concept of gender is today explored
and deployed within the postmodern context
of difference often cast within the notion of
gender scepticism. For many historians, and
as John Tosh has pointed out, it is now axi-
omatic that both females and males become
gendered in particular ways under certain

cultural circumstances. Most notably French feminist philosophers and critical theorists Luce Irigaray and Hélène Cixous, along with Judith Butler, Diane Elam, Teresa Brennan, Mary Poovey and Donna Haraway, have explored the process of cultural absorption into a dominant gendered discourse, raising questions about how gender historically defines sex and **agency(/structure)**.

Gender is now firmly fixed as a part of the history industry's many new features – the family, fatherhood, war, men's studies, work, masculinity, AIDS, lesbianism, homosexuality and queer theory, masturbation, transsexualism and transvestism – but is now fused with the whole range of mainstream historical concepts already noted through the exploration not just of difference but also of identity. For example, explorations that link sexuality, gender and nationalism are revealed in texts like George L. Mosse's *Nationalism and Sexuality: Middle Class Morality and Sexual Norms in Modern Europe* (1985) and the multiple-authored *Nationalisms and Sexualities* (1992). On gender, race, imperialism and colonialism see Anne McClintock *et al.*, *Dangerous Liaisons: Gender, Nations, and Postcolonial Perspectives* (1997) and Ida Bloom, Karen Hagemann and Catherine Hall, *Gendered Nations: Nationalisms and Gender Order in the Long Nineteenth Century* (2000). See also Marina Warner's blend of history, gender and fairy tales *From the Beast to the Blonde* (1996).

Gender as a category of historical inquiry has shown itself to be a classic instance of **constructionist history**. As Alice Kessler-Harris says,

historians have created a new interpretative stance that enriches our view of the past, enabling us to construct a fuller portrait of historical change and to comprehend it more completely. Employing a complicated notion of gender, imbricated with race and class, historians have revealed it as an important axis of power. .... Gender is, I want to make clear, not the only axis we need to understand, but one among

the several (including class, ethnicity, political structures, ideology, economic institutions and, more recently, race) whose consequences are already the subjects of analysis. Gender is embedded in these axes, even as it remains analytically distinguishable.

(Kessler-Harris, 2002: 99)

This is, possibly, one of the best descriptions not only of how gender as a historical concept is used today, but of the nature of mainstream history thinking and practice – specifically how analytical concepts are deployed to prise open the meaning that is presumed to exist in the empirical world of what once was. Like all the concepts that historians use, gender is yet another modelling device (and the more we have, perhaps, the greater is the richness we have in history) for organising and then representing the past. As always, this is done for reasons that have as much to do with the historians' preferred **narrative** structure for history, and their vision of what is history as a discipline, as with explaining the nature of the past itself. Kessler-Harris concludes in such terms. In 'new empiricist' argot (the effort to meld the empirical-analytical with the narrative-linguistic), she maintains that gender history is a way of looking at the past that expands our vision of it especially if we use the insights of the postmodern, though not, as she says, 'its rejection of the material' (ibid.: 108). As these comments suggest, historians always start in the present with their choice of epistemology and their prefigurations and work backwards to create, in this case, 'the-past-as-gendered-history', while always looking over their shoulder at what they are doing with, and to, the discipline.

Further reading
Alcoff, L. and Potter, E., 1993; Alexander, S., 1984; Bloom, I. *et al.*, 2000; Bock, G., 1989; Brennan, T., 1993, 1992; Burkitt, I., 1998; Butler, J., 1991, 1990; Cixous, H. and Clément, C., 1986 [1975]; Corfield, P.J., 1997; Curthoys, J., 1997; Epstein, J. and Straub, K.,

1991; Firestone, S., 1971; Fuss, D., 1991; Gardiner, J.K., 1995; Haraway, D., 1991, 1988; Irigaray, L., 1985; Kelly, J., 1984; Kessler-Harris, A., 2002; Maynard, S., 1989; Melosh, B., 1993; Mitchell, J., 1974; Mitchell, J. and Rose, J., 1982; Mosse, G.L., 1985; Parker, A. *et al.*, 1992; Poovey, M., 1988; Riley, D., 1989; Rinehart, S.T., 1992; Rowbotham, S., 1974; Scott, J.W., 1996b, 1988, 1986; Shoemaker, R. and Vincent, M., 1998; Smith-Rosenberg, C., 1985; Stanley, L., 1992; Stearns, P.N., 2000; Tosh, J., 2004; Williams, C.D., 1997.

GENRE

In the discipline of history genre is taken to represent a (generic, genus) category of inquiry characterised by a specific relationship between **form and content**. Genre thus provides the epistemological and methodological shape or design of the history as constituted by the individual historian as they endeavour to provide some sort of **narrative** meaning for the (content of the) past (see EPISTEMOLOGY). A historical genre is, in effect, an epistemological **discourse**. Historians choose (and occasionally create within) a genre for functional reasons and, hence, all genres of history have been constituted with fitness for purpose in mind (see ARGUMENT; EMPLOTMENT; EXPERIMENTAL HISTORY; BIOGRAPHY AND LIFE WRITING; CONSTRUCTIONIST HISTORY; RECONSTRUCTIONIST HISTORY; DECONSTRUCTIONIST HISTORY; STRUCTURALISM). Genres of history are also, of course, products of time and place. Clearly, fitting a form to a particular body of content (past **events**, happenings, intentions, processes) cuts to the heart of the historical project.

Arguably, given the above definition, there are at least four major genres of history: Reconstructionist(ism), Constructionist(ism), Deconstructionist(ism) and today we might offer Postist(ism) or Endist(ism) histories (the kind(s) of history 'after history' that is created in an epistemologically sceptical and narratively self-conscious **post-structuralist** universe). The case for these broad genre definitions has been explained and argued for by Keith **Jenkins** and myself (Jenkins and Munslow 2004). Ours is certainly not an exhaustive treatment of the notion of historical genre but is, rather, a reasonably detailed examination of how historians consciously locate themselves within the intellectual structure of the discipline. Genre in history represents the constructed relationships that emerge as a consequence of the different attitudes toward epistemology, the utilisation of diverse theories and concepts, and the different kinds (bodies) of empiricism invoked by historians. Most historians (even constructionists), because they are realists, would immediately say that you cannot have genre in history (at least in the sense of a formal and fixed structure of four genres). This is because of the incredibly complex empirical nature of the past and history's constantly developing practical responses to it. But this, of course, ignores the fact that history is first and foremost the product (and a practice) of an epistemological choice.

In (usually fictional) literature, genre is defined as a category of writings constituted by a range of shared practices and literary conventions. Genre in non-historical written works is used to define the fundamental types or kinds of literary activity (narrative, drama) as well as forms of composition (prose, poetry) and a substantial range of minor categories defined (confusingly still called genres) according to criteria that include structure (sonnet, epic), authorial intention (parody, lampoon), subject matter (magic realism, fairy/folk tale), type of action (tragedy, romance), etc. Genre in literature is a formal mapping of literary practice. It is also, of course, historicist in the sense that all genres of literature are imprinted by time and place (see HISTORICISM). The emergence of the novel is time- and place-specific, just as is, for example, the modal common history form of **gender history**, or 'race history' or 'economic history', or 'history from below'.

Genre in history reflects the epistemological decision of the historian to organise knowledge about the past in ways that satisfy their preferred cognitive, **aesthetic (turn)**, ideological and **representation**al aims. What we might call 'modal history forms', such as economic history, **cultural history**, race history, social history, **intellectual history**, military history, **gender** history, **oral history**, international history, **post-feminist history**, political history and **postcolonial history**, can be cast within any one of the genres of Reconstructionist(ism), Constructionist(ism), Deconstructionist(ism) history. The fourth genre – Postist(ism) or Endist(ism) history(ies) – is, of course, the one that critiques the first three and challenges itself.

Because the genre chosen by the historian determines the meaning that will be generated from the **sources** within their chosen modal form, this inevitably raises the question of how the genre produces different kinds of historical narrative (or something beyond history if it is postist/endist in orientation). Although the history narrative is not a discoverable given but is always a choice available to the historian, that choice is always genre 'in-formed'. So, rather than ask a historian why he or she is an economic or international historian, it is always more helpful to find out why they prefer to write in one genre rather than another and how this then 'in-forms' their narrative choices. So why, indeed, do historians generally prefer one genre to another?

It would be unfair to suggest that historians today are more self-conscious about what they do than previous generations or have some kind of 'higher' appreciation of what is history. The point in creating history as a coherent discipline (over the past two hundred years in its modernist form) was, and is, to be self-conscious about our engagement with the past. But today, in an era of epistemological scepticism and ever conscious of the purposes to which cultural discourses are put and the material influences upon them, historians are aware of what they do in ways that are different from (though not necessarily 'better' or 'worse' than) previous generations. In the end, why a historian chooses to work within one genre rather than another and then translate it into a particular modal form is presumably a mix of where they were trained, who supervised their graduate degree(s), what other historians influenced them and their thinking through of the pros and cons of each genre. And this self-consciousness is probably what dictates why historians choose to work in one genre rather than another – or if they wish to make out an intellectual case for some kind of mixed-genre approach (which is always going to be problematic, given how the genres appear to work).

But what might be more important and more worrying is the number of customers for history who do not recognise the genre of history they are reading, listening to or watching. If the point of genre in history is that it should assist the reader/consumer in understanding the kind of 'text' they have in front of them, if the consumer–historian loop is broken because there is a deficiency in understanding the nature of the genre (by either the historian or the consumer), knowledge of the way in which meaning is being produced is lost. Importantly, if consumers do acquire experience with a genre they should start to understand better how the genre encodes its modal common forms. For historians – always depending on their level of genre competency – such knowledge allows them to invoke 'generic rules' to cue the reader. By the same token historians can transgress the genre rules if they so wish, but this is rare given the professional and peer pressures not to (see EXPERIMENTAL HISTORY).

'Uneducated' consumers miss the cues (and clues) that will allow them to read the epistemological 'message' in the economic, social or whatever history they are reading. And the additional complexities of the communication medium in which the genre is cast – book, **film (and history)**, digitised, or TV – can compound this failure 'to read the nature of the performance'. By performance I mean, of course, the epistemological decisions that dictate emplotment, figuration, argument, authorial voice, ideology and so forth. The four main kinds of historical genre constitute the terms of the epistemological contract between the historian and the consumer. The history genre is thus an intellectual construction that, to operate efficiently in transmitting meaning, must operate successfully in both its production and its consumption. As the history of the four genres evidences, they also propagate and mutate. Hence constructionism mutated from reconstructionism, and deconstructionism and endism in similar fashion. The theory of history genre reveals not merely how the discipline is always in a state of development, but also its epistemological tensions.

Further reading

2004 'Interchange: genres of history'; Chamberlain, M. and Thompson, P., 1998; Chatman, S., 1978; Derrida, J., 1992; Frye, N., 1957; Genette, G., 1990 [1983], 1986 [1972]; Jenkins, K. and Munslow, A., 2004; Kellner, H., 1989; Munslow, A., 2003b; Rigney, A., 2001, 1990; White, H., 1987; Williams, R., 1977.

H

HEGEL, G.W.F. (1770–1831)

History is central to the German **Enlighten-ment**-inspired and anti-positivist philosopher G.W.F. Hegel (Beiser 1993: 270). Rather than viewing philosophy as the universal master discipline with history its handmaiden, Hegel turns to history as the only genuine basis for knowledge of reality. The irony is all the stronger, therefore, that Hegel has never been attractive to English-speaking empiricist (see EMPIRICISM) or reconstructionist historians (see RECONSTRUCTIONIST HISTORY). In part this is because of his idealist conviction that empiricism alone cannot find **truth**, that concepts (see CONCEPTS IN HISTORY) have priority over objects, and his belief that the historian is the key to the study and writing of the-past-as-history. In addition, Hegel fails to appeal to constructionist historians (see CONSTRUCTIONIST HISTORY) because there are now so few large-scale system-building members in that guild to find his totalising and deterministic pattern-seeking history plausible. In sum, although Hegel turned to history as the only true foundation for knowledge, historians have largely rejected him. In fact his influence has been limited to the minority of idealist historians who placed empathy and thought at the centre of the historical undertaking, like R.G. **Collingwood** and Benedetto **Croce**, the former largely pro-Hegel, the latter anti-Hegel. Furthermore, because there is seemingly little in his contribution to the study of the past, it is difficult to offset some of his more outlandish notions concerning non-historical peoples. His praise for the Great Man theory of history and his unre-served reverence for the state find little appeal in a postmodern (see POSTMODERNISM) world that has little time for such intellectual grandstanding.

The fundamental problem with Hegel is that his theory of historical knowledge (his **epistemology**), which is that the reality of the past is to be found through the mind of the collective subject, which he refers to as the logic of the 'spirit' (*Geist* in German), not only sounds far-fetched today, but what is worse is founded upon the notion that the spirit must ultimately unify subject with object. Hegel apparently diminishes the importance of the empirical in favour of jacking up history to the level of a philosophy, that is, understanding the big mechanism of ideas or concepts rather than being satisfied with discovering the meaning of **facts**. Most empiricists are worried by R.G. Collingwood's commentary on Hegel that 'all history is the history of thought' (Collingwood 1994 [1946]: 115). To empiricists conflating history with philosophy is not a good idea at the best of times, but it becomes just plain silly when the aim is to suggest that the end of history can be reached in the blending of subject with object.

The independently derived, yet collective or organic, gift of self-knowledge that leads to the realisation of the 'World' or 'Absolute Spirit' demonstrates to Hegel our human progress toward a rationalist (and nationalist) community of belief (which Hegel believed happened to exist in the Prussian state in which he lived). For Hegel human activities and events have a design *because* of their spiritual direction. While mainstream historians today view this sort of mystical thinking as of archaic interest at best, deconstructionist historians (see DECONSTRUCTIONIST HISTORY) regard it as nonsense given their antipathy not so much to the unity of subject and object (which is not really a problem), but to grand explanatory or teleological (goal-orientated) **narrative**s translated as (knowable) history. Through his idealism Hegel believed he knew the reality of history. Empiricists are more at ease with his conclusion than with his method, and deconstructionists favour the method but not the conclusion.

Although most historians today thus reject Hegel's notion of the Absolute Spirit and historical determination through ideas, a good many nevertheless still find attractive his basic method whereby ideas come into conflict – the dialectic. Its allure is due to two factors: the notion of it as a kind of scientific procedure, and the often quite unself-conscious assumption that the dialectic exists as a 'natural' feature of humanity, namely it is the destiny of human beings to struggle and overcome opposing forces in order to achieve. This double potential in the dialectic for objective history and/or emplotting history as the overcoming of tragedy by beating life's obstacles has a potent charm (see EMPLOT-MENT; Hayden WHITE).

For Hegel, however, the dialectic has only one purpose, to demonstrate the progressive conflict of opposing ideas revealed as the steps toward the highest stage of historical development. Hegel thus found history lit-tered with examples of strife and conflict as he pursued his big idea of the fulfilment of the human spirit. Nevertheless, when shorn of its Hegelian spiritual aim this dialectical principle retains a strong law-like epistemo-logical elegance – the notion that each step, phase or epoch in history contains within itself the source(s) of its own dissolution (see Michel FOUCAULT; EPISTEME). The essence of Hegelianism, the determinism of ideas in progressively creating *the* pattern of real historical change, is dumped in order to retain the dialectic as a neutral mechanism of historical explanation (see HISTORICISM).

What makes Hegel unfashionable is not just his spiritual determinism (his ideal-ist dialectic), but in addition what he sees as the necessity for an activist historian in the constitution of the-past-as-history. Like everyone else in the early years of the nine-teenth century, Hegel was in a dialogue with Immanuel **Kant**'s theory of knowledge. Both philosophers wanted to know what it is that drives history along. According to Kant it was nature. Nature, defined as things-in-themselves, can be known but only through the screen of the concept. Hence knowledge comes from sense-experience as it is shaped by human, or in our case the historian's, categories of thought. This is the so-called epistemological basis of knowledge – that reason can discover both its foundations in the knowing subject and its limits in the cat-egories the human mind deploys to carve up reality (hence the description of Kant's thinking as non-empirical transcendental ide-alism). Hegel's response was to extend Kant's limits of (rational) knowledge beyond that of the conceptual. Hegel deployed reason differently. He chose to believe we could know things-in-themselves because rational thought can give access to the world beyond the appearance. Because things-in-themselves do exist so our concept of existence must make things knowable.

If Hegel had ended at this point he might well have kept an irresistible appeal for empir-icists everywhere – the greater our knowledge of reality through sense-experience the closer we shall get to the **truth** of reality. But he did not end there; instead he pushed his line of thinking toward absolute idealism. The logi-cal conclusion of his premises is that if the real is open to rational conceptualisation then everything must be ultimately knowable *through* the thought of the historian. It is this extraordinary universalism that destroys the Kantian distinctions of subject and object, **form and content** and **a priori/a posteriori** whereby the (a priori) form provided by the mind is given its (a posteriori) content by historical experience. For Hegel our knowledge *is* reality because concepts (like those used in history) represent the rational mind at work. So history becomes knowable through the unfolding of the logic of conceptualisation (as Hegel liked to argue, what is rational is real and what is real is rational); indeed history *is* the unfolding logic of conceptualisation via the dialectic (concepts in conflict). R.G. Collingwood concluded Hegel was right that 'there is no history except the history of human life, and that, not merely as life, but as rational life, the life of thinking beings' (Collingwood 1994 [1946]: 115).

Like many of the other major historical thinkers of the Enlightenment, Hegel also considered the connections between epistemology (knowledge) and aesthetics (art). Along with **Vico**, **Nietzsche** and Croce, Hegel philosophised about history as revealed as a form of writing cast in the historian's preferred figurative style. As Hayden White describes Hegel's vision of history, it is written in the form of a tragic drama unfolding into comedy (White 1973b: 81–131). Hegel's views on language are, therefore, instructive in the context of today's postmodern (see POSTMODERNISM) reversal of content and form in history. Hegel argues that no matter how much the historian strives to reproduce actual historical facts (and he/she must attempt to do this), he/she has to infuse them with his/her own creativity in order to make the content of the past vivid as history. Language, as used by the historian, mediates between consciousness and reality and, it follows, history must be close companion to poetry and, specifically, to drama. The function of the historian's language is to seek out the inherent idealism in the prosaic or literalist world (see TROPE/FIGURATION).

Hegel thus offered a grand metaphysical (see METAPHYSICS) and deterministic framework for the understanding of the-past-as-history that has been rejected by almost every historian of whatever stripe. He is rejected because of the 'corruption' of his esoteric idealism (his over-emphasis on knowledge through rational thought), because of his unwarranted teleological assumptions, and, while there is still a residual appeal for his dialectical mechanism for constructionists, the resolution of opposites in the pursuit of closure is abandoned by deconstructionists (D.D. Roberts 1995: 87). The Hegelian appeal to the totalising or grand narrative to which the idealistic dialectic leads is cast out in favour of accepting otherness, alternatives and constantly deferred meaning (there are no 'ultimates' whether in meaning or as the Absolute Spirit) (see Jean-François LYOTARD). The realist philosopher of history Michael Stanford claims that today 'hardly any historian is a Hegelian' (Stanford 1998: 197). However, although speculative history of the Hegelian kind may be out of fashion, it should not obscure the fact that it was Hegel who, almost on his own, made history an occupation worth undertaking.

Further reading
Adorno, T., 1983 [1966]; Beiser, F.C., 1993; Collingwood, R.G., 1994 [1946]; Hegel, G.W.F., 1975 [1821]; Knox, T.M., 1975; O'Brien, G.D., 1975; Popper, K., 1962 [1945]; Roberts, D.D., 1995; Stanford, M., 1998; White, H., 1973b.

HERMENEUTICS

Originally a post-Reformation practice of Biblical textual explanation (exegesis), developments in the nineteenth and twentieth centuries redefined hermeneutics as the theory (or philosophy) of interpretation rather than as an interpretative textual practice (a methodology). Although it was recognised in the nineteenth century that the rupture between the reader and the **author** can create a cloudy, if not at times an impenetrable, barrier to meaning/understanding, that did not stem the desire to recover the text's 'real' meaning. In the twentieth century, however, the relativism immanent in the author–reader relationship has been generally viewed as inevitable, suggesting that meaning is probably a cultural variable rather than a discoverable given. Historians, as interpreters of the textual **evidence** of the past, live in this uncomfortable situation of knowing it is impossible to recover *the* meaning of the past, yet being pushed constantly in that direction by the professional culture of getting the story straight.

Most (practical realist) historians today are still wedded to a crude kind of **Enlightenment** hermeneutics. There is a strong urge to believe that there is probably an original meaning in the evidence, but the circumstances under which they labour to reconstruct the past will never permit that original meaning to emerge – and even if it did they would not be able to recognise it (see RECONSTRUCTIONIST HISTORY). Nevertheless, the aim remains to objectively serve the evidence within our historical **narrative** (see OBJECTIVITY). Serving the evidence entails an engagement by the historian but one that is rigorously controlled by **truth**-conditional statements (see JUSTIFIED BELIEF), propositional logic, strict rules of **inference**, referentiality, the contextualisation of evidence, the deployment of a limited range of explanatory theory and **concepts in history**, and keeping one's distance from the object of study (separation of knower and known). The most that can be said is that historians today are only just starting to engage with the broader issues of how we understand – in philosophical terms (see EPISTEMOLOGY; INTELLECTUAL HISTORY). The shift away from being solely concerned with the impossible dream of *the* truthful interpretation, recovering through various kinds of **empiricism** and varieties of sophisticated constructionist methodologies the givenness of the past, is an immense step for today's historians (see MODERNISM). It is a move that radically changes the conception and character of the discipline by injecting into it a fundamental ontological aspect to the historian's work – that there is a case to be made for the fruitful collapse of subject and object (see FORM AND CONTENT; ONTOLOGY; EXPERIMENTAL HISTORY; FILM AND HISTORY).

Recognition (by post-Hegelian (see G.W.F. HEGEL) **continental philosophy**) that language cannot fix meaning, that in practice power and perspective do replace objectivity and rationality, that truth is situational and culturally and epistemologically relative, suggests not merely that texts have multiple meanings, but that the big issue is the nature of our being-in-the-world. How we think about that question as historians infuses the history we write with our individual and collective senses of what we want out of the future (see TELEOLOGY). While it is still a minority pursuit, more and more historians are displaying an interest in teleology, replacing the profession's traditional preoccupation with the discovery of original meaning with a re-casting of the discipline.

This potential reorientation of history is indebted for its philosophical foundations to the German phenomenologists and hermeneuticists Martin Heidegger (1889–1976) and Hans-Georg Gadamer (1900–). Heidegger suggests that we all possess a foresight; a pre-critical understanding that makes all our acts of interpretation also acts of inquiry about our own existence. From Gadamer historians observe that our prejudices and pre-judgements are not capable of suspension, but are an integral part of what we do. What Gadamer calls the 'effective-historical consciousness' is the recognition, as we interpret the documents of the past, of the 'horizon' of our cultural situatedness. History is about our own existence as much as about the past. Historical interpretation – hermeneutics – is not just about practice (empiricist methodology) or epistemology (knowledge), it is about ontology (existence).

This divorce of truth and method (truth from method?) does not yet convince many practical realist historians. It has not, for example, convinced the likes of E.D. Hirsch or Jürgen Habermas, the major critics of Heidegger and Gadamer. Habermas insists that there is room for, indeed it is vital that there be, a *rapprochement*, within the field of hermeneutics, of methodology and epistemology. As Hirsch argues, without this – established through the correspondence (theory of knowledge/interpretation) of meaning and author intentionality – we are rudderless in a sea of ideology and cultural relativism. Paul Ricoeur's contribution to hermeneutics is also important in his work on the nature of the historical imagination, especially the functioning of memory and symbolism. Because historians rarely read any philosophy of history, the philosophical thinking and debates about hermeneutics of Heidegger, Gadamer, Hirsch, Habermas and Ricoeur have tended not to make it into the mainstream of the profession's consciousness. This can be rectified by reference to the 'Further reading' below.

Further reading

Gadamer, H.-G., 1998; Heidegger, M., 1962; Hirsch, E.D., 1976; Müller-Vollmer, K., 1986; Palmer, R.E., 1969; Pickering, M., 1999; Ricoeur, P., 1981; Thompson, J.B., 1981.

HISTORICAL EXPLANATION

Historians tend to ask three questions about the events, processes and people of the past. These are: what happened (discovering the facts), how did it happen (historical interpretation), and why did it happen in the way the evidence suggests it did (see CAUSATION)? Historical explanation requires addressing and answering all three: what, how and why in the-past-as-history? The kind of explanation any individual historian appeals to in answering these questions informs their perception of history as well as their cache of historical knowledge, and determines the kind of historian they are. The complementarity of the entries in this book should give some sense of the interconnected nature of historical explanations, involving as they do a great many of the key features of the historical project (see CONSTRUCTIONIST HISTORY; DECONSTRUCTIONIST HISTORY; EMPIRICISM; EPISTEMOLOGY; HISTORICAL IMAGINATION; HISTORICISM; INFERENCE; NARRATIVE; OBJECTIVITY; ONTOLOGY; POSITIVISM; RECONSTRUCTIONIST HISTORY; STRUCTURALISM; INTELLECTUAL HISTORY).

Before getting to historical explanation, however, a brief preliminary word about explanation in general terms, and then scientific explanation in particular. To explain something is to describe it (to act epistemologically by creating knowledge), and to justify its existence (its ontology) at a certain time and place (to be in touch with reality – the metaphysical) (see METAPHYSICS). Explanation at a general everyday level is, therefore, a fearsomely complex thing, but in order to get on with life we assume that explanation simply means that events and occurrences follow on from other events (see EVENT) and occurrences (which we might call preconditions or antecedents) in a sequential order, and that we describe such occurrences to each other in the shape of a narrative: 'this happened, then that, because . . . '. This explains why, for most historians, narrative is the form of explanation – specifically, to explain historically is to discover *the* story (Gallie 1964) or, more radically, to impose one that is invented as much as found (White 1973b) (see FORM AND CONTENT).

How does this shape up to so-called scientific explanation? Thanks to the work of Karl Popper and Carl Hempel the dominant view of scientific explanation holds, although it has been increasingly challenged since the 1980s, that a scientific explanation means subsuming an explanation under a law of nature. Water freezes and bursts central heating pipes when, in an empty house, the temperature falls to a certain level. This hypothesis is testable empirically and accountable for by an appeal to a universal law of nature. The premises, which are known in philosophy as the *explanans* (that which does the explaining

– the temperature level) predicate a certain known outcome (based on previous empirical experience), which is called the *explanandum* (that which is to be explained – burst pipes). The *explanans* contains a universal or covering law (see COVERING LAWS) to which appeal is made for the purpose of demonstrating that the *explanandum* had to happen. This kind of explanation contains all the features we would expect of a conventional scientific explanation: it is subject–object in architecture, inferential – specifically hypothetico-deductive (or propositional-inferential) – referential, realist, foundational, capable of re-testing, empiricist, factual, rational, objective, has no room for interpretation, is cause–effect in character, endorses the correspondence theory of knowledge, and is, therefore, predictive. As Carl Hempel said, somewhat dismissively, if historians do not make an appeal to a general or covering law, they are just talking in metaphors. In a clean fight over **truth** a deductive empiricism will always beat imagination (see TROPE/ FIGURATION).

But is Hempel correct? Is this hypothetico-deductive inferential model appropriate for the study of the-past-as-history? Can historians infer necessary consequences from the data? Although, while agreeing with Hempel to the extent that history is indeed an empirical project, is it also not about the one-off and the contingent rather than the universal? Doesn't history explain unique and differentiated events in a sequential order? Positivists counter, saying that every individual micro-level event in order to be explained must be subsumed, at some point, under a universal (at the macro-level) (see POSITIVISM). But, the humanist historian responds in turn, where there are no universal laws of nature involved, as in history and the rest of the humanities and social sciences, the deductive-nomological model (which is the philosophical description for Hempel's scientific model described above) surely must give way to another form of argument, a fuzzier, less deterministic model? Explaining why, for

example, the process of capitalist industriali-sation *tends* to occur uncertainly, presumably requires a different model of explanation from the scientific. At best we are looking here for a statement of statistical probability, rather than an immutable law of economic and/or human behaviour. Such a model would not be classically scientific, and certainly not predictive. It would be a model of explanation that is after-the-event and inductive, meaning that, from a range of examples having a common feature, the historian generalises to further unobserved instances. As the historian might say, 'from this evidence it seems likely that . . .'. This is much closer to the way historians explain things.

Given certain initial conditions of time and place, is it more or less likely that capitalist industrialisation will occur? By examination of the evidence, did it occur? Were there discoverable patterns to it? Is there a universal law of capitalist industrialisation? Explanations suited to this kind of problem conform, then, more to the inductive-statistical model (as it is known) in which the *explanans* requires that we inductively infer a high (or low) probability in the *explanandum*. The fewer the number of assumptions I have to make in order to arrive at my explanation, the more I can be justified in the veracity or truth of my explanation. The way to reduce the number of assumptions, and to offer a workable compromise with covering-law positivism (if a compromise is what I want), is for me to produce as wide a spread of contextualising evidence as possible so as to define and refine my hypothesis so that I can draw reasonable inductive inferences and make justifiably true historical statements. This particular inductive inferential mechanism – evidence steered by a suitable social theory resulting in the truth-conditional statement – leads me to (one of the huge varieties of) constructionist history (see CONCEPTS IN HISTORY). My preference for one form of constructionist history over another usually depends on my own criteria as to what it is that constitutes genuine knowledge. That, of course, is likely to be influenced by my politics, my age, my **gender**, my professional training, my **class** affiliations and my views on human nature (if I believe there is such a thing).

The problem with covering laws in historical explanation (usually referenced as concepts, categories or appeals to theory) seems to be that they are either so broad and plastic that they become meaningless, or so narrow and rigid as to barely qualify for the title. Moreover, much of history is concerned with the actions of individual human beings (and their attendant hopes, desires, fears, intentions and a whole variety of psychological states) to which proclaimed universal laws of behaviour do not regularly apply. So what are the alternatives if history does not conform to a scientific model of explanation? It suggests the need for some more elastic kind of framework. William H. Dray has been influential in proposing that historians apply criteria of rational behaviour to people's actions in the past in order to provide solid criteria for historical judgements and interpretations (Dray 1957). Developed from R.G. **Collingwood**'s notion that historians can usefully re-enact the thoughts of historical agents, rational action theory helps to account for agent **intentionality** and leads to a reconstructionist history which assumes that historians can explain (given enough evidence and a degree of empathy) why something very probably happened, or why a historical agent took a certain course of action for explicable reasons. In practice, explaining the reasons for a historical agent's actions usually also means invoking some kind of judgement about the broad generalities of human behaviour. Thus we end up with the dominant form of history today – a hybrid, a sophisticated practical realism that carries within it appeals to various kinds of argument that, based upon empirical research, purport to explain human behaviour from the level of the rational individual acting intentionally, up to that of major event, social structure, institution, process, nation or empire (see AGENCY/STRUCTURE).

Given the fuzzy nature of historical explanation as I have described it so far, no historian claims to tell the absolute truth about the-past-as-history. Clearly this is not possible given its inferential and indirect evidence-based nature. The sensible and moderate aim of most historians is to establish a high degree of probability that things actually happened as we say they did in our narratives, and hence their meaning becomes demonstrable. We do this through the conjunction of our data with our sophisticated explanatory conceptual hypotheses. This conjunction is achieved by the referentiality demonstrated in the correspondence theory of knowledge – what we describe corresponds to the evidence and, ideally, through a statistical correlation in the case of numerical data. In practice historians seek to explain the past by discovering and narrating the real causes of the social institutions and structures inherent in society that influence events, people and processes. What do we mean by causation/causality? I take it to mean the understanding I have of the determining relations between events, processes and people's actions. Historians tend to talk of primary and secondary causes, and necessary and sufficient conditions for occurrences to take place. Necessary causes are found in the majority of cases generating a particular effect, whereas a sufficient cause alone can be taken to account for a particular event. Causation is complicated further in that it has to embrace explanation at different levels: that of the actions of individual people (invariably named), of collectivities like classes or occupational groups, and also of large-scale social, economic and political practices, processes and structures.

But regardless of the level of causal explanation, the past becomes history through the correspondence theory of knowledge: the empirical discovery of the real structures that are believed to have governed the choices of historical agents, and which in their turn were influenced by those choices. This methodology assumes a realist position on the epistemological problem of how accurately our categories and concepts can capture the real world (see G.W.F. HEGEL; Immanuel KANT). It assumes that words, discourses and narratives cannot change physical realities, actual events, social structures, so our representation is of secondary significance (see REPRESENTATION). The historical narrative (if written with due care and attention to the evidence and appropriate theory) is taken to be homologous to the actual narrative found in the structural and causal arrangement of the past. A mountain is still a mountain, and the independence and partition of India still occurred on 15 August 1947, even if I describe the first from several different physical locations, or the second from competing ideological perspectives.

The thrust of much postmodern (see POSTMODERNISM) argument is to problematise that thinking by offering an a priori (see A PRIORI/A POSTERIORI) challenge (to this practical realist foundationalism in explanation), by re-examining the nature of language, representation, the historical narrative and inference. All our knowledge in the humanities and social sciences comes to us in narratives composed from words, sentences, discourses (see DISCOURSE; NEW HISTORICISM), emplotments (see EMPLOTMENT) and language. The historian's self-imposed dependence upon a sophisticated process of empiricism and conceptualisation cannot alter the fact that he/she is directly implicated in the process of knowing through what is a description of a highly mediated experience of the past. For this reason it is held that objectivity-in-knowing is a position that must be surrendered. What this means for historical explanation is the rejection of the epistemological subject–object model in favour of (what is claimed to be) an unavoidable subject–subject relationship (see WOMEN'S HISTORY). It must also mean that in its creation of facts history is ultimately dependent upon a severely flawed methodology – inference to the best explanation – if the stated aim of history is to reproduce *the* meaning of the past.

Historians conventionally work, then, by drawing inferences. At its most straightforward this means that interpretations and explanations are capable of being (and are supposedly) amended according to the latest available evidence, although in practice this often seems to be the result of the most plausible and popular current tweak to our theory. There are, in fact, three types of inference that historians deploy: two have already been mentioned, the deductive and inductive. The third is the abductive. Although induction, as I have noted, is generally regarded as the primary mechanism of historical explanation (along the lines of the statistical-inductive model), strictly speaking abductive inference is *the* characteristic feature of historical explanation and the historical imagination. Where a statistical correlation is inappropriate or incapable of demonstration, it falls to the historian to generate a pattern of meaning (see COLLIGATION). It occurs to me that the present interest in narrative's role in historical explanation derives in part from the failings of abductive historical thinking defined as inference to the best explanation, in addition to the difficulties with the covering law. It also derives from the belief I noted at the start of this entry, that historical explanation is taken by most historians to be fully understood only through the narrative form.

If the historian presupposes an objectivist history then the explanation will take the form of a factual (proper historical) narrative. If he/she entertains a different presupposition, the form of his/her history will change, and the nature of explanation will also. Hayden **White**'s model of the historical imagination, for example, presupposes a prefiguration (tropes) and connected levels of historical explanation: emplotment, argument and ideological preference. It is White's (now famous) argument that the tropes anticipate and structure these other elements of the historical explanation. White thus denies that historical explanation emerges primarily from referential correspondence/inferential thinking, but believes instead that it arises through the process of prefiguring the data by the mental processes of analogue, similarity or difference (hence tropes = different types of metaphor). White is suggesting that although historical explanations may possess referentiality (in abundance), and reasonable inferences can be drawn, ultimately we cast it all into a narrative, and no individual emplotment, argument or ideological explanatory connection can be more truthfully described than any other. White is saying that narratives cannot be true or untrue just because they do or do not correspond with past realities. This rhetorical constructionism is certainly not a view shared by narrativist and realist philosophers like W.B. Gallie and C. Behan McCullagh, who between them defend narrative and historical explanation as capable of being either true or false (McCullagh 1998: 127–8). Perhaps all we can say is that historical explanation is not yet a settled matter. One reason for this is the fact that historians do not read much of what is written on the philosophy of history. A great deal of pertinent thinking about historical explanation tends, therefore, to be neglected by its practitioners. Historians might benefit by consulting the following key thinkers on how historical explanation could work.

Further reading
Achinstein, P., 1983; Appleby, J. *et al.*, 1994; Atkinson, R.F., 1978; Black, J. and MacRaild, D., 1997; Brown, C.G., 2005; Cannadine, D., 2002; Carr, E.H., 1987 [1961]; Collingwood, R.G., 1994 [1946]; Daddow, O., 2005; Danto, A., 1968a; Davies, S., 2003; Dray, W.H., 1957; Evans, R.J, 1997a; Fulbrook, M., 2002; Gallie, W.B., 1964; Gardiner, P., 1961 [1951], 1959; Graham, G., 1983; Green, A. and Troup, K., 1999; Hempel, C.G., 1965; Hesse, C., 2004; Hoffer, P.C. and Stueck, W. W., 1994; Hughes-Warrington, M., 2000; Iggers, G., 1997; Jenkins, K., 2003, 2003 [1991], 1999a, 1999b, 1997, 1995; Jenkins, K. and Munslow, A., 2004; Jordanova, L., 2000; McCullagh, C.B., 1998; MacRaild, D.M.

and Taylor, A., 2004; Mandelbaum, M., 1977; Marwick, A., 2001; Munslow, A., 2003b; Munslow, A. and Rosenstone, R.A., 2004; Oakeshott, M., 1933; Perry, M., 2002; Popper, K., 1959; Roberts, Clayton D., 1996; Roberts, G., 2001; Ruben, D.-H., 1993, 1990; Snooks, G.D., 1998; Southgate, B., 2003, 2000, 1996; Thompson, W., 2004; Topolski, J., 1991; Tosh, J., 2001; von Wright, G.H., 1971; Walsh, W.H., 1984 [1967]; White, H., 1973b; Williams, R.C., 2003.

HISTORICAL IMAGINATION

The human mind has the capacity to bring forth things that are not directly accessed by the senses and to address that which is not real. That this power of imagination is particularly important to the process of historical interpretation is attested to by the number of philosophers and historians who have addressed its nature and functioning in the creation of historical meaning. Historians regularly exercise the mental power of rehearsing possible past cause and effect relationships, connections and situations.

I assume, therefore, the historical imagination to be the application of the general capacity of the human mind for comparison, connection, analogy and difference to the study of the past and its **sources** (see EVIDENCE). This is actually a metaphoric process that allows the historian to relate different domains of knowledge in many general and particular ways toward the aim of interpretation and understanding. As the philosopher Peter Strawson suggests, our perception of objects owes its character to the internal links that we bring into being through our preferred metaphorical descriptions (Strawson 1974: 53). What I am suggesting here is that the historian normally and regularly crosses the line between **inference** and imagination. The act of historical re-creation means picturing the linkage possibilities in the past. The peculiar form that this picturing of links takes is the figurative **narrative** (see TROPE/FIGURATION; Hayden WHITE; REALITY/REALISTIC EFFECT).

It follows that to gain some kind of understanding of the historical imagination we must examine the historian's narrative composition process and the manner in which historians deploy metaphor to 'fix' meaning. This directs me to the cognitive value of metaphor/trope and troping, and its potential for **truth** in historical knowledge. How do metaphor, trope and troping function within the historical imagination? Metaphor, along with its two main forms of metonymy and synecdoche, is the transference principle of all language use. It allows historians to re-describe patterns perceived between different domains of experience and evidence. The narrative, being the vehicle for this process of re-description, permits the historian to 'see' and compose/configure a set of relationships that did not previously exist between events.

The historian imagines a cognitive relation in a figurative sense between a new/borrowed word and the proper meaning of the deliberately absented word. The meaning of this relationship is the 'reason' for the substitution. This 'reason' takes the form of a figurative substitution. In metaphor this has the form of a structure of resemblance. As the French narrativist philosopher Paul Ricoeur describes it, metaphor is representational in object-to-object terms, metonymy is reductive in part-to-part correspondence or contiguity terms, and synecdoche is integrative in a part-to-whole essentialist or connective way (see REPRESENTATION; Frank R. ANKERSMIT). Necessarily each of these is protean in the potential range of relationships they permit. Thus metonymy – the relationship of correspondence – allows historians to deploy cause to effect, propensity to action, sign to signifier. Synecdoche connects one to many, species to genus, or species to individual (Ricoeur 1994 [1978]: 56).

Now, the question here is that given this is just a substitution between terms and no new information is provided in the text, surely troping is just rhetoric and not cognitively useful to historians? Presumably it cannot give access to the truth of history? It has been argued, however, that if truth is what you seek, figurative language need not stand as an obstacle because metaphor works at a secondary imaginative level consequent upon the initial reference. Truth can be obtained, therefore, via the metaphorical acts of the historical imagination. The issue, therefore, is not simply one of explanation through empirical correspondence but, as Paul Ricoeur argues, rather analogue, resemblance or substitution (Ricoeur 1984: 3). This would also seem to reinforce the point made by the philosopher of metaphor Donald Davidson, that metaphor allows us to make new connections and create new theories that lead to knowledge, rather than being knowledge itself (**Rorty** 1991: 163).

Hayden White also argued the case for the historian's choice of figurative styles as rhetorical models of historical representation, implying that form is as significant a feature of historical study as content (White 1973b) (see FORM AND CONTENT). Metaphor, for White, is *the* means for explaining human intentions/actions, operating through the displacement of meaning as analogy, imitation, resemblance, essence and/or contiguity at the level of words and sentences (the money to finance the Civil War came in at first like a trickle from a faulty tap . . .), and again structurally at the level of the emplotment (the history of these events was a tragedy . . .). How we tropically imagine the emplotment creates explanatory coherence out of the jumble of the past at the level of the chosen word or sentence, but it also organises such coherence in a particular way, with an end in mind that will result in a prefigured emplotment and/or argument and/or ideological position (see TELEOLOGY).

Realist philosophers of history, like C. Behan McCullagh, indict White's rhetorical constructionism on several counts: for what is claimed to be his failure to address content and for his failure to accept that truth derives from the contextualisation of sources, but mostly for his failure to accept that the truth-conditional statement makes historical descriptions reliable. McCullagh is happy to acknowledge that metaphor has a role to play in doing history. It is his argument that the metaphoric historical imagination can be truthful but only at the level of the singular descriptive statement. Truthful statements originating in the historical imagination can be established by substantiating truth conditions and inference, leading to conclusions that are then translated into language both literal and/or metaphoric (McCullagh 1984: 4–44; 2004). This is done through the formation of an explanatory hypothesis – the singular descriptive statement – and the inference or deduction of testable consequences of that hypothesis according to the principles of fewest suppositions, probability, plausibility, contextualisation, etc. So it is that language can accurately represent past reality through either a literal or a metaphoric rendition.

McCullagh agrees that the historical imagination works through analogies that are helpful in establishing possible connections between things in the past. Among examples that McCullagh gives are the comparison, of the slave plantation and the Nazi concentration camp, made by American historian Stanley Elkins to explain the infantile nature of black slaves. The two sets of circumstances generated the same effect. Another example he offers would be to describe the debates in Parliament between Gladstone and Disraeli as a duel. Such a description is true if, in the context of the public mind at the time, their relationship manifested some of the salient characteristics of a duel. Equally, there is another context, that of a shared language and culture between the historian and the reader (see EPISTEME; Michel FOUCAULT). For a metaphoric statement to be metaphorically true, the reader must share in the meaning of the terms of the metaphor with the historian. So historians can

offer true and fair interpretations, according to McCullagh, by deploying metaphor when the metaphor displays an adequate resemblance or saliency between statements and objects, and such statements are adequately contextualised. Rejecting what he calls a naïve correspondence, McCullagh allows himself the argument that while metaphorical statements cannot be literally true, they can be metaphorically true.

Historians know the narratives they write are not wholly accurate pictures of past reality, yet they write them on the assumption that the past is an object that is given and independent of the descriptive discourse through which it is appropriated. As Ricoeur drily observed, 'If history is a construction, the historian instinctively would like his construction to be a reconstruction' (Ricoeur 1984: 26). Although the historian is implicated in the writing, he/she is not permitted by canonical law to intrude on the factualism of the real past. The important issue is the one that White alerted us to, namely the absenting of the figurative modes in which the historical imagination is framed. The result is the vain attempt, as Roland **Barthes** claims, of most historical narratives at degree zero writing: a style barren of figurative language that assumes the world can be represented accurately through the word.

In his evaluation of the historical imagination, R.G. **Collingwood** rejected any conception of history that depended on empiricism (the authority of the evidence) to the exclusion of the historian's imagination. For Collingwood the idea of history was of an imaginary picture of the past in the form of a Kantian-type a priori (see A PRIORI/ A POSTERIORI) that all humans possess (Collingwood 1994 [1946]: 248). No matter how fragmentary or faulty might be the results of the historian's work, for Collingwood the idea which governed its course was 'clear, rational and universal. It is the idea of the historical imagination as a self-dependent, self-determining, and self-justifying form of thought' (ibid.: 249). However, in spite of this bold idealism, ultimately Collingwood also makes the representationalist choice (along lines similar to McCullagh and Ricoeur) endorsing the ultimately impermeable barrier between the linguistic world and the world of things and their perception – metaphoric truth is still truth.

Collingwood's endorsement of the absolute centrality of metaphor as a cognitive instrument for the characterisation of the historical narrative is not, in his lights, incompatible with referentiality and truth. Naturally (ironically?), Collingwood's thoughts about metaphor were cast figuratively. Employing the picture metaphor, he argued that the historical narrative should construct a picture of things as they really were. In another metaphor he described the historian as a lawyer placing his/her evidence in the witness box. If the evidence is unforthcoming or the source offers false witness, then the authority is rejected and the historian makes his/her own connections between the fixed points of the statements of the sources (Collingwood 1994 [1946]: 238–49). To do this, Collingwood argues, we deploy the human mind's universal faculty for imagining relationships between the selected fixed points (statements of the sources). So history, because it is in large part the product of the historical imagination, is constructive because it works by interpolating and inferring connections between the evidence of the sources, or the other thoughts and statements implied by them.

In another metaphor Collingwood describes this process as the creation of a 'web of imaginative construction' (ibid.: 242). But he insists that the historian him/herself fixes those points as he/she interrogates the sources through contextualisation and verification, and so he/she 'constructs an imaginary picture' that becomes coherent and continuous, and which eventually becomes its own touchstone and measure (ibid.: 242–5). Not surprisingly perhaps, Collingwood argues at this point for the resemblance between the historian and the novelist. Both the novel and the history are self-explanatory,

self-justifying and autonomous. The 'only' difference, but one that is crucial, of course, is the historical narrative's requirement to produce a picture 'of things as they really were and events as they really happened' – 'is like' rather than 'looks like' (ibid.: 246). But this constraint must also exist in tandem with the fact that, as he says, every generation 'must re-write history in its own way' (ibid.: 248) (see Geoffrey R. ELTON). So what is there in the mechanisms of the historical narrative, as the product of the historical imagination, that inclines us toward one reading rather than another to fix the statements in one way or another?

To illustrate how metaphor might drive the historical imagination I will take one of the most famous interpretations of American history, Frederick Jackson Turner's 'The significance of the frontier in American history' (1893). Turner was writing at a time – the 1890s – when America was undergoing a cultural crisis brought on by disruptive industrialisation, mass immigration, wholesale political corruption, metropolitanisation, the emergence of **class** conflict and the 1890 Bureau of the Census declaration that the western movement was now over. This is the era of progressivism and the crusade for social justice. How did his historical imagination work at such a time?

At the level of the single historical descriptive statement Turner said, 'The existence of an area of free land, its continuous recession and the advance of American settlement westward explain American development' (Turner 1961 [1893]: 1). You will recall that metonymy and synecdoche shape our statements of relations of cause and effect and inference. In metonymy the name of an attribute is substituted for the thing itself – reductively the part stands in for the whole. Free land is presented here metonymically to stand in for the frontier, and eventually in Turner's imagination for the generic characteristics of American democracy. It is an association by contiguity.

But even the most strictly referential metonymic sentences are located within the larger literary artefact of the emplotted historical narrative. Reminder: the historical narrative reveals the historian's thinking about difference and resemblance. It is not, therefore, only a matter of the single statement that, in this instance, conveys metonymic meaning, but the epistemic and culturally disciplined intertextuality of the historical narrative itself (see Frank R. ANKERSMIT). How does Turner compose his 1890s narrative during a time of cultural conflict and division? At this point, as a historian-**author**, I speculate that Turner's objective in his fixing of the role of free land in the pushing back of the frontier was to judge its significance in the subsequent creation of a unified American national identity. This, in turn, is likely to be dependent upon the epistemic character of the historical context in which both Turner and his reader existed – the episteme that embraced the 1890s. Turner's history was in harmony with a contemporary popular consensus on the unique character of American identity as demonstrated in the evidence of a substantial nationalist literature (see NEW HISTORY).

From the available evidence, for example, he chose to quote from Peck's *New Guide* to the west, where the wave metaphor is dominant. Turner evidences his argument with phrases like 'another wave rolls on. The men of capital and enterprise come. . . . Thus wave after wave is rolling westward' (Turner 1961 [1893]: 19–20). This selection of the evidence on Turner's part I take to be a demonstration of his imaginative creation of a narrative of inexorable and unstoppable nation-building, the tide of nationality as he says at one point. Before Turner the historical literature had not created the links that Turner's history did. This demonstrates, I think, that the fictional narrative can rarely construct a fiction so convincing as the historical narrative given the latter's presumed association with the referential (see JUSTIFIED BELIEF).

In his search for a relevant past upon which to build a national popular culture Turner used a rhetoric that matched his own and his culture's prefigured vision of America as an exceptional historical creation. Turner's language evidences the existence of White's deep structural level to the historical narrative that is specifically linguistic in nature, and which serves as the pre-critically accepted model of what a distinctively 'historical' explanation should be (see AESTHETIC TURN; LINGUISTIC TURN).

America in the 1890s needed its own utilitarian history, an exceptional (i.e. a non-European) history. Turner provided this in his argument that America was a new frontier; 'free land' was its essence and, by inference, *the* causal factor in America's exceptionalism (see CAUSATION). Unlike metonymy, synecdoche operates integratively, suggesting a qualitative relationship among the elements of a totality. By injecting a class analysis at this point, I am suggesting that the demands of the emergent and rapidly dominant industrial bourgeoisie necessitated that Turner reconfigure free land at the structural level of the narrative. The narrative is now re-cast, therefore, in the archetypal trope of synecdoche so as to meet contemporary cultural and epistemic demands for coherence, and class unity. At a second-order cultural or mythic level Turner's history, therefore, signifies America's exceptional historical creation through its classless frontier-inspired unity.

Having speculated on the nature of the historical imagination I do not know if Turner's history is generating the truth, either metaphorical or literal, at either the level of the single statement or the finished narrative. I have no measure except, perhaps, plausibility. I suspect that his use of metaphor is cognitive, but whether or not it apprehends reality, I do not know. I do not know if this is *really* how the historian's imagination works. However, if we agree that historical knowledge is primarily, or in substantial part, the metaphoric creation of the historical imagination, historians should reorientate themselves epistemologically, to consider form as anterior to content. If the historian's imagination is built upon his/her assumptions about life and how it worked in the past as well as now (assumptions Turner had), then the historical imagination allows us not only to create different pasts dependent on how we choose to relate the evidence within its historical context and upon whatever particular theory of human behaviour we invoke to connect action with structure, but also to broaden the forms through which we can create historical knowledge.

Further reading

Ankersmit, F.R., 1994; Auxier, R.E., 1997; Collingwood, R.G., 1994 [1946]; Curthoys, A. and Docker, J., 1997; Davidson, D., 1984; de Man, Paul 1983; Fiumara, G.C., 1995; Hesse, M., 1983; Johnson, M., 1981; Lorenz, C., 1998; McCullagh, C.B., 2004, 1998, 1984; Munslow, A., 2003b, 1992; Ricoeur, P., 1994 [1978], 1984; Rorty, R., 1991; Sachs, S., 1979; Strawson, P.F., 1974; Taylor, B., 2004; Turner, F.J., 1961 [1893]; White, H., 1973b.

HISTORICISM

Historicism is a troubling concept (see CONCEPTS IN HISTORY) because its definition is so fluid yet it is acknowledged to be central to how historians do history. Indeed historicism is taken by many to be the essence of historical method. To make matters worse, historicism has been appropriated by other disciplines and this has further muddied the waters. For the sake of explanation, however, historicism seems to have three related meanings: for most historians it is the primary historical act of perceiving historical periods in their own terms rather than any imposed by the historian; second and relatedly, it means accepting that every historical period had its own standards through which it determined what was trustworthy knowledge and warranted **truth**; third, that there are inclusive, demonstrable and determining patterns in the process of historical change.

In its primary meaning historicism refers specifically to Friedrich Meinecke's judgement that historians should aim to understand the events (see EVENT), actions and thoughts of people at their own historical moment – the observation and report of the individual occurrence when and as it actually happened. This leads to understanding people as they understood themselves rather than through the imposition of present-day concepts and categories of analysis. By this argument historians empathise with the social conditions that gave rise to actions that occurred at a particular place in time. Historical understanding is thus entirely derived from within that place and time. It is, moreover, this process that reveals the nature of change and continuity, and allows us to rationally locate past things and put them in their proper (temporally sequential) order.

This is a contextualist or 'then and there' variety of historicism that can be traced back at least to Wilhelm Dilthey and R.G. **Collingwood**, who, in their different ways, suggested that historians had to insert themselves into the lives and stories of people in the past, escape the present and restrain their own powers of **narrative**. Although they tend to dispute this empathic process, reconstructionist historians (see RECONSTRUCTIONIST HISTORY) find an appeal in what is a definition of historicism that rejects extra-historical (extra-historicist) **covering laws**, social theories, too many and complex concepts that beg questions and a role for language beyond that of simple referentialism. Such things, they believe, can only be alien impositions on past times and places (from present times and places). History thus serves the strata of chronologically laid down **evidence**. A sceptical **empiricism** is the central feature of this view of how to do history, and its corollary is a suspicion of any history not done in this way, that is, done with the needs of the present or future in mind (see TELEOLOGY; POST-MARXISM).

Historicism thus defined pushes historicism toward its second meaning, which takes on a more relativist hue (see RELATIVISM). In understanding the past on its own terms (the 'then and there' approach), historians quickly came to realise that each historical epoch possessed its own standards by which it judged what was reliable knowledge and verifiable truth. Each period was/is thus unique in the process of its generation of knowledge, that there are no universal extra-historical or transcendental standards by which we can judge the past, so every person, event and process was/is historically unique. What particularly distinguished historical periods was the manner in which each age symbolically and metaphorically expressed itself to itself (see EPISTEME; TROPE/FIGURATION). Of course, in reconstructing the past in its own terms the historian has again to be aware of, and be able to control, his/her own forms of expression. To be a historicist in this second meaning of the term means, therefore, also escaping from any kind of here-and-now linguistic determinism.

The nineteenth- and twentieth-century reaction against the then-and-there varieties of historicism came with positivist (see POSITIVISM), constructionist (see CONSTRUCTIONIST HISTORY) and structuralist (see STRUCTURALISM) thought. This reaction assumed that science offered a transcendental method, which permitted the rational study of human behaviour by spectators standing apart from the object of observation, who could 'really see' what was going on. Positivism holds, for example, that it is feasible and proper to account for human activity in accordance with recurring covering laws of behaviour.

This logic, when viewed through the events of the twentieth century, persuaded the philosopher Karl Popper (1902–97) to radically redefine historicism (effectively giving it a personal definition) as a dangerous belief in historical determination and the existence of universal patterns in historical processes. Popper specifically had Marxism and fascism in mind as examples of this dubious universalising tendency in history. His book, *The Poverty of Historicism*, is, in fact, dedicated to the memory of all who 'fell victims to the fascist and communist belief in Inexorable Laws of Historical Destiny' (Popper 1957). Popper's personal redefinition of historicism suggests not just that the meaning of historicism is not fixed, but by implication neither is that which is conventionally to be history's proper methodology.

What is at issue with historicism is the question of epistemological relativism: how accurately can we represent the-past-as-history through our words and concepts in the here and now (see EPISTEMOLOGY)? The American pragmatic philosopher Richard **Rorty** has claimed it is no sort of answer to say that historical accuracy can be assured by the good historian who judiciously and fairly represents what they find in the archival record (Rorty 1998: 73). That they do not misrepresent the record says nothing about the reality of past events, nor the truth conditions of the statements they make, nor the **hermeneutic** or interpretational character of the discipline.

In spite of the claim that we can know the reality of the past above and beyond what we write about it, history's puzzle must lie in its intertextuality. At what point can/does the historian break into the seemingly eternal and closed loop of evidence and written interpretations – the hermeneutic intertextual circle? Is it possible that historians can distinguish the *real* meaning of the evidence from the meaning *it held for* people at the time, and then from the overlaid *interpretations of subsequent generations* of other historians? If historians can break the circle – escape from intertextuality – to achieve foundational truth (*the* meaning of the text) then the relativist implications of historicism can be avoided. If not, they cannot. This position declares the epistemological bond between the past and its accurate representation to be an assumption. The language used by historians is epistemologically autonomous and cannot accurately represent history's content (see FORM AND CONTENT; REPRESENTATION; AESTHETIC TURN). If this is a correct view, then any 'logic' to historical method is akin to literature's critical evaluation of a text rather than the discovery of objective reality, and the essence of history is hermeneutic not factual, linguistic not empirical, fictive not real.

From this perspective it is impossible to accurately recover the past, and all we have is the-past-as-history because historicism (if defined as the proper historical method of telling it as it really was) ignores its object's poetic, presentist and intertextual nature. History *is* conceived in the historian's mind, history *is* literature, and history *is* generated in the here and now. There is no reason, therefore, not to abandon historicist approaches to history defined in the three ways I have indicated. None of them carry any baggage that is significant to the-past-as-history. If we choose to abandon historicism – or do what Popper did and redefine it, but now in a postmodern or hermeneutic fashion by recognising that we 'style the-past-as-history' and use the present to understand it – we may become more open to the idea that referentiality, rather than determining our rhetoric, may be the result of it (form is prior to content). This does not, of course, mean that we are destined to go off the rails or lose that sanity that can *only* be assured by empiricism.

Some historians experience further confusion with historicism since it has been appropriated by literature in the shape of the **New Historicism**. Just as history has made a **linguistic turn** so literature has made a historicist turn. This is literature's turn toward interpreting the literary text in its historical context (the world external to it) rather than evaluating it primarily as a text (its internal world). In certain respects this has a parallel with developments in history's 'old' historicism. While I may elect to redefine historicism (and therefore history) by accepting that history cannot be hermetically sealed off from either its linguistic conventions in the here and now or the purposes for which it is written, New Historicism is characterised by the literary critic's awareness of the historical traditions of literary criticism and how changes in its methods have *in the past* served

special interests – like those of white, middle-class males, or the forces of imperialism (see POSTCOLONIAL HISTORY). These are sensitivities that, when directed at written history, are, of course, shared with many post-colonial and feminist historians (see WOMEN'S HISTORY; POST-FEMINISM). I could suggest that there is now a post-empiricist historian's version of historicism that we might call history's New Historicism, and which effectively ceases to worry about historicism – but to have two New Historicisms would surely over-egg the pudding?

Further reading
Berlin, I., 1976; Collingwood, R.G., 1994 [1946]; Dilthey, W., 1976; Hamilton, P., 1996; Meinecke, F., 1972; Popper, K., 1957; Rorty, R., 1998; Veeser, A.A., 1989; Worton, M. and Still, J., 1990.

HISTORIOGRAPHY

The term historiography is normally taken to refer to the act of the writing of history, the collective writings of history (or writings on the past if you prefer), and the history of such activities over the centuries. A now classic definition of historiography by Keith **Jenkins** draws out the self-reflexive aspect of the activity with his distinction (which he makes regularly) between 'the past' and 'history'. Jenkins's use of the term directly addresses the philosophical problems that arise for history given its essential interpretative and written form. As he says, echoing Michel de Certeau, history is a **discourse** about, but different from, the past. Jenkins suggests, 'It would be preferable, therefore, always to register this difference by using the term "the past" for all that has gone on before . . . whilst using the word "historiography" for history' (Jenkins 2003 [1991]): 6).

By this way of thinking, history becomes merely an umbrella term for the whole enterprise of studying the past in all its facets, in other words, the past plus dedicated methods/concepts plus historiography equals history. For Jenkins the last two terms in the equation – historiography and history – are synonymous. If this is so, then the act of writing history produces many questions that focus upon the impositional role of the historian, the nature of the social construction of reality, the character of **historical explanation**, the art of interpretation and the constitution of the **historical imagination**, the relationship of **form and content** and the problems of **representation** and the **linguistic turn** (see Frank R. ANKERSMIT). Questions are also raised about cultural and historical **relativism** and the cognitive links between history and literature, history and theory, and the philosophy of history more generally (see EPISTEMOLOGY; ONTOLOGY; INTELLECTUAL HISTORY; NEW HISTORICISM).

The centrality of historiography to the historical enterprise, which is made amply clear with Jenkins's claim, is confirmed by the editors of the *Blackwell Dictionary of Historians* who seem to be suggesting that it is so important that it does not even require them to offer a generic defining entry. Because writing history is what historians do, it is enough to acknowledge the act by the many entries on national historiographies (from Australia and Austria through to Scandinavia), and also the historiography of themes/periods (with entries on black historiography, classical historiography, Jewish historiography, and feminist historiography) (Cannon *et al.* 1988). This heavy emphasis on historiography ought not, however, to be read as support for Jenkins's position that history consists in the works of interpretation of historians. The logic would seem to be that to know the past we should begin with what historians tell us about it – the discourse of historians – but I suspect it is meant to denote a body of interpretation rather than the act of interpretation.

This is an important point. It is one also made (I'm not sure whether wittingly or unwittingly) by Joyce Appleby, Lynn Hunt

and Margaret Jacob in their book *Telling the Truth About History* (1994), when they explicitly argue that proper history (that which for them seeks a necessarily pragmatic access to a knowable past reality) can be (or certainly is in their case) compatible with the creation of a national (which for the United States is also a democratic, open and multi-cultural) identity. Telling the **truth** about history (a historiographical act to be sure, but one that gets the **facts** straight) for them means having discovered and written down the truth of the **event**s of 200 years of American history. Happily these point to the achievement of its multi-cultural democratic heritage. So history, historiography and now a moral positioning also conveniently coincide (see ETHICAL TURN). Appleby, Hunt and Jacob get the US history they want to write.

If history is historiography (defined as the act of writing the-past-as-history) then it is reasonable that we understand the material and/or ideological situatedness (translated as moral choices and/or attitudes) of the historian who writes (shapes, structures, emplots, forms, interprets?) the past (see EMPLOTMENT). But there is a big problem here. Not all historians accept the ultimate logic of the equation historiography equals history. E.H. **Carr** in *What is History?* (1987 [1961]) seemingly accepts that the historian 'is of his own age, and bound to it by the conditions of human existence' and that 'The very words he uses . . . have current connotations' (Carr 1987 [1961]: 26). But he immediately goes on to deny any association with the result of an inevitable present-centred, pragmatic or relativist history that can have 'an infinity of meanings' as if it were 'spun out of the human brain' (ibid.). Like Appleby, Hunt and Jacob, Carr understands that historians write history, but this element does not mean that 'the facts of history are in principle not amenable to objective interpretation' (ibid.: 27). Making sense of the facts remains the ordinance. Carr is trying here to square this modernist epistemological circle with an inevitable appeal to the legacy of **empiricism** (the existence of a real past that is factually knowable by objectively observing, by rational, non-future-anticipating or teleological historians) (see the ENLIGHTENMENT; MODERNISM; TELEOLOGY).

A substantial foray into the nature of historiography is Michael Bentley's edited *Companion to Historiography* (1997). Here again the issue of history as the discourse of historians is recognised with entries on the ancient, medieval, the early-modern and modern styles of historical writing (historical periods!) sub-divided into national historiographies. There is also a sizeable section on the writing of history with explorations of the connections between history and **narrative**, and related disciplines like archaeology, anthropology, philosophy and women's studies (see WOMEN'S HISTORY; GENDER). The obvious point is made in this collection that historiography is a contested terrain at many levels, not least that of competing interpretations, but also at the level of the assumptions that historians make about what constitutes particular varieties, versions, visions, re-visions and conceptions of history (see METANARRATIVE).

Further reading

American Historical Association, 1995; Ankersmit, F.R., 1994, 1989; Appleby, J. *et al.*, 1994; Bentley, M., 1997; Breisach, E., 1983; Cameron, A., 1989; Cannon, J. *et al.*, 1988; Carr, E.H., 1987 [1961]; de Certeau, M., 1988 [1975]; Iggers, G., 1997; Jenkins, K., 2004, 2003, 1997; Jenkins, K. and Munslow, A., 2004; Kozicki, H., 1993; McCullagh, C.B., 2004; Munslow, A., 2003b; Munslow, A. and Rosenstone, R.A., 2004; Momigliano, A., 1990, 1985 [1966], 1977; NeSmith, G., n.d.; Roth, P.A., 1992; Stanford, M., 1994; Topolski, J., 1999; Warren, J., 1998; White, H., 2000; Zagorin, P., 1990; Zammito, J.H., 1998.

I

INFERENCE

Conventional historical understanding depends on the way in which historians choose to infer conclusions from the **evidence** (see SOURCES). They try to provide the most likely explanation of an object of study (**event**, process, action or whatever) that is justified by the sources of information available to them about that object. Why is it important to historians, and to society more widely, that their conclusions are grounded in the sources? The argument is that to seek the **truth** in the past not only must we be justified in what we believe (see JUSTIFIED BELIEF), we must know that other people (past and present) are justified in what they claim. The sources, it is assumed, provide the foundation for this justification. Axiomatically, therefore, historians are interested in the epistemological process of inference that, it is believed, has the power to distinguish assertion from historical knowledge, thus providing access to the truth of the past (see EPISTEMOLOGY).

Modernist historians and realist philosophers argue that historical explanations and descriptions are true if they can be verified by other explanations that are themselves supported by sources (McCullagh 1998: 20–3) (see CONSTRUCTIONIST HISTORY; MODERNISM; RECONSTRUCTIONIST HISTORY). Hence the conclusions we infer from the evidence as to its meaning (in the shape of historical descriptions) can be true if they meet these conditions. Historians – even deconstructionist historians (see DECONSTRUCTIONIST HISTORY) – accept that much about the past, certainly at what I would call the almanac(ish) level, can

be true. I cannot think of any historian who would deny that, according to the evidence, on 13 April 1846 the Pennsylvania Railroad received a charter or that on 3 December 1947 Tennessee Williams's play *A Streetcar Named Desire* opened in the American city of New Orleans. These are simple descriptive statements amply supported by the evidence. For all intents and purposes they are truthful descriptions.

Historians usually work at a much higher level than this of course. We draw inferences so as to construct interpretative narratives but only initially by reference to the most recently available evidence. This constructionist history process is informed by a priori theorising (from premise to proposition) that eventually launches us into the realms of interpretation (see A PRIORI/A POSTERIORI). Inference is a form of logic, therefore, that consists of the connection between the premises and the conclusion of a logical argument. Put another way, it is the drawing of a conclusion from premises that support it either deductively or inductively.

Strictly speaking there are three types of inference that we need to distinguish: deductive, inductive and abductive. Deductive (or logical) inference is generally regarded as inappropriate for the study of the past. This is because such inferences are established without reference to the empirical to reach a truthful (or a false) conclusion (see EMPIRICISM). Deductive inferences follow on from premises that, if true, mean that the conclusion reached is valid – if A, then B. Deduction, therefore, has two stages: initially we must understand the premises, and then we draw a conclusion. There is, however, a further optional stage whereby we are free to test the validity of our deductive conclusions empirically – the process of model-testing. Constructionist historians – those of a social scientific persuasion – often do indeed infer (i.e. set up) models to be tested. But the majority of historians believe history to be content-led, hence they operate primarily through some kind of induction. The evidence, they claim, guides their conclusions and their 'models' are really just the categories and concepts of analysis suggested by the evidence itself (see CONCEPTS IN HISTORY).

Inductive inferences are commonly drawn when a historian reads the available evidence to reach an interpretation about its intrinsic meaning. An inductive inference is at best only probably true. Unlike deductive inferences, inductive inferences offer conclusions that broaden and deepen knowledge beyond the simple level of the initial premises, but cannot guarantee truth. With inductive inference we are not deriving logically true statements (all Xs are Ys, all Ys are Zs, therefore all Xs are Zs), but statements that may be truthful when judged empirically (by the nature of what X, Y and Z actually represent). The process of induction is fourfold: initially it requires the historian to discover and observe the event, process or action (the source/evidence as a text); next he/she sets up a hypothesis (an explanation/proposition) that tries to account for the data referring to the event, process or action within a wider circle of evidence (the context); then he/she is expected to recognise and explain how his/her conclusion/interpretation takes us beyond the available evidence and existing conclusion/interpretation; and, finally, he/she will evaluate that fresh conclusion/interpretation by reference once more to the evidence. Clearly, inductive inference exists within an empirical loop grounded in the material world. This becomes the ultimate guarantor of **objectivity** in the work of the historian. His/her interpretations serve the evidence. Although historians are increasingly loath to deploy them, inductive inference is also the means for inferring **covering laws** or general statements of behaviour – inference from the particular to the general. Suspicion about covering laws derives precisely from the fact that, unlike deduction, induction cannot guarantee its conclusions. It cannot certify laws of behaviour and/or theories, but can only suggest possible causes *post hoc* from events, imply meaningful analogies and propose the best (the most likely) explanation (see HISTORICAL EXPLANATION; HISTORICAL IMAGINATION).

The peculiar method of inductive inferential reasoning by which the historian speculates as to what constitutes the best explanation without generalising is abduction (see COLLIGATION). Abductive historical reasoning, unlike induction that leads to covering laws and general explanations, accepts conclusions/interpretations on the grounds that they explain the *particular* event that is to hand. Historians observe the evidence of the event and then set up a hypothesis to explain an apparent anomaly or surprising situation they believe they have 'found' therein, and then inductively test the explanation/supposition via further evidence. As the American pragmatic philosopher Charles S. Peirce described it, the abductive inferential process is characterised by the inductive mind-set of realism, discovery and anti-scepticism to arrive at the conclusions that best explain the available evidence (Peirce 1958: 89–164).

An example may be helpful. Historians find they are surprised that Terence V. Powderly, in the 1880s, became such a successful leader of the American trade union, Knights of Labor, given that, in most respects, he appeared unqualified and, therefore, unlikely to succeed. But we suppose (hypothesise/propose?) that his actual success came about perhaps because he had a long and varied career in local politics before he became a trade union leader. If we accept that this was indeed a valuable training, then his success as a trade union leader is more explicable. So by that union leadership success there is good reason to believe (*post hoc* or literally after the event) that his local-government career was a good training. Abduction, therefore, allows for imaginative if not indeed surprising conclusions about specific cases. In this example the historian (with surprise) notes Powderly's successful union leadership, then frames an explanation (after the event) from which a particular inference flows – most plausibly as no other hypothesis or supposition seemingly can explain Powderly's union success as well. It follows that we are justified in believing that his local-government career is the correct explanation for his union leadership success.

A postmodern (see POSTMODERNISM) or deconstructive vision of inductive and abductive inferential historical explanation points out, of course, that as a foundationalist or realist-inspired reasoning process it must be subject to an infinite regress of justified beliefs (see JUSTIFIED BELIEF; NEW HISTORY). By following the logic of history's inductive-abductive inferential method the assumption cannot be made that at some point the historian will discover the original source of meaning – the correct supposition – upon which all later justified explanation is built (e.g. Powderly's local-government career). Historians know they cannot deduce or infer any original truths or explanations about past experience simply through the observation of the evidence. There is no empiricist originary point of knowing. So it is admitted that there is no absolute, truthful or given meaning to be discovered. It follows that, because historical explanation is abductive, history's conclusions must be provisional no matter how extensive the reservoir of either old or new evidence. It cannot be other because there can be no bedrock of empirical knowledge that grounds all other historical knowledge. The post-structuralist critic points out that this means that historical knowledge is propositional and incapable of ultimate justification (see POST-STRUCTURALISM). History is subject, at best, to only highly localised verification, and remains a petty narrative.

This critique is usually pushed further with the claim that, because historical expla-nation is inductive-abductive, history's interpretations are at best just sophisticated guesswork that only exist in a reality-effect (see REALITY/REALISTIC EFFECT) universe generated by forces other than merely the (intrinsically laden with meaning!) evidence, such as the historian's own ideological situatedness and the historian's preferred social theories (see Roland BARTHES). It follows that explanation (and meaning) in history is as much about form as about content (see FORM AND CONTENT). It means that in a non-justifiable universe of historical knowledge **facts** become beliefs that can only be 'justified' relative to the arbitrary preconceptions, prefigurations or desires of the historian and his/her culture (see TELEOLOGY). It also means that historical explanation should primarily be construed as a **narrative**-fictive process that is concerned as much with the needs of the present or the future as with those of the past. It reveals that the idea of a real and knowable past about which true or false statements can be made is, at best, just another in a long line of modernist suppositions about how we know things. Accepting this means not just ceasing to believe in the reliability of inferred historical descriptions, but accepting that history is not a legitimate or privileged epistemology by virtue of its inferential methodology. We believe in the truth of historical knowledge only to the extent to which we believe in the abductive form of inference.

There are at least five criticisms now regularly offered against an inferentially based and truthful history. They are: that history can at best only represent the past through concepts that are primarily language-based and language is a notoriously poor conductor of meaning; that in his/her use of concepts the historian unavoidably imposes his/her present culture on the past and so cannot understand the past in its own terms; that he/she imposes him/herself on the past through his/her individual ideological and moral perspective; that the writing of history has an epistemic (knowing) priority over the content of the past inasmuch as the historian must eventually compose the past as (an invented) narrative; and, finally, that the modernist investment in the unified knowing subject can be demonstrated to be little more than a Western metaphysical (see METAPHYSICS) wish-fulfilment (see the ENLIGHTENMENT). All we can know of the past are our present, cultural, linguistic and ideological descriptions of it. The drastic conclusion is that we can never know the past except in the ersatz version of it we choose to call the-past-as-history.

Further reading

Audi, R., 1998; Hanson, N.R., 1958; Josephson, J.R. and S.G., 1994; McCullagh, C.B., 2004, 1998; Peirce, C.S., 1958; Rorty, R., 1998, 1991.

INTELLECTUAL HISTORY

According to a leading contemporary intellectual historian, Dominick LaCapra, intellectual history consists of a variety of activities including (but not restricted to) a history of intellectuals and the critical reading of their texts (LaCapra 2004a: 510). More strictly, intellectual history is that performative activity through which historical practitioners (intellectually) constitute or articulate their engagements with the past. It is hardly surprising, therefore, that there are trends in intellectual history just as there are in all other forms of historical work as its practitioners continuously revise the relationship between it and dominant forms of historical practice. How and what ideas are brought to bear on the process of constituting 'the-past-as-history' is the essential territory of intellectual history and the intellectual historian.

Hence the study of the **aesthetic turn**, **linguistic turn**, **critical theory**, **ethical turn**, **agency and structure**, **epistemology**, **ontology**, **cultural history**, **post-structuralism**, **New Historicism**, **mimesis**, **New History**, **positivism**, **author**, **postmodernism**, **trope/figuration**, **post-feminism**, **episteme**, **metanarrative**, **truth**, **discourse**, etc., etc. all fall within the purview of intellectual history because as topics, and along with individual intellectual historians like Benedetto **Croce**, Carl **Becker**, R.G. **Collingwood**, Arthur O. Lovejoy, Hayden **White**, Keith **Jenkins**, and Frank R. **Ankersmit**, they helped situate and orientate history as an intellectual, cultural and, more recently, language and linguistic activity (see Giambattista VICO). Indeed, the text you have before you is an intellectual history insofar as it is a self-conscious exploration of the interface between the past and history produced in accordance with a contemporary 'postmodern perspective' or paradigm. However, by the nature of its being such a literary artefact, it is using a language over which 'I' the 'author' ultimately have no control mainly because it is part of the bigger discourse (its discursive context) of 'what is history thinking?' that you (as well as 'I') inhabit – and you will 'receive' my words infusing them with meanings I cannot even imagine. I have no control over the meaning of this text because I cannot control its reception by you – as you read it you also rewrite its meaning (see DECONSTRUCTIONIST HISTORY). This text may also qualify as intellectual history because of the mundane nature of its claim to classify historians and thinkers within intellectual systems, **genres** and a variety of forms illustrating how they provide pictures (**representations**) of past reality, which they constitute historically (see HISTORICISM; HISTORIOGRAPHY).

But it would be a misleading oversimplification to equate intellectual history with the history of ideas. This is because intellectual history is only in a very limited fashion interested in the history of an idea, although an exception might be made if that idea is 'history'. The founder of the history of ideas Arthur Lovejoy produced his key text *The Great Chain of Being: A Study of the History of an Idea* in 1936 as an examination of the 'doctrine of plenitude' from Plato to the early part of the nineteenth century. This is an exercise in idealist history inasmuch as one believes that the study of the past can be reduced to R.G. Collingwood's ascription that all history is the history of thought (and not, therefore, a science – see POSITIVISM; CONSTRUCTIONIST HISTORY).

Like every genre and form of history, intellectual history is historicist and, therefore, subject to contemporary 'intellectual fashion' as well as being – as you will see – the subject of discourse. By way of illustration, the changes in the understanding of intellectual history in the past thirty years or so can be readily seen in four short (chapter-length) surveys of the field (though there are many examples to choose from) to which I shall refer. All are anglophone. In 1972 Felix Gilbert examined the aims and methods of what he said was hardly a new historical undertaking if defined as an interest in the nature of historical scholarship and history of ideas. What was new was 'the manner in which it is treated' (Gilbert 1972: 143). He said that intellectual history had 'broadened' its scope to investigate the interconnected nature of thought and communication, thus making itself 'equal in importance to then traditional genres of political, diplomatic, and economic history' (ibid.: 145). For Gilbert, intellectual history in the early 1970s was no longer simply the study of the history of ideas but was also increasingly concerned *about* history thinking – but essentially still the ideas of the individual thinker or a range of social groups and their literatures, and also in the (early 1970s) role of the social sciences and intellectual dominance of social history. There was no overt epistemological self-consciousness or epistemic scepticism in Gilbert's comments and certainly nothing about the way in which language expresses ideas – moves us from naïve epistemology into ontology.

By 1980, when Michael Kammen edited (for the American Historical Association) *The Past before Us: Contemporary Historical Writing in the United States*, the ground of history as a discipline had clearly shifted. In his generally upbeat introduction Kammen noted 'a creative proliferation of new historical literature' that was 'altering our perception of the past' (Kammen 1980: 20). He noted that 'During the 1970s a marked transition occurred within the guild of historians in the United States . . . a changing of the guard took place . . . [and a] historiographical whirlwind' had transformed the profession (ibid.: 20–1). What Kammen distinguished was the emergence of the computer, the 'discovery' 'of women, blacks, ethnic groups, the labouring and so-called dangerous classes; . . . the application of social theory and psychoanalysis . . .' and other fresh areas of research such as historical geography, the 'new economic history', the 'new political history', and grass-roots history known as 'history from the bottom up' (ibid.: 21) (see CLIOMETRICS). Kammen mentioned only briefly what became known as the linguistic turn (and it was not a description he used) in his brief reference to Hayden White, which was to say that no one could complain any more as White did in the mid-1960s that there was a resistance 'throughout the entire profession to almost any kind of critical self-analysis' (ibid.: 33). Kammen's own agenda for the 1980s was – essentially – to balance agency and structure, which was, he said, 'essential in achieving a fully rounded perception of the past' (ibid.: 39) (see AGENCY/STRUCTURE).

Writing the chapter on 'intellectual history and cultural history' in Kammen's collection, Robert Darnton (who became President of the American Historical Association in 1999) began by saying that a malaise was gripping American intellectual historians. But the problem had started, he said, some twenty years before that when intellectual history was 'the queen of historical sciences', but 'she seems humbled' (Darnton 1980: 327). The reason in 1980 was that realignment produced by 'sociocultural history' and its bewildering language: '*mentalité*, episteme, paradigm, hermeneutics, semiotics, hegemony, deconstruction, and thick description' (ibid.). He said that intellectual history, of the Lovejoy kind, had been shaken, quoting a 1979 circular sent by Dominick LaCapra to colleagues to the effect that social historians were suddenly asking questions that intellectual historians could not answer. Darnton further noted how 'Europeans do not speak of intellectual history in the American manner' and how the rising tide of the European social history journals *Past and Present* and **Annales** were a *mentalités* axis that had swept all before it. Not surprisingly, perhaps, Darnton's conclusion, after a brief survey of the state of US history between the mid-1940s and late 1970s, was that the US version of intellectual history was alive and thriving in all its four major variants. The variants he noted were

the history of ideas (the study of systematic thought, usually in philosophical treatises), intellectual history proper (the study of informal thought, climates of opinion, and literary movements), the social history of ideas (the study of ideologies and idea diffusion), and cultural history (the study of culture in the anthropological sense, including world views and *mentalités*).

(Darnton 1980: 337)

In all this Darnton also briefly acknowledged the work of Hayden White, along with Nancy Struever, Maurice Mandelbaum, Donald Kelly and Lionel Gossman as critics who 'have gone beyond the older historiographical concerns to a fresh consideration of time consciousness and the linguistic nature of thought in the past' (ibid.: 341). He went on to say that US Europeanists 'seem more sensitive to European currents of philosophy – analytical philosophy in England, post-structuralist thought in France – while the Americanists respond primarily to the American strain in the sociology of knowledge and anthropology' and, in a footnote, Darnton said that Foucault 'stands out among the closely watched avant-garde for Europeanists' (ibid.) (see Michel FOUCAULT). He judged

White's overtly structuralist 1974 article (which influenced cultural and intellectual historians in the 1980s and 1990s) on popular culture and engagement with Foucault to be 'unhistoric' (White 1974). But Darnton did also alert his readers to the work of Quentin Skinner and John Pocock, especially the way in which meaning in the past can be recovered only by shifting from text to context, thus connecting language with time and place.

The fourth and most recent effort at explaining what is intellectual history that I have selected appeared in the edited collection *What Is History Now?* (2002). In her chapter 'What is intellectual history now?' Annabel Brett argued that today intellectual history is about unravelling the relationship between thought and action predicated on two things: first, how human action and agency are connected to language and discourse and, second and through the issue of textuality, how humans represent reality (Brett 2002). In this chapter Brett bears out Darnton's belief of almost a quarter of a century earlier that European intellectual historians have (and probably since the middle of the last century) been more 'philosophical' in their thinking about intellectual history. Brett invoked the 'Cambridge School' that worked from the 1960s on language, thought, agency and time (especially Quentin Skinner) and specifically what one intends when using language as opposed to what one seems to be saying – so-called speech act theory. This **intentionality**, claimed Skinner, was recoverable through the contextualisation of the utterance. So, while Gilbert and Darnton were explaining intellectual history, its basis was already shifting toward what today might be viewed as a revolutionary move in intellectual history – from the unstated assumption that thought was independent of the words used to express it. Today, intellectual history is concerned with language as the constitutive of thought and action as well as acknowledging the death or decentring of the self-agent-author.

The advent of the postmodern critique of historical thinking and practice that emerged in the later work of Ludwig Wittgenstein, and then in Hans-Georg Gadamer, Michel Foucault, Jacques **Derrida**, Hayden White, Frank Ankersmit, Keith Jenkins and Dominick LaCapra, has substantially altered the epistemological orientation of intellectual history. It has fully encompassed the narrative-linguistic paradigm of history as the aesthetic, linguistic and ethical turns have become increasingly influential. As Dominick LaCapra perspicaciously noted in his *Rethinking Intellectual History* (1983) and others like David Harlan subsequently argued in the late 1980s, historians must embrace the linguistic turn and, in effect, recognise that history is always an empty signifier. Developments in intellectual history during this period mediate the tensions that have grown within the wider discipline/practice and the 'spill over' of history into adjacent disciplines such as literature and psychology and growing postmodern epistemological concerns. Though quite possibly a cliché, there is no intellectual history *per se* any more because all history is today intellectual. Surely, all historians today must recognise that doing history is as much an intellectual and philosophical act as it is anything else? Well, you would hope they would.

Further reading

2004 Dominick LaCapra, *Rethinking History: The Journal of Theory and Practice,* themed issue; Bevir, M., 1999; Boas, G., 1969; Brett, A., 2002; Darnton, R., 1980; Forum *AHR*, 1989; Gardiner, J., 1988; Gilbert, F., 1972; Harlan, D., 1989; Kammen, M., 1980; Koselleck, R., 1985; LaCapra, D., 2004a, 2004b, 1989, 1987, 1983; LaCapra, D. and Kaplan, S.L., 1982; Lovejoy, A.O., 1936; Rorty, R. *et al.*, 1991 [1984]; Skinner, Q., 1969; Stromberg, R.N., 1994; Toews, J.E., 1987; White, H., 2000, 1998, 1996, 1995, 1992, 1987, 1984, 1978, 1974, 1973a, 1973b; Wickberg, D., 2001.

INTENTIONALITY

Intentionality is the connection between a state of mind (a mental state), its expression or representation (signifier), and that to which it refers (referent) (see REPRESENTATION). Historians regard intentionality as one of the central features of **historical explanation** and specifically of the study of **causation**. The British philosopher-historian R.G. **Collingwood**, for example, stressed that historians seek out the thought behind the action in order to get at the **truth** that lies in the past. While the second-hand nature of history means that observation of the **evidence** does not permit the *real* character of events or processes and individual actions to be known through the deployment of **inference**, historical explanation demands that historians give a plausible and supported account of agent intentionality (and the extent of free will) (see AGENCY/STRUCTURE; SOURCES). To be truthful in history we are expected to seek the correspondence between the mind and the fact. This requires that we explain the reasons why, for example, Stalin wanted to put Leon Trotsky on trial, why Harry S. Truman in March 1947 promulgated the doctrine that bears his name, why Hitler invaded Poland, why the Nazis acted as they did toward Europe's Jewish population and why the Cold War occurred. Historians should, therefore, understand the motivation, purposes and intentions of individuals before adequate explanations of **events** and processes can be made.

However, in pursuit of Collingwood's notion that to comprehend human actions we must understand the intentions they manifest, historians have to face the dilemma that to know intentions means having to infer mental states from the evidence of actions. Determining what certain actions or events signify (what they mean) in terms of the mental states that may have given rise to them is notoriously difficult. Working on the principle of purposive and rational action seems to most historians to be the only way to approach it; that is, by assuming people act in such a way as to achieve a specified objective (see TELEOLOGY).

For example, why did the American president Abraham Lincoln issue the Emancipation Proclamation (1 January 1863)? Was it because slave labour was useful to the Confederate cause? Or because low morale in the North necessitated an injection of high moral tone? Or Northern public opinion demanded it? Or ending slavery would preclude the support of Britain and France for the Confederacy? Or was it a strategic thing to do because General Lee had been expelled from the North after the battle of Antietam? So what was the objective in emancipating the slaves? Conventionally, historians are contextualists who, in this example, are likely to assume all these reasons/causes were intertwined, and all were related by an ultimate purpose or objective – which will, of course, constitute *the* explanation (see COLLIGATION). But is this a reasonable assumption? Can we really expect to 'discover' *the* explanation? Can we make our decision about what is *the* explanation only by forming yet further sets of assumptions, in this case about Lincoln's intentions, within the wider framework of events based on our personal selection from the available evidence? Each set of assumptions that conventionally is meant to bring us closer to the truth is, in fact, moving us further into speculation and supposition.

This seems fair enough, perhaps even unavoidable if, as a historian, you are predisposed toward believing that people's intentions are the central feature of historical explanation and that they can be knowable (see LIBERAL HUMANISM). It seems quite wrong if you do not make this assumption (i.e. you reject the idea of consciousness determining being), or if you believe it is ontologically (see ONTOLOGY) (as in the construction of reality) and epistemologically (see EPISTEMOLOGY) (as in the construction of knowledge) impossible to know how intentionality fits in with the context, or what the agent's motives were, or what *we think*

their objective was. In fact, to explain the intentions of people in the past requires the presumption that they are the same as we are and that it can be demonstrated that they, like us, were capable of making explicable rational decisions (!) or, given their circumstances, they displayed behaviour that can be explained by their failure to be rational. And it also demands that the textual evidence can be deciphered so as to reveal all relevant hidden intentionality, their likely mental state and consequent motive and purpose.

Of course, if we believe we cannot recover the intentionality of the author of the evidence, it implies several significant things about doing (or not doing!) history: it suggests that we cannot know the original or primal meaning of the evidence; it means rejecting the correspondence theory of knowledge; it casts doubt on the idea of **objectivity**; it challenges conventional notions of history as a legitimate empiricist undertaking; it questions the possibility of a knowable historical reality; and it means that evidence (as texts) can only be studied for their multiple meanings or their **reality/realistic effect** (see COVERING LAWS; EMPIRICISM; Jacques DERRIDA). But all this may be the unavoidable price that historians have to pay if they choose to invoke the *post hoc* argument that we know people in the past are likely to have thought in such and such a way because our world thinks the way it does (see BIOGRAPHY AND LIFE WRITING).

'Discovering' agent intentionality depends, therefore, largely on how the historian conceptualises or represents the intentional act linguistically (see CONCEPTS IN HISTORY; LINGUISTIC TURN; Hayden WHITE). The thoughts that generated an action are states of mind presumably directed at things in the real world. But the historian can only explain them a posteriori (see A PRIORI/ A POSTERIORI) through the evidence of the intention as ink stains on paper – the word that references the action. In practical terms agent intentionality presents itself to the historian as a function of language rather than as a direct plug-in to the mind of the agent. Historians are, consequently, always subject to the intentional fallacy of assuming an access to the **author's** real motives from which we can deduce the person's true intentions. This is especially so if the historian claims to be using an authoritative piece of evidence when it is, in fact, only a trace of the author's act of self-reflection – just another text the meaning of which is forever deferred.

So how should we deploy agent intentionality? It seems to depend on both the **form and content** choices made by the historian. Hayden **White** and Frank **Ankersmit** suggest that because history is essentially a literary commodity historians use the history story form prior to the 'discovery' of agent intentionality. For White what this means is that there is nothing in history's empiricist methodology that requires *or permits* historical narratives to relay the past realities of human intentions and beliefs. Our prefigured preferences will, in fact, largely determine how we trope or emplot the individual and his/her intentions even if, following Collingwood's advice, we have tried to rethink the thoughts of the historical agent and measured them referentially

against the evidence (see EMPLOTMENT; TROPE/FIGURATION).

The philosopher Arthur Danto has also concluded that language, being opaque and cloudy, means that linking language to intention is usually a reduction too far. It would appear that the truth or plausibility value of the historian's written sentences about mental states can readily be altered if one replaces certain expressions or metaphors by others. We can only believe in knowable intentionality, therefore, if we accept that there are real stories that were once lived, that they are available to be 'discovered' and now retold accurately and so correspond to the **facts**. If, however, we choose to interpret mental states as what they manifestly are – representations – as in words, sentences, paintings and graphs, then we have the same problems of deciphering them as we do with any texts in history.

Further reading
Ankersmit, F.R., 2000, 1983; Bevir, M., 1999; Collingwood, R.G., 1994 [1946]; Danto, A., 1981; Dray, W.H., 1957; Olafson, F.A., 1979; Roberts, G., 1997; Searle, J.R., 1983; Weber, M., 1957 [1947]; Wilson, G.M., 1989.

J

JENKINS, KEITH (1943–)

The low esteem in which historical theory and philosophising about history is still held by some historians (particularly in Britain and the United States) is an indication of the continued strength of the modernist 'let's get on with the real business of research' stance as well as a determined head-in-the-sand attitude. However, that some of these historians have started to admit, though (increasingly more rarely these days) with curmudgeonly ill-grace, that history is not solely an empirical-analytical activity but might be considered to be a presentist cultural **narrative representation** of the past, is due in large part to the pressure put upon their position by the British epistemological sceptic Keith Jenkins (see also Frank R. ANKERSMIT; Hayden WHITE). But (still all too often) these historians then go on to say either that this argument is now old hat and for that reason can, in effect, be forgotten, or that we have always known the situation, but so what? They then continue to do history as though the past thirty or forty years of debate over the nature of history never happened. Not only is this an odd attitude for historians who also tend to think we should be able to learn useful things from the past – but clearly not where their own practice is concerned – but it also reveals a persistent desire to deny the reality of what 'doing history' entails.

Since the early 1990s Keith Jenkins has attempted to confront this determined desire (which is still there) among many practitioners to ignore the nature of historical inquiry as if it had little to do with their work. Despite this importunate indifference to his-

torical theorising among such members of the historical profession in Britain, Jenkins's first polemical text, appropriately enough called *Rethinking History* (Routledge, 1991), became (and remains) a best seller (and his publishers have elevated the text to the level of a 'classic'). This is probably because of the nature of the postmodern message it contained which was new, challenging, voguish and seriously damaging to the cosy epistemological torpor of many in the profession. In several subsequent texts, including *On 'What is History?' From Carr and Elton to Rorty and White* (1995), *Why History? Ethics and Postmodernity* (1999) and *Refiguring History* (2003), he has developed a substantial critique of both the attitude and professional practice of such historians. It is this mix of taking no rustic empiricist hostages plus the bluntness of his 'message' that has justifiably made him the best-known as well as the most combative contemporary British historical theorist.

He declared at the very beginning of *Rethinking History* that the discipline of history was as much about what it hid about its true nature as what it revealed. This, he then claimed, meant that most historians lived (as too many still do) in denial of the narrative and representational logic of their enterprise. Deliberately casting himself as an outsider, he stated and re-stated his belief that history was a constructed literary, philosophical and cultural activity that *produced* knowledge about the past. Rather than discovering *the* meaning of the past in its empirical traces and then passing it off as a truthful copy or facsimile called history, Jenkins blistered the profession (and its university and institutional centres of epistemological lassitude and 'let's get back to the archive' and 'telling the truth about history' fixations) with his postmodern re-thinking of history as a constructed discourse.

The intellectual backwardness that was prevalent among the early 1990s British historical profession resulted directly from the relatively slight impact that postmodern ideas had made at that time. In the recent 'classic' edition of his book which was prefaced with an interview with your author, he replied, in response to my question asking whether the book's success had surprised him, that the discipline of history, because it was 'rabidly anti-theoretical', was 'a niche market . . . which *needed* to be opened up' (Jenkins 2003 [1991]: xvii). His aim was overtly disobedient and disruptive inasmuch as he believed students ought 'to know something about the product they are making . . . And they still do' (ibid.). Delivered in a no-nonsense style, his argument was that history students should have the right to understand and, if they choose, to escape from the archivally industrious yet perpetually stultified empirical-analytical vision of what history is (see POSTMODERNISM).

He began by making the point that the past and history are different things. But while the backwoods historian says this is a truism, Jenkins went on to point out what the rustic did not wish to pursue, that history is a discourse – a different category – to that 'which it discourses about' (Jenkins 2003 [1991]: 7). But even more than this the past and history 'float free of each other' as, he says, there are many ways to read a discourse' (ibid.). This was a distinction that he has pursued exhaustively in a variety of texts that, over the years, have become more complex, as he cited a whole variety of the misconceptions professional historians had about what they do. Among the major of these misconceptions was the failure to understand that the history they write is, plainly, *just another text* and one that is not privileged in terms of truthful knowing simply because of its referential pretensions. Most historians still do not fully comprehend that the shift from the past to

history entails the move from **epistemology** to **ontology**. This is unavoidable because we historians (like everyone else) cannot escape our narrative-making universe in order somehow to checklist how our texts correspond to 'reality'. We cannot escape the gravity well of representation/narrative making. We can obviously refer to past reality – but this should never be confused with some bizarre kind of escape back to it by going into the archive, as if this insulated us from our present existence.

Now, while plenty of philosophers of history had long been exploring the consequences of this, especially the epistemological 'foundations' of history as a truth-acquiring discipline (and a good many hold serious doubts about it), it was Jenkins who brought this to the attention of historical practitioners (see Jacques DERRIDA; Michel FOUCAULT; Roland BARTHES; Richard RORTY; R.G. COLLINGWOOD). He claimed, though it wasn't a surprise for most philosophers of history, that history was primarily a philosophical activity, which was more than just epistemologically fragile. By this he meant the curious attempt to know the truth about something that no longer exists from its traces. While historians can provide ample evidence that something happened (by reference to the **sources**) such knowledge can never resolve the fundamental quandary of knowing what it truthfully means (in other words to acknowledge that the past and the historian have a shared ontological status that severs the presumed epistemological connection between experience and **truth**). But true knowledge through simple reference was and is precisely what they (or most of them still) are trying to do. The fact that there are so many different interpretations of the same past (using essentially the same sources and evidence) is indicative of the failure to square this circle. That 'truthful interpretation' is an oxymoron is still quite lost on too many historians.

The ontological status of history results, for Jenkins, from the situation historians always find themselves in. First, they cannot be other than selective in their choice of evidence. Second, they cannot copy the thing-in-itself as a discourse (in other words all we have is other history discourses). Third, they cannot escape being an involved 'narrator' who constructs *their* vision of the-past-as-history. And, finally, they cannot break out of their temporal location in the present with all its retrospective knowledges and resultant creations. All this is a broadside against **objectivity** and their favourite oxymoron. The perplexity, fear and loathing engendered by this assault in the minds of most empirical-analytical historians resulted in the claim that Jenkins was proposing a manifesto that would no longer permit historians to 'tell the truth about history' as the American historians Joyce Appleby, Lynn Hunt and Margaret Jacob described it (Appleby *et al.*: 1994). And of course they were and are right to be fearful, but not for the empirical-analytical reasons they gave and still give. What Jenkins was saying was yes, historians couldn't tell the truth 'about history' – that it is epistemologically impossible to tell the truth about a representation (in the form of a history narrative) depicting/referring to something that no longer exists. To deny this would suggest that art historians can 'tell the truth about the Mona Lisa' or literary critics can 'tell the truth about Shakespeare's *Macbeth*' or, equally, that history book reviewers can avoid pandering to their prejudices simply by referring to what is said on a particular page. To repeat what is surely a very simple point, reference is not truth.

Until *Why History?* (1999), Jenkins had broadly conceived ideas usually associated with postmodernism because he believed their anti-foundational deconstruction at least offered the possibility of radical, emancipating histories. These ontological histories, he believed, might aid in 'legitimately' *producing* the past historically in more generous and in different media and genres (**post-feminist, post-structuralist, post-Marxist**, etc.). He appeared to hope the result would be the construction of reflexive, positioned, radical texts. But with *Why History?* his tone and

direction changed. He began to argue that we could now forget history – given its arguably moribund condition – and live among the ample and agreeable imaginaries provided by postmodern-type theorists – say Roland Barthes, Michel Foucault, Gilles Deleuze, Jacques Derrida, Jean-François **Lyotard**, Jean **Baudrillard**, Richard Rorty, Elizabeth Ermarth and others. He now began to promote the notion of an 'emancipatory rhetorics such that we no longer need any kind of foundational – or no-foundational – past' (Jenkins 1999a: 10).

In *Refiguring History* (2003) Jenkins further developed the 'end of the need for history' theme. He argued for a new way of thinking about history – if we still wanted such a cultural artefact – drawing (in Ch. 3 of the book) on ideas by Edward Said, Alain Badiou, Jean Baudrillard and Elizabeth Ermarth, to suggest fresh refigurings of the 'past' outside/beyond conventional historisations. These concerns have since developed in two directions, both of which constitute his present/future work. First, he is concerned to compose a figure of an *intellectual* who might be able to think around/beyond current histories, and second he appears interested in writing utopian-type alternatives for refiguring 'the past' (or, as he now always prefers to refer to it, 'the before now').

It seems that Jenkins has always wanted to make a difference to the way 'The Nature of History' is seen, particularly writing for undergraduate students and never just for scholars/scholarly reasons. His work has always been very deliberately 'popularising' so that 'young' students can access difficult theorists' ideas at a simplified level before going on to read them – and hopefully apply them – in their own work. Over and above that, he seems to hope that his argument (best expounded in *Why History?*) about the 'end of history' is one he *believes* is an accurate (?) analysis of how things currently stand in relation to the 'condition'/state of 'history today'. This is a project which, no doubt, will be greatly to the continued annoyance of many if not most historians.

Further reading

Appleby, J. *et al.*, 1994; Jenkins, K., 2003, 2003 [1991], 1999a, 1999b, 1998a, 1998b, 1997, 1995; Jenkins, K. and Munslow, A., 2004; Jenkins, K. *et al.*, forthcoming 2007; Zagorin, P., 1999.

JUSTIFIED BELIEF

What do reconstructionist and constructionist historians think provides the foundational principles of their discipline (see RECONSTRUCTIONIST HISTORY; CONSTRUCTIONIST HISTORY)? First, they would claim that it is possible to know the reality of the past and, second, that it is equally possible to translate that knowledge into the historical **narrative** (see REALITY/ REALISTIC EFFECT). Both these expectations are based on a/the simple inferential procedure through which the meaning of the empirical **evidence** of the past is derived (see INFERENCE; EMPIRICISM; EVENT; EPISTEMOLOGY). All this is based on the realist belief that the past itself shapes the historical narrative through the correspondence of present word and past world – that history is an epistemological act (see EPISTEMOLOGY; SOURCES; FACTS; FORM AND CONTENT; COLLIGATION; MIMESIS; REPRESENTATION; TRUTH; NARRATIVE; HISTORICAL EXPLANATION; MODERNISM; Richard RORTY).

The connection between evidence and inference is realised in the sentence-length statement of justified belief. As the philosopher of history C.B. McCullagh has argued, it is by virtue of the empirical-analytical method that historians can be secure in the knowledge that they have discovered what really happened in the past (McCullagh 1984: 2). As John Tosh says, 'refining the inferences that can be legitimately drawn from the sources' is, essentially, what historians do, and only by that mechanism can the facts of history 'be said to rest on inferences whose validity is widely accepted by expert opinion' (Tosh 2001: 113).

In several books dedicated to the defence of history as a truth-acquiring and -transmitting discipline, the philosopher of history C.B. McCullagh has provided historians with an exhaustive and detailed analysis of how they justify their beliefs concerning the reality of the past. McCullagh makes six basic assumptions through which he maintains that historians can have 'faith in the truth of their conclusions about the past' (McCullagh 1984: 1). These assumptions are empirical-analytical in character and are widely accepted not merely among historians, but more broadly by everybody. The six assumptions are, first, that the existence of the world is independent of our beliefs about it; second, that our perceptions, by and large, offer an accurate impression of its reality; third, that reality is structured, generally, according to most of the concepts by which human beings describe it; fourth, that our rules of inference are a reliable way of arriving at new truths about reality (ibid.); fifth, that the historical world is an extension of the present and can be conceived of in the same ways (ibid.: 5); and sixth, that we can determine with fair accuracy the intentions/actions of people in the past (McCullagh 1998: 209–39) (see INTENTIONALITY).

As he says, most historians accept these six assumptions in their bid to 'discover what actually happened in the past' (McCullagh 1984: 2). It is these assumptions that require historians to be accurate in their use of evidence and which hopefully produce the fair and reasonable inferences they draw from it. As he says, the pursuit of truth is dependent upon the assumptions that underpin the empirical-analytical method. Without this, history would simply be propaganda or literary fiction, where narrative coherence is more important than adherence to the evidence of what actually once happened. He maintains that, if historians abandoned the pursuit of truth and were content with narrative coherence or, worse, a preferred theory/ideology, then their writings would be partial and misleading. In the end, the veracity of history is dependent upon high standards of 'historical justification' (ibid.: 3).

So how do historians justify their beliefs about the past? In other words, how can we produce honest, credible, fair and reasonable historical descriptions? Beyond the six assumptions there exists a methodology the whole point of which is to provide us with these truthful historical descriptions. However, to be an empiricist is also to be a sceptic inasmuch as one always doubts what the evidence is telling you. Hence the perpetual state of scepticism about the 'meaning' of the evidence and, consequently, the need to continuously compare and contrast evidence and verify that what you have is actually what you think it is. The other dampener, as empiricists (as well as postmodernists, for that matter) know, is that there is no concept of absolute proof in any description. Plainly, as Frank R. **Ankersmit** points out, a description is not *the* 'thing-in-itself'; it is a description or representation *of* some 'thing-in-itself', idea, process, person or whatever. So, like a painting, no matter how realistic the intention behind it is, it is still a painting. Hence, when you read David Loades's *The Reign of Mary Tudor* (1991 [1979]) or Geoffrey **Elton**'s *England under the Tudors* (1991 [1955]) you are never doing anything else other than reading books *about* the Tudors. However, empiricists reject this as a dereliction of the duty to be 'professional' and 'proper' historians – which it is perfectly possible to be – when it comes down to historical descriptions being very probably true given the six assumptions and the nature of evidence and inference.

As realists like McCullagh and others (as various as Jack Hexter, Isaiah Berlin, Arthur Marwick, Martin Bunzl, Keith Windschuttle, Richard Evans, Gertrude Himmelfarb, etc.) argue, when historians produce reliable descriptions based on the available evidence with a fair and honest intent, it is reasonable to believe that those descriptions are true in a correspondence sense. In other words there are certain 'truth conditions' that make for historical statements of justified belief. These truth conditions are the state(s) of the real world. What historians then believe validates their descriptions is the correspondence between the truth condition (past reality) and the justification of their historical description based on evidence from which an event can be inferred (historical method). In a nutshell, justified belief (for those historians I have described as reconstructionist and constructionist) derives from the correspondence (match) between reality (the world) and its description (the word).

Now, critics of justified belief have tended to say that the correspondence or match between the world (the evidence) and the word (historical description) are always fraught with problems – not least the collapse of the relationship between signifier and signified – but also that the logic of history is not primarily that of the empirical-analytical but of the narrative-linguistic (see POST-STRUCTURALISM; Jacques DERRIDA; Keith JENKINS; Jean BAUDRILLARD). Some critics go so far as to suggest that we cannot rely on historical descriptions to deliver truth about the past in any correspondence sense at all. This is not to say that we cannot know what happened – clearly this is not the issue so long as we have the data relating to the past which is verifiable – but rather it concerns how we can know what it 'really means'. Clearly, this is a very important issue not just for the nature of history as an intellectual practice that makes implicit truth claims about the knowability of the *meaning* of the past (because it knows what happened), but also for a profession with vested interests whose practitioners wish to continue earning a living as 'truth-telling historians' rather than doing anything else. For deconstructionist historians, however, these issues remain irresolvable and some kind of 'coming to terms' with history understood as a narrative-linguistic undertaking is required (see DECONSTRUCTIONIST HISTORY).

The post-structuralist critique (see Roland BARTHES; Michel FOUCAULT; Jacques

DERRIDA) that there cannot be any essential or fixed relationship between signifiers and signifieds and the 'death of the **author**' suggests that meaning (in this case the meaning of 'the-past-as-history') can only be determined by the reader intertextually, that is, reading texts against each other rather than against a given, originary and discoverable meaning/story. Why? Because as I suggested above, all we have are texts that are examples of historicist cultural and language practices though they may be heavily referential (see HISTORICISM). So, using the same evidence, for Elton Mary Tudor's reign was a 'disastrous failure' (Elton 1999 [1955]: 223) and for Loades she committed 'errors of judgement' (Loades 1991 [1979]: 403). From a narrative-linguistic perspective, therefore, our knowledge about what the past means does not simply originate in an approachable reality that exists outside language (if it did there would only be one knowable Mary Tudor?), but only in (past and present) language – a structure that is unstable and relativistic (unhappily maybe, but that is how it is) (see METANARRATIVE; METAPHYSICS; MODERNISM). As Hayden **White** has long argued, determining the meaning of the past is always dependent upon how the narrative is written. Moreover, Frank R. Ankersmit has reminded us that it is important to distinguish a description (which can be justified according to McCullagh's assumptions if you accept the assumptions) from what history actually is – a representation.

No deconstructionist historian would deny that there once was a real past about which historians can say things that are true (or false), but they add that this does not bottom out what is history. To suggest that history is basically just an empirical-analytical undertaking neglects the 'aboutness' or narrative representation dimension to doing it. To apply the logic of linguistic expression, which is used to denote things in the past at the level of a statement of justified belief, cannot be cranked up to the level of the narrative (a book of 90,000 words, or an 8,000-word article, or a 2,000-word lecture, or the words and images in a website). History is not just a collection of linguistic or graphical expressions of past reality. It is a far more complex production that includes historical debate, figuration, ideology, **emplotment**, characterisation, conceptualisation, description, theorisation and argumentation (see CONCEPTS IN HISTORY). To acknowledge all this and then say 'ah yes, but reference overcomes all these issues' is hardly convincing.

The deconstructionist implication of viewing history as a representation of the past is that it short-circuits the epistemological argument that history's only job is to connect present words to past things. Rather, the history (as a constructed representation about the past) is ontologically logically prior to the statements of justified belief contained within it. The conclusion must be that aesthetics (figuration, emplotment, argument, ideology) precedes empiricism. So we are left with the question, is it only through our understanding of the substance of the historical narrative and its construction that we can determine what in history is useful, moral, just or unjust, convincing or implausible, rather than simply stick at 'what happened' and by this assume that we can know what the past really means?

Further reading
Ankersmit, F.R., 2005a, 2005b, 2000; Appleby, J. *et al.*, 1994; Berlin, I., 1997; Bevir, M., 1999, 1994; Bunzl, M., 1997; Carr, D., 1986a; Davidson, D., 1984; Dummett, M., 1978; Elton, G.R., 1991 [1955]; Hexter, J., 1972; Loades, D., 1991 [1979]; Lorenz, C., 1998, 1994; McCullagh, C.B., 2004, 1998, 1984; Marwick, A., 2001; Munslow, A., 2003b, 1997a, 1997b, 1997c; Novick, P., 1988; Putnam, H., 1988, 1987, 1983; Quine, W.V., 1990; Ricoeur, P., 1984; Rorty, R., 1998, 1991, 1979; Saari, H., 2005; Searle, J.R., 1995; Sellars, W., 1997 [1956]; Tallis, R., 1998; Tosh, J., 2001; White, H., 1998, 1995, 1992, 1987; Windschuttle, K., 1995.

K

KANT, IMMANUEL (1724–1804)

Immanuel Kant was one of the key philosophers of the eighteenth-century **Enlightenment**. What makes Kant's **metaphysics** so important is his **epistemology**, namely the foundational belief that reason has the power to probe and establish its own boundaries (*Critique of Pure Reason*) (see G.W.F. HEGEL; INTELLECTUAL HISTORY). Kant's contribution to the modernist (see MODERNISM) project lies in his assertion that knowledge is grounded in the knowing subject. Kant claimed that such a knowing and rational subject could save us from the competing sways of illusion, scepticism and **relativism**. Kant's basic aim was to demonstrate that a reality exists (the world) independent of our representations of it (the word). In addition he thought at great length about ethics (see ETHICAL TURN), (*Critique of Practical Reason*), aesthetics (*Critique of Judgement*) (see AESTHETIC TURN), politics (*Ideas on the Philosophy of the History of Mankind*), and history (*What Is Enlightenment?* and *Idea for a Universal History with a Cosmopolitan Purpose*). Kant tried to overcome what he saw as the problems of David Hume's sceptical empiricism and G.W. Leibniz's extreme rationalism by arguing, following Descartes, in favour of a transcendental idealism, that the mind has pre-programmed categories, intuitions and concepts that command, construct or order our understanding of the real world. This is undertaken by the unified self through the adding together (synthesis) of perception with perception according to given rules that determine in advance how the object will appear to us.

With this thinking Kant offers us the central modernist intellectual expression, that there are given and natural conditions through which we experience reality. Such categories (he proposed a fourfold division – Quantity, Quality, Modality and Relation – with three categories in each) are the filters of reason offering the synthetic a priori (see A PRIORI/A POSTERIORI) foundation with which we make sense of experience. Through these filters we can know the reality behind our experiences. Under Relation we have, for example, substance and accident, cause and effect, and reciprocity. The circularity in this lies in the fact that as we place this grid of categories on our lived experience, those features of existence that derive from the categories/intuitions must correspond to reality as we experience it because they are universally prior to it. Our minds are created in a certain way and we perceive the external world accordingly. Our reason creates the conditions for our experience – the epistemological paradigm. So, rather than believing that our knowledge corresponds to the world of things, things conform to our means of knowing (time is conceived of as one-dimensional, space as three-dimensional, cause before effect, and so on). Our knowledge, therefore, is derived from sense-experience as formed and filtered through our categories (see POST-COLONIAL HISTORY; RACE).

Kant claimed in the opening to his *Critique of Pure Reason* that it was beyond a doubt that all knowledge begins *with* experience, but this does not mean it derives *from* experience. There is a component part of knowledge independent of experience that he terms a priori, which stands to be distinguished from empirical knowledge (from the senses) (see EMPIRI-CISM). How can we further distinguish what is pure a priori from what is empirical? Kant's fortification against Humean scepticism resided in the transcendental ego, which is the human mental source of this rationalist power. In following his stated objective to discover how it is we can objectively know, his route was to posit the two worlds of that which appears to us (phenomena), and that which undoubtedly exists, things-in-themselves (noumena) that, while they are knowable, are not subject to reason. This means that the human mind can discover the **truth** of the world only as it appears to us, not the world as it is in reality. We cannot ever know for certain that the objects we perceive are organised by our categories, but we know the categories exist and we believe they organise our sensory input. We cannot escape this situation. We cannot escape from the categorical form of our knowledge into the world or content of reality (empirical realism) (see FORM AND CONTENT).

This rejection of an empiricism that insists that what we know can only be derived through unmediated experience is the basis of Kant's legacy for historians. Also clearly significant in that legacy is what is usually taken by historians to be Kant's assurance that while the mind is a processing mechanism that renders the stream of data intelligible (and making reason transcendent in the process), this does not mean that our knowledge must be subjective or contingent. It is possible, therefore, for the historian to derive objective knowledge. While for Kant the form of our experience is what we know a priori (mental categories or forms independent of experience), the content is always derived a posteriori (according to the **evidence** of experience) (see SOURCES). It is only when we deploy both form and content that we can hope to derive objective knowledge of the real world. As rational creatures we know objects universally through these forms. Kant's transcendental idealism led him to the conclusion that all forms or ways of conceiving the historical process are, therefore, imposed by the rational mind in the shape of the preferred **emplotment**s of historians.

But, and it is a big but, we cannot know for sure that the content of the real world is organised according to our category forms of emplotment, because we only know content through the forms. All we can know is that the content of the world seems to conform to the forms. In the ironic Kantian universe we cannot escape the form of our cognition to see if the emplotments do really apply. So we are left with the ironic situation that there *must be* a correspondence of form and content, even if we cannot be *really* sure about it. Whatever we think of this, it is the relationship of the form and the content of history that remains central to the connection between **narrative** and **objectivity**.

Experience (the-past-as-history?) taught Kant that humanity had not, at least to his satisfaction, demonstrated that historical change was necessarily smooth or continuous (our lives are subject to chaos, especially the dislocation of wars) but, nevertheless, the advance toward rationality is a moral demand that all must obey. Kant believed history was an ethical imposition. Obeying this demand led him to the three rational conceptions of the historical process that historians could choose to endorse – progress, degeneration and/or stasis – which match the emplotments of Comedy, Tragedy or Epic. For Kant history represented the human mind's capacity to impose different forms on the process of historical change. Any wish to secure the truth must, therefore, be understood through these aesthetic categories. This imposition raises all kinds of questions, not least whether the narrative form for producing a particular kind of history is a category that corresponds with reality because it *is* a condition of knowing. Some history *really* is Epic, other *really* is Tragic!

Kant was a product of his age (as, I assume, we all are) and one of his key assumptions, which was outlined in his short article *What is Enlightenment?* (1784), written for the 'enlightened' emperor Frederick, was Kant's bourgeois celebration of individual freedom and his belief in the essential autonomy of the free agent. While the early 1780s in Europe were not an especially enlightened age, or so it seems to me, the way was opening for men (if not for women) to free themselves from what Kant called self-imposed tutelage. His ideological commitment to human (male) freedom influenced his vision of history, and unavoidably this inflected his message to later generations of historians. He rationalised his bourgeois ideological commitment, arguing that since men have been endowed with the powers of reason, so history must demonstrate the development of mankind toward ever greater levels of intelligence. The ultimate success of rationality is defined in the *Idea for a Universal History with a Cosmopolitan Purpose* in the forms of a republican state, political liberalism, individual emancipation, equality, liberty, free will, the principles of right – what Jean-François **Lyotard** would later describe as **metanarrative**s – the stories Enlightenment philosophers (like Kant) elected to tell about emergent-dominant bourgeois Western European culture.

Built on Kant's basic premise, then (the match or correspondence between subjective categories/concepts and objects), is his contribution to the study of history and the work of historians. It resides in his combined belief in rationality, objectivity, a particular **teleology**, the form/content duality, an emergent bourgeois ideological positioning, the knowing subject, and that it is clearly not possible to accept a crude variety of empiricism. The circularity in his arguments (the ideological content of his logic) is the basis of much deconstructive debate. What happens if we place object before subject, or argue that form always precedes content? So it is today that we can and do debate whether the historical narrative corresponds to *the* (real and genuine) story, or whether it merely reflects an emplotted invention of the historian (see Hayden WHITE).

Further reading

Beck, L.W., 1963; Cassirer, E., 1981; Fackenheim, E., 1956/57; Guyer, P., 1992; Kant, I., 1933 [1781]; O'Brien, K., 1997; Reiss, H., 1991 [1970]; Yovel, Y., 1980.

L

LIBERAL HUMANISM

Although the Renaissance advanced respect for the individual, and the decline of the feudal system assured it, it was not until René Descartes' insistence on the thinking self, and the **Enlightenment**'s progression toward the victory of **modernism**'s bourgeois industrial capitalism as a social and economic system, that the modernist conception of the human individual burgeoned. But it was not until liberalism emerged, as the political, economic and intellectual force most closely associated with the Enlightenment and nineteenth-century scientificism, that this individual was placed at the centre of everything. This revolutionary (literally in some cases) and all-powerful individual was cast in humanist fashion as the rational man. He was accompanied by popular sovereignty, equality of opportunity, the free market and, most importantly, the ability to control the creation of knowledge. Humanism as a philosophy developed, therefore, within the context of an emergent capitalism, new **class** relations and a new human-centred framework for the comprehension of reality. This man was privileged because 'he' (the pronoun is apt given the patriarchal inclination of modernity) (see WOMEN'S HISTORY) was at once the median and the high point of the historical process. In what was quickly appropriated as a bourgeois conception, man was regarded as a unified, coherent and stable, but above all atomistic, self-acting human agent. This subject at the heart of the Enlightenment project was supplied with the will, the ability and the power (the freedom) to make rational social, political and economic choices about the real world out there (see Benedetto CROCE; G.W.F. HEGEL; Immanuel KANT; Friedrich NIETZSCHE).

This liberal humanism, as the bourgeois ideology of the age of capital may be called, found it (socially, culturally, politically, philosophically and economically) necessary to generate what soon found its shape in Enlightenment philosopher Immanuel Kant's rational autonomous subject (as opposed to one possessing a collectivist consciousness) who could carve his place in the universe through his capacity to know. In the 1890s the American historian of the frontier, Frederick Jackson Turner, supplied what is for me the definition of the modernist subject with his description of the early nineteenth-century American pioneer. The frontier pioneer, as a Modern Man, possessed

> acuteness and inquisitiveness; [and] that practical, inventive turn of mind, quick to find expedients; that masterful grasp of material things, lacking in the artistic but powerful to effect great ends; that restless, nervous energy; that dominant individualism, working for good and for evil, and withal that buoyancy and exuberance that comes with freedom
>
> (Turner 1961 [1893]: 37)

The dominant entrepreneurial and exploitative nature of the individual demanded that he be given – as a natural right – command over his environment, and that history should recognise and map his progress toward self-realisation.

Liberal humanism defined man as the engineer, the maker of history, the creator of empires, the founder of nations, the subduer of lesser peoples, the author and master of language, and his identity would not be fragmented or dissolved by forces greater than himself. The ideology of liberal humanism takes for granted a world in which conflict and dispute can be arbitrated by the knowing subject, nature can be chastened and knowledge can be compartmentalised but, above all else, man has dominion over language. The self, as the mainspring and origin of consciousness, understanding, meaning, knowledge and agency, can overcome all obstacles, particularly when the knowing self is linked to science and technology (see INTENTIONALITY). Liberal humanism in the defence of its self, therefore, has a major stake in the philosophy of reason and science as it pursues knowledge and, equally, in denying the arbitrary social, cultural or linguistic construction of the individual, or that nature (the real world) will ultimately determine his actions. Liberal humanism has no time at all for the idea that knowledge of the real world may be unobtainable or inconsistent, or that the real world cannot be discovered and represented as it actually is.

Historians within this liberal humanist tradition are locked into this image of the man in control: the man who can offer the **truth** of the past, which his power over the **sources** and method has disclosed. This is achieved by the paradox of humanism, the exclusion of the historian, so 'history' may reveal its own truth through disembodied narration, displaying it rather than speaking it, as a report rather than a conversation (see Roland BARTHES; NARRATIVE; REALITY/REALISTIC EFFECT). The form of the liberal humanist-inspired history text is seen in its attempt to obliterate itself (see FORM AND CONTENT). The text tries to diminish its own existence to the point at which it is not history that speaks, but the past. The historian remains there, of course, but as a pale if not shadowy facilitator in the background who invites the reader to accept the reality of his/her invisible text. That reality that the historian has mastered is

offered clearly, transparently and in an unmediated fashion to the reader as another way of extending the realm of the knowing subject. The reader of history is thus sucked into the ever-widening and 'self-perpetuating' world of the unified knowing subject. The assumptions of liberal humanism seem to present few problems to reconstructionist historians (see RECONSTRUCTIONIST HISTORY; AGENCY/STRUCTURE) and, for that matter, much conventional practical realist or **constructionist history** also fosters the liberal humanist ideological perspective that embraces **empiricism**, the methodological individualism of rational-action theory (the belief in agency/intentionality), **objectivity**, factualism, **representation** and truth-conditional narratives.

Further reading
Branstead, E.K. and Meluish, K.J., 1978; Bullock, A., 1985; Carroll, J., 1993; Cox, C.B., 1963; Davies, T., 1997; Margolin, J.C., 1989; Roberts, D.D., 1995; Rockmore, T., 1995; Sartre, J.-P., 1989; Turner, F.J., 1961 [1893]; Williams, C.D., 1997.

LINGUISTIC TURN

The term 'the linguistic turn', which according to Richard **Rorty** was coined by the Austrian realist philosopher Gustav Bergmann, has been used by advocates and critics alike to describe the shift in **historical explanation** toward an emphasis on the role of language in creating historical meaning (Rorty 1992 [1967]). The debate over the linguistic turn hinges on the extent to which one believes **objectivity** and **truth** are possible in historical descriptions. As an **epistemology**, as a theory of knowing, defenders of the linguistic turn ask, are there **facts** to be discovered and captured outside language and, moreover, can the historical **narrative** accurately represent this factualist reality as genuine knowledge? Because of its inherently figurative nature and the manner in which textual meaning is constantly deferred, is language destined to remain the ultimate barrier (through which we cannot pass) to the discovery of reality (see EMPLOTMENT; Jacques DERRIDA; TROPE/FIGURATION)? Or can historians access the real by curing language of its figurativism so that it mirrors the reality beyond itself by means of the logical form of the propositional sentence? The alternative is to adopt Ludwig Wittgenstein's position that language is a set of games each possessing its own rules for constituting truth (see RELATIVISM; MIMESIS).

In general, historians still tend to move in a particular epistemological direction regarding language as an adequate representational vehicle, and so the linguistic turn to an anti-realist orientation is not an option (see EPISTEMOLOGY; REPRESENTATION). The American philosopher of history Hayden **White** is often regarded as the leading advocate of the linguistic turn in his comparison of the past to a text that needs interpretation (see HERMENEUTICS). Through his recognition of the power of language to create meaning he has described how the form of the language we use as historians has a determining effect on the meaning we 'extract' or, to be more accurate, we 'impose' on the-past-as-history (see FORM AND CONTENT). As the philosopher Frank R. **Ankersmit** describes it, the historian translates the text of the past into the narrative text of the historian, the-past-as-history, guided by the four major tropes (the figurative devices of metaphor, metonymy, synecdoche and irony (Ankersmit 1994: 64). In his book *The Content of the Form* (1987), White argued that the choices the historian makes in organising the-past-as-history are less to do with the reality (see EVIDENCE; SOURCES) and more to do with the historian's own **ontology** (his/her understanding of the nature of being), ideology, epistemology and emplotment choices. The narrative shape selected by the historian, therefore, carries within it its own prefigured agenda. As Hayden White describes it, the form provides for the content of the past.

The term has been notorious among reconstructionist (see RECONSTRUCTIONIST HISTORY) and mainstream constructionist (see CONSTRUCTIONIST HISTORY; GENRE) historians since the early 1980s because of the widespread misunderstanding of Hayden White's position on what was taken to be his supposed turn to anti-realist linguistic relativism. Although he is still often accused of this by hard-hat reconstructionist historians like Arthur Marwick, what White is actually saying is that language operates within the framework of a **discourse** (the narrative beyond the level of the single sentence), which unavoidably influences how we create the-past-as-history (Marwick 1995; White 1995) (see Roland BARTHES; EPISTEME; Michel FOUCAULT; HISTORICISM; REALITY/REALISTIC EFFECT; NEW HISTORICISM). The linguistic turn is not anti-realist but is post-empiricist in the sense that it questions the notion that social and material forces always have a primacy over cultural and linguistic structures. The linguistic turn offers up to historians several disquieting arguments – that the past consists of texts that are largely self-referential, that aesthetic decisions are as important as the evidence in generating a narrative (see AESTHETIC TURN), that the **intentionality** of the author cannot be known with any certainty, that history beyond the sentence is all interpretation, and that the correspondence theory of knowledge is too frail to support all that is claimed for it. By not addressing these arguments history opens itself to the charge of endorsing a coarse **empiricism** that is, in practice, hard to combat as it is usually cast as a highly refined, sophisticated and suitably sceptical methodology. But at the end of the day history will seem to remain an epistemologically unreflective process of objective knowing and objectified meaning if it does not turn to the consideration of its own linguistic and philosophical features.

Further reading

Ankersmit, F.R., 2005b, 1994; Brown, C.G., 2005; Chandler, D., 2002; Fay, B. *et al.*, 1998; Harlan, D., 1989; Hollinger, D.A., 1989; Iggers, G., 1997; Jenkins, K., 1997; Jenkins, K. and Munslow, A., 2004; Joyce, P., 1991a; Kellner, H., 1989; LaCapra, D., 1995; Lorenz, C., 1994; Marwick, A., 1995; Mink, L., 1970; Munslow, A., 2003b, 1997a; Roberts, M., 2004; Rorty, R., 1992 [1967]; Toews, J.E., 1987; Vann, R.T., 1987; White, H., 1995, 1987, 1973b.

LYOTARD, JEAN-FRANÇOIS (1924–98)

Though a philosopher of postmodernity from the 1980s, Lyotard began his academic career as a Marxist in the 1950s and 1960s. His major post-Marxist interest was in theorising the nature of 'difference', culminating with his two best-known books *The Postmodern Condition: A Report on Knowledge* (1979) and *The Differend: Phrases in Dispute* (1988, originally published in 1983) (see POST-MARXISM; POSTMODERNISM). His turn from Marxism was also signalled early on in his *Libidinal Economy* (1974), in which he proposed a Freudian-inspired libidinal economy replacement for the political economy. Lyotard's contribution to postmodern thinking and the critique of modernism can be divided into two main areas. First, theorising the nature of difference in modern technological societies and, second, that because knowledge (scientific, technological, aesthetic, historical) is constituted its rationale is always disputed.

Lyotard's fame (or infamy, depending on your perspective) arises primarily from his argument that we now live in a post-**Enlightenment** or postmodern milieu characterised by a crisis of intellectual/epistemological certainty, authority, uniformity and direction (progress). The epistemological scepticism that is characteristic of our age Lyotard summarises as incredulity toward what he calls grand or 'metanarratives'. He meant that today it was no longer feasible to adhere to the one-time modernist great narratives of emancipation and progress whether they were, for example, religion, Marxism, science or history. There were no longer any totalising foundations to our existence which is henceforth conditioned by experimentalism, a lack of rules, the ludic (happenstance), a lack of sense of period/time, the aestheticisation of existence and politics, local/micro narratives and situational ethics (see AESTHETIC TURN; ETHICAL TURN). He argues that the disappearance of totalising grand narratives has the effect of allowing the differential nature of single **events** to become more obvious. The consequent end of consensus means greater freedom from enforced agreement and the exercise of power toward conformity.

It is at this point that Lyotard articulates the theory of the 'differend' as his contribution to the analysis of the nature of **truth**, freedom and generally getting along in a universe without metanarratives. The differend is – in the case of history – the recognition that the (modernist) conflict between two parties (or between ideas, ideologies, epistemologies or historical interpretations) is always structured in the dominance of the conventions and rules of one of them. This means that the wrong suffered by the subordinate party cannot be acknowledged. Lyotard describes this as the clash between each party's language game (discourses or phrases in dispute), which cannot recognise the legitimacy of the terms of the other (discourse or phrase), and consequently there is no universal language to which a disinterested appeal can be made. Thus, while we have to make a decision we must do so without agreed and just criteria (an agreed two-party rule) and so we are thrown back on the only realm we have which is the aesthetic. Here we enter our postmodern world. Only through aestheticism can we try to avoid the political violence that dictated our modernist totalising existence, by now respecting difference and rejecting the authority of all such metanarratives.

So does anything go? Well, not exactly,

because in our postmodern world all views are permissible so long as they do not close down competing views – future differends or language games (phrases in dispute). So we all continue to 'play the game', to be 'in dispute' and this is the essence of freedom (from the terror of the unjust). We now exist in a continuous game of the just and unjust. So the point about American, Russian, English or Nazi Holocausts ('Trail of Tears', Wounded Knee massacre, pogroms, Boer War 'concentration camps', Auschwitz, etc.), is not that there is a differend (as between Nazis and Jews or between President Andrew Jackson and Creek Indians), but that there is not! The reason is that in each case there has been the imposition of a master narrative by one party over the other (Jews and American Indians), and because there was no possibility of an appeal to a disinterested arbitrator.

What does this mean for history and historians? It means that in a broad sense history cannot be the disinterested arbitrator about the meaning of the past simply because it collects empirical knowledge of 'what happened'. At one obviously vital level, knowing the nature of the evidence that demonstrates the existence of some thing is imperative to avoid the banality that flows from denying that it happened, but such empirical knowledge cannot 'resolve' what it means. The past cannot be 'known' just through empiricism or its analysis, no matter how much of it we have. This is not to say that you cannot or should not deploy empiricism in an honest and sincere way to 'find out' what actually happened, but to imagine that by coming to reasoned conclusions based on the evidence the historian is somehow vindicating history as the best means for truthfully knowing what the past means is seriously naïve. It is this one-dimensionality that makes the grievous error of believing that history is a detective story and equating cognition with truth.

Through his analysis of the differend Lyotard has extended our appreciation of the cognitive boundaries of history. His argument is that knowledge of past events comes not from the events as such (simple empiricism cannot resolve the differend or disputed language), but that such knowledge is a sign of the historian's state of mind and her or his epistemological, methodological and/or interpretational preferences. Hence the meaning or 'true representation' of the American Revolution, Ronald Reagan's presidency or 'the war in Iraq' cannot be 'found' in the events that make it up. This is because every history (and by implication every past event) is an example of the differend, of the silencing of one competitor in a language game. For the modernist historian, referents (gas chambers, fields of battle, diary entries, attested events) not only do, but they *must*, equal history in a more or less uncomplex manner. This is because they endorse the epistemological 'phrase', 'language' or 'discourse' (see EPISTEMOLOGY). But if one refuses this 'modernist language' (with its characteristic rules and practices) history as a phrase regime becomes disputed – a differend.

For the postmodernist, clearly, the referent is not enough for 'doing history'. This is because such referents have to be represented figuratively (usually in some form of language) (see TROPE/FIGURATION; AESTHETIC TURN; REPRESENTATION; Frank R. ANKERSMIT; Keith JENKINS; Hayden WHITE; MIMESIS; NARRATIVE; REALITY/REALISTIC EFFECT). For modernists this is simply not an issue. This is because that which is knowable about the past exists only in their statements of **justified belief** – phrases that through correspondence refer to what is knowable and real. It is this dispute over knowable reality that gives rise to the 'history differend' and which Lyotard has examined to such disturbing effect.

Further reading

2004 'Historians and ethics', *History and Theory*; Benjamin, A., 1989; Bennington, G., 1988; Callinicos, A., 1989; Drolet, M., 2004; Jenkins, K., 2004, 1999b; Kearney, R. and Rainwater, M., 1996; Lyotard, J.-F., 2004, 1997, 1988, 1979; Readings, B., 1991.

M

METANARRATIVE

Literally a **narrative** about narratives, the term was popularised by Jean-François **Lyotard** in his book *The Postmodern Condition: A Report on Knowledge* (1979), in which he argued that metanarratives or master narratives, the stories told about how we gained and legitimated knowledge in the past, underpinned human progress and history. Such stories or narratives are various and broad, encompassing philosophical, political, economic and cultural processes like Hegelianism, Marxism, liberalism, **hermeneutics**, modern science/scientific knowledge, the **Enlightenment**, the free market, the power of language to represent accurately, even the very notion of transcendent legitimacy. According to Lyotard, all have reached the end of their useful life in what is now the postmodern era (see POSTMODERNISM). The fact that we can no longer depend on such grand stories as universal benchmarks against which we can measure or ensure **truth** is what supposedly characterises our postmodern condition – there are no foundational truths, no epistemological givens (see EPISTEMOLOGY). What we are left with are numerous 'little narratives' or performances/practices that effectively become self-legitimating, and that by their nature cannot offer our culture transcendent or unqualified access to the reality of the world as it actually is, or was. It follows that these narratives about narratives cannot guarantee **objectivity** in the study of the past.

The effects of such a sweeping rejection of the master narratives have been nothing less than a total questioning of the conditions under which we generate knowledge and understand our situation in the world both present and past. This general anti-Cartesian or post-empiricist orientation has been explicit in all realms of study – from philosophy (Richard **Rorty**'s postmodern pragmatism) and feminism, to our construction of time, and the collapse of representation in written history, hence postmodernism's 'anti-historical' stance (see Roland BARTHES; Michel FOUCAULT; Hayden WHITE; POST-FEMINISM; REPRESENTATION).

The challenge to the concept of the metanarrative prompts many questions for those who write history. Do we continue to narrate even if no one believes in narration or its use? Can we stop narrating? Do we narrate our lives to ourselves as we live them? Do historians retell *the* story of the past (according to the given metanarrative or canon of **empiricism**) or do historians tell *a* story about the past (invoking selected and even invented metanarratives, thus ditching empiricism in favour of some other performance or individual practice(s))? Posing and answering these kinds of questions has produced an extensive literature on metanarratives since the mid-1980s.

Further reading
Ankersmit, F.R., 1994; Ankersmit, F.R. and Kellner, H., 1995; Berkhofer, R.F., 1995; Bertens, H., 1995; Carr, D., 1986a; Ermarth, E.D., 1992; Jenkins, K., 2003 [1991]; Lyotard, J.-F., 2004, 1997, 1988, 1979; Norman, A.P., 1991; Putnam, H., 1992; Scott, J.W., 1996a; White, H., 1987.

METAPHYSICS

In philosophy the term conventionally designates the broadest of inquiries into reality,
being, what exists and how we can classify or
categorise it (see A PRIORI/A POSTERI-
ORI; CAUSATION; EPISTEMOLOGY;
EVENT; FACTS; OBJECTIVITY; ONTOL-
OGY; INTELLECTUAL HISTORY). The
metaphysician (the knowing subject, the 'I')
asks the ontological question 'What is there
"out there" to be known?' Next, the metaphysician asks the epistemological question
'How can "I" delineate those categories into
which everything "out there" can be divided?'
The answers to these two questions eventually
translate into a methodological procedure.
Unfortunately, given the highly abstract
nature of metaphysics, there has never been
any general agreement not only as to the
nature of reality, but also as to what constitutes the categories of knowledge, how the
categories are related, how useful they are
as representations of reality and, in the late
twentieth century, what is the point of it all
when critics increasingly doubt the existence
of the knowing subject (see REPRESENTA-
TION). So metaphysics pushes the questioner
into ontology, epistemology and methodology. For example, explaining the causes of
the American Civil War covers all three areas
– the process of causation exists in the real
world of ontology, and explaining its nature
is supposedly an epistemological and methodological process of thinking about and
organising that past reality. 'I' then place it
into categories and conceptual schemata to
interpret and explain it (see CONCEPTS IN
HISTORY).

As might be imagined, around 2,000 years
of thinking about the nature and organisation
of reality has generated a number of different
conclusions about its nature and our catego-
rial access to it. Aristotle initially defined
metaphysics as the search for first causes
aimed at proving the **truth** of the existence
and nature of God (the Unmoved Mover).
But, for Aristotle, metaphysics also sought

out the meaning of those very general concepts or categories that are the foundations of
all other disciplines. **Enlightenment** thinkers
(rationalists like Descartes, Spinoza and Leibniz) vastly extended the realm of metaphysics
to include a new range of issues prompted
by developments in science (the mind–body
duality), experimentation (empirical inquiry)
(see EMPIRICISM), and mathematics (Cartesian geometry). The attempt was made to
unify this new world of metaphysics as the
study of the nature of 'being'. As one might
anticipate, the centre did not hold and metaphysics collapsed into a new configuration of
subject matters that eventually became the
modernist (see MODERNISM) disciplines
that, in their different ways, have assessed that
nature of human being and existence.

The Enlightenment metaphysicians proved
to be somewhat quarrelsome, taking up a
number of separate positions on the character and knowability of reality. In opposition
to the rationalist argument that the human
mind can discover truths about itself and
the real world by reason alone (and that the
senses are not to be trusted), other metaphysicians argued that knowledge founded on
sensory input and experience was superior
to that obtained from reason. These empiricists (Locke, Berkeley, Hume) did not doubt
that there must be some a priori (derived by
reason) truths that are knowable independent
of experience; but that ultimately knowledge
of the metaphysical (real) world must be
empiricist because all our knowledge of reality has to be reducible to experience, that is,
it must be a posteriori (derived from experience). For propositions and concepts to be
truthful they must, therefore, be grounded in
the actual world, in other words they must be
factually based.

Immanuel **Kant** offered the insight that
understanding in the metaphysical world
requires a connection to be made between
innate rational concepts *and* sensory input
(producing a compromise or new synthesis
of the rationalist and empiricist positions).
The raw data, he argued, is processed by our

concepts to generate an object of knowledge. That object is, therefore, only accessible to us through our cognitive faculties. So, in the Kantian metaphysical word, the empirical is organised rationally. Neither can act alone to create genuine knowledge of reality. Kant's reconciliation of the rationalist and empiricist minds lay in his argument that we can know about the real world a priori, even though such knowledge of the real world cannot go beyond its appearance to us. We can have such knowledge thanks to our practical distinction of **form and content**. The form of our sensory input (data, **evidence**, **sources**) is knowable a priori while the content is provided a posteriori. Only with form and content together can we make a reasonable stab at knowing reality. It is by this means that our knowledge transcends the merely sensory (hence the description of Kant's metaphysics as transcendental idealism).

Metaphysicians since Kant have not agreed on the meaning of his legacy. Some argue that the structure of our thought substantially reflects the world as it is: thought is the mirror of nature (see MIMESIS). This is the opinion of those we might call metaphysical realists. Other metaphysicians emphasise Kant's argument that all we know is what our concepts represent to us (or tell us): nature is the mirror of thought – a view held by those we might call metaphysical relativists. Your position on this debate depends on how you answer the following question: is what I discern as an object primarily the result of how I conceptualise and represent it to myself? The extreme version of this is, of course, idealism. This holds that all I can apprehend are my concepts and representations (of an assumed real world) and how I fit them into the pictures I have of reality, or the stories about reality I tell myself. Reality is, in effect, a string of statements put into a **narrative**. Truth is measured in the plausibility of the story. Of course, the question then becomes, are we creatures that tell invented stories, or are we creatures that exist in real stories that can later be retold as 'the history'? Is this story, for example, just my story?

There is a weaker version of the idealist variant of metaphysical relativism. One does not have to be an extreme idealist to accept that reality is only ever viewed through the grid of our concepts. Through concepts we invoke Kant's Quantity, Quality, Relation and Modality, or we may deploy others, like the four primary tropes (see TROPE/FIGURATION). According to this weaker position we are to some extent always constructing reality. Accordingly, no one can provide undisputed, genuine and unmediated knowledge of the structure or nature of reality. Although time and circumstance have eroded their initial Enlightenment conservatism (so they are more amenable to this general neo-Kantian position), the response of rationalists and intractable reconstructionist (see RECONSTRUCTIONIST HISTORY) empiricists is to point out that this metaphysical constructionist (see CONSTRUCTIONIST HISTORY) position is built on a paradox (which is far worse for idealists). If we cannot know reality except through what our concepts represent to us about reality, how can we know we are constructing adequate conceptual schemes? If concepts inevitably stand between us and the full representation of a real object why should we allow the constructionist's request that we accept their conceptual representation? This is not, of course, just the response of the sceptical empiricist or rationalist, it is also the response of the postmodern (see POSTMODERNISM) deconstructionist (see DECONSTRUCTIONIST HISTORY; POST-STRUCTURALISM).

But there is a meeting of reconstructionist and constructionist minds in their ultimate agreement on the big epistemological question of the essential objective knowability of past reality. The empiricist reconstructionist historian (the archetypal metaphysical realist) argues that proper history continues to speak reasonably about the metaphysical past, its events, people, processes, more or less as they happened, rather than just as they are worked out in our concepts and/or narratives.

For the metaphysical constructionist also, the past remains finally knowable in a mind-, culture- and language-independent way. The concepts and social theory deployed by constructionists, they claim, are less an obstacle to knowledge than they are actually tools for breaking out of the prison-houses of mind, culture and language. Both metaphysical realists and constructionists agree, therefore, that while it may be difficult to discover the truth of the reality out there, in their different ways it should not be impossible. Reality can be described accurately.

The metaphysical debate continued with the two post-Kantian German philosophers Georg Wilhelm Friedrich **Hegel** and Friedrich **Nietzsche**. The metaphysical question was still the same: how can we know the nature of reality when all we have are its appearances? Which concepts are most realistic? Hegel argued that our concepts could be valid for both things-in-themselves (reality) and their (its) appearance. For Hegel there exists an absolute unity of intellect and reality, and this unity that transcends subject and object means that our concepts are valid not just for appearances. In Hegel's metaphysics to know the concept is to know the reality, is to know the truth, is to be objective. History is of prime importance in Hegel's metaphysical world because of his argument that to know the world (i.e. get at truth) we must begin with the act of rational knowing – cognition – and the historian is the cognitive knowing subject *par excellence*. Moreover, the prime vehicle for this knowledge is history through its prime mechanism, the dialectic (thesis, antithesis, synthesis). Contrary to this, Nietzsche maintained that our concepts possess no universal validity and have no symmetry with reality. Concepts are all perspectives generated by our cultural situation. No conceptual schema can offer truth, and no such schema can be objective. The mind of the knowing subject cannot unify or capture the reality of the world.

It should be starting to be clear by now how this short history of metaphysics translates into something that is important to historians. Metaphysics, like history, is about the study of reality. What has emerged from this history of metaphysics is that history distinguishes three main orientations: metaphysical realism, metaphysical relativism and a form of idealism I call post-empiricism. At the risk of over-simplification there is a homology here with developments in what I have called reconstructionist history, constructionist history and deconstructionist history. Each poses the metaphysical question, 'how can we know the reality of the past?'

Metaphysical realist conceptions of the world tend toward the belief that reality is rather too complex for the conceptual constructionist's best efforts (see POSITIVISM), while deconstructionists are just off-the-wall idealists who have wrapped themselves in the (once, and now, it is said, much less) fashionable cloak of postmodernism. When cast in the shape of a reconstructionist historian, the metaphysical realist tends to claim that particular things located in time and space (people, events, buildings) can be understood, and the true meaning of past experience can be inferred through their general attributes, made usually in a subject–predicate sentence (see INFERENCE). Take the sentence, 'Napoleon Bonaparte was misogynous'. The truth of that description inheres, for the reconstructionist historian, in the correspondence of the sentence's linguistic structure to the way the world was. Both subject and predicate are referenced in the real world by their respective bodies of evidence – that Napoleon Bonaparte existed, and he hated women. The realist position would also hold for the sentence, 'Napoleon Bonaparte was fearless', because fearlessness is a universal that can be attributed to that particular historical figure. There is, therefore, everything a realist could want here: attribution (predicates express universals), correspondence, referentiality (evidence-supported inference), truth, factuality, historical transcendence (Bonaparte hated women then, now and always until new evidence to the contrary comes along), and adequate representation and objectivity because the description is independent of the mind of the historian and his/her social situation.

The metaphysical realism that underpins reconstructionist history thus effectively divorces ontology from epistemology, detaches subject and object, and disconnects the knower from that which is known. Such history insists that its empirical inferential methodology permits the historian (as a knowing subject, the 'self', the 'I') to dispassionately detect the truthful interpretation located in the past's documentary evidence, and then to relate it appropriately in a transparent narrative. What they do is also mind-, culture- and language-independent. For the reconstructionist historian metaphysical realism translates directly into objectivity. For the neo-Kantian constructionist, however, it is always more messy than this, knowing that reality is a mix of **relativism** and realism. The 'practical realist' appellation coined in the mid-1990s to describe the sophisticated mainstream historian of today is a useful description of this individual (Appleby *et al.* 1994). The metaphysical realist middle position is well described as practical realism or constructionism.

The metaphysical relativism that supports constructionist history assumes that the realist cannot gain truthful insights into the experience of the past without the application of the right social theory (categories of analysis). All history, constructionists claim, is ineluctably theoretical and must be presentist inasmuch as the theory is constructed and applied in the here and now. Nevertheless, constructionist history can also be truthful because it endorses the epistemological position that facts can be derived through theory by the sophisticated neo-Kantian knowing subject (a.k.a. the practical realist historian). The empirical has to be organised in some way, and when the organisation is appropriately done through our concepts then we can truthfully represent the past. For the constructionist historian history is interpretation

so, by definition, it cannot be reconstruction. Historical knowledge emerges relative to both theory and evidence.

As soon as this position is reached the historian is immediately shifting into what is, to be fair, at least a situation of moderate anti-realism. Constructionist historians do not doubt that the real past existed, just that it does not exist now, hence the need for theory to help recapture it. None of this, however, invalidates the truthfulness of the interpretation for constructionists, nor does it cast doubt on our powers of historical representation; indeed hypothesis-testing makes it more likely to be truthful. So the constructionist is a hypothesis-tester, an empiricist and a realist (his/her interpretations are mind-, culture- and language-independent), believes in referentiality and is objectivist, and some hardened social science historians will display their tendency toward **positivism**, statistics and **structuralism**. The slide into relativism is not unavoidable; it can be stopped at this point. It has to be stopped!

But once we break out from a metaphysical realist position where do we draw the line if we want to find the truth? Can we, in fact, find the truth any more? How can we stop history collapsing into full-blown relativism? And if we cannot is this actually a problem? The issue seems to be that historical interpretation, once we abandon an absolutist metaphysical realist position, becomes unavoidably mind-, culture- and language-dependent. This raises doubts about all the central features of the reconstructionist and constructionist positions. Once we challenge inductive inference, the correspondence theory of truth, objective knowing and representation, what happens to history? Can we still have truthful history without these realist attributes? If we assume a particularly sceptical, idealist, postmodern or deconstructionist position about the constructed social, cultural, political, gendered, racial and ideological nature of our categories for the organisation of past experience and assume there can be no adequate representation of reality as a result, then we simply cannot do reconstructionist or constructionist history. In fact we are living in a world without modernist history (see MODERNISM).

The most significant attack on the Western metaphysical tradition after Nietzsche came in the twentieth century with the advent of **continental philosophy** and certain aspects of **critical theory**, and particularly French philosopher Jacques **Derrida**'s assault on the metaphysical notions of the unified knowing subject, knowable reality and the adequacy of representation. Derrida is suspicious of the idea that words are stable in their reflectivity of original meaning and that when we hear or write them an imposed meaning is already present in our minds. Instead of this 'metaphysics of presence' Derrida invites us to consider the cultural intertextuality of words and concepts as well as the slippery and fictive textuality of narratives. He claims that Western metaphysics is based on the fundamental illusion that there is a unified knowing subject and that the 'I' has full control over language and original meaning. This critique applies to adherents of both realist and relativist metaphysics because, while they may argue like squabbling siblings, both assume that they can (through their own individual epistemologies and methods) reach and represent the extra-discursive (non-linguistic) exterior world of reality (see DISCOURSE).

Doubting knowable reality, because we believe the categories are inadequate to the task of representation (metaphysical presence is an illusion), does not mean we can simply replace them with others that are better, because this swings us back on the route to realism, presence and just another interpretation of past reality. If sceptics do want to practice what they preach, then they have to radically change their notion of what is history. In a postist universe there are no empirical foundations for knowing, positivism is a deficient epistemology and we cannot know anything independently of our mind, language use or culture, and so we cannot know the past, and all we have is the-past-as-history. With the collapse of the knowing subject (the conflation of subject and object, and form and content) we are no longer in history but only ever live on the outer edge of a wave of time.

Losing touch with the reality of the past is a grim vision for reconstructionist and constructionist historians. But whether we endorse this post-empiricist position or not, we cannot escape the fact that history (not to be confused with the past) does not exist until the historian composes it as a narrative. In the narrative the historian chooses events and places them in a preferred order so as to tell a (or, if they prefer to see it this way, the) story. Regardless of the burden of empirical referentiality, range and sophistication of the concepts employed or the hypotheses tested, historical explanation exists only in the form of a narrative. In the wake of the **linguistic turn**, therefore, the reality of the past exists only in its story. And, as no story can be fully comprehensive, as the philosopher Arthur Danto points out, we can never hope to 'know' the past in the fullness of its meaning; at best all we can have is a highly selective, poorly represented and ideologically influenced set of beliefs about the past. And anyway, history is still going on so we can never have a final truth of any event (Danto 1985). There is much for historians to debate here. Is the past knowable as history? Is history only about language as opposed to **class**, **gender** or **race**? Is history primarily a conceptualisation process that is then represented in language? It comes down to the question of whether there is a knowable meaning to be found in the reality of the past and how we can acquire it and, if there is not, how we invent it and for what purposes.

Further reading

Appleby, J. *et al.*, 1994; Bunzl, M., 1997; Collingwood, R.G., 1940; Danto, A., 1985; Derrida, J., 1978, 1976; Loux, M.J., 1998; Putnam, H., 1987; Roberts, D.D., 1995; Walsh, W.H., 1966.

MIMESIS

For most historians history reflects the reality of the past as accessed through the **evidence** and the **sources**. The connection between the past and history is usually accounted for by the correspondence theory of **truth** and the referential nature of history prose (what is assumed to be the essentially transparent relation between past action and the words used by the historian to 'relate' it). What this is, in effect, is a demonstration of a belief in mimesis (from the Greek *mimēsis*, which means 'imitation'). Mimesis defines that state or object of aesthetic **representation** that, it is believed, resembles what it represents (as in *trompe l'œil* painting or the art movement of verism) (see AESTHETIC TURN). History is, in this sense, an imitation of past reality; literally history is the re-presentation of the past in another form (specifically a **narrative**). Now this is a 'down to earth' (to use a classic realist phrase) realist understanding of what is history. Moreover, this view assumes that the historian is essentially just a cipher in this re-presentation. At the same time, and somewhat paradoxically, it is also recognised that the historian is, in a crucially important sense, also the **author** of the history. In other words, he or she is a writer who, through their narrative-making/literary constructionism chooses to imitate the empirically attested-to past in a particular way as they create an aesthetic object (see LINGUISTIC TURN).

This mimetic tradition (that informs the realist perception of history) is found in the belief that history discovers and re-presents *the* story of human beings in action. The **postmodern** critique of Jean-François Lyotard, Jacques **Derrida**, Hayden **White** and Frank R. **Ankersmit** has, however, provided grounds for the rejection of the mimetic theory of representation. Once the metanarrative 'that art must imitate reality' is rejected through the casting out of the transcendental signified or the knowable originary past, and the consequent elevation of the figural, then history can no longer be viewed as simply the product of mimesis, but results from an aesthetic act that is not merely the function of the empirical.

The most detailed analysis of change over time and of support for mimesis is that provided by the French philosopher Paul Ricoeur, who maintains that the fundamental nature of our engagement with the past exists in the ability of historians to construct and follow a story, and it follows that history is itself most appropriately understood as a narrative-making process – though for Ricoeur it should still be seen as ultimately referential. For Ricoeur, therefore, explanation in history is much more than just following a story. This is the crux of the debate about what is history. What is the balance between the empirical-analytical and the narrative-linguistic? Responding to this, many narrativists (and even a few non-narrativists) have pointed out, though most notably William Gallie, that history must possess its own narrative coherence rather than simply (crudely) reporting what happened according to archival research. So, in addition to **evidence**, we have **trope**, **argument**, ideological preference and conceptualisation (see CONCEPTS IN HISTORY).

Ricoeur, in *Time and Narrative* (1984) (Vol. 1), maintains that there is a fundamental and indissoluble link between 'telling a story' (theory of the history text) and the reality of change over time (the temporal nature of human life encapsulated in the theory of action). The link between these is provided by his model constructed out of three definitions of mimesis (what he calls threefold mimesis): mimesis$_1$, mimesis$_2$ and mimesis$_3$. Mimesis$_1$ he takes to encompass all those prior understandings that we must possess before we can create a narrative. These include the concept of an 'action', a pre-understanding of **agency/structure** of what constitutes an **emplotment**, and the nature of **causation** and change over time (note how many temporal adverbs there are in history – 'since', 'before', 'after', 'later', 'during'). We must know what agency/structure, emplotment and causation are in order to turn them into a plausible textual representation. In other words, to understand a story we must have a sense of what it means 'to act' (to be, or not to be . . .) and to understand the range or forms of action we can deploy within our own culture. For an action to be located in a 'meaningful' (meaning-full) story, historians need to be aware of what our society, or what we believe a past society, may have regarded as noble or ignoble actions. Some actions are culturally slotted into tragedies, for example, while others are not. Armed with this knowledge we can turn the data of the past into a story/plot – mimesis$_2$.

By mimesis$_2$ Ricoeur refers, then, to the ordering of events as the emplotment of the narrative. Emplotment – literally the central function in making history – turns the minutiae of the past into a story of a particular kind cast within a particular literary genre with all its attendant understandings about action and cause. Mimesis$_2$ refers to the ordering and organisation of events, takes the contingent and gives it a meaningful shape – a 'followable' story with an ending (have you ever noted the number of history books the final chapter of which is called 'Conclusion'?) which is constructed according to the historian's accrued data, preferred argument, ideology, concept and/or trope. In effect, mimesis$_2$ connects or, more accurately, mediates between mimesis$_1$ and mimesis$_3$. Mimesis$_3$ is what Ricoeur refers to as the 'application' or reception of the (history) text by the reader/audience. All histories do their work (whatever that turns out to be) in this three-fold mimesis interface between the once real action and its reception as a textual structuring. Eventually, and mimesis$_3$ indicates this, it is the reader who finishes off the text. But, as Ricoeur notes (and Derrida for that matter but with a different purpose in mind), no language structure is entirely devoid of reference to that which exists beyond its self.

History thus remains referential, so Ricoeur insists, but it is at the level of the sentence-length statement of **justified belief**. However, as Frank R. Ankersmit maintains, texts like history, though they make truth claims, at this

level are always poetic. Ricoeur would not go so far as to suggest that this dimension allows historical narratives to re-inscribe the reality of human action in as many ways as there are authors. He would maintain that as the referential text describes actual action, this makes such texts (like history) realist – history brings experience *to* language. While acknowledging the significance of emplotment in making history, it is not just a poetic/imaginative and semiotic act. Hence it remains possible for historians to view their narrative-making as a truthful, candid and straightforward attempt to represent *the* nature of past action and of cause and effect. The historian can thus view the act of narrative-making as a complex mime of the intentional acts of historical agents and/or the evidentially revealed structures of change over time. Ricoeur reinforces this point by assuming that people in the past always constructed their lives as emplotted narratives. So it is that historians, he concludes, can find out *the* story shape of the past as it appeared to the minds of historical 'actors' and imitate it in the history texts. This debate shows few signs of ever being capable of a resolution and you will have to make up your own mind.

Further reading
Ankersmit, F.R., 2005a, 1998a, 1988b, 1983; Auerbach, E., 1953; Danto, A., 1985; Derrida, J., 1982; Gallie, W.B., 1964; Girard, R., 1978; Ricoeur, P., 1984; White, H. 1998.

MODERNISM

There is no single or easy definition of modernism. Usually the term is taken to refer to the aesthetic or cultural dimension of the historical period of modernity (see AESTHETIC TURN; LINGUISTIC TURN). Modernity is, unfortunately, almost impossible to date, but may be regarded as being constituted out of a series of events around the time of the **Enlightenment** and it has been regarded as continuing up to the present. This implies that it is just a period of European historical change, but this would be an inadequate definition. It may be helpful to consider modernism more broadly as a **discourse**, a highly complex yet coherent **narrative** containing assumptions about how it is possible to represent the state of nature as supported by a new realist historical consciousness of change over time (see Michel FOUCAULT). This suggests that modernism is a conception of a world continuously being brought into existence through a set of beliefs, significations, cultural practices and spoken and unspoken 'rules' that became its own essence. Modernism, therefore, signifies changes to the aesthetic practices of modernity. In fact modernism overpowered ancient ways of thinking, knowing and believing in all fields of human endeavour: in technology, science and the social sciences as well as philosophy, history, literature and the visual arts.

Perhaps the central feature of this widespread reorientation of mental life from the seventeenth century is modernism's self-reflexive nature that recognises the enormous complexity and paradoxes inherent in controlling technological, industrial and urban existence. Jürgen Habermas's definition of the Enlightenment serves as a useful commentary on the broad nature of modernism when he says its primary feature is the control exercised by human beings over both objective reality and human nature (see EPISTEMOLOGY; ONTOLOGY). This suggests that all fields of knowledge (including history) are constructions that involve the exercise of a regulatory power. Indeed, Michel Foucault argues, in his linkage of power and knowledge, that viewing modernism as a discourse is the key to understanding its identity. For Foucault knowing how a discourse works, as a cultural regime for authenticating and controlling the process of knowledge creation, is essential to an understanding of modernism (see EPISTEME; NEW HISTORICISM). From Foucault's perspective modernism is best

summarised as the Enlightenment-inspired drive to **truth** through the domestication of the world out there by the (European and male) human mind. While modernists subsequently have debated whether this meant that representation (form) was secondary to reality (content), for Foucault the important point is that the will to truth (the will to know) is inextricably connected with the Will to Power (see REPRESENTATION).

Given its Enlightenment origins modernism possesses a long list of characteristics all based on the idea that solutions are always available to the rational, technologically educated and realist human mind. As Immanuel **Kant** had pointed out, however, giving organisation to the world does not mean that it is possible to know what its content really means or how it actually comes to be what it seems. Nevertheless, the characteristic features of modernism have proceeded from the principle that there is always a way of finding out the truth. Its principles include **empiricism,** with its investment in the correspondence theory of knowledge, the verification of **evidence** through comparison and the derivation of **causation** through **inference** to the best explanation. Other key modernist principles include the belief in human **intentionality** and **agency/structure**, naturalism (science will explain), scepticism (translating eventually into pragmatism), secularism, progress and newness. Modernism (as the master narrative) also gave birth to other 'big' narratives such as **historicism** and liberalism, and eventually Western imperialism, fascism, Marxism, paternalism and the global dominance of bourgeois capitalism. All these are modernist ways to acquire power and all have claimed to tell the truth (see POSTCOLONIAL HISTORY; POST-MARXISM).

Modernism was thus influenced by the challenge it offered to itself. This is illustrated by the problems associated today with the term postmodern (see POSTMODERNISM), as in 'postmodern history'. The term postmodern is regularly used to denote the succession of the postmodern over the modern. In the case of postmodern history it means the appearance of a variety of properties associated with historical study that have occurred subsequently (hyphenated post-modern) but this is not so. The origins of much that is described as postmodern already existed in nineteenth-century modernism's criticism of its own founding principles. For example, there is nothing postmodern in Friedrich **Nietzsche's** deconstruction of causality, which is that the effect is primary in the search for cause. Modernism's auto-criticism means that the features we associate with postmodern history tend to derive from modernism's self-reflexivity over content, form, **objectivity**, ambiguity in knowing and being and the idea that language constructs rather than reflects reality.

The contribution, for example, of much twentieth-century **continental philosophy** and **critical theory** has been built on the work of Nietzsche confronting and criticising modernism as a description of Western **metaphysics**. The critique has concluded that modernism has outlasted its intellectual utility and that greater attention should now be paid to the final collapse of objectivity and the instability of representation through language (as the only access we have to constructed reality). Modernism has existed fitfully, therefore, in the midst of its own self-determined and self-imposed dialectical (opposing) directions: reason and unreason, concealment and disclosure, freedom and terror, **liberal humanism** and anti-humanism, reality and myth, certainty and mutability, history and fiction, past and present, object and subject.

This self-reflexivity of modernism so far as the discipline of history is concerned has, therefore, produced a super-modernist (though it is more often called a postmodernist) critique. This critique has had rather more impact in mainland Europe than in the United Kingdom or the United States where Anglo-American **hermeneutics** are entrenched. Enlightenment rationality has had a chequered career in Europe in the past 200 years, being more often turned to vicious de-humanisation than in either the United States (slavery and the native American genocide notwithstanding) or the United Kingdom (its imperial adventures apart). This may help explain why modernism is less intellectually secure in Europe. This was evidenced in the 1990s and 2000s debates on how to represent European modernist events like its alarmingly regular holocausts. Many twentieth-century European thinkers, therefore, have seen modernism as a failed experiment in living and thinking.

In the United Kingdom and the United States 'modernist history' remains (for the majority) the means for continued intellectual advancement and square dealing with the past. Indeed, the argument runs that by relativising history we can no longer grasp the significance and meaning of the present. This is the claim usually made by the more militant reconstructionist historians (see RECONSTRUCTIONIST HISTORY). But modernism has produced at least two other main varieties of historian, each of whom remains in dialogue with their reconstructionist colleagues as well as with each other. These are the twentieth-century positivist-inspired social theory devotees of **constructionist history**, whom it may be useful to think of as 'late-modernist' historians; the third type is postmodernist or deconstructionist historians (see DECONSTRUCTIONIST HISTORY). This last group are very much the product of the present generation who have taken their cues from **post-structuralism** and the works of Frank R. **Ankersmit**, Roland **Barthes**, Jacques **Derrida**, Michel Foucault and Hayden **White**.

While accepting modernism's recognition that uncertainty exists in knowledge, not all historians slavishly followed the empiricist model. In the United States the historians Carl **Becker** and Charles Beard in the 1930s pointed out the cultural relativism inherent in writing history, as did R.G. **Collingwood** and Benedetto **Croce** in Europe. In its more recent self-reflexive state, modernism's realist constructionist historians like Appleby, Hunt and Jacob have acknowledged that there is an unavoidable perspective in writing about the past, that the historian's social theories are always compromised by the present, that inference does have severe failings, that the telling of a myth can possess a hard reality, and that the historian is an **author** as much as a disembodied observer. But, when push comes to shove, the argument is still made that empiricism remains the best way of objectively coming to terms with the past in the present.

None of this convinces the deconstructionist post-empiricist critics of modernist and late-modernist history. They maintain that no amount of experimentation with form avoids the fact that even the most sophisticated and self-reflexive of historians still pursue the epistemological model. That is, they seek adequacy in their representation, reject the **linguistic turn** against objectivity, proclaim knowability through referentiality, deny the rupture of the signifier–signified relationship, accept the need for truthful interpretations, regard **historiography** as secondary to methodology, deny that the **emplotment** of the narrative has primacy over factualism in generating historical knowledge and, withal, remain unwilling to accept that there is no mind-independent reality.

Self-critical and self-reflexive modernism, especially in the literary and artistic worlds, has long generated experiments in, and outright rejections of, modernism: impressionism, futurism, cubism, Dadaism and surrealism in art, movements in literature from naturalism to postmodernist subjectless fiction, and the development of absurdist drama. But not in history until the relatively recent advent of **experimental history**. Dadaist, pastiche, montage or absurdist history has yet to arrive even from the word-processors of the deconstructionists. While for the majority of historians history is still in the age of 'pointing' (a term I have borrowed from sculpture used to describe the long-established method for mechanically transferring as exactly as possible the proportions of a three-dimensional model to another model), the experiments of

the deconstructionists do not fully exemplify the anti-modernism that is the signature of a radically different approach to the past. No historian has yet produced an overtly anti-modernist work of history the equivalent of Marcel Duchamp's scandalously successful 1913 painting *Nude Descending a Staircase*, or of Antonin Artaud's work in the theatre, or of the writer Alain Robbe-Grillet's highly self-conscious text *In the Labyrinth*. There are few outlets for such activities, which are still viewed by many obdurate empiricists as either pointless or feckless.

It seems unlikely that there will be a major surge in experimental history until historians embrace the idea that history can be freed from the restraints of maintaining the gap between process (form) and its product (content). Only once history's invention and theatricality/performaticity is accepted and exploited can 'history as process' take over from 'history as product', and the anti-modernist historian will finally have the chance to reflect upon the infinite regress of meaning and the nature of history's existence. Anti-modernist experiments in historical process will, I suspect, be prompted only by the disquiet of historians about what can genuinely be known in a representational literary form and the slow realisation that our 'mass mediated' age is actually doing away with 'the history book'. The ontological character of future anti-modernist history will be revealed not in asking how we can know about the past but, perhaps, in asking how we can live without a modernist historical consciousness at all.

Postmodern history, so-called, often fails to deliver its promise. Why? It seems to be because of the nature of the experiments with form that retain a referentialist connection. Experiments in postmodern history do, of course, acknowledge the aesthetic nature of historical writing in which the form of the statement is one of the prerequisites for the truth of the statement (Ankersmit 1994: 170–2). In postmodern historical writing form is increasingly recognised as just as important as content. It follows that postmodern historians often claim to be no longer primarily interested in the real story hidden in or between the lines of the evidence, but work instead on the principle that evidence signposts not the past, but other interpretations of the past. In pursuit of this claim the act of postmodern history sometimes begins with the historian's present construction of the evidence. He/she looks for its gaps and silences and injects his/her own needs as well as those of his/her present cultural, epistemic and teleological context. Such historians do not fill the gaps and silences exclusively with inference to the best explanation founded on an assumed knowable reality. Such history tends to be both historiographic and psychoanalytic and is far more complex than empiricism conceives it.

The ultimate denial of modernism may well be to move beyond the incipient deconstructionism of historians like Hans Ulrich Gumbrecht, Simon Schama, Natalie Zemon Davis, Mary Poovey and George Duby, to take up a thorough anti-modernist stance that demands not only the disavowal of experiments with form, but also the denial of a history defined in any way as a referential text in favour of studying the absurd nature of the metaphorical relationship of the present to the past. Indeed, future history may require a wholly new non-written form and a content that is allusive and metaphorical, and which will expand our capacity to grasp meaning as well as make ethical decisions in the present (see ETHICAL TURN).

This may be too heady a brew for some (or, depending on their opinion, just a pointless waste of time). Alternatively, and somewhat less radically, it might be that so-called postmodernist history, as a kind of metafictional historiography, will prevail. In this 'history' historians will reflect upon their own status as historians and authors, and they may choose to disrupt the flow of narrative in order to confront the constructed nature of what they write, yet all the while they still reference a generally recognisable and knowable real past. Disruption of form is not, of course, a disruption of the modernist historical consciousness; more often than not it merely illustrates its self-reflexivity. By exposing the fictive nature of history by foreclosing on the epistemological model and denying the gap between process and product, deconstructive historians may more effectively dispute the sustainability of the modernist distinction between history and fiction, but in so doing they are not necessarily denying the historical consciousness that is the discourse of modernism's greatest legacy.

Further reading

Ankersmit, F.R., 1994; Appleby, J. et al., 1994; Bradbury, M. and McFarlane, J., 1976; Brown, C.G., 2005; Danto, A., 1998, 1997, 1985; Davis, N.Z., 1987a, 1987b; Duby, G., 1993; Ermarth, E.D., 1992; Eysteinsson, A., 1990; Ginzburg, C., 1982; Gumbrecht, H.U., 1997; Habermas, J., 1987; Jenkins, K., 1999a; Poovey, M., 1988; Rosenstone, R.A., 1995a, 1995b; Schama, S., 1991.

N

NARRATIVE

Narrative is central to **historical explanation** as the vehicle for the creation and **representation** of historical knowledge and historical explanation. What is narrative? For the historian it is the telling of an **event** or connected flow of events, by a narrator/**author** (the writer/historian) to a narratee (the actual/imagined reader) and rarely is it so abstruse (akin to a scientific narrative) that it is cast in other than a relatively jargon-free language. The historical narrative, because it is composed within the realist mode, is normally invested with a naturalism concerning **truth** that more obviously fictional narratives do not claim – although there is a substantial contemporary debate about the truth-carrying characteristics of fictional narrative. The cognitive functioning of narrative is an important topic among philosophers, psychologists and literary and artificial-intelligence theorists – rather more so, unfortunately, than it is among historians.

Prior to the historian's act of narration, the given events and **facts** are arranged as an **emplotment** according to an understanding of their causal connections (see CAUSATION; COLLIGATION). In the case of realist-inspired narratives like history it is assumed that the causal connections parallel the actuality of the events and facts described, hence narrative usually takes the shape of 'this happened, then that, because . . .'. Normally the narrator of historical narratives (the historian) is a voice cast in the third person. This is a conscious act intended to reference the **objectivity** of the undertaking, by confirming that the required distance exists between historian, real event and accurate description.

So far as the historical narrative is concerned, the historian traditionally has only one position – that of the dispassionate observer – and it is this position that ensures the truthfulness of that which is recounted/interpreted. In summary, the historian's narrative is the vehicle for plainly stated historical facts, and while the historian arranges the facts, the arrangement will, if done properly, uncover *the* real story (*the* real narrative) in, and according to, the **evidence** or **sources**. This is the commonly accepted understanding of the nature of the historical narrative, one that is founded on a particular epistemological position, namely that **empiricism** has the power to reveal the past as it actually happened by getting the story straight (see EPISTEMOLOGY). This, indeed, is the cognitive or knowledge-making function of narrative. Narrative (form) effectively references and relates the past (content) as history (see FORM AND CONTENT; GENRE). Narrative thereby provides the dedicated means for articulating the given nature of the past.

Why is narrative important to historians? The answer ought to be clear by now. It is accepted by most historians that narrative is significant because it is through it that we establish the cognitive link between form and content, the word and the world. Narrative acts as the (aesthetic) expression of (in the case of history) an evidenced and, therefore, knowable past material reality (see AESTHETIC TURN). Through it we accurately interpret and relate the discoveries we have made in the archive. From this perspective the term 'narrative historian' really has no meaning because all historians tell stories about people in the past who themselves 'naturally' led narrativised lives. Adding the term narrative to historian is simply redundant. Life is narrative-shaped and so it can best be understood (and analysed) as a narrative (see BIOGRAPHY AND LIFE WRITING).

Working within this logic, form must follow the historian's avowed function, which is to truthfully explain the content of the past. It follows that, because life is narrativised, narrative possesses the power to disclose *the* story of the past as history – always presupposing that the proper methodological rules have been followed at the research and archival stage. Thus narrative does not present an obstacle, in the words of Peter Gay, to Ranke's 'celebrated wish to relate the past as it actually happened'; neither will it permit Ranke's history to be 'a fantasy nor a concealed ideology' (Gay 1988 [1974]: 199). As Gay describes it in evidencing the case of Gibbon, his 'ironic vision equipped him to penetrate the fraudulent machinations of Roman politicians, and the all-too-human pettiness of the Church Fathers' (ibid.: 199–200). If the intention of the historian is to get the story straight (as Ranke and Gibbon are presumed to have wished), then narrative construction will not get in the way of accessing the truth of the past. Indeed, for Gay, what makes the task of the historian special is the precise fact that his/her science is, and can only be transcripted as, a narrative couched in an appropriate style of rhetoric. Style and truth are compatible because, as Gay concludes, 'Style is the art of the historian's science' (ibid.: 217). For Gay form does indeed follow function – getting at *the* story and getting it straight.

This is a position famously established by William B. Gallie, that historical narratives may be judged correct inasmuch as we believe them to be 'supported on every main point by evidence of some kind' (Gallie 1964: 21). Gallie insists that there is only *one* true story to be discovered. By **inference** to the best explanation according to the evidence the historian can (if he/she does the job properly) reasonably expect to discover *the* particular

story-shape pre-existing in the past: the one and true emplotment. For Gallie historical understanding rests on the reader being able to follow *the* story so carefully reconstructed through the hard work of the historian actively seeking the truth as he/she arranges the facts according to the available evidence (ibid.: 105, 108) (see RECONSTRUCTIONIST HISTORY). The role of the historian as interpreter is, therefore, like that of the foreign-language translator (the past is a foreign language, not just a foreign country!), who renders the text as accurately as possible so that its true meaning will emerge. All this adds up to the fact that the historian's narrative conveys knowledge – it does not constitute it.

What then is narrative's relationship to the **discourse** of the historian (see NEW HISTORICISM)? From what I have said so far it would seem unproblematic. Put another way, we ought to know where exactly is the line between the discovery and constitution of knowledge in the historical narrative. Most historians, in accepting that history and narrative have much in common for the reason just noted, would also accept that because evidence is not a collection of building blocks past reality cannot be reconstructed unproblematically. But they would not endorse the claim of American philosopher of history Hayden **White** that attention to the way in which a historical narrative is constructed may tell us rather more about the historian's emplotment choices than about the past. Because of this, much mainstream **constructionist history** is built on the argument that it is better to relate the past in a non-narrative form. This has led many such historians to write the past in ways they believe break with the above description of narrative, that is, by means of thematic or concept-led approaches (see CONCEPTS IN HISTORY).

Needless to say, the truth-claims that 'non-narrative historians' make for their written history also remain intact. Indeed, some constructionist historians find it tempting to suggest an even higher level of truthfulness for their 'non-narrative historical analyses'. Marxists, for example, tend to hold that the complexities of the model(s) they construct out of the evidence allow for a complex structural and functional crosshatched historical explanation that is particularly faithful to the past as it actually happened. Marxist history, like virtually all other kinds of constructionist history, is thematic, topic- and/or concept-based, and often non-chronological. Even in such histories, however, I would suggest, following the work of the narrativist theorist Jerome Bruner, that there is an irreducible narrative dimension to our understanding of reality past or present (see Roland BARTHES; EPISTEME; Michel FOUCAULT; TROPE/FIGURATION) (Bruner 1990; 1992).

Like most aspects of what historians do, the role and functioning of narrative has been increasingly discussed of late, especially Gay's insistence that style is not necessarily incompatible with *the* truth, as well as Gallie's notion that the historian's narrative is capable of rendering *the* true story. Leaving aside the general and detailed criticisms of the representational and referential character of language that have surfaced as part of postmodern (see POSTMODERNISM) developments, and that highlight, among many other things, the **reality/realistic effect** of history writing and the possible incommensurability of style and truth, the major concerns about narrative have centred on its supposed inherent capacity for objectivity and 'truthful interpretation'. This focuses on the parallel that it is said can be reasonably assumed to exist between lived experience and its accurate representation (see POSTCOLONIAL HISTORY). Hence the greater the parallel the more truthful the historical knowledge. So just how adequate is the historical narrative as a form of explanation? To what extent does the narrative itself determine its content? To what degree does the historian impose a narrative on the past through the process of his/her emplotment?

We already have Gallie's answer to the question of the adequacy of narrative as historical explanation – generally it is adequate because the narrative and what actually happened share the same story-shape. This assumes that narrated conceptions of **intentionality** and **causation** operate in an isomorphic relationship (one-to-one correspondence of shape and structure) with their real counterparts. As already noted, it is a precondition of this view of historical narrative that the historian be omitted from the process except to acknowledge that it is he/she who is midwife to that culturally neutral isomorphic product called history. The fact that this is a rather difficult position to sustain has not deterred historians and a few philosophers of history from defending it. The question of whether viewing the historian as midwife undersells the extent of his/her interventionism in researching and then configuring the past, has engaged a good number of commentators ranging from those such as William B. Gallie, David Carr, Arthur Danto, William H. Dray, Andrew P. Norman, John E. Toews, Geoffrey Roberts, C. Behan McCullagh, M.C. Lemon, Dorothy Ross and Peter Munz – all of whom, in varying ways, accept that history is story-shaped and is recoverable through narrative pretty much as it actually happened – to others less convinced like Paul Veyne, Hayden White, Keith **Jenkins**, Louis Mink, Paul Ricoeur, Frank R. **Ankersmit** and Hans Kellner, Michel Foucault and Jacques **Derrida**.

The two at the extremes in this debate are David Carr and Hayden White. Both, as narrativists, insist that narrative and explanation are coincident. For Carr this is because narrative and real life are coterminous; for White it is because it is the preference of the historian to view them as such (see BIOGRAPHY AND LIFE WRITING). Both agree with Peter Munz's position that the past was once real, but that the stories historians tell about it are constructions (Munz 1997: 851–72). Where they differ is over the truthfulness of those constructions. In Carr's words the structure of narrative inheres 'in the events themselves' and, far from being any kind of distortion, a narrative account 'is an extension of one of their primary features' (D. Carr 1986a: 117). This is the isomorphic relationship – a community of form as Carr has it between action, event and the narrative constructed to explain them (ibid.: 117).

In opposition to this view Hayden White maintains that the past does not *necessarily* conform to a given, and therefore discoverable, 'true narrative'. He claims that we do not live stories; at best we give meaning to our lives by (retrospectively) casting them in the form of stories. It comes down to whether you believe the emplotment is discovered or imposed (or invented as White says) by the historian. In both cases the assumption is that the essence of the historical narrative is the historian's emplotment. Because the past for White is not shaped according to a given narrative that is discoverable through the evidence, then it is the historian who must provide it with the emplotment. Indeed, for White, the historian is more like an author and their emplotted historical narrative is, as a result, also an instrument of ideological construction. History is not only an emplotted narrative but, because it is the-past-as-history, it is also always a political text of dissent or affirmation even though its author may proclaim to be in pursuit of the truth. Historical narrative as it exists today is the result primarily of the bourgeois **Enlightenment** and its Marxist critique. White views both as efforts to control and domesticate the past either through the correspondence theory of knowledge (rather than aestheticism), or constructionism (rather than as an acknowledgement of the sublime and ineffable) (White 1987: 67–8). Neither view takes the cognitive nature of narrative adequately into their accounts; historians ought, therefore, to rethink the logic of history as that of narrative-making.

Further reading

Ankersmit, F.R., 2005b, 2001, 1994, 1983; Ankersmit, F.R. and Kellner, H., 1995; Bruner, J., 1992, 1990; Callinicos, A., 1995; Canary, R. and Kozicki, H., 1978; Carr, D., 1986a, 1986b; Chatman, S., 1978; Curthoys, A. and Docker, J., 1997; Danto, A., 1985; Derrida, J., 1979; Dray, W.H., 1970; Foucault, M., 1977; Friedlander, S., 1992; Gallie, W.B., 1964; Gay, P., 1988 [1974]; Genette, G., 1990 [1983]; Heise, U.K., 1997; Jenkins, K., 1995; Jenkins, K. and Munslow, A., 2004; Kellner, H., 1989; Klein, K., 1995; Lemon, M.C., 1995; Lipton, P., 1993; McCullagh, C.B., 1998, 1984; Maza, S., 1996; Mink, L., 1978, 1970; Munslow, A., 2003b, 1997a, 1992; Munslow, A. and Rosenstone, R.A., 2004; Munz, P., 1997; Norman, A.P., 1991; Ricoeur, P., 1984, 1985; Roberts, G., 1996; Ross, D., 1995; Stone, L., 1979; Toews, J.E., 1987; Veyne, P., 1984; White, H., 1998, 1987, 1984, 1978, 1973b; Zagorin, P., 1999.

NEW HISTORICISM

Historicism has been defined (ignoring Karl Popper's definition) as the belief that all knowledge, including 'historical knowledge', is time- and place-specific. It follows that such knowledge is epistemologically relativist inasmuch as we can only represent such knowledge as 'the-past-as-history' (see EPISTEMOLOGY; RELATIVISM; Richard RORTY; Keith JENKINS; LINGUISTIC TURN; AESTHETIC TURN; REPRESENTATION; OBJECTIVITY; Frank. R. ANKERSMIT; TRUTH; Hayden WHITE; Michel FOUCAULT; Roland BARTHES; POST-STRUCTURALISM). This means that historical knowledge is always opaque and presentist. This has led a good many historians and cultural critics to think about and practice history experimentally in a variety of new forms of which the new cultural history is one (see, for example, the journals *Common Knowledge, History and Theory, Representations, Rethinking History: The Journal of Theory and Practice* and *Culture, Theory and Critique;* there are also many others).

The perennial issue of 'history as representation' and the disputed nature of originary knowledge lead us, therefore, to the 'New Historicism' defined as a broad intellectual movement across literature, politics, art, anthropology and history that recognises and explores the consequences of the inescapable nature of representation by viewing cultural change through its 'poetics'. As the anthropologist Clifford Geertz famously argued over thirty years ago, society is an ensemble of texts, which are in turn ensembles. Reading textuality and symbolism is now popular among social scientists and humanists in trying to understand cultural change past and present. New Historicism is a way of exploring the constructed nature of cultural discourses and practices through literature (factual and fictional can be read as textual practices) and other forms of media. This acknowledges and relies on the notion of 'intertextuality'. By this is meant the reading of a text (which is now defined more widely as a cultural practice rather than just a written text) 'against' others. This is done in order to work out what they have in common in terms of the power and ideological connections which are not always that obvious when read in 'realist' or materialist terms. Reference 'hides' reality. Hence no text is autonomous or 'out of or distanced from history/language/**discourse**'. Hence we have the collapse of disciplinary boundaries, the rise of challenges to a variety of **genre** definitions, the redefinition of the **author**, etc. As for history, when it is 'read intertextually' it is no longer a self-contained, authorially independent, ideologically freed, empirically driven, 'out of time and place' objective and largely unproblematically truthful 'insight' into the reality of the past (see EMPIRICISM; MODERNISM).

The implication of all this for history is substantial and can be summarised as producing five consequences. First, and perhaps most dramatically, it removes history from any privileged position vis-à-vis 'the past'. 'History' is now seen as just another text *about* the past of which there are a good many available today and probably more will emerge in time. While conventional (modernist) notions of history rely upon honouring its referential and rational orientation, once it is accepted that its meaning flows from its intertextuality this privileging ceases (see INFERENCE; SOURCES; MIMESIS). This is never to deny the utility or importance of reference to the archive – but merely reminds us that all such referencing is to be understood intertextually. Second, it directs our attention to history as what it palpably is, a piece of literature. As such history can be viewed as both connoting (implying meaning) as well as denoting (apparent factual meaning). Connotation in history is the realm of further associations that a referent/historical concept possesses beyond its 'accepted' definition. Hence when a historian talks about a 'shift' in a government's policy this is more than a simple denotation. It carries more 'textual meaning' – ideologically and possibly emotionally – in the mind of the reader than the reference to 'what happened'. Third, it locates the historian/author at the centre of the 'knowing what the past means' process through their choice of language. Conventionally the historian writes as if she or he is legitimating the weight of *the* 'given meaning of the past', *the* story. Historians are viewed as merely allowing the past to speak again (and for itself). Now, however, the historian is heavily implicated (as a participant) in creating the text and, therefore, what it might mean, though 'according to the evidence'. But our postmodern situation requires us to acknowledge the historian-as-author. This leads directly to the fourth outcome of 'reading history' as a text. This is, by definition, the direct inclusion of the reader/audience/viewer in the process of 'making sense' of what the historian intends to tell us about the past. Once we doubt that the historian is offering us the real (or even the most likely) meaning of the past then we are all drawn into the construction of history's meaning as a text. Following Roland Barthes' arguments history cannot be viewed as ever producing a finished reading. History is never just a 'readerly text' that offers a given and unalterable meaning, but it is always 'writerly' whereby the reader can 'overwrite' or even reformat it. So, finally, given the reader's cultural and ideological context we now have a new economy of participation, as readers of history splice themselves into the meaning of the past. As there is no discourse, whether imaginative or referential, that gives us access to 'truthful knowing', we must take responsibility for our complicity in creating a meaning for the past.

If you accept the assumptions upon which 'intertextuality' works, these five consequences reveal something of the crisis that has afflicted modernist conceptions of history in the past thirty years or so. Of course, if you choose not to accept the assumptions then you will be likely to ask what crisis 'the post-modernists' are talking about and be inclined to say 'let's get back to the archive and get on with doing history'. But it seems doubtful that developments such as new historicism have left or will leave conventional empirical-analytical notions of history unchallenged and, therefore, unchanged. The rise of the new cultural history has demonstrated that there is little fear that history, as a professional practice, will disappear (though some commentators like Keith Jenkins would have welcomed such a development). Perhaps in part because of, or despite, this critique, the thinking and practice of history has changed immeasurably in the last generation. Yet there remains, as Ricoeur has tried to demonstrate in his analysis of mimesis, a strong belief in agency/structure, and in a knowable past that can be inherited and represented adequately by us. If we no longer have *the* story, historians will still strive to create plausible other stories – and still deploy detailed reference to the past.

Further reading

Bann, S., 1984, 1983; Berkhofer, R.F., 1995; Burke, P., 1997; Cannadine, D., 2002; Carrard, P., 1992; Chartier, R., 1997; Gallagher, C. and Greenblatt, S., 2000; Geertz, C., 1983, 1973; Hunt, L., 1989; Kloppenberg, J.T., 1989; Maza, S., 1996; Munslow, A., 1992; Palmer, B., 1990; Pittock, J.H. and Wear, A., 1991; Poster, M., 1997; Veeser, A.A., 1989; White, H., 1987, 1978.

NEW HISTORY

It seems that every generation of historians produces a 'new history'. And every generation says to itself that the realm of historical study is expanding at a dizzying rate (Burke 1991: 1). Every so often there appears a spate of books that survey the historical scene and usually conclude that it is both refreshed and vigorous. Our own period is, however, different because of the extensive critique of history from an epistemologically sceptical perspective (see EPISTEMOLOGY; META-NARRATIVE; ONTOLOGY; POSTMOD-ERNISM). For the first time there has been a sea change from all the previous 'new histories' that have tended to be about 'new approaches', or 'new methodologies', or 'new theories', or 'new orientations', or 'new tendencies' but never before has there been a debate over the rejection of epistemology. Take, for example, the 'new history' that emerged in the United States around the end of the nineteenth and start of the twentieth centuries (Novick 1988: 86–108). Perhaps because he was writing from the perspective of the late 1980s and well into the debates over postmodernism and history, Peter Novick detected no direct challenge to the then turn-of-the-century 'prevailing norm of **objectivity**', though he thinks he sees a subtle undermining of the idea (ibid.: 87). However, this does not seem particularly convincing from the point of view of epistemic sceptics today as, arguably, it was not until the 1970s and later that the notions of objectivity and **truth** were challenged within the profession.

At any rate, Novick notes how the turn-of-the-century debate among US historians was over the so-called 'germ theory' of Teutonic origins of American cultural and historical development. Essentially the popular theory of US and English democratic and liberal institutions was that they developed from an institutional germ, which grew in the long distant forests of Germany and was carried to England in the fifth and sixth centuries. By exterminating the Celtic heritage the Teutonic germ eventually migrated to America to emerge in the 'town meeting'. This was the generally accepted theory for explaining American history by the 1880s. Then along came Frederick Jackson Turner's alternative explanation with his homespun US 'Frontier Thesis' of expansion westwards and the 'free land' that was available. According to this 'theory' (given in 1893 in a lecture before the American Historical Association) American history was home-grown and with his theory he attempted to elevate the national character-shaping effect of the advance westwards of the frontier – a wilderness history for the United States. Now, while this was a dramatic re-orientation of the origins of American national history and it was also cast in the early stages of what became known as 'The New History', which dramatically extended the range and scope of US historians' interests beyond the political, it hardly constituted what today might be regarded as a genuinely 'new history'.

Turner appeared to be establishing something radically new in what turned out to be an interdisciplinary and social science approach to the past with his emphasis on joining environment, geography, culture and thought. And because Turner was extending the **discourse** of history beyond the political and constitutional it was claimed that he threatened objectivity. From our perspective this is hard to credit. But as with all apparent threats to the sway of empiricism and the notion that historians 'select' **evidence**, the reaction especially among the historical establishment was one of shock and horror. However, the reaction of the Turner-inspired other 'new historians', like James Harvey Robinson, Charles Beard and Carl **Becker**, was unapologetic. Not only did they encompass a fresh social science methodological

approach to the past, they were also plainly ideologically committed to liberal reformism. The new historians who were also called Progressive Historians did their history with the 'common man' in mind. The message of Turner, that each age writes history anew with reference to the conditions of its own time, was clear. As he said in his 1910 American Historical Association Presidential Address (sometimes radicals get into the establishment) he was not surprised that socialism showed noteworthy electoral gains as well as the popular demands for political reforms, because they were efforts to find substitutes for what had been the former safeguard of democracy – the now disappearing free land of the West. Moreover, Turner went on to point out that history is not simply the effort to 'tell the thing exactly as it was' because of the needs of contemporary society. Though not providing an obvious challenge to empiricism, Turner was clearly indicating the **historicist** nature of historical inquiry.

As this example indicates, history is subject to the fads (if not the fancies) of historians, and what they perceive to be the needs of society. But it is also self-conscious as to the needs and functions of the discipline itself. There are many examples of 'new histories' that were and are overtly concerned to 'do history' differently. Examples would include the French **Annales** School starting in the 1920s and continuing up to the present, the old and new economic histories (see CLIOMETRICS) from the pre- and post-1960s, the new social history from the 1960s, the rise of **women's history** and then **gender** history from the 1970s, the French *nouvelle histoire* (the new history) from the late 1970s, the emergence of **Post-Marxism**, the appearance of cultural history from the 1980s and its more recent incarnation as the New Cultural History. However, the latest manifestation of a new history – in the United Kingdom – is the self-conscious, self-proclaimed and deliberate effort to reinvigorate 'the discipline in the wake of the epistemological challenges that have brought into question many of the foundational assumptions of historians' (Editorial: *Cultural and Social History* 2004: 1).

Published by the Social History Society (itself not founded until 1976) in the United Kingdom, the journal *Cultural and Social History* (2004 onwards) grew out of the Society's *Bulletin* and is now establishing itself as a platform for bringing together cultural and social history, and also responding to the latest 'new history' and 'postsocial history', which has been generated by our condition of epistemic scepticism (that is emblematic of our postmodern circumstance). Sounding somewhat recherché to a postmodern ear, in its first editorial, while proclaiming the need to incorporate the cultural in the social (and vice versa), it commits itself to 'the craft' of history (Editorial: *Cultural and Social History* 2004: 5). Trying to be both all-inclusive and all things to all social and cultural historians, the journal welcomes discussion but shuns 'unnecessary polemic' (warning off postmodernist wreckers?). Whether this will turn out to be a forlorn hope remains to be seen, though it did publish Peter Mandler's realist defence of cultural history method which he elected to cast in the trope of ennui, saying, 'It seems to me . . . that most of us are exhausted . . . Tired of hearing over and over again how little we know and how little we can say, we are ready for a compromise, to begin reconstructing what we can know . . .'. (*Cultural and Social History*, 2004: 1: 94) (see RECONSTRUCTIONIST HISTORY). This was followed in the second issue by Carla Hesse's commentary on Mandler's piece ('The new empiricism', *Cultural and Social History*, 2004: 1: 2: 201–7) in which she tried to make that compromise between 'realist and anti-realist practitioners of cultural history' by proclaiming herself to be a 'chastened realist', one who is aware of the dangers of reverting to naïve empiricism and the intellectual world before what she called the discursive turn (see CONSTRUCTIONIST HISTORY; DECONSTRUCTIONIST HISTORY). If this 'new (combined social and cultural) history' is to thrive it might be better for its adherents to argue (in language and sentiment similar to that of George Santayana) that if epistemological scepticism is the chastity of the historian's intellect it should not be given up until it can be securely exchanged for fidelity or happiness. In the interim, we all await the next 'new history'. There is bound to be one.

Further reading
Bentley, M., 1997; Black, J. and MacRaild, D., 1997; Burke, P., 1991; Cabrera, M.A., 2004; Editorial: *Cultural and Social History* 2004; Hesse, C., 2004; Joyce, P., 2002, 1998, 1995, 1994, 1991a; Kammen, M., 1980; Mandler, P., 2004; Munslow, A., 2003b, 1992, 1986; Novick, P., 1988.

NIETZSCHE, FRIEDRICH (1844–1900)

Some of the ideas of the German philosopher Friedrich Nietzsche have been particularly important to historians in the late twentieth century. His interpretation of Immanuel **Kant** to argue in favour of perspectivism (*not* to be confused with **relativism**) is especially significant for a re-casting of the nature of history and what it is that historians do. Essentially Nietzsche suggests that our categories or forms of knowing have no transcendent or universal validity, and **concepts in history** are interpretations largely determined by our cultural situatedness, perspective and/or bias. Nietzsche concluded that there are no absolutes, no origins, no **facts**, no answers, no given meaning; that all is fiction, all is false, and all attempts to organise and systematise knowledge are merely expressions of a will to control (which he described as the Will to Power). His famous claim that God is dead in *The Gay Science* (1882) refers to this belief that there is no longer any absolute authority for **truth** (faith in God equals truth). This constitutes a wholesale rejection of **modernism** and the **Enlightenment** project.

Nietzsche's approach to philosophy, history and life was one of irony and scepticism. In *On the Genealogy of Morality: A Polemic* (1887) he claims that scepticism sprang up in his life 'so early, so unbidden, so unstoppably, and which was in such conflict with my surroundings, age, precedents and lineage that I would almost be justified in calling it my "a priori"' (Ansell-Pearson 1994a: 4–5) (see A PRIORI/A POSTERIORI). Such a comment served clear notice of his opinion of Kant, modernism and rationality. There is also a strong tongue-in-cheek sense, as the American philosopher of history Hayden **White** argues, of Nietzsche's self-awareness of the fictive nature of his ironic perceptions (White 1973b: 69), and how this translates into his belief in the fictive nature of the historical enterprise. In his second text, *Unfashionable Observation* (1874), for example, Nietzsche questioned whether or not historical knowledge was in and of itself useful. He concluded that it was, but only when it was pursued, not for its own sake, but as an art form that can allow us to forget! Such a position is profoundly antagonistic to the modernist conception of history as the way to the truth. Although Nietzsche continued to believe that research in the archive could lead to the de-bunking of myths (i.e. religion), the general tenor of his unfashionable observations sets the stage for his career attitude toward history and historians.

Interestingly, given the emphasis Nietzsche always placed on language as an obstacle to knowledge, his written style is difficult (see LINGUISTIC TURN; AESTHETIC TURN). His aphoristic style emerged first in *Human, All Too Human* (1878/79), which he later acknowledged ironically by claiming that one needed 'to be a cow' rather than a 'modern man' to read him, by which he meant that we have to acquire the power of 'rumination' (Ansell-Pearson 1994a: 10). Though difficult and idiosyncratic, his narrative style is the perfect vehicle for his philosophy of history. As he breaks the literary philosophical conventions Nietzsche's contribution to the study of history is revealed to be important because his written form reinforces notions that are a direct challenge to the very concepts and language in which Enlightenment or modernist (especially Kantian) philosophy poses its problems. Put straightforwardly, Nietzsche maintained that the rational analysis of the world – such as that claimed by Kant – could not resolve all problems of knowledge; indeed rationality and language soon reveal their severe limitations.

Most significantly for historians, Nietzsche argues that what we take as fact is actually nothing more than a layered earlier interpretation that has somehow managed to throw off its referent, be it empirical or interpretative. He was, of course, particularly scathing about the Christian religion in this respect, maintaining that Christian moral precepts were merely conveniences to make life more tolerable for the mass of people (which he metamorphosed as the herd, and for whose moral behaviour he coined the term the 'herd instinct'), or to constrain those who would otherwise rightly reject organised religion's proclaimed moral Christian universalism (the *Übermensch*).

So the universal or transcendental categories that Kant proposed (like space, time, perception and causality), because they are valid for all rational people (subjects), are consequently objective, are rejected or literally deconstructed by Nietzsche. He claims that Kant's a priori categories have no foundation except in other than cultural convention. This means they are ultimately arbitrary. They are interpretations or value positions dependent upon personal perspective, psychological need, ideological orientation, desire for power and/or cultural situation. What often confuses is the fact that, in addition, certain positions/ interpretations become fixed over time. Particularly where certain key cultural texts are concerned, they can become concretised as 'facts'. As already noted, they lose their interpretative anchorage. Nietzsche uses what he calls his genealogical method to demonstrate this process of how 'facts' are really unavowed interpretations (see Michel FOUCAULT). *The* facts cannot exist, and no single interpretation can be definitive; hence there is no such thing as *the* text. For Nietzsche both **form and content** and, therefore, all meaning are attempts to impose an order on our experience (see AESTHETIC TURN). In respect of history, Nietzsche was determined to view it as an act of tragic aestheticism, as in 'Use and abuse of history' (1874). Why? Because he conceived the **emplotment** of Tragedy as the best means available to demolish the idea of an objective stance from which historians can access truth.

We should be aware, therefore, that any methodology or **epistemology** is in practice *free to claim access* to the real world if it so wishes, and we should be wary of all that do, because there are no universally valid perspectives. We cannot peer round our forms to see what is actually happening. We must, of need, treat all claims to *the* truth with scepticism. This means there are no disinterested historians, no historical concepts that can lay a claim to reconstructing the past as it actually was, and no historical method (construed literally as a metahistorical method) that can overcome this perspectival condition of knowledge (see CONSTRUCTIONIST HISTORY; DECONSTRUCTIONIST HISTORY; RECONSTRUCTIONIST HISTORY). The apparent success of **empiricism** (with its disinterested historians on a voyage of discovery in the archive) resides not in its access to *the* truth, but because it has successfully supported the modernist bourgeois power superstructure that has grown up in Western society. Indeed, it is because of empiricism's referential claims to a knowable independent reality and the common-sense correspondence of the word and the world that it has ensured the survival of that culture. This is why it remains so central to it. But, for proper historians, because Nietzsche casts his dismissal within his own peculiar history of morality (in *The Genealogy of Morals* (1887), in which he argued against a foundationalist goodness in humanity), his view of historical

knowing seems to sanction (under the appeal to truth) any old nonsense cast as morality and history. Ironically, of course, this is probably the point Nietzsche is making.

The further response of proper historians is that even if we grant that truth (truthful historical interpretation) is indeed influenced by a Will to Power or by personal or ideological preference, this does not *necessarily* mean that the correspondence theory is wrong. The existence of a particular **teleology** (history written with an end product in mind) does not mean that we cannot hold up a mirror to nature (see MIMESIS). Another flaw in Nietzsche's position is also fairly obvious. Every time we point out that there is no absolute truth because everything is perspectival, surely we have to do so from our own particular point of origin – the self-conscious, rational, knowing subject? So, as we claim there is no truth, we are making a claim that we believe to be truthful! In postmodern (see POSTMODERNISM) terms, of course, the decentred subject does not, *in fact*, exist. For Nietzsche the truthfulness of this resounds in the Will to Power, by which I think he means that no interpretation can be an impartial reflector of the facts – especially given they do not exist anyway. We get out of the text what we put into it. What we get out of the past is the history we put into it.

Nevertheless, Nietzsche's view that truth is perspectival resounds in a profoundly imaginative and interpretational discipline like history (see HISTORICAL IMAGINATION). In his rejection of the *error* of the 'old conceptual fairy-tale' (Ansell-Pearson 1994a: 92) of the rational knowing subject of knowledge in favour of the realm where reason is firmly excluded, it may become more difficult to sustain the idea of history as being merely the accurate and literal translation of the archive. For Nietzsche (as later for Jacques DERRIDA) the pursuit of knowledge is forever clouded by its embedded linguistic and specifically metaphoric structure. What we take to be our knowledge of the world (and the past), derived from the correlation of empiricism and conceptualisation, is merely the collected tropic conventions of representation (see TROPE/FIGURATION; REPRESENTA-TION). To grasp what is the past, we have first to understand that history is merely an invented match between facsimile and concept. There is no extra-linguistic platform upon which we can stand in order to exert leverage on reality.

Nietzsche's attitude to language was that it seduced humanity into a dream-like state with which we cloak the horrors of everyday existence. We have art so as not to die of the truth, that is, knowing there is no truth. All forms of knowing are ultimately metaphoric, and phenomena simply exist as images possessing no referentiality beyond themselves. Debating the epistemological bases of history, as Nietzsche does, eventually means addressing – as many have done – the narrative form of historical writing and the **metanarrative** form of historical study. Practical realists accept the reconstructionist position of knowing that the past as it actually was is not tenable. They tend to do so, however, on grounds that explicitly reject Nietzsche's sceptical arguments. Certainty, it is accepted, is not possible in history because it is always a second-hand and interpretative experience, and the historical narrative is never a perfectly reflective mirror. But **objectivity** is possible because of rational Kantian categories of knowing, which are themselves reflective of the reality out there. There is, consequently, a high correlation between form and content. While there may be something of a fissure between the word and the world, this does not mean, as Nietzsche seems to be saying, that there must be ontological uncertainty (about our state of being) (see ONTOLOGY).

Apart from the rump of hard-hat reconstructionists, most historians accept that the notion of truthful interpretation reads somewhat more awkwardly these days than previously, when history was unembarrassingly in the grip of unreflective empiricism, covering laws, the social sciences and **cliometrics** (see POSITIVISM). The Nietzschean

world-view has had its impact – one where it is agreed that objective truth is impossible because no system or historical methodology can guarantee truth. While we may not exist in a constant flux of being, it follows that while historians generally still prefer to imagine history as rooted in the evidence of a knowable external reality, the line between fact and interpretation is often too fine to draw with certainty.

The point at issue is not just that everything is interpretation. It is that some interpretations and meanings, under the hand of historians and because of the way we use language (subject–predicate, correspondence of sign and signifier), take on the appearance of facts. Interpretations like the Cold War, the Industrial Revolution, the war on terror and the Monroe Doctrine – but much worse, interpretative concepts like **class**, **intentionality** and **evidence** – have become facts. The **discourse** of constructionist history in particular is prone to confusing facts with concepts. The metaphoric nature of language means reality and, therefore, truth are not directly or objectively accessible. As Nietzsche famously claims, truth is a 'mobile marching army of metaphors, metonymies and anthropomorphisms' (Norris 1982: 58). Because of this, the story offered about the past by the historian is imposed as he/she looks at his/her own life and the ideology he/she serves. **Historiography** becomes history. History, as the ultimate form of knowing and sense of what we want from the future, is thus imposed on an unknowable past. The irony is that because the past becomes the subject of history, so it can be emplotted however the historian chooses, with whatever ending he/she has in mind (see EMPLOTMENT).

Further reading
Ansell-Pearson, K., 1994a, 1994b; Danto, A., 1965; Derrida, J., 1979; Magnus, B., 1993; Magnus, B. and Higgins, K.M., 1996; Megill, A., 1985; Nehamas, A., 1985; Norris, C., 1982; Rabinow, P., 1999; White, H., 1973b.

O

OBJECTIVITY

In the early 1970s the Belgian literary critic and philosopher Paul de Man argued famously that the bases for historical knowledge are not **facts** but written texts, even if they masquerade as wars or revolutions (see Carl BECKER; NEW HISTORY). Shortly after that bald deconstructionist (see DECONSTRUCTIONIST HISTORY) pronouncement Hayden **White's** book, *Metahistory*, appeared with its now famous message that writing history is about configuring stories as we order the **events** of the past, not about objectively discovering *the* given **truth** that is presumed to exist in the past (White 1973b). This judgement is central to deconstructionist history and the **linguistic turn**, being not just another theory or conceptualisation about how we do history but commentary on the present conditions in which we generate historical knowledge.

White's argument would not persuade all historians, largely because the concept of objectivity is not regarded as a disputable concept in history (see CONCEPTS IN HISTORY). However, I would suggest it has several different meanings. At the naïve extreme of **reconstructionist history** it means the pursuit of genuine knowledge of the past thing-in-itself, and the translation of this knowledge (of the past as it actually happened) into an accurate and unbiased historical **narrative** based on the sources (see EMPIRICISM). At this extreme, objectivity and historical truth are synonymous. This is revealed in the strange case of the effacement of the historian from the written text. Objectivity is thereby regarded as a function of proper historical thinking. The realist philosopher of history C. Behan McCullagh offers us a clear summary of how to achieve a state of reconstructionist history objectivity when he says 'Most historians . . . see themselves as trying to discover what actually happened in the past' and why historians 'pay such attention to the accuracy of their observations of evidence and to the adequacy of their inferences from it, and why they refuse to put forward any descriptions of the past for which there is not good evidence' (McCullagh 1984: 2) (see INFERENCE).

Most constructionist historians (see CONSTRUCTIONIST HISTORY) (those within the practical realist mainstream) view objectivity as somewhat less cut and dried than McCullagh seems to think it is, but still have an investment in conceiving objectivity as the opposite of **relativism**, which is viewed as an attack on truthful knowing. This is the vision of E.H. **Carr** and the American social and cultural historians Joyce Appleby, Lynn Hunt and Margaret Jacob (Appleby *et al.* 1994: 241–70). Appleby, Hunt and Jacob elect to defend what they maintain is the sensible constructionist middle-ground, warning against the 'fluid scepticism' that now appears to cover 'the intellectual landscape' (ibid.: 243) and denies the goals of truth-seeking and objectivity. The roots of this are supposed to be those disillusioned social and historical constructionists and deconstructionists who recklessly doubt that a knowable reality exists, and/or that the world can indeed be mind-independent. While acknowledging the subjectivity of much historical interpretation Appleby *et al.* maintain a core belief in the referentiality of the historical narrative (the accuracy and completeness of the observations rather than the perspective of the historian) that ultimately guarantees its veracity, accuracy and objectivity (see JUSTIFIED BELIEF). While a gap undoubtedly exists between the record and the interpretation, this does not cast us into a state of ontological relativism with an inability to judge reality from fiction, or mean that no knowable referential correspondence exists between the word and the world (see ONTOLOGY).

Upon what basis do naïve and/or practical realists still claim genuine historical knowledge (see EPISTEMOLOGY)? There are three epistemological principles of standard history: namely, the belief that the past once really existed; that that which constitutes historical truth is found in the correspondence of the historians' facts to that reality through the empirical reconstruction of agent **intentionality**; and that the facts precede interpretation, confirming the process of inference as central to historical interpretation (except when social-theory constructionists argue that inductive and deductive reasoning cannot operate independently). The four corollaries to these three principles are that there is a clear division between fact and value, that history and fiction are not the same, that there is a clear separation between the knower and the known, and that truth is not perspectival. The adherence to these principles with their corollaries determines the understanding of objectivity in historical practice, and together is taken to constitute the objectivisation of the-past-as-history.

Having said that, the post-empiricist challenge's success is evidenced by the fact that very few historians today accept these principles and corollaries at face value. To do so would be to endorse a naïve if not brutal realism that ill fits the sophisticated levels of analysis to which most historians aspire. The majority of historians are empiricist (rather than epistemological) sceptics. As Mark Bevir has suggested, historians know they make observations under the influence of their current opinions, and that the facts of history are

ultimately squeezed out through the mental filter of categories of analysis and a priori (see A PRIORI/A POSTERIORI) theories (Bevir 1994). The realist-inspired philosopher David Cockburn endorses this view, arguing in favour of a qualified realism, promoting a historian's emotional sensitivity that does not preclude a rendering of the past faithfully (Cockburn 1997). Cockburn's position is that of most constructionist historians. It is predicated on a perception of **evidence** not as statements of reality, but as collectivities of **sources** from which we can infer their true meaning by verification and comparison within a known context and through the use of appropriate social theory. Our knowledge may not be direct, but it can be truthful (ibid.: 247–8).

Historians may, therefore, distinguish factual from normative (assumptive) statements in their work, that is, recognise the two planes of the historical enterprise: research and the narrative explanation of what it means. However, as we know, facts alone cannot determine historical understanding. As a hermeneutic process (an act of textual interpretation) history is subject to the ontological beliefs held about society by historians, and to the ideologies to which they subscribe, and to what they anticipate their audience will wish to hear and/or read (see HERMENEUTICS). These expectations usually translate into beliefs about the nature of **causation** and of the character of temporal change. It is at this second level of interpretative statement that the conflict of objectivism couched as realism and relativism arise.

It seems clear that, while historical understanding is not viewed as a rough and ready empirical enterprise, most historians still follow E.H. Carr and Appleby, Hunt and Jacob in drawing back from the logic of their thinking. As practical realists most historians argue that the reality of the past is prefigured by reference to the evidence and not by the fictive narrative inventions of historians as Hayden White would have us believe. History is generated by *the* narratives inherent in the evidence of the past, what the

American historian Sarah Maza has called 'stories in history' (Maza 1996: 1493). The historian-observer relates *the* story that he/she has sensitively witnessed in the evidence rather than authored and on which he/she has placed no prior value (see AUTHOR). This echoes British historian Geoffrey Roberts's argument that there are 'real stories in the past to which historical narratives can correspond, and the narrative structures . . . of historians . . . mimic or resemble the action/story/narrative of past happenings' (G. Roberts 1997: 257). This is a classic statement of history as **mimesis**.

Ultimately, then, the purpose remains the same even if the standard model has been modified. History remains about discovering, as the philosopher William Gallie insists, *the* real story that is then retold *accurately* (Gallie 1964: 105; Mink 1978: 129–49; D. Carr 1986a: 117–31). The narrative is discovered by the historian in the events themselves and is objective and realistic because, as realist philosopher of history George Iggers confirms, it possesses referentiality (Iggers 1997: 12). The American philosopher of history David Carr summarises this view with his conviction that there is a correspondence between history as it is lived (*the* past) and history as it is written (*the* narrative). Narrative and history are homologous.

But as the philosopher Martin Bunzl asks, can we leave 'the status of facts undisturbed' when we turn to the consideration of writing history (Bunzl 1997: 27; M. Roberts 2004: 233–4)? How reasonable is it to expect that narrative historical interpretations are likely to be correct, not because we have generated factual accuracy, but because our lives are narrativised and the past itself conforms to the discoverable structure of narrative? Are past lives story-shaped? It is an important question if you choose to believe that historians impose stories rather than 'discover' stories that have hitherto lain hidden from history, but which nevertheless pre-exist as cultural narratives, either as Maza's stories in history, or as White's figuratively determined emplotted historian's narratives (see EMPLOTMENT; TROPE/FIGURATION).

White reverses the Maza position, arguing that the narrative does not pre-exist but a narrative is invented and provided by the historian. Of course the situation is complicated by the fact that the historian's narrative may itself be culturally provided because it at present exists intertextually as a cultural discourse (see EPISTEME; Michel FOUCAULT; NEW HISTORICISM). Consequently, for White, there are many different yet equally legitimate stories to be told about the same facts, the same events, the same past. While still constrained by what actually happened, as the French historian Paul Veyne suggests, the meaning of history as a story comes from a plot, which is imposed, or as Hayden White insists invented, as much as found by the historian (Veyne 1984; White 1978: 82).

Hayden White's point, which he made almost thirty years ago, has now become a commonplace assumption for many historians, that when we attempt to explain the facts of the French Revolution or decline of the Roman Empire, 'What is at issue . . . is not What are the facts? but rather, How are the facts to be described in order to sanction one mode of explaining them rather than another?' (White 1978: 134; M. Roberts 2004: 233–4). White is suggesting here that facts are far more complex than McCullagh, for example, imagines. In the view of White historical facts are always constituted a second time in the form of a rhetorical or narrative structure that is invariably written for a particular purpose – hence his well-known emphasis on the content of the form (see FORM AND CONTENT; FILM AND HISTORY).

Such a prefigured emplotment may well be the wish to 'discover' the 'real' cultural narratives that existed in the past. Arguably this has been the agenda of cultural historians like Judith Walkowitz with her narratives of sexual danger (Walkowitz 1992), Elizabeth

Deeds Ermarth and her disquisitions on time (Ermarth 1992), Natalie Zemon Davis's pardon tales from sixteenth-century France (Davis 1987a) or Mary Poovey's deconstructive feminism (Poovey 1988), while even more open to the sublime and self-reflexive nature of the historical enterprise is Robert Rosenstone's multi-voiced study of cultural engagement between the United States and Meiji Japan (Rosenstone 1988) (see EXPERIMENTAL HISTORY).

If it is as much at the level of writing as at that of research that understanding and meaning are created, a **reality/realistic effect** may thus be generated as we emplot the past (see Roland BARTHES). No matter how well done is our technical recovery/discovery of the past in the verification and authentication of sources, or in the contextualising process, or in the accurate rendition of the meaning of individual texts or, for that matter, in the recovery of author intentionality and/or agent action in our creation of historical facts, it may be that unless we accept the realist narrative conception – that *the* story pre-exists in *the* action – *a* meaning is always going to be imposed by an ideologically aligned and rhetorically and/or socially theoreticised constructionist historian.

Where then is the objectivity and guarantee of truth in this? I submit that any truth that we can find is at best an epistemological truth. Any corroborated evidence-based historical narrative on the political career of 1930s and 1940s would-be US president Thomas E. Dewey has referentiality and is in an obvious sense objectively true. But it is only an epistemic truth. If we pose questions of meaning – what is the meaning of Dewey's career? – then such a question still has referentiality but cannot be answered cognitively. When we put real events into an interpretative narrative we shift to another plane of knowledge creation because we are creating meaning within a larger cultural and intellectual discourse.

If we reject the correspondence theory with its assumption that our forensic scrutiny of the evidence somehow ensures that our

descriptions refer accurately to their presumed inherent narrative shape, then our image of the historian as the impartial observer, ultimately unmoved by his/her situatedness and simply relating the facts, requires me to ask how many of us do believe we are writing *the* story, whether it be national, **feminist**, subaltern or **class**, rather than *a* story.

The debate on objectivity and the written historical narrative resolves no questions. It does not invalidate the pursuit of objectivity, truth and the self-effacement of the historian (should that be what you want). It merely exposes the limits of these aims. Whether an event was real or not is no longer relevant when it is placed in a narrative, unless one believes the past possesses, or is shaped according to, one particular story. All historical narratives in that sense are fictional artifice, quite unverifiable at the ontological level for their objectivity or their truthfulness. From this perspective, I submit, the principles and corollaries of standard history start to look even more precarious than before.

Further reading
Ankersmit, F.R., 1994; Appleby, J. *et al.*, 1994; Bevir, M., 1994; Bunzl, M., 1997; Burke, P., 1997; Callinicos, A., 1995; Carr, D., 1986a; Cockburn, D., 1997; Davis, N.Z., 1987; Ermarth, E.D., 1992; Evans, R.J., 1997a; Forum 1991; Gallie, W.B., 1964; Iggers, G., 1997; Lorenz, C., 1994; McCullagh, C.B., 1991, 1984; Maza, S., 1996; Mink, L., 1978; Munslow, A., 2002, 1997a, 1992; Novick, P., 1988; Poovey, M., 1988; Popper, K., 1979; Roberts, G., 1997; Roberts, M., 2004; Rorty, R., 1991; Rosenstone, R.A., 1996, 1988; Sellars, W., 1997 [1956]; Veyne, P., 1984; Walkowitz, J., 1992; White, H., 1978, 1973b.

ONTOLOGY

Rather too many historians, while they may be methodologically sophisticated, still tend to share the naïve empiricist (see

EMPIRICISM) reconstructionist (see RECONSTRUCTIONIST HISTORY) suspicion of philosophy fostered by, variously, Geoffrey **Elton**, Keith Windschuttle, Jack Hexter, Gertrude Himmelfarb, Arthur Marwick, Richard Evans, Neville Kirk and Peter Mandler. Many within the profession endorse their collective misgivings about what Elton has called the dangerous cocktail of German philosophy and French *esprit*, by which I think he meant idealism and twentieth-century **continental philosophy** (see CRITICAL THEORY). In addition to dubious and doubtful thinkers like Martin Heidegger, Theodor Adorno, Hans-Georg Gadamer, Roland **Barthes**, Jacques **Derrida**, Hayden **White** and Michel **Foucault,** the naïve empiricists have also named and shamed Benedetto **Croce**, R.G. **Collingwood**, E.H. **Carr**, Robert A. Rosenstone, Keith **Jenkins**, Frank R. **Ankersmit** and even occasionally your author (although I have just the odd walk-on part). Elton *et al.* reject critical theory, **hermeneutics**, **structuralism** and deconstructionism (see DECONSTRUCTIONIST HISTORY; POST-STRUCUTURALISM), maintaining that **truth** in history is discoverable in the **event**. While most historians will not accept their hard-hat reconstructionism, they would agree with them that history is about serving the **evidence** and **sources**. What most would agree is that history is not a philosophical disputation on the ontological condition of either the mind of the historian or his/her construction of past relationships of being, space and time. The historian is dedicated to discovering the reality of the past rather than to debating **metaphysics**, that is, disputing the nature and construction of reality and being.

Ontology is that branch of metaphysics that addresses the general state of being, the nature of existence, and how the human mind apprehends, comprehends, judges, categorises, makes assumptions about and constructs reality. For the historian ontological questions arise when we address how to create historical **facts** within the larger ontology of our own existence, that is, the condition(s) of being under which we create or construct the-past-as-(the discipline of)-history. While the historian is necessarily an ontological creature who has prejudices, preconceptions and beliefs about the nature of existence (past, present and future), for Elton *et al.* this does not mean that he/she cannot escape them when researching and writing history. Such an escape from ontology is warranted for Elton by our being constrained by the authority of the evidence (Elton 1991: 43, 49).

This empiricist-objectivist perspective views history as primarily concerned with those practices dealing with the evidence that permit us to acquire genuine and, therefore, mind- and **discourse**-independent knowledge about the past; history is perceived exclusively as a methodology that allows escape into the past. The issue of **epistemology** (the nature, theory, foundations, conditions, limits and possibilities of knowing), if raised at all, rarely gets further than formally re-stating the assumption that historical knowledge is discovered through evidence-based **inference** and the delineation and specific application of social theories/categories of analysis that 'naturally' emerge from the evidence. Ontological questions are largely ignored. The reason according to conventional wisdom is that historians are insulated from their present conditions of existence by their skills/inferential methodology (see EMPIRICISM).

It is quite possible, therefore, to have truthful historical knowledge. The routes to 'ontology-free' justified historical knowledge can take and have taken many forms. Examples of such routes might include **covering laws** (the positivist (see POSITIVISM) 'social science' route), service before the evidence (the 'empiricist-objectivist epistemological' route), practical realism (the 'lots of things in history are relative' route), truth conditions (the 'induction does work' route) or the gendered re-casting of time (the 'regendering time can produce a new and really proper history' route), etc., etc. The upshot, anyway, is that the reality of the past is accessible.

However, the ontological conditions of historical inquiry are at present more fiercely debated than ever before (Ankersmit 2005b). Historians are asking and answering questions about the bases of their theories of explanation that form the a priori (see A PRIORI/A POSTERIORI) grounds or ontological presuppositions of the discipline. Having said this, most historians still find it hard to imagine a history other than the 'normal' one. What would a history written by reversing the being and knowing or content and form polarity look like (see FORM AND CONTENT)? Indeed, can history be history if it is viewed as a series of ontological rather than resolvable methodological (or occasionally epistemological) problems? The most obvious example is probably the **linguistic turn** that, in reversing content and form, makes history more than a little like literature; that is, it denies the knowable reality of the past.

Such a radical construal of history – reversing the polarity – means that our knowledge is not necessarily discovered in the real past (see EXPERIMENTAL HISTORY). While historians are happy to endorse Immanuel **Kant**'s view that philosophy cannot grasp reality, fortunately history can – it has the methodology. Consequently, most historians are still not prepared to accept that any form of genuine, useful or plausible historical understanding may be achieved without benefit of an objective evidence-based (science-like) methodology. Of course, as sceptical empiricists they all know of the perennial and substantial problems that are part and parcel of the inferential method. Although our knowledge is, therefore, indirect and evidence-dependent, the hypothesis-induction-deduction, truth-conditional mechanism is rigorous and sophisticated (see CAUSATION; COLLIGATION)

This conception of what are the proper means for acquiring historical knowledge deliberately brackets off the ontology of history. Denying the need to philosophise on the status of history permits the comforting notion that history is a truth-acquiring discipline. It invariably also leads to an uncritical acceptance of referentiality, factualism and the correspondence theory of knowledge, as well as the belief that a history that prioritises being is certain to degenerate into a dangerous subjective anti-history idealism that might fool the unwary into believing it could still be history.

Once we doubt that useful knowledge can emerge only from rational explanation and knowable objects, then we are admitting that knowledge must, to some extent, be subjective and perspectival – and here historians enter the murky world of Friedrich **Nietzsche** and a kind of history that is no longer an independent reconstruction, but is historian- or observer-relative (see AUTHOR). Reversing the polarity also means losing faith in the accuracy of our **representation** of the past, for how can we write about the real past when we do not 'know' that our language is an adequate vehicle for relaying the truth that, we assume, is out there? Frank R. Ankersmit has continued to point out the historicist nature of history (see HISTORICISM). This means we must think of historians and what they write 'not in epistemological but ontological terms' (Ankersmit 2005b: 197). There is, rather, contiguity between the historian (subject) and the past (object). They share the same ontological sphere. In practice it may be, then, that we do not really have a choice, for the notion that language constitutes both ontological and epistemological states has already destabilised our priority of knowing over being. The reversal means that ontology, whether it is called our present condition, our ideology, historicism, **reality/realistic effect** or the constant deferral of meaning, will always get in the way of 'knowing the past'.

Further reading

Ankersmit, F.R., 2005b; Elton, G., 1991; Evans, R.J., 1997a; Grossmann, R., 1992; Hexter, J.H., 1972; Himmelfarb, G., 1994; Marwick, A., 1989 [1970]; Mensch, J.R., 1996; Munslow, A., 2003b; Pihlainen, K., 1998; Windschuttle, K., 1995.

ORAL HISTORY

In the past fifty years or so, oral history can be understood as the practice of interviewing eyewitnesses to past events. The practice most often (though not invariably) entails interviews with representatives of groups who might otherwise have escaped the scrutiny of historians. These have tended to be members of the non-literate labouring classes, or indigenous or minority cultural groups. Of course, such interviews have then to be placed (as with all the **evidence** related to the past) within what the historian believes to be an appropriate **narrative** framework. An additional range of inter-disciplinary skills, which the historian has had to borrow (from sociology, psychology, ethnography, social anthropology and often linguistics), usually supports this activity. But oral history also – so it is claimed – places a new emphasis on the mediatory role of the historian. It is, for example, impossible to ignore the heavily constructed character of oral histories, specifically the ideological functioning of the historian who wishes to recuperate certain voices rather than others. Using history as a way to empower certain groups is – surprisingly perhaps – still a controversial aim. Although this is not really that unusual as all historians select their range of evidence, in oral histories silence can often mean forgetting and it is the historian who regularly has to act as 'stage prompt'. Moreover, the ethnographic practices of the historian can make 'listen, record and narrate' a hugely complex and necessarily fictive history-making process (see NARRATIVE).

For such reasons, as a practice for engaging with the past, oral history is still often regarded with suspicion and scepticism, especially by those who are distrustful of the 'new social history' (which is modernist historian's code for postmodern inflected social history) (see DECONSTRUCTIONIST HISTORY). As the **reconstructionist** historian Arthur Marwick has said, while oral testimony can give us access to information about

the recent past we would otherwise not have, 'oral accounts are particularly subject to the fallibility of the human memory' and are, he maintains, severely limited in their utility to historians. Moreover, he regards the argument that oral testimony, memoirs and autobiographies are special and need expert treatment as 'specious nonsense' (Marwick 2001: 136). In other words, oral testimony is at once a highly problematic source and certainly does not require an arcane set of skills (see SOURCES). Oral history is often dubious because it all too easily relies on the stories people tell about themselves and pays too little (if any) attention to the many different kinds of primary source, which are (claimed to be) the real basis of 'proper history'. The riposte to this – the document-driven history of reconstructionists – from oral historians has long come from Jan Vansina, who maintains that where there is no written documentation oral traditions must bear the brunt of the reconstruction of the past. But far more importantly, it is dangerous to undervalue oral testimony because it can correct or support the perspectives historians can obtain from sources of other kinds.

But many historians still remain unconvinced. Essentially, 'proper history' must be based on documentary evidence because its artefacts can be compared, contrasted and verified with each other (just as 'history films' have to use documentary footage shot of the events to which reference is being made) (see FILM AND HISTORY). Documents also do not get confused over when things happened – the things to which they refer happened chronologically. And, of course, oral testimony cannot account for change over time. Oral testimony is essentially just a matter of 'this happened, then that happened', and is delivered infused with inexplicable and unstable emotion. Any challenge to document-driven and 'artefactually' inferential history is to be avoided because it loosens up the strict regime of professional modernist history. Once this happens we (will surely?) end up with all kinds of serious problems.

These include the invention of traditions, epistemic **relativism**, fictive stories, overt **author**ship, the figuration of the past, the collapse of **objectivity**, uncertainty over what is **truth** and untruth and, eventually, mystification over what is 'right' and 'what is wrong'.

This opens up the key issue with oral testimony/history. Do we think that people retell pre-existing stories or are they so unreliable that they simply 'invent' them about their own past? Such invention (if we assume it is invention) can result from false memories, wishful thinking and ideological conviction. We might also encounter the unconscious repetition of a cultural narrative, a desire to obfuscate, self-indulgence and/or simple confusion. So what can historians do when faced with oral testimony? Do they still think they are able to 'discover the actual stories that exist in the past' by supplementing oral testimony with other 'documentary sources' (see EMPLOTMENT; REPRESENTATION; MIMESIS)? However, and this is a major consideration, whatever sources are used, the historian still has to substitute their narrative emplotment for the past regardless of whether they like to call it a 'reconstruction' or a 're-telling'. At this point oral history, given its particularly disputed nature, demands that the historian consider the implications of the relationship between **form and content** in generating their history. The empirical fragility of oral testimony, including issues of interviewing technique and choice of questions (the face-to-face relationship between source and historian), forces historians to examine the content, purpose and design (including their analytical strategies of explanation) of their history text. The form of oral history is clearly different from that of other forms and **genres**.

But a very important related point about oral testimony is what seemingly makes it different from other kinds of source. It is that interviews – the content – appear 'already formed' *as* narratives. Though they are usually generated as a series of responses to individual questions, oral testimonies are typically cast within a narrative framework that has already been created by the witness as well as – in part – by the historian's choices of question. The witness's narrative is constructed like any other, and is subject to the same formal influences (voice, distance, perspective, timing and focalisation). In oral history the 'reference' comes already as an event under a description, as an interpretation – authored and subjective. It comes to us *as* a history rather than a document out of which a history is (supposedly) constructed. Of course, oral testimony is actually no different from other documentary forms inasmuch as all sources are narrativised to some greater or lesser extent (as when they are archived, for example, or grouped together by the historian). It is merely that oral testimony so obviously mixes up the historical, narrative and cultural contexts (past and present) in their creation. Because of this, oral sources only appear to possess a different sort of (dubious) quality from other kinds of source. But this is wrong. That argument privileges those other 'documentary' sources as if they were 'proper' and 'factual' (see FACTS) and oral testimony is inferior and suspicious. What is confused (and forgotten) is that sources of all kinds have an ontological dimension that makes them of a kind. All sources are simply sites for meaning-creation. Surely, it is hard to claim objectivity for certain sources over others? The mere existence of a source does not endow it with 'objectivity' or 'truth', whether it is documentary or oral. All history has a purpose, it is constructed for someone and, arguably, it is in the nature of oral history to forcefully remind us of that central feature of the historical undertaking.

Further reading

Chamberlain, M. and Thompson, P., 1998; Dunaway, D.K. and Blum, W.K., 1996; Genette, G., 1990 [1983]; Grele, R.J., 1999, 1991; Marwick, A., 2001; Perks, R. and Thomson, A., 1998; Prins, G., 1991; Samuel, R., 1994; Thompson, P., 1978; Vansina, J., 1985.

P

POSITIVISM

This is an **epistemology** or theory of knowledge developed by the nineteenth-century French sociologist Auguste Comte as part of his grand three-stage theory of progressive historical evolution (the theological, the metaphysical and the scientific or positive stage). The final stage (which Comte saw himself as ushering in) is characterised by the verifiable or empirical measurement and predictability of the relationship between discrete phenomena. As an extension of established notions of **empiricism**, positivism insists on no speculation about natural phenomena. Because positivism assumes uniformity in scientific method it allows for the analytical study of human behaviour – a science of society – by observers who stand outside that which is being observed. In terms of the study of the past, positivism assumes that it is possible to characterise human experience according to discoverable and repeatable laws, namely **covering laws** of human activity that allow for the creation of categories of both people and analysis, the functions and structures of which are determined by such laws (for example **gender**-, **class**- and **race**-determined behaviour). This is the essence of the inductive empirical method whereby observation of repeated occurrence suggests patterns of human behaviour (see INFERENCE). This observation and measurement requires no impositionalism by the historian.

Among the practical consequences of positivism is the belief in the facticity of the past: historical **evidence** can be discovered, evaluated and objectively constituted as **facts**. Beyond the simple level of **event**s positivism spurs some historians to seek out the infrastructural laws that guide, constrain and/or determine human society and its progress (see CONSTRUCTIONIST HISTORY). This means understanding the motors of history prior to a close scrutiny of its content. This may involve hypothesis-testing whereby the historian seeks to test an explanation in the crucible of the evidence. Or it may, more likely, mean offering an interpretation already brought to a corpus of evidence by the examination of other evidence, and/or by a pre-existing mental state or set of beliefs (interpretation preceding evidence) (see ONTOLOGY; TELEOLOGY).

Further reading

Berkhofer, R.F., 1995; Braudel, F., 1980; Burke, P., 1993; Forum 1991; Gardiner, P., 1959; Hempel, C.G., 1942; Kolakowski, L., 1972; Lloyd, C., 1993; Lorenz, C., 1998; Novick, P., 1988; Roberts, D.D., 1995; Snooks, G.D., 1998; Tosh, J., 2001.

POSTCOLONIAL HISTORY

Given the epistemological conditions under which we at present construct the past, our post-imperial engagement with largely non-European cultures has given rise to that branch of historical study generally referred to as postcolonialism or postcolonial studies (see EPISTEMOLOGY; POSTMODERNISM; STRUCTURALISM; POST-STRUCTURALISM; CONSTRUCTIONIST HISTORY; AESTHETIC TURN; ETHICAL TURN; LINGUISTIC TURN; REPRESENTATION). Given the variety of 'turns' that history has undergone in the past forty years or so under the impact of post-structuralism and epistemic scepticism, conventional post-imperial history has given way to a variety of fresh analyses and understandings. These have stressed the linguistic and cultural avenues through which historians can attempt to escape from their Eurocentric conceptions of history in both its theory and its practice. Through, in particular, the use of the languages of power, Antonio Gramsci's concept of cultural hegemony, the notion of **discourse** and the use of myth, a new generation of historians has re-addressed the history of Western imperialism. But, in so doing, they have also helped reconstitute the nature and 'history of history' in the West (see Michel FOUCAULT).

Central to this reformulation has been what is now called postcolonial history. This has developed under the impress of the key postmodern emphasis upon the ways in which the world or the real, and the word or language, are made to connect. That the re-casting of the relationship between the methods of literature and history has raised the question of **truth**, once we assume that history is a form of literature, has made the historical **genre** of postcolonialism a crucial development in thinking about history. The specific reason for its importance resides in the manner in which historians and other writers have reconstituted the concepts of 'cultural identity' and 'difference'. In specific terms this has pivoted on a variety of key concepts such as **race**, feminism (postcolonial feminism) and **gender**, as addressed in postcolonial literary and well as historical theory, but also in **critical theory**.

Perhaps the key text in postcolonial history was that of the Jerusalem-born neo-(possibly pseudo-)Marxist Palestinian critic Edward Said, published in 1978, *Orientalism*. In this text Said indicated how historians, rather than 'the past', constitute history and its objects of study. Working in the tradition of Foucault and in some ways anticipating Jean-François **L**y**otard**'s incredulity toward metanarratives and acknowledging the possibility noted by Jacques **Derrida** of multiple histories constructed from different perspectives, Said argued in favour of the essentially historicist nature of history (see HISTORICISM). Doing this in the context of European imperialism, Said pointed out that history always has a vantage point and invariably seems to isolate and work in opposition to 'the other'. He noted the failure of historians of European colonialism to engage in an epistemological critique of the hegemonic connection they made (which was ethno- and Eurocentric) between world history and their own (historicist) perspective. In essence what Said was pointing to was the confederacy of academic history with the institutionalisation of modernist epistemological thinking.

Although the debate centres specifically on the construction of postcolonial history, the bigger stakes concern the notion that historical knowledge (all knowledges in the humanities and sciences?) consists of discursive formulations of power. It has been suggested that any discipline that does not adequately examine its own discursive operations will never be able to escape its own constraints. Unless it genuinely critiques itself, history can never hope to understand that it creates the reality it purports to describe. Unless historians address the nature of historical representation they will never escape their own disciplinary solipsism. Of course, we can hope that there may be an escape back to the real (in the case of Said the 'real Orient' rather than the Western construction of it). But being aware of history's self-construction suggests that this is epistemologically impossible. In a universe where we cannot connect to the real, how will we get back to it? So if there is any way out of this conundrum we must acknowledge two apparently incommensurable positions: that there is no 'real' connection between 'the past' and 'history' and yet that there is no practical distinction between 'the past' and 'history'. This is because we can only appropriate the former through the latter.

Said's work has generated the minor industry of postcolonial history and studies which has been further developed by a range of historians and critical theorists including Homi K. Bhabha, Gayatri Chakravorty Spivak and Dipesh Chakrabarty. Homi Bhabha has added and developed a variety of dimensions to postcolonial history incorporating psychoanalysis and developing a medley of conceptual refinements (mimicry, hybridisation, ambivalence and resistance). The Marxist deconstructionist feminist Gayatri Spivak has illuminated not only the nature of postcolonial history but also the way in which history itself is made to work through its narrative construction – an exercise in what she has referred to as epistemic violence. For her, history seemingly has no existence beyond itself as a narrative representation. She is also known for her appropriation of Antonio Gramsci's concept of the 'subaltern'. She takes this to designate women and those of inferior rank who, though marginalised, have been redeemed 'in history' to reveal the nature of opposition to imperialism. And, by extension, the term is used to refer to those intellectuals who are themselves working to bring history face-to-face with its own epistemological crisis that other, apparently oppositional, historians such as Marxists so conspicuously fail to do (see Keith JENKINS). Dipesh Chakrabarty has pushed on from subaltern studies to explore the 'end of history' in the West (though its end has not yet been announced in India). It seems appropriate to close this entry with a reference such as this, as, arguably, any failure to resolve the ironies in engaging 'realistically' with the past must end in silence.

Further reading

Ashcroft, B. *et al.*, 1994, 1989;
Bhabha, H.K., 1994, 1990; Chakrabarty, D., 1992; Dirlik, A., 2000; Fanon, F., 1968 [1952], 1961; Gramsci, A., 1972; Jenkins, K. and Munslow, A., 2004; MacKenzie, J.M., 1995; Mohanty, C. *et al.*, 1991; Pieterse, J.P.N., 1990; Said, E.W., 1993, 1989, 1978; Spivak, G.C., 1990, 1988, 1987; Young, R., 1990.

POST-FEMINISM

There is no ready definition of post-feminism to hand. However, it may be broadly defined as that range of academic discourses, not simply in history but throughout the arts, humanities and social sciences (and certainly beyond in the public and political realm), which explore the implications of the encounter between feminism and **post-structuralist** theory. Post-feminism developed in the 1980s and 1990s in that 'phase' of feminism often called Second Wave Feminism. Historians of the female experience and of **gender** soon recognised that incorporating women into the discipline of history in terms of both its **form and content** required substantial changes in terms of new themes and topics. But, even more significantly, it also meant rethinking the nature of historical research and confronting history's traditional, modernist, male-orientated empirical-analytical **epistemology** (see WOMEN'S HISTORY; MODERNISM).

The challenges presented to the history profession by **continental philosophy**, **critical theory**, the **linguistic turn**, the **aesthetic turn** and literary theory generated a crisis in the 1980s and 1990s that has changed the nature of historical scholarship profoundly (see POSTMODERNISM; Jacques DERRIDA; Jean-François LYOTARD; Jean BAUDRILLARD; Michel FOUCAULT; CULTURAL HISTORY; DISCOURSE; DECONSTRUCTIONIST HISTORY; HISTORICISM; POST-MARXISM). The emergence of epistemic scepticism that coincided with the second wave of feminism (actually less a coincidence and more cause and effect) can be seen in the work most particularly of Joan W. Scott and above all in her radical book collection *Gender and the Politics of History* (1988). In certain respects Scott established the intellectual agenda for what later became known as post-feminism when she said that for her gender meant sexual *difference* but that knowledge of this was never absolute or true but always relative to the epistemic frame in which it was produced. She insisted that while gender was about sexual *difference* it did not reflect 'natural physical differences' (Scott 1988: 2). Most importantly, and very plainly, she spoke to the trial that history as a discipline was going through and which, of course, it still does. This is that, in the instance of gender and feminism, history does not simply record the history of sexual *difference*, but is directly implicated – a participant – in the production of knowledge *about* sexual *difference*.

She went on to say that how this happens demands that historians attend to their assumptions, practices and rhetoric, which, up until then, had not normally been on the disciplinary agenda. Among these assumptions was that history can 'faithfully document lived reality, that archives are repositories of **facts**, that categories like man and woman are transparent' (Scott 1988: 2). She went on to make the point that the language of history was implicated in the construction of power and gender relations. The construction of historical texts as well as the politics of the discipline needed to be addressed. She concluded that for her history was as much the object of attention as it was a method of study (ibid.: 3). In other words, to do feminist history meant she had to pursue theoretical questions as well as be avowedly political.

To do new feminist history Scott said she sought a new epistemology:

A more radical feminist politics (and a more radical feminist history) seems . . . to require a more radical epistemology. Precisely because it addresses questions of epistemology, relativises the status of all knowledge, links power and knowledge, and theorises these in terms of the operations of difference, I think post-structuralism (or at least some of the approaches generally associated with Michel Foucault and Jacques Derrida) can offer feminism a powerful analytic perspective.

(Scott 1988: 4)

She pointed out the basic idea behind post-structuralism, which is that there are no clear and common meanings to cultural concepts (or historical concepts, including the concept of 'history', as this book clearly indicates!), that meanings are not fixed but are always in flux, that what we signify is always arbitrary at a basic level. This state of affairs also suggests that 'signifying meaning' is also a political activity. In whose interests is history written and for what purposes? The mask of **objectivity** and factualism needs to be torn away (which is *not* the same as doing away with knowing what happened) to reveal the historical acts and constructions beneath – of which most (all?) are nakedly political, national, gendered, racial, etc. What needed to be confronted was the historian's assertion that through knowing what happened a stance of intellectual neutrality could be obtained. This is hard to sustain not only because of the inevitable selectivity of data but, just as importantly, because of the manner in which the data is represented (see REPRESENTATION). So being self-aware and reflexive demands more than understanding that the facts can be misleading.

The mood of epistemic scepticism (reflected in Scott's attack) means today that when students of history ask what it is, the answer can be manifold. But it is never simply that it is an organised body of empirical data referring to the past, the meaning of which can be inferred (largely unproblematically) (see INFERENCE). How we frame our questions, what consciousness(es) we bring to bear on the activity, how we write the meaning of history into the past (how we create 'the-past-as-history'), how historians personally make the connection between knowledge and power, are all central issues in defining what is history (see LINGUISTIC TURN; ETHICAL TURN; AESTHETIC TURN).

This anti-epistemological approach has allowed feminist historians (and increasingly historians working in other historical **genre**s) not just to 'do history' differently (or to question whether we need it at all) but to do it by being intellectually self-conscious at a level that takes them beyond the simplicities of reconstructionism (see RECONSTRUCTIONIST HISTORY). But it should also take us beyond the presumed sophistication of constructionism (see CONSTRUCTIONIST HISTORY). Any definition of history today should allow us to ask questions about how we deconstruct meaning and author(ise) those definitions and categories of analysis through which we create the-past-as-history (see AUTHOR; DECONSTRUCTIONIST HISTORY).

Unhappily for those who would want to fix meaning for their own benefit or in the name of **objectivity** and **truth** (in terms of what 'the past' most likely means), this is now an uphill task in a sceptical universe that in the genre of feminist thinking has feminist epistemology(ies), feminist philosophy(ies), feminist theories of psychoanalysis, feminist social science, feminist aesthetics, feminist ethics, feminist literary criticism, feminist jurisprudence, feminist theology and so on and so forth. The post-feminist intellectual revolution has generated libraries of analysis and criticism in all these areas and numerous others. Several key thinkers, not least Luce Irigaray, Hélène Cixous, Julia Kristeva and Judith Butler have generated this work. Irigaray and Kristeva are cultural theorists and psychoanalysists who have explored the notion of sexual difference. Cixous has examined the language of phallogocentrism and, more recently, Butler has promoted the notion of gender as performative, which has contributed much to 'queer theory', by arguing that sexual roles are social rituals as well as being hegemonic.

History is still rarely seen as a political act. Indeed it is usually regarded as being the exact opposite. But writing history is, nevertheless, the premier cultural site for the creation and recognition of, and debate over, competing systems of meaning and the definitions of *differance*, as Scott and others have indicated. Indeed, the more recent way in which the concept of post-feminism has been appropriated and 'turned' against its liberationist and inclusionist sentiments, especially by the political right, reveals how adjacent are the concerns of history to politics. Denying the Derridean concept of difference for women (that meaning is the result of fixing signifiers within a structure of difference by which 'true meaning' is always deferred) allows again the fixing of the meaning of what it is to be female for purposes of cultural dominance (see ETHICAL TURN).

The philosopher Edith Wyschograd suggests that the historian's account of the past is not the result of an inert and lifeless relation to the past but is the product of the desire for and love of those in the past who need to speak – to relate 'that-which-was' (Wyschograd 2004: 28). Historians remain constrained by the rules of evidence and the ideal of making true statements about what happened. But, as she says, this view presupposes that the original and narrated events are homologous, yet this is wrong. While still seeking verisimilitude (resolving the problem of 'narrative truth'), what the post-feminist episode has indicated is that historians need to recognise that this issue lies at the heart of the historical project. Disclosing the meaning of the past is something that facts cannot settle. The rise of post-feminist history has done this valuable service to historians – forcing us to recognise that reference does not equate with meaning – our aesthetic, linguistic and ethical choices are the prisms through which reality is refracted. The only people who do not seem to realise that are those who simplistically claim that reality has precedence over its representation.

Further reading

Alcoff, L. and Potter, E., 1993; Aldrich, R. and Wotherspoon, G., 2001; Alexander, S., 1984; Antony, L.M. and Witt, C.,

1993; Baker, M., 1998; Beauvoir, S.
de, 1952 [1949]; Butler, J., 1991, 1990;
Cixous, H. and Clément, C., 1986 [1975];
Code, L., 2000, 1991; Curthoys, J., 1997;
Downs, L.L., 2004; Duran, J., 1997;
Elam, D., 1994; Firestone, S., 1971;
Garry, A. and Pearsall, M., 1996; Hall, C.,
1992; Haraway, D., 1991, 1988; Kemp, S.
and Squires, J., 1997; Laslett, B. *et al.*, 1997;
Mitchell, J., 1974; Mitchell, J. and Rose, J.,
1982; Mohanty, C. *et al.*, 1991; Moi, T.,
1986; Nelson, L.H., 1990; Rendall, J.,
1991; Scott, J.W., 1996a, 1996b, 1991,
1989, 1988, 1986, 1983; Stanley, L., 1992;
Wyschograd, E., 2004.

POST-MARXISM

As with all self-avowed 'postist' (literally
'after') intellectual developments in the past
twenty to thirty years post-Marxism is
defined as a revision (even a rejection) of a
given set of ideas and beliefs about the inter-
section of the past (reality) and history (its
representation) in the train of **post-
structuralist** theory. Post-Marxism developed
in the mid-1980s specifically as a critique of
'classical' Marxism but it did so within that
broad sceptical epistemic movement called
postmodernism. Just as with **post-feminism**,
post-Marxism offered a commentary on, and
a rejection of, central elements of **Enlightenment** thinking, specifically several of the key
ideas of Marxist analysis and the view of
historical change and historical analysis associated with it (see MODERNISM; FORM
AND CONTENT). Inevitably, as a realist
and essentially empirical mode of social and
economic investigation, Marxism was vulner-
able to this form of criticism as was its materialist conception of socialism, the nature of
the working **class**, the concept of 'Socialist
Revolution' and 'class consciousness' (see
EMPIRICISM). What was now fully at risk
in the Marxist analysis was the realist/materi-
alist idea of certainty and, therefore, 'history'
itself. The 'realities' of social and economic

life under the capitalist mode of production
that were claimed to result from the base and
superstructure relationship between relations
of production and class relations were now
regarded as uncertain, plural and the product
of a fluid late twentieth-century 'political
imaginary'. The old modernist verities and
master narratives subsequent to the French
Revolution, for example, could no longer be
counted on (see MODERNISM; POST-
MODERNISM; CULTURAL HISTORY;
DISCOURSE; DECONSTRUCTIONIST
HISTORY; HISTORICISM). What had to
be explained at a time of new epistemological
uncertainties was the 'failure' of the Marxist
revolution (see EPISTEMOLOGY).

Most accounts of post-Marxism have
begun with the analysis of Ernesto Laclau
and Chantal Mouffe in their book *Hegemony
and Socialist Strategy: Towards a Radical
Democratic Politics* (Laclau and Mouffe 1985).
As they said,

> What is now in crisis is a whole conception
> of socialism which rests upon the
> ontological centrality of the working class,
> upon the role of Revolution ... as the
> founding moment in the transition from
> one type of society to another, and upon
> the illusory prospect of a perfectly unitary
> and homogeneous collective will that will
> render pointless the moment of politics.
> The plural and multifarious character of
> contemporary social struggles has finally
> dissolved the last foundation for that
> political imaginary.
>
> (Laclau and Mouffe 1985: 2)

They went on to say that their analysis was
not innocent of its own 'discursivity' and their
aim was to focus on certain discursive categories of which the key one was that of the
Italian-Sardinian Marxist Antonio Gramsci's
notion of hegemony, 'considered as a discursive surface and fundamental nodal point of
Marxist political theorization' (ibid.: 2–3)
(see DISCOURSE). With this resuscitation
of Gramsci's effort to account for the fail-

ure of the Socialist Revolution, Laclau and Mouffe interred 'historical necessity' in favour of contingency upon which a new politics for the Left could be developed based upon 'the project of a radical democracy' (ibid.: 3). They called their aim 'a deconstruction of the various discursive surfaces of classical Marxism' (ibid.). They even acknowledged that their new project was not itself essentialist. Indeed, it could not be 'in an era [when] normative epistemologies has come to an end' (ibid.).

In, as they said, scaling down the pretensions and the validity of Marxist theory they were breaking with something deeply inherent in that theory, namely its claim to capture 'the underlying meaning of History' (Laclau and Mouffe 1985: 4). In doing this they were denying the connection between **ontology** and **epistemology**. At that point they acknowledged that what they were attempting took them into a post-Marxist terrain though they still insisted on the Marxist orientation of the theory (of hegemony). While there was no more objective science of historical development that indicated a given metahistorical course for Marxist historical analysis, this still left them with the notion that they could use history to suggest what might still happen in the present and future (see POSITIVISM). As a result of the post-Marxist moment the theory and nature of Marxism has been dramatically confronted. The classical economistic approach has been replaced by the demand for a radical democracy as seen in the debates that involve or invoke Ludwig Wittgenstein, Theodor Adorno, Hannah Arendt, Louis Althusser, Jürgen Habermas, Jean **Baudrillard**, Julia Kristeva, Michel **Foucault**, Roland **Barthes**, Jean-François **Lyotard** and Jacques **Derrida**.

Laclau and Mouffe were among the first to realise the improbability of being able to compromise (as many 'new empiricists' are still trying to do today) access to reality with its construction. That they were never able to satisfactorily resolve this problem is no criticism of their heroic efforts to eliminate the question of representation, but is, rather, a

commentary on its unresolvability. Viewing **objectivity** as part of the bigger issue of representation is no help. That we may wish to know what mechanisms create change over time, no matter what ideological, theoretical and personal commitment we have to them, does not alter the way representation works. Though they take the view that we exist in a world where there is no 'ultimate fixity of meaning' their retention of some measure of knowable reality upon which we can fix (partial) meaning remains an unsatisfactory notion. That the alternative must be 'partial fixations', otherwise we could not recognise difference at all, is not convincing either (Laclau and Mouffe 1985: 112). It is precisely this incommensurability that makes the 'new empiricist' historians' position untenable and illogical. Why they are unconvincing is because they neglect to grasp the point (as ultimately do all realists) that beliefs about reality (ultimate or partial) have to be represented first. And, of course, this means not just a degradation of 'knowing' into 'telling'. It means mechanisms of knowing always come through telling (see AESTHETIC TURN).

Wishing to maintain the emancipatory logic of Marxism can, of course, remain as a guiding light. But, in a postmodern universe, the old Marxism is gone once and for all and, indeed, what replaces it may not be Marxist at all. But does this now happen to all metanarratives? The debate on whether post-Marxism has reduced the reality of class conflict to the level of the contingent and ultimately unknowable and unrepresentable will probably never be resolved, at least not under the epistemological considerations that for many still seem to exist today. Meanings in history can only ever be understood 'relatively', always over-determined by other meanings that co-exist in the social and cultural imagination. The classic Marxist base and superstructure metaphor is a clear case in point. The 'truth' of that metaphor is not 'fixed'. This is not because of the application of fresh doses of data and new analytical procedures, but because it is a meta-phor. Whatever the metaphor refers to, 'it' is a representation – and we cannot escape that. The point is well made perhaps if you think of 'class' or even 'society' as not being *things*. They are 'constructions' or, perhaps more 'realistically', they are 'prefigured'. Neither can possess a meaning in perpetuity. These 'things' are all empty signifiers.

All objects in the past are, therefore, con-tinuously reprocessed as history. Perhaps the only function that history has is to re-signify (strictly speaking 're-vision') 'things'. And it is here that we would acknowledge the precise functioning of language as the logic of his-tory – aesthetics always preceding empiricism. Historians of the French Revolution can always cast the Rural Code of 27 September metonymically as part of the bigger move to agrarian individualism or not, as they 'imag-ine' the connections between events. It is their narrative-making choice and it never does any injury to 'what happened'. The examples of this logic in history are, of course, almost endless. As Laclau and Mouffe maintain, all 'discourse ... becomes metaphorical: literality is, *in actual fact*, the first of meta-phors' (1985: 111). In that sense history is the first metaphor for the past. The tradition upon which this belief rests is, as Laclau and Mouffe suggest, a long one that includes vari-ously Heidegger, Wittgenstein, Derrida and Baudrillard, all of whom acknowledged that it is impossible to fix ultimate meanings. This, in effect, is the same as saying it is impossible to fix anything – all we have are temporary meanings in history.

There remain many realists who point out the 'limitations' to postmodernist thinking, the most important being (of course) its pri-mary argument (or metaphor?) that we can only represent past reality through present language. Understanding past reality as an endlessly creatable and interpretable text is said to ignore the actual differences between reality and texts. Texts are not merely said to be interpretative systems of meaning but they are also 'real objects' and we learn to write them, buy them, borrow them and read them in 'real time', and in real places, because they are part of our 'real existence'. What is more important, they are objects that reveal the nature of the economic, social and cul-tural system. Before we can babble on about endless chains of signification we must first understand the real constraints on those activities. Basically the material world will always intrude into the metaphorical and ide-alist. So we really must learn to 'get back' to 'reality'.

Yes, the anti-representationalist would respond, history texts are authored and real objects but they are written about the evidence of reality (see AUTHOR). The anti-representationalist (Marxist or other-wise) would never deny the existence of the real (this isn't the issue and it never has been – I accept I am writing a real book after all) nor claim all we have are ethereal texts. They (and I) would, however, remind the realist that once we (which includes them) shift up to the coherent representation of the past – as we must if we are to write history rather than merely list what happened – at that point a fundamental epistemological change occurs. Not only do we move from 'knowing' to 'tell-ing' but the unavoidable 'narrative feedback loop' means all we have is representation at any level beyond that of being run over by a bus. This inescapable shift is the site of the narrative logic of history, whether it is Marx-ist, post-Marxist or history of any other kind (see GENRE).

Further reading
Arditi, B. and Valentine, J., 1999; Beardsworth, R., 1996; Bennington, G., 1994; Bowman, P., 2005, 2002; de Man, P., 1978; Derrida, J., 1994; Goldstein, P., 2005; Laclau, E., 1996, 1993, 1990; Laclau, E. and Mouffe, C., 1985; Laplanche, J. and Pontalis, J.-B., 1988; Lechte, J., 1994; Mouffe, C., 1996; Mowitt, J., 1992; Sim, S., 2001, 1998; Torfing, J., 1999; Townshend, J. and Tormey, S., 2005; Weber, S., 1987; Žižek, S., 1989.

POSTMODERNISM

Postmodernism is a general description for the conditions of our present existence – what might better be called postmodernity. According to the French cultural critic Jean-François **Lyotard** postmodernism is distinguished by its denial of grand or metanarratives (see METANARRATIVE) as deployed since the **Enlightenment** to explain and justify the Western conception of human progress. Our postmodern age is characterised generally by a self-conscious reaction against the vehicle for the Enlightenment's notion of progress, its cultural product, **modernism**. But the act of rejection is only found in certain spheres of intellectual activity. In others it is manifest, as the philosopher Michael Stanford has pointed out, as modernism's self-reflexion, or a case of modernism turning to challenge its own shortcomings (Stanford 1998: 246–63).

Such a situation has generated a number of claims and counter-claims about what this means for the discipline of history. These arguments are, as one would expect given the above definition of our postmodern condition, couched in terms of rejection and/or self-reflexion. Our postmodern condition, because it has destabilised the foundations of understanding, meaning and existence, has spawned, in the view of 'proper' or 'normal' historians, a series of anti-history developments (see Jean BAUDRILLARD). These include the rejection of representationalism in favour of the **linguistic turn** whereby the written form of history is as important as the past's content in creating meaning (see AESTHETIC TURN; FORM AND CONTENT; REPRESENTATION; POST-MARXISM); the acceptance of **relativism** rather than **objectivity**; and the willing loss of the knowing subject resulting in the destruction of a sense of reality and referentiality because of the disruption of the signifier–signified relationship (see DECONSTRUCTIONIST HISTORY; REALITY/REALISTIC EFFECT; FILM AND HISTORY; INTELLECTUAL HISTORY). The result is that postmodern history

is no longer an empirical enterprise but arguably a variety of fiction that is wholly dependent upon self-referentiality for its meaning (see EMPIRICISM). Hence postmodern historians argue we must defer interpretational closure because we are all cut adrift by the inadequacy of language and **narrative**. So it is that such historians are predisposed to prioritise **historiography** over the past through the arrangement, configuration and **emplotment** of the data (form rather than content as the source of meaning) (see TROPE/FIGURATION; Hayden WHITE).

In the literature-based humanities postmodernism is characterised, however, less by these rejections than by a modernist self-reflexiveness, the kind of modernism that makes its methods and the nature of its perceptions an object of study. This has been most apparent in developments generally in **continental philosophy** and **critical theory** and especially in the challenges to the Enlightenment realist assumption of, among other things, universal and fixed meanings (hence the challenge to representation), the correspondence theory of knowledge (the challenge to empiricism), **truth** conditions (the challenge to analytical philosophy), the priority of knowing over being (the challenge to **epistemology**) and that the stories we tell cannot capture the reality of the past or present (the challenge to narrative). It also disputes several realist epistemological (knowing) and ontological (being) dualisms: the separations of knower and known, observer and observed, subject and object, form and content, and fact (see FACTS) and value (see ONTOLOGY). Postmodernity, as our condition of not knowing the true origins or foundation of knowledge or its trajectory, has produced (whether we like it or not) a state of ontological drift and epistemological uncertainty, and the ungluing of methodological confidence.

Even though I have my doubts about modernist conceptions of objectivity, **inference**, truth, representation and finding firm foundations to knowledge in the humanities, I still agree with my realist colleagues that there remains a strong need in our Western culture to come to terms with the past by understanding it. But what I am saying is that this is no longer (if it ever was) an option in epistemological terms. Postmodern history is not just a negative anti-realist 'anti-the-past club' that we can join if we want. Rather we are being forced by our present conditions of existence to rethink how we construct 'the-past-as-history'. Postmodern history is a history effectively liberated from what Keith **Jenkins** and Robert A. Rosenstone have called History (upper-case H) and history (lower-case h) (Jenkins 2003 [1991]; Rosenstone 1996).

History (upper-case) is the central Western cultural metanarrative, a modernist speculation that we traditionally assign to chance **event**s a trajectory and significance determined by the bigger programmes of historical development and progress – Marxism, liberalism, capitalism, socialism, nationalism or whatever. Upper-case History, in order to be plausible, has had to annex lower-case or university-level professional history's features: its investment in **positivism**, reason, rationality, **inference**, probability and truth-conditional descriptions, reality, objectivity, explanatory closure and common-sense factualism. But this is no longer the only way to study the past. H/history in our postmodern era is now being placed in inverted commas. 'History' eschews H/history in favour of problematising the whole idea of historical knowledge by placing ontology before epistemology, and studying the past without the urge to write the indescribable or reconstruct the inaccessible (see EXPERIMENTAL HISTORY).

For me postmodern 'history' is no longer about domesticating or controlling the past without acknowledging why you are doing it, why you choose to deploy one ontology, epistemology or methodology over another, or what you hope to get out of it. It does not bother me at all if my realist colleagues choose to work on the assumption that their methods permit a match between **concepts in history** and events in the past. After all, they can

believe that particular fiction if they want. I only get uneasy when they tell me it is through their methods alone that we can properly understand the past (i.e. match history with the past). From my position I question the assumptions that underpin that view, usually beginning by pointing out the substantial epistemological failings of the inferential method that is H/history's foundation (and that most historians tacitly admit anyway). It is not, as my realist friends still sometimes claim, a matter of me not recognising the existence of the material world but is rather a recognition on my part that the connection between the real and its representation in **discourse** and language is not fixed by a privileged method (their method). As an act of faith I choose to believe in the reality of the past. I do not believe the past has no substance other than being just another text or linguistic entity. But understanding the meaning of history, like all the literature-based humanities, is a figurative/linguistic activity (see Roland BARTHES; Jacques DERRIDA; HISTORICAL IMAGINATION; Giambattista VICO). It is not, as many proper historians claim, a matter of postmodernist historians trashing the past (defined, as I have suggested, as the-past-as-history) and then not being able to offer a better historical practice. The point is that under our postmodern conditions there is no practice or set of rules of the kind normal historians insist upon (i.e. extra-historical) that can exclusively reveal the truth(s) of the past.

Further reading

Ankersmit, F.R., 2005a, 2005b, 1994, 1989; Appleby, J. *et al.*, 1996; Attridge, D. *et al.*, 1987; Bann, S., 1984; Baudrillard, J., 1983; Bauman, Z., 1998, 1997; Belchem, J. and Kirk, N., 1997; Bertens, H., 1995; Connor, S., 1989; Domanska, E., 1998a; Drolet, M., 2004; Ermarth, E.D., 1992; Harvey, D., 1989; Heise, U.K., 1997; Hollinger, D.A., 1991; Hutcheon, L., 1988; Jenkins, K., 2003 [1991], 1999b, 1997, 1995; Jenkins, K. and Munslow, A., 2004; Jenkins, K. *et al.*, forthcoming 2007; Klein, K., 1995; Lechte, J., 1994; Luntley, M., 1995; Lyotard, J.-F., 1979; Marshall, B.K., 1992; Marwick, A., 1995; Mensch, J.R., 1997; Munslow, A., 1997c; Munslow, A. and Rosenstone, R.A., 2004; Norris, C., 1990; Poster, M., 1997; Roberts, G., 1997; Roberts, M., 2004; Rosenstone, R.A., 1996; Southgate, B., 1996; Spiegel, G.M., 2005, 1992; Stanford, M., 1998; Zagorin, P., 1990; Zammito, J.H., 1998

POST-STRUCTURALISM

Developments in **continental philosophy**, recent versions of pragmatism, **structuralism** and **intellectual history** have been central to the emergence of the philosophy and practice of post-structuralism along with its most intoxicating form, that of deconstructionism. As an epistemically sceptical intellectual movement of the late twentieth century, initially responding to Saussurean structuralism and its mid-twentieth-century incarnation in the social sciences (mainly in anthropology – see the work of Claude Lévi-Strauss) and psychology (psychoanalysis – see Jacques Lacan), post-structuralism is, in many respects, the key development mediating our postmodern/anti-epistemological age. Represented most obviously in the work (in a tradition traceable back to Friedrich **Nietzsche**) of the later Michel **Foucault** and Roland **Barthes**, Jean François **Lyotard**, Jean **Baudrillard**, Richard **Rorty** (a kind of pragmatic, American, liberal version), Keith **Jenkins** (directed toward the 'end of history' argument) and pre-eminently Jacques **Derrida**, post-structuralism is a both a philosophy and a theory of literary criticism. Inevitably there are reactions against orthodoxies and the post-structuralist reaction against **structuralism** (as the highest of most recent attempts at providing a scientific system for knowing) was violent and radical.

The post-structuralist attack on structuralism challenged its key assumption that language was a semiotic and referential mechanism that connected 'knowing', 'telling' and 'meaning'. Barthes' move in which he argued that the relationship between signifier and signified was not fixed and, hence, meaning is always unstable was probably the key shift toward post-structuralism. Other moves were made as well, not least the understanding that texts derive meaning from their relationship to other texts (intertextuality) rather than simply from the intentions of their **author**s (death of the author). The role of the reader was also acknowledged in the process of creating textual meaning. Barthes, for example, notes texts as being either writerly, where the reader is active in creating meaning, or readerly, where they are passive and they accept a provided meaning. Clearly, the history text would 'read' differently according to the role of the reader.

It was Derrida, however, who provided the main development in post-structuralist thinking with his argument that the sign is constantly unfinished and so, as a result, is meaning. Meaning is always deferred because signifiers can only refer to other signifiers in a never-ending chain of signification. Meaning is always postponed. Derrida coined the term *différance* to express this unfixed nature of meaning. In terms of history as both a textual **representation** of pastness and a discipline built expressly for knowing the **truth** about the reality of the past, Derrida's deconstruction of the sign is devastating, though hardly convincing if you are a hard-core materialist like the Marxist historian Bryan D. Palmer who sees all this as a crude 'descent into discourse' (Palmer, 1992). Deconstructing history means accepting not just indeterminacy of textualised meaning but that history is not privileged above other kinds of text that may wish to engage with the time before now, like **film**, TV, hypertext, re-enactment, graphic novel, experiential museums, pop-up books, CD-ROMS, computer games, etc. As Baudrillard might say, we construct our sign and our media in order to destroy the reality with which we do not wish to engage. The subsequent 'loss of reality' can only then breed ever better simulations. So, while we proliferate our histories, none of them is ever closer to the 'real past', they are just more (or less) convincing simulations that are constructed out of public records. The recent enhanced trend toward ever more empathic and 'interactive' museums is illustrative as is what has been called 'prosthetic memory' (memory as a media effect).

Viewing history as just another (i.e., deprivileged) text/simulation/media effect waiting its turn in the queue for engaging with the past means it is subject to all the questions that can be asked about any **narrative**. Can it reveal anything useful (let alone truthful) about the past by matching present word and past world (see TRUTH)? Or, like every other text, does its meaning derive entirely from its functioning as a representation rather than as a facsimile that happens to be written or otherwise mediated? Clearly, that the history text is referential does not mean it is just a list of references. The **emplotment**, which is at the heart of any historical narrative, is the key rhetorical device for 'making' sense ('making' as in 'building', not 'finding') of the past. But even while every emplotment is deployed to construct and offer a meaning, the reader must be as involved as the author in 'forming' events to 'make sense' of the past. This is why history is about re-visions and why some are better received by the readership than others. That there will always be more new **evidence** and smarter **inference** is largely irrelevant to 'making history' and its reception.

If we assume that historical knowledge is created rather than discovered then the logic of history is that of its narrative construction, and we are able to see history for what it is – a representation. Making history is, for that reason, coterminous with assembling a narrative. We may happily assume the past existed and that it can be referred to, but making history means there are pasts that are deliberately not referred to. That they are not is because of the pressing needs of the present for 'suitable' and 'usable' histories. We may

want a '**class** history', a '**gender** history', a '**postcolonial** history', a '**women's history**', etc., but by the same token we forget those histories we do not want to produce (see CONCEPTS IN HISTORY).

Post-structuralism has attracted many other thinkers who have engaged – sceptically – with the basic tenets of **epistemology** (see the list in the first paragraph above for the key thinkers). These others have questioned many of the conventional tenets of **Enlightenment** thinking such as the prioritising of speech over writing, the role of the 'I' (the subject) in 'writing knowledge', the subject–object distinction, the notion of 'otherness', simulacra, the nature of referentiality, the role of theory and concept in understanding, issues of truth and objectivity, and grasping the character of ontology of the text and the nature of representation. Among the other major theorists of post-structuralism are Gilles Deleuze and Emmanuel Lévinas, and there have been innumerable historical practitioners who have attempted to 'do history' informed by post-structuralist ideas (though inevitably some have been 'more post-structuralist' than others). Working variously and often experimentally in **genres** such as **race**, class, film and feminism, see, for example, Patrick Joyce, Gareth Stedman Jones, Greg Dening, Joan W. Scott, Edward Said, Anne McClintock, Robert Rosenstone, Denise Riley, Patrick Finney, Oliver Daddow, David Harlan, Alun Munslow, Miguel Cabrera, Elizabeth Deeds Ermarth, Wendy Slater, Sven Lindquist and Carolyn Steedman. And be prepared for a bumpy and often disconcerting ride.

Further reading
Baynes, K. *et al.*, 1987; Bernstein, R., 1983; Brown, C.G., 2005; Cabrera, M. A., 2004; Caws, P., 1997; Culler, J. 1982; Curthoys, A., 1996; Daddow, O., 2005, 2004; Dant, T., 1991; Deleuze, G. and Guattari, F., 1984 [1972]; Dening, G., 2004, 2002, 1992, 1966; Dews, P., 1987; Dosse, F., 1997; Ermarth, E.D., 1992; Finney, P., 1998; Goodman, J., 2004; Harlan, D.,

1997, 1989; Hawkes, T., 1977; Jameson, F., 1976; Jones, G.S., 1983; Joyce, P., 2002, 1998, 1994, 1991a, 1991b; Kearney, R. and Rainwater, M., 1996; Landsberg, A., 2004; Lechte, J., 1994; Lindquist, S., 2004; Lloyd, C., 1993; McClintock, A. *et al.* (eds), 1997; Munslow, A., 2003b, 1997a, 1997b, 1992; Munslow, A. and Rosenstone, R.A., 2004; Palmer, B.D., 1990; Poster, M., 1989; Riley, D., 1989; Roberts, D.D., 1995; Rosenstone, Robert A., 2003, 2002a, 2002b, 1996, 1995a, 1995b, 1988; Said, E.W., 1989; Saussure, F. de, 1959 [1916]; Scott, J.W., 1996a, 1996b, 1989, 1988; Slater, W., 2005; Snooks, G.D., 1998; Steedman, C., 2001; Stromberg, R.N., 1994; Sturrock, J., 1979; Tallis, R., 1998; Walker, J., 2004; Ward, C., 2004a, 2004b; Williams, R., 1983.

R

RACE

Race is yet another one of those **concepts in history** devised and deployed by historians to organise the data of the past. Like all concepts, that of race is derived only in part from the **sources** that contain references to it. It is, equally, an invention built to meet the insatiable demands of historians for 'new and better mechanisms of explanation', but also for larger political purposes. Inevitably historians re-view and re-construct such ideas as the needs of contemporary society and, therefore, history change. For this reason, like all concepts employed in history, race is both found (in the **evidence**/sources) and also continually re-imagined and re-invented. That the concept of 'race' is now going out of fashion among historians not merely flags what is now, certainly from the 1970s, increasingly regarded as its crude nature as a mode of explanation, but also once more testifies to its continuously re-fabricated and utilitarian nature.

Accordingly, the reason why the historian John Davidson is doubtful about the concept of race is that it is too clumsy to describe, as he says, the complexities of 'biological distinctions' within 'races', which 'is as great as differences between races' (Davidson 2004: 205). But, arguably, just as important in doubting the utility of 'race' is the fact that the fabricated nature of concepts is not always pleasing to historians. As Davidson says, 'race exists as a socially constructed reality' which means it is subject to the popular public sphere (ibid.). This suggests that historians have to construct their concepts as closely as possible to what the sources allow

them to infer. That this neglects the nature of **representation** is an obvious blunder.

Race has now been increasingly challenged (as an organising concept) by 'identities', 'ethnicity' and 'otherness'. Each is claimed to emerge from the sources but while this sounds right and proper, every definition of 'identity' emphasises an element of human difference that has an appeal to the particular historian, anthropologist or sociologist using it, not least because of the ideological and ethnocultural perspectives they want to pursue (the collapse of **epistemology** into **ontology**). The understanding and use of 'identity', or race as it still seems to be used by Audrey Smedley, Saul Dubow, Thomas Gossett, Edward Said, Frantz Fanon, George M. Frederickson, Kenan Malik, W.E.B. Du Bois, Ronald Takaki, Paul Gilroy, David Theo Goldberg, Zygmunt Bauman and John Solomos (a list that could be chosen randomly from any reading list on race and history), are all different, though they (almost certainly will) use exactly the same sources (see GENDER; POST-COLONIALISM; CLASS; WOMEN'S HISTORY). Some historians meld concepts together to produce fresh ones like Edward Said's notion of 'orientalism' or the Marxist deconstructionist feminist Gayatri Spivak's definition of race in the context of post-colonialism. So all concepts in history are **historicist** and clearly have their own histories that cannot be disconnected from their own life and times (see FORM AND CONTENT).

Constructed to make sense of both the past and the proposed history **narrative**, race has been deployed over the last four hundred years in a variety of forms that might just be recognisable to historians today even though they are being superseded by new definitions. It seems to me (for the purposes of this narrative I will suggest that) the origins of the concept of race and what constitutes identity are probably ancient and deep-rooted in the past. Ideas about race emerged with others about language, territory and cultural and religious descent. Then, from the fifteenth century and the advent of the European Age of Reconnaissance and from the seventeenth century and the **Enlightenment**, we have the emergence of race as a construction that helped define and explain empirical events such as conquests, imperialisms, colonial conflicts, economic necessities, wars, intellectual superiorities, etc. Race and ethnic distinctions of various kinds, though noted in the sources, were re-invented and contrived afresh to meet changing national, economic, social, migrant, slave, imperial and political contingencies.

Aristotle famously thought that human characteristics both physical and temperamental resulted from climate differences, especially cold and heat, but there was no connection for him between slavery and race. Environmental and cultural distinctions appeared to be more important than race, although toward the close of the Roman period questions were being asked about the nature of the differences between, say, Germans and Libyans. The Catholic Church when it started its missionary work emphasised the unity of mankind, although religious prejudice eventually began to fracture non-racial sentiment. This was seen in the attitude toward the one-time Chosen people, the Jews. Soon the persecution of the Jews became – arguably – almost indistinguishable from our contemporary conception of 'racism'. The historian of race Thomas F. Gossett quotes Peter the Venerable of Cluny as saying 'Really I doubt whether a Jew can be human' (Gossett 1997 [1963]: 11).

When the early European adventurers and explorers first landed in America they at once encountered a 'race problem' with the aboriginal Indians. Were the natives 'men' or beasts?

Very soon the determination was that whatever they were, they were not European and, therefore, were inferior. For the Spanish conquistadors the natives were idolatrous and libidinous (Gossett 1997 [1963]): 12). Social and economic relationships were defined quickly according to race differences. Despite the minority appeal of the concept of the 'Noble Savage' the distinction between 'savagery' and 'civilisation' became a central tenet in the growing thinking of Enlightenment racism. Undoubtedly, however, the defining feature of race and racism lay in the relationship between the white man and the Negro. The 'race problem' was compounded and deepened when in 1619 the first English colonists imported a boatload of Negro slaves. The significance of Negro slavery in creating race theories probably cannot be overestimated (given the available evidence and the present needs of Western society).

Thus it was in the European and American Enlightenment (most historians choose to believe) that race became a significant idea in explaining historical change. Arguably a key move was that of French physician François Bernier who, in 1684, classified the races of mankind. This classification bore the imprint of the poverty of contemporary understanding of biology. Despite the emphasis upon reason and rationality, the philosopher David Hume writing in 1742 equated nationalism with race when he said he had no doubts that 'the Negroes (were) naturally inferior to whites. . . . There never was a civilized nation of any other complexion than white' (Hume quoted in Kramnick 1995: 629). Approving of Hume's comment, Immanuel **Kant** writing in 1764 maintained that the 'Negroes of Africa have by nature no feeling that rises above the trifling' and so fundamental 'is the difference between these two races of man . . . it appears to be as great in regard to mental capacities as in colour' (Kant quoted in Kramnick 1995: 638). The historian James Long writing in 1774 said in *The History of Jamaica* that Negroes are 'marked with the same bestial manners, stupidity, and vices, which debase their brethren on the continent, who seem to be distinguished from the rest of mankind . . . in possessing . . . every species of inherent turpitude' (Long quoted in Kramnick 1995: 644–5).

Though there were attacks on the notion of slavery by a variety of thinkers ranging from Thomas Paine to William Wilberforce, the historian Edward Gibbon reinforced the notion of racism with his comparison between what happened to Rome and what might befall the Europeans and their colonies. It was his claim that the balance of power might be upset should the enemies of civilised society – the savage nations of the globe – become too powerful. The sedimentation of ideas on race was further laid down throughout the nineteenth century with the debates between scientists over the status of the races but all of them generally acknowledged the superiority of whites and inferiority of all others. Indeed, the racial world-view had become the dominant paradigm in the new social sciences. Piggybacking on the theories of polygenesis (theory of multiple creation), Darwinism and the fashionable nineteenth-century appeal of 'stage theories' of historical change, the idea of natural selection was elevated into a support for so-called 'scientific racism'.

Scientific racism presumed to explain 'scientifically' the classification of races and the existence of dominant and subordinate races. This (inevitably?) appealed to the mind of contemporary historians and social scientists like Paul Broca, Hebert Spencer, Sir Francis Galton, Madison Grant and William Z. Ripley, with imperialism, colonialism, the struggle for survival, class conflict and the rise of the eugenics movement culminating in the perverted 'race science' of the German Nazi regime in the 1930s and 1940s. Although there have been occasional efforts to reinvigorate race attitudes in science even up to the present, scientific racism was increasingly challenged, especially from the middle part of the twentieth century, with the developments in genetics, human heredity studies and biology. The upshot has been to rethink the concept of race, recognising human variability without the concept (and classification system) of race.

The role of historians in all this, it might seem, has largely been to simply document such developments with as much precision and objectivity as possible. But this would, of course, be a misunderstanding. As with all histories – the creation of narratives about the past – the historian does not simply refer and describe. Historians configure their narratives for purposes beyond that of simply recording. In creating a history narrative the historian poses questions and it is those questions that create their particular narrative. They ask questions such as 'why was there a challenge to scientific racism after the First World War?' and 'how was race reconceptualised as a result of this challenge?'; or 'is ethnicity just a polite way of referring to racial difference?'; or 'why has white ethnicity not been investigated until recently?'; or 'is racism universal or are there different types?; or 'what are the main elements of Marxist, liberal, postmodern and multiculturalist conceptualisations of race and racism?'; and 'what is "new racism" and why is it criticised?'. In other words – as with all history-making – we get *a* history of race *through* the questions we ask about it. It is plain that changing social attitudes will influence how historians write race. The problem, if there is one here, is not that history is historicist, but that consumers of history (and still many practitioners!) expect historians to provide the objective **truth** that is somehow insulated from their present lives and the epistemological conditions under which they work today (see HISTORICISM). How concepts are derived clearly reveals the oddity of this belief.

Further reading
Anthias, F. and Yuval Davis, M., 1992; Back, L. and Solomos, J., 2000; Balibar, E. and Wallerstein, I., 1991; Bauman, Z., 1989; Bell, B.W. *et al.*, 1996; Bulmer, M. and Solomos, J., 1999; Centre for Contemporary

Cultural Studies 1982; Davidson, J., 2004; Dubow, S., 1994; Fanon, F., 1968 [1952], 1961; Feagin, J.R., 2001; Frederickson, G.M., 2003; Gilroy, P., 1987; Goldberg, D.T., 2002, 1990; Gossett, T.F., 1997 [1963]; Kramnick, I., 1995; Lentin, A., 2004; Malik, K., 1996; Ruiz, V.L. and DuBois, E.C., 2000; Said, E.W., 1993, 1989, 1978; Smedley, A., 1999; Solomos, J., 1993; Takaki, R., 1994.

REALITY/REALISTIC EFFECT

A concept explored at some length by Roland **Barthes** in his essay 'The discourse of history' (1967), it is his argument that the connection between language and history does not rely on any genuine conformity between **evidence** and its constitution as historical fact (see FACTS; SOURCES). This means that what historians take for the actual past is only a reality effect generated by our assumption that the correspondence theory of **truth** allows us to adequately reconstruct the past (see Frank R. ANKERSMIT; RECONSTRUCTION-IST HISTORY; NEW HISTORICISM). In this essay Barthes claims that written history is only one **narrative** among many, and is in no way epistemologically privileged (see EPISTEMOLOGY). As Barthes' interpreter Stephen Bann comments, the 'rhetorical analysis of historical narrative . . . cannot grant to history, a priori, the mythic status which differentiates it from fiction' (Bann 1984: 5).

In 'The discourse' Barthes begins by stating the issue that strikes at the very existence of history as an epistemology. History, he notes, is usually legitimised by the principles of 'rational' exposition but, he asks, does this type of narration really differ in some distinctive way from imaginary narration, as found in the novel or drama? He goes on to challenge the authority of the historian based not only on his/her access to the sources, but more importantly on their translation into historical knowledge and meaning as a narrative of historical interpretation – the translation

of the object into a subject of study. Barthes' challenge takes the shape of a critique of the structure of the historian's **discourse**. The examples he offers include the deployment of lots of the minutiae of **events**, what in the history of art is called the *trompe l'œil* principle whereby such detail aims to give the sense of reality. Barthes further probes the collateral process whereby the historian absents himself/herself from their discourse to create the impression of realism through direct access to the referent, from

> where there is in consequence a systematic deficiency of any form of sign referring to the sender of the historical message. The history seems to be telling itself all on its own. This feature . . . corresponds in effect to the type of historical discourse labelled as 'objective' (in which the historian never intervenes). . . . On the level of discourse, objectivity – or the deficiency of signs of the utterer – thus appears as a particular form of imaginary projection, the product of what might be called the referential illusion, since in this case the historian is claiming to allow the referent to speak all on its own.
>
> (Barthes 1967: 65–75; trans. Bann 1981: 11)

The epistemological status of historical discourse is thus asserted. The historical fact is privileged by being placed in the specially reserved position of a superior claim to truthfulness as warranted by both a plain language and an independent research methodology as supported in the references – the scaffolding of proper historical methodology. Barthes is suggesting that history is performing an epistemological trick through which the referent is placed in a privileged world of the real beyond arbitrary signification. As he says, in classically structuralist terms, 'The historian is not so much a collector of facts as a collector and relator of signifiers; that is to say, he organises them with the purpose of establishing positive meaning' (Barthes

1967: 65–75; trans. Bann 1981: 16). Following Barthes we may also acknowledge the issue of **representation** and the troping of the real as central to creating historical meaning (see DECONSTRUCTIONIST HISTORY; TROPE/FIGURATION; Hayden WHITE; Jean BAUDRILLARD).

Further reading

Ankersmit, F.R., 2005a, 2005b, 2001, 1994; Bann, S., 1984; Barthes, R., 1967; Berlin, I., 1997; Bunzl, M., 1997; Carr, D., 1986a; Iggers, G., 1997; Lorenz, C., 1994; Putnam, H., 1988, 1983; Ricoeur, P., 1984; Searle, J.R., 1995; Tallis, R., 1998; White, H., 1998

RECONSTRUCTIONIST HISTORY

Reconstructionist history describes the self-proclaimed metaphysical (see METAPHYSICS) realist, common-sense, empiricist, referential, truth-conditional, objectivised, inferential, non-theory and non-ideological professional history produced in the wake of the **Enlightenment** in the mid- to late nineteenth century after the advent and rejection of **positivism** (see Geoffrey ELTON; EMPIRICISM; EVIDENCE; FACTS; HISTORICAL EXPLANATION; INFERENCE; OBJECTIVITY; SOURCES; TRUTH). This modernist-inspired (see MODERNISM) scientific model for the study of the past resulted directly from the severing of **ontology** from **epistemology**, a move that demanded the separation of subject and object, and the observer from that which is observed. Reconstructionist history insists that its methodology (underpinned as it is by this philosophical position) allows the historian to disinterestedly discover the most probably truthful (and also, therefore, morally certain) interpretation inherent in the documents of the past, and write it up in a monograph. It is claimed that the true intentions and voices of people in the past will speak to, and through, the reconstructionist

historian (see INTENTIONALITY; ORAL HISTORY).

The success of this approach to any kind of history has been such that by the end of the nineteenth century it had become culturally embedded as the proper way to reanimate the past. The present generation of historians have, however, experienced a challenge to that model. This has taken shape as a postmodern (see POSTMODERNISM) rethinking of history's literary form as a cognitive (knowing) instrument and consequently raised questions about history's legitimacy as an independent epistemology. Baldly stated, this challenge has confronted history as an inferential procedure through both the **linguistic turn** and the **aesthetic turn** which have been underpinned by developments in **continental philosophy**, **critical theory** and **post-structuralism**. That challenge emerged in the past thirty years as a part of our postmodern conditions of knowledge creation. The habit of history writing in the West was fixed originally and firmly in the correspondence theory of knowledge (common-sense empiricism). It has become so entrenched that any questioning of it generates reconstructionist claims of, at the very least, moral degeneracy in the questioner. It also carries with it the conviction and certitude that there is only one way to 'do history'. The anticipated truthfulness in its accounts (reconstructing the past as it actually was, or to use Ranke's dictum of *wie es eigentlich gewesen*) emerges because it was/is built upon the primary sources and, so the reconstructionist argument runs, we are capable of writing truth-conditional descriptions in everyday language. History has, quite simply, a formal and generally accepted assortment of operations and practices that permit genuine knowledge about the past.

Empiricism, as the methodology of reconstructionist history, assumes that its mode of explanation springs from the skills of the historian in addressing the **evidence** (see SOURCES). Reconstructionist historians substantiate their factual knowledge of the past, in large part, because they claim they can remain unmoved by their perception of it – what the most vociferous of reconstructionists, G.R. **Elton**, described as the 'rational, independent and impartial investigation' of the evidence (Elton 1991: 6). The reconstructionist methodology of interrogating the evidence through comparison, verification, contextualisation and authentication entails rejecting both R.G. **Collingwood**'s idea that writing history can involve an intellectual re-enactment in the historian's mind (producing the danger of **relativism**), and the misplaced idea that we can never have a genuine knowledge of the real past because of the instability of language and its fabricated **narrative** form (see FORM AND CONTENT).

The greatest mistake historians can make, so Elton and more recent reconstructionists like Richard Evans, John Warren and Arthur Marwick argue, is to deny the possibility of objectivity because of the unavoidable imposition of the voice of the **author** (Evans 1997a; Warren 1998; Marwick 2001). Placing his defence within his rejection of the positivist wing of reconstructionism (an important border skirmish on the road to reconstructionism's purist empiricism), Elton offers the example of how objectivity disappears when social science theories are imported into history. He argues that such imports arrive at their dubious results by setting up a theoretical model that their makers then claim to either validate or disprove by an 'experimental' application of factual detail, a process Elton believes to be honoured more in the breach than the observance (Elton 1991: 10). When probed, Elton's careful attention to the archive that reconstructionists insist upon rests on several related beliefs: that the past was once real and because of that it is knowable now because truth corresponds to that reality through the unearthing of the facts in the evidence, that there is an unambiguous distinction of fact and fiction, that truth to be truth must be derived independently of the historian and (consequently) that truth is not perspectival. Elton summarises the reconstructionist view of knowledge creation when he says (ibid.: 52),

We are looking for a way to ground historical reconstruction in something that offers a measure of independent security – independent of the historian, independent of the concerns of his day, independent of the social and political conditions imposed on him. And the obvious answer to this quest, as it has always been and must continue to be, lies in the sources he has at his disposal.

In the past three decades a practical realist consensus has developed in response to the postmodernist attack on reconstructionist history. This new consensus has, by and large, not been raised in defence of Eltonian reconstructionism, but rather to modify the crudities of naïve empiricism – also to tactfully and tactically point out what is often claimed to be the straw-man nature of the object of the postmodernist attack. This consensus of constructionist historians (see CONSTRUCTIONIST HISTORY) of various stripes (sociological, anthropological, conceptual, new empiricist) claims to inject into the debate a more sophisticated and sensible appreciation of the difficulties of researching and writing history. After all, so the new consenting empiricists argue, no one these days really practises the absolutist kind of history that old-fashioned reconstructionism represents. This reasonable (in tone) and rationalist new practical realist or constructionist voice stresses the complexity of the relationship between facts and interpretation. It acknowledges the central problem of written history's poor fit with the realities of the past. The precursors to this new practical realism emerged in the United States in the 1930s with the first (pre-Eltonian) reaction against nineteenth-century positivism led by the two American historians Carl **Becker** and Charles Beard. Influenced by the Italian historian Benedetto **Croce**, Becker and Beard contested the possibility of an objectivist history that claimed to be above and beyond present cultural concerns. Becker summarised his idea of **relativism** by arguing that historical thinking 'is a social instrument, helpful in getting the world's work more effectively done' (Becker quoted in Novick 1988: 98).

In a suitably sceptical new practical realist fashion the American intellectual historian David Hollinger has argued that the historian's personal leanings are less a constraint and more an imperative that makes historical interpretation possible (Hollinger 1989: 613). Historians, but not of a crude reconstructionist kind (the straw-man hypothesis holding that there are none around any more), are now fully aware of the hermeneutic (see HERMENEUTICS) circle. This is a situation of which, so Hollinger claims, critics like Joan Scott and David Harlan seem not to be aware. In other words, the historian today knows how tricky hermeneutics is, and that we can never encounter an Archimedean point of a grounded or true historical object, and cannot, therefore, reconstruct the past as it actually happened. Hollinger accepts the difficulties historians have in translating the documents into facts and generating an appropriate interpretation of events (see EVENT). Along with all new practical realists (i.e. simply all historians), Hollinger claims to recognise that the historian cannot be insulated from the construction(ist history) process as reconstructionists like Elton once naïvely believed. Hollinger insists, speaking for practical realists and, by implication, also for reconstructionists, that our theories about the past must be tested in the crucible of the evidence, and while our measures of agent intentionality are not absolute, the voice of the past remains in the documents. Postmodern concerns about our ability to know and to represent what we believe we know are not convincing enough to cast genuine doubts about proper history for the reconstructionist historian. As Hollinger concludes, 'I do not understand the mystery of knowing, but I believe this mystery has survived the return of literature' (Hollinger 1989: 621). Or, as another reconstructionist historian is quoted as saying, try punching a postmodernist in the face and see if he can explain why it hurts (Colin Richmond quoted in Warren 1998: 191).

Further reading

Ankersmit, F.R., 2005b; Appleby, J. *et al.*, 1994; Beard, C., 1935, 1933; Becker, C., 1931; Berkhofer, R.F., 1995; Bunzl, M., 1997; Carrard, P., 1992; Collingwood, R.G., 1994 [1946]; Croce, B., 1970 [1927]; Domanska, E., 1998a; Elton, G., 1991 [1955]; Evans, R.J., 1997a, 1997b; Harlan, D., 1997, 1989; Hexter, J.H., 1991; Hollinger, D.A., 1991, 1989; Hunt, L., 1989; Jenkins, K., 2003 [1991]; 1999b, 1997, 1995; Kellner, H., 1989; Lorenz, C., 1994; McCullagh, C.B., 1991; Marwick, A., 2001; Mink, L., 1978; Munslow, A., 1997a; Norman, A.P., 1991; Novick, P., 1988; Poster, M., 1997; Roberts, G., 1998, 1997; Scott, J.W., 1996a; Topolski, J., 1991; Warren, J., 1998.

RELATIVISM

Adherents of **postmodernism** tend to hold that conventional history can no longer be regarded as an objective method for the discovery of the **truth** of the past (see EMPIRICISM; OBJECTIVITY). Postmodern thinking certainly maintains that we can no longer be assured a posteriori (see A PRIORI/A POSTERIORI) that correspondence or **representation** theories of knowledge work despite the claims of practitioners of **reconstructionist history** to the contrary. This means there are no solid meanings, no certain **facts**, no foundational knowing subject, and we are witness to the collapse of various dubious binomials: knower and known, subject and object, fact and fiction, **form and content**, etc. The representational connection between the word and the world is rejected as a naïve assumption. So the grandest modernist **narrative**, history, is revealed to be a hollow and illicit **epistemology**, the last refuge of **modernism**'s empiricist delusion. Such anti-historical opinions, according to the empiricist response, open the floodgates of moral relativism because they indicate a failure to ground truth as conforming to reality and, what is worse, permit the anti-representationalist argument, for example, that the Nazi Holocaust or the ethnic cleansing of Kosovan Albanians by the Yugoslav Serbs can only be understood as a text and as such trivialise genocide. Fortunately, so the reconstructionist argument runs, relativism can be easily diagnosed and, if proper action is taken early enough, it can be cured.

Relativism comes in two varieties: metaphysical (see METAPHYSICS) and epistemological. Metaphysical relativism doubts that there is a reality 'out there' independent of our minds. For such a full-blooded relativist it is not a matter of the adequacy of our **concepts in history** to grasp reality, but that our concepts actually create reality for us. Metaphysical relativists believe that what we call reality is only an appearance in our mind's eye. All objects are mental fabrications, representations, semblances, linguistic constructs. Reality cannot be known (if it exists) independently of our minds and those inventions we call our organising concepts.

Epistemological relativism falls somewhat short of the fully matured metaphysical variety, suggesting that our knowledge of the real world has to be assisted by our mental constructs. But our situation in the world and, therefore, our conceptualisation and representation are affected by many forces beyond our control: how old we are, our **race**, the **class** we think we belong to, our **gender**, our ideological preferences and the historical time and place in which we live. To argue that these constraints have at least some effect on how and what we think is hard to dispute. They are bound to affect how we think about the past and influence how we write history. But most epistemological relativists, in acknowledging such constraints, stop well short of denying that there is no approximate truth in history. They are content to distance themselves from the metaphysical relativism found in much postmodernist thinking (Appleby *et al.* 1994).

The roots of postmodernist relativism are to be found in the **historicism** of Friedrich **Hegel** and Karl Marx, and in the inspira-

tion of Friedrich **Nietzsche** as digested by Ludwig Wittgenstein and more recently Jean **Baudrillard**, Richard **Rorty**, Keith **Jenkins**, Hayden **White** and Jacques **Derrida**. Historicism, as understood by Hegel, assumes that truth is relative to time and place. Marx took up a similar relativist position in his base–superstructure metaphor through which he imagined truth to be contingent on economic structures via false consciousness. But, the likes of Hegel and Marx apart, historians have tended to express their faith in their craft by investing in the certainty of representation while being judicious about the stories it tells of the past.

However, no amount of judicial circumspection about historical narratives or, for that matter, feelings of moral superiority can deny the nature of linguistic and cultural relativism. Linguistic relativists maintain that what counts as truth is at best the product of grammatical rules and structures. Ludwig Wittgenstein famously argued from this perspective that language creates our apprehension of reality. Just as air is the medium in which birds fly, so language conditions how we exist. Wittgenstein called the codes structuring a language a 'game' that we all must play when we express ourselves through a language. Playing the 'language game' means we are participating in a particular life. So when we write history – as a conditioning part of our life – it too is formed by our language use. As the French cultural critic Jean Baudrillard has suggested, the sign according to modernist thinking has been taken (by representationalists) to be capable of being exchanged for true meaning (history is thus seen as an exchange for the past). That exchange has conventionally been guaranteed by the referential power of representation, which permits historians to know through **inference**, the **intentionality** in the mind of the historical agent.

But what if we call the bluff of representation? If we do, then surely is not historical representation, by definition, a constant simulation? In Baudrillard's terms, history is nothing more than a gigantic simulacrum. This does not make the past unreal but it does make the-past-as-history a simulacrum, a simulation exercise, pretence and/or a hyper-real version. So, although it can never actually exchange itself for what was once real, the empiricist claim for such an exchange continues to be made with its charge of moral relativism if it cannot (see Roland **Barthes**; **reality/realistic effect**). What reconstructionist empiricists and even more sophisticated constructionist historians (see CONSTRUCTIONIST HISTORY; CARL BECKER) have in common is their bedrock belief in knowable reality, so both reject the postmodern idea of history as an uninterrupted interpretative circuit, a fictive intellectual process ultimately without reference or boundary. Empiricism denies (by its definition) that we can only 'know' history through history, in other words, only through a perspective that is within history. Empiricists tend to regard as sinister the postmodern vision of the world 'back there' as just a jumble of signs and symbols, the meanings of which are constantly deferred and self-referential, with signifiers signifying only themselves.

Based on the thinking of Baudrillard, for example, I can imagine several stages (of representation) through which history passes in its descent into simulacra. History begins by being conceived as the mirror image of the reality that exists in the archive; next history dissembles and corrupts past reality as the historian domesticates, prefigures, configures, plans and organises it; next it necessarily (and cunningly?) disguises its growing lack of contact with past reality through the device of referentiality; finally, with its bluff called, it is shown to have lost all connection to past reality (see MIMESIS). It has become a simulacrum – a TV programme, re-enactment, film, etc. History has achieved its ultimate state of relativism when it can only be judged by itself as when historians judge each other, and the past becomes forever unknowable. At this postmodern point there is no longer a foundational standard by which we can judge the-past-as-history.

In his book *Philosophy and the Mirror of Nature*, the American philosopher Richard Rorty declared dead modernist (i.e. foundationalist, representationalist, grand narrative) philosophy (see Jean-François LYOTARD). In applying Rorty's thinking to history, Keith Jenkins makes the point that Rorty (who, like Baudrillard, is starting from a Nietzschean position that doubts the knowability of the real world) is saying to historians that we have to come to terms with a compromised correspondence theory of truth, and that the past can only be usefully understood as **historiography**. This means that any claims history makes to an epistemological hold on the past should be seen at best as spurious, and at worst as dangerous, repressive nonsense. How many times has the phrase 'empirical reality' been used to defend the morally indefensible or the politically expedient?

After Baudrillard and Rorty (and others like Southgate, Jenkins, White and Derrida) it is reasonable to ask if in our postmodern age, with its demise of the knowing subject, we can ever again claim to experience the unalloyed joy of empiricist and meaningful history? Most historians argue that we can overcome this lurch into relativism by maintaining a 'bystander' theory of historical knowledge. They believe they can avoid (both varieties of) relativism by endorsing the 'common-sense' or 'natural' empirical wish to give credence to a knowable and real past 'by standing' outside the language and belief game. This is then reinforced by their regular empirical drills of **evidence** verification and comparison, contextualisation, **colligation**, establishing **causation** and intentionality (rational-action theory) and the argument that relativists try to retain to themselves what they deny to everyone else with relativism proposed as the true way of seeing reality(!). In being self-referential, deconstructionist (see DECONSTRUCTIONIST HISTORY) historians are being inconsistent – to be relativist you have to accept the relativism of your relativist position. Mainstream sophisticated, if sceptical, representational empiricist historians accept a degree of perspectivism in their work, but as a group they do not give up on the idea of deriving meaning through representation and, therefore, objectively discovering the truth of the past. Historians, in spite of all the pitfalls of relativism, can still, so the majority believe, produce truth-conditional sentences. When the evidence is adequately supported by appropriate social theory historians can escape from the relativism of beliefs, language and simulacra.

Further reading

Appleby, J. *et al.*, 1994; Baudrillard, J., 1983, 1976; Bernstein, R., 1983; Davidson, D., 1984; Finney, P., 1998; Harris, J.F., 1992; Jameson, F., 1976; Krausz, M., 1989; Putnam, H., 1981; Quine, W.V., 1969, 1960; Rorty, R., 1991, 1982; Sellars, W., 1997 [1956]; Southgate, B., 2000; Warren, J., 1998; Wittgenstein, L., 1995 [1921].

REPRESENTATION

Today, the nature of representation is the single most important issue in our understanding of what is history. How we think and practice the discipline depends upon both our knowledge of and/or our epistemological orientation toward our engagement with the past (see EPISTEMOLOGY). As a result of the **event**s of the past century many of the 'foundational' beliefs that have underpinned Western culture – science, **truth**, **objectivity**, purpose and progress – have been viewed with increased scepticism and in some instances rejected. The consequence of our late modern condition of epistemic scepticism has been to challenge afresh the 'principles of knowing' that have come to inform disciplines particularly in the humanities, arts and social sciences. All this has produced several 'turns' and developments – the **linguistic turn**, **ethical turn** and **aesthetic turn** – plus advances in **critical theory**, **continental philosophy**, **poststructuralism**, **intellectual history** and **cultural history**. The consequence has been a re-thinking that distinguishes history from the past at a fundamental epistemological level.

Often 'postmodern history' is regarded simply as an acknowledgement of the cognitive consequences of its written, rhetorical, composed and configured form (see POST-MODERNISM). But it is far more than that. Understanding history as what it is, a representation of the past, historians are well overdue re-aligning the discipline as an aesthetic *as well as* an empirical and analytical activity. It is time that historians caught up with modernist literature's effort to comprehend and probe the limits of 'reality' and 'objectivity'. To be a historian today is not to assume that knowing what happened is the primal basis for knowing what it all means. The concept of 'truth' is far more complex than that. This is the context for the 'crisis of representation' that has prompted the effort to challenge **empiricism**'s belief that we can know the reality of the past independently of our representations of it.

However, several distinctions have to be sorted out before we can develop our understanding of what history is as a representation. These include the distinction between an event and its representation, between **sources** and histories, between histories and their cultural contexts, between 'literal' and 'figurative' language, between the past (as a referent) and the history (as a **discourse**), and most importantly we must sophisticate our understanding of the difference between the 'fictive' (narratively constructed) and the 'factual' (see EMPLOTMENT). Though single statements of **justified belief** are and remain referential, they are still descriptions that can only be given a meaning when they are represented in a **narrative**. Therefore, while events happened, their representation takes them to a level of understanding that possesses the characteristics of literary subjects (see FORM AND CONTENT; Frank R. ANKERSMIT).

Collapsing the above distinctions manifestly complicates our understanding of the supposed difference between history and literature, but it also has the therapeutic benefit of freeing us from the correspondence theory of truth. To exist in a universe characterised by an endless crisis of representation is to be always suspicious of the easy claims of 'empirical truth' as the facile connection is made between what was/is and what it *must* (have) mean(t). The exclusive property right history has had on 'knowing the truth about the past' is now ended. Not that this is really news. The 'crisis of representation' has been with us, on and off, since Plato, although the Nietzschean advance of irony and scepticism and the Kantian critique of reason thrust it forcefully onto our agenda (see Friedrich NIETZSCHE; Immanuel KANT). Henceforth history really should be viewed as a set of empty aesthetic signifiers that we fill with our empirical knowledge and, because of that, what we believe the past means can *only* be generated through the history we write about it.

The major contemporary theorist of historical representation is the Dutch philosopher of history Frank A. Ankersmit. He has answered the most common criticisms of the crisis of representation straightforwardly. The primary (and foolish) claim of historical realists is that if we cannot represent past reality as it actually was then we cannot know its truth, and this means we are free to say whatever we want and claim it as 'truth' (see RELATIVISM). Ankersmit's first response is to reject this notion as specious. While he recognises that the problem of textual representation is unavoidable because it is clearly impossible to represent anything completely or even adequately he accepts that historians (like painters) can and do refer. But we cannot scrape our representations to 'get back to' the thing in itself. If we scour the paint off Albert Bierstadt's *The Rocky Mountains* (1863) we won't 'get back to' anything but the canvas on which the oils were applied. Histories are no different. Like brush strokes, statements of justified belief can give a sense of heightened realism, but that is all they can do. Historical narratives are not just congeries of such statements.

We can say, for example, 'upon the death of Henry I in 1135, the Norman nobles at first offered the Duchy of Normandy to Theobald'. But we must recognise that this description uniquely identifies people and recorded events and the description refers exclusively to them. Quite plainly, however, this does not work with historical narratives. Descriptions such as 'the foundation of the English Common Law' or the 'picaresque proletarian' (Linebaugh 2003: 119), or 'the last years of Henry VIII' or 'the French Revolution' or 'the war on terror' cannot refer in the sense just noted – to a unique and highly specific event or person or precise and strictly limited situation. If you read a history *text* on the foundation of the English Common Law what can such a text refer to? It will possess lots of references but what, after all, exactly is the English Common Law? Is it what Henry II had in mind, or what the historian F.W. Maitland had in his mind? What makes it what it is represented as? What can we historians include in it or leave out when we use that phrase? Do we include/leave out the 'King's peace'? 'Eyres' (visits of Royal Judges)? Record keeping?

The English Common Law isn't over yet either. A history requires historiography and we cannot know what it is going to become for historians yet to write about it. The topic has also to be turned into 6,000-word articles or books of 80,000 words. What does this do to that chunk of 'the past' we represent as the 'English Common Law'? Clearly, we cannot use the notion of reference for something that is ultimately unknown and subject to historical debate. There is, for example, no unique *essence* to, say, 'the war on terror'. If there were it would only have one *meaning*. To refer, as we have seen, is to note what is absolutely unique about the object. We can, obviously, refer to the other histories (narratives) written by historians because they are unique, but of themselves they cannot pin down *the* essence – *the* meaning – of, say, the 'last years of Henry VIII'. We might well argue everything we know about the founding of the English Common Law and which historians can agree upon are merely necessary but cannot ever become sufficient conditions for the description to refer (Ankersmit 2005: 23–33) (see TRUTH; CAUSATION; HISTORICAL EXPLANATION; HISTORICAL IMAGINATION; RECONSTRUCTIONIST HISTORY; CONSTRUCTIONIST HISTORY; DECONSTRUCTIONIST HISTORY; SOURCES; Hayden WHITE; EMPLOTMENT; COLLIGATION).

Clarifying reference does not, however, clear up the issue of representation. There is also the not so small matter of truth. As shorthand we can define truth as propositions that are in agreement with knowable reality. We can 'truthfully' say, for example, that William Gladstone's first government was between 1868 and 1874. The subject of this sentence is Gladstone and the predicate was his first government from 1868 to 1874. This statement is true because the subject and predicate denote a state of reality and so it is a statement of justified belief. But there is no automatic cranking up from this level to that of the connotative narrative. No narrative, by this logic, can be 'truthful'. The reason is simply that the subject of the sentence (Gladstone) is ascribed properties (the predicate of his first government) but this truth cannot work at the level of large-scale historical narratives. This is because, while we can assume identifiable connections between subject and predicate in a sentence, that logic does not apply to a narrative. The history text cannot be connected to the past in subject–predicate terms. So sentences can refer, but narratives cannot. They can only be *about* the past – hence we create 'the-past-as-history'. Of course, in all reasonableness, there is probably some kind of sliding scale between description and representation – there are complex clauses, paragraphs, descriptions that range from tight referential ones to greater generalisations. We weigh some justified beliefs more heavily than others; different historians combine them in diverse ways. Truth in a narrative is not ever as straightforward as justified belief. It is this situation that gives opportunities, among other things, for **experimental history**.

So histories can, and invariably do, contain referential sentence-length descriptions. And this disposes of the misapprehension that accepting the 'crisis of representation' means being unable to refer to what we feel justified in believing happened – 'the past'. But to then assume willy-nilly that we can now 'tell the truth' in a narrative is akin to saying that we can 'tell the truth' of *The Rocky Mountains* as a painting, or that we can 'tell the truth' about *Macbeth* as a play. Descriptions allow historians to refer and attribute properties, but not at the level of representations. The clearest illustration of this is that of a photograph that is intended to be a realistic representation of a person. In such a photograph you cannot distinguish what refers to the person and those parts that attribute properties to them. In other words, representation is not reference; it is *about* its subject. That history contains references does not authorise our access to the past's meaning. And, of course, 'references to what happened' are almost always contested anyway. History is certainly about interpretation, but not just at the referential level.

Only historical representations can be narrated – that is, prearranged, reasoned, emplotted – and thereby become plausible. To argue there is coherence in *a* history is not the same as saying it reconstructs *the* coherence of past reality. The key issue in historical analysis is not the correspondence between the narrative and the past for, as a representation, we know history cannot undertake this task. What history (defined as that narrative we create *about* the past) can do is simply generate *a* connection between representation and what it purports to represent. This is not the same as description, which has no concern for coherence, emplotment and plausibility. Accordingly, it would be wrong to dismiss the representational as opposed to the descriptive character of history. Most importantly, what we choose as our conceptualisation of past reality at the level of representation actually determines what we will 'find' on the level of the represented (past reality). This does not mean all we can have is some kind of ridiculously relativist magic realist history (well, of course we can, if we want to write it that way and agree to call it history) (see RELATIVISM). But what it does mean is that the (aesthetic) decisions we make about our narrative representation will directly affect what (the data descriptions) we eventually choose to put into it and what we make them mean.

The conclusion seems clear. There are two basic forces in making history – those descriptions we feel justified in believing refer to what was once real *and* the representation we call our narrative. Those historians who fail to grasp this can be identified because, typically, they tend to make the claim that 'history can tell the truth about the past though be it through a glass darkly'. They also have a propensity to refer to 'history' when they should talk of 'the past'. This is because they make the category mistake of connecting knowing what happened with meaning. What they do not understand is that *a* meaning for the past (assuming it can be generated at all) derives from the process of its representation. There is a simple way to remember this: every referential statement has to be signified. That is to say, the historian has to create a meaning for them. Or, as the historical theorist Michel de Certeau describes it, we must all 'envision the operation that turns the practice of investigation into writing' (de Certeau (1988 [1975]: 86).

Further reading

Ankersmit, F.R., 2005a, 2005b, 2003a, 2003b, 2002, 2001, 2000, 1998a, 1998b, 1994, 1989, 1983; Ankersmit, F.R. and Kellner, H. 1995; Appleby, J. *et al.*, 1994; Auerbach, E., 1953; Bann, S., 1984; Barta, T., 1998; Barthes, R., 1988, 1986, 1984 [1967], 1983, 1981 [1967], 1977, 1975, 1974, 1972, 1967, 1957; Benveniste, E., 1971; Brown, C.G., 2005; Chartier, R., 1988; de Certeau, M., 1988 [1975]; Evans, R., 1997a; Friedlander, S., 1992; Fulbrook, M., 2002; Jenkins, K., 2003; Jenkins, K. and Munslow, A., 2004; Kellner, H., 1989; Linebaugh, P., 2003; Marwick, A., 2001; Munslow, A., 2003a, 2003b, 1997; Munslow, A. and Rosenstone, R.A., 2004; Nye, A., 1998; Pihlainen, K., 2002; Popper, K.R., 1979; Putnam, H., 1992; Rigney, A., 2001; Rorty, R., 1992 [1967], 1979; White, H., 2000, 1998, 1996, 1995, 1992, 1987, 1984, 1978, 1974, 1973a, 1973b.

RORTY, RICHARD (1931–)

Although originally an analytical philosopher trained to pursue the **truth** conditions of propositions and the logical structure of thought, in the second half of his career from the late 1970s Richard Rorty began to question the conventional categories of analytical philosophy – knowable reality, **objectivity**, truth and **epistemology** (theory of knowledge). He replaced these interests with a postmodernist rendering of pragmatism in the tradition of the **continental philosophy** of Hans-Georg Gadamer, Martin Heidegger, Jürgen Habermas, Jacques **Derrida** and Michel **Foucault** as well as his own rendition of the work of the American pragmatist John Dewey (see HERMENEUTICS; INTELLECTUAL HISTORY; CRITICAL THEORY). Rorty's philosophical ideas are important to the humanities in general but especially to literary theory and history (see NEW HISTORY). His significance as a key thinker in postmodern (see POSTMODERNISM) philosophy lies in his rejection of reasonless foundationalism in all its disguises: grand theories, notions of truth and meaning, the autonomous knowing subject, **empiricism**, limpid **representation** leading to unclouded or mirror-like referentiality, distanced objectivity, the correspondence theory of knowledge and knowable reality (see MIMESIS).

Instead of this verism Rorty favours the sceptical acceptance of contingency and uncertainty, the necessity for perpetual dialogue rather than truthful or absolute answers, the parochial rather than universal nature of truth (localised truth effects), situational ethics (see ETHICAL TURN), the irresolvable polarity of appearance and reality, and the **relativism** associated with the inability of the human mind to stand outside its own terms of reference (in order to mirror reality). But Rorty rejects as a misunderstanding of his position (associated with critics like Christopher Norris) the idea that he is either sceptical or relativist, arguing instead that he is merely pointing out the anti-representational/description-dependent, gendered, ethno-cultural and historical situatedness of knowledge. Rorty's argument is that just because our beliefs are constituted within our situation, this does not mean we cannot rationally justify our views. Moral truths may not be objectively derived but we can still tell the fascists from the good guys and that holocausts occurred in the past and are occurring in the present. What Rorty is saying is that how we narrate such **event**s influences the meaning we derive from them (see DISCOURSE; NARRATIVE; NEW HISTORICISM).

Analytical philosophy, as the central twentieth-century tradition of Western **metaphysics**, tried, in the work of Bertrand Russell and the younger Wittgenstein, to expose reality's logical form – attempting to demonstrate that language is essentially representational and transparent. Through language, specifically the grammatical sentence, analytical philosophers told us we could access the real world of our present and past existence. In later years Wittgenstein rebelled against this, taking up what has been called ordinary-language philosophy, and in the process stimulated a fresh interpretation of the connections between language, philosophy and knowledge. Rorty's post-epistemological radicalism (that is, a state wherein knowledge cannot precisely represent reality) is derived from the anti-representationalist view he has of language. This view is derived from the pre-postmodern and pre-post-structuralist critique of the representational language of Friedrich **Nietzsche**, Ferdinand de Saussure, John Dewey, Wittgenstein (later in life), Donald Davidson and W.V. Quine. During his own working career Rorty has been influenced by the deconstructionism of Derrida, Foucault and Roland **Barthes**. The point here is the simple one that once we move from the single statement of fact (the factual sentence) to the level of discourse (the interpretation), that which we believe we know and that which we metaphorically create are no longer completely separate entities and, significantly, the subject–object binary effectively disappears (see HISTORICAL IMAGINATION; TROPE/FIGURATION).

Rorty's most influential book is *Philosophy and the Mirror of Nature* (1979), in which he argues against essentialist and representationalist thinking in philosophy. For historians Rorty's message is that **empiricism**, the correspondence theory of truth and **inference** to the best explanation are not universally valid methods because they are constantly jeopardised by the historicist nature of language (see HISTORICISM). In his book *Consequences of Pragmatism* (1982) he rejects the description of him as a relativist in favour of that of pragmatist, arguing that the search for absolutist methodologies that will deliver *the* truth is a fruitless exercise and should be abandoned. Instead he favours the pragmatic pursuit of the useful and prods us toward accepting that knowledge is subject to the context of its production/construction. In his book *Contingency, Irony and Solidarity* (1989) Rorty turns to face the issue of the intellectual's private imaginative construction of knowledge, the sharp edges of which are publicly held in check by the political ethics he associates with liberalism.

Language is no longer the vehicle to deliver truth. Instead it is an elastic medium for self-realisation and for the creation of new kinds of expression. Conventionally language is used by historians as a largely unproblem-atic way of organising our perceptions of the content of the past, the organisation of which permits the use of the logic of inference. But Rorty argues that perception and inference are the somewhat limited consequences of viewing language as the medium for express-ing the inexpressible. Instead Rorty suggests that by recognition of the power of lan-guage to turn meaning – through the rule of the metaphor – we can rethink language as a mechanism that can re-form our historical truths by the translation of the metaphoric into the literal (see LINGUISTIC TURN). In this way the American historian of the frontier experience Frederick Jackson Turn-er's waves of Western pioneers expressed the inexorable movement of American national-ism, and the American race leader and social historian William E.B. Du Bois's key meta-phor of the veil of **race** served to describe a whole culture's historical experience. Neither use of language is 'wrong' because they serve liberating purposes in writing history.

While it is possible to remain relaxed about the fact that such descriptive language is a form of knowing, the historian becomes what Rorty calls an 'ironist' only when he/she faces up to his/her doubts about language and the influences exerted over him/her by being born at a certain time in a certain place (Rorty 1998: 307). Rorty's 'liberal ironist' thus speaks of 'truths' ill recognised and constantly doubted rather than merely stretching the expressive powers of language. In the postist world the 'real', as Hayden **White** suggests, is always cast in a self-consciously sceptical tone, the intention of which is to constantly bring forth the relativism of the 'real' (White 1973b: 37). Irony is, therefore, the intellec-tual form of postmodernism: that phase of consciousness in which the cloudy nature of language has been finally grasped and in which reality can only be expressed through the negation of the literal (see EPISTEME). Irony should not, after all, upset the already sceptical empiricist as it often seems to; rather it should assist them in taking that extra step

that will extend their scepticism to the lan-guage they use.

The fact that a continuing ironic narra-tive thus replaces universal truth ought to strengthen the historical consciousness, because the historian can now only touch base with the past once he/she has realised that language no longer faithfully represents transcendent or universal truths. However, it is not unalloyed good news for historians – especially reconstructionist historians (see RECONSTRUCTIONIST HISTORY). By accepting a Rortyan post-epistemological position it becomes increasingly difficult to sustain the notion of reaching not just final, but any genuinely truthful, conclusions about what actually happened in the past. The aim in a Rortyan world is to acknowledge and welcome, even celebrate, the indeterminate and interpretational nature of history as a linguistic dialogue about the past, rather than try to empirically domesticate it by trying to find out what really happened (hence the oxymoron of the definitive interpretation!). In this way post-epistemological historians are allowed to see themselves as authors (see AUTHOR) who intervene and re-create the connection between reality and writing. They no longer *have to* see themselves as objective explorers who can only infer and theorise according to the **evidence**.

Experimentation rather than definitive truth-seeking is now the keystone of this new version of (Rortyan) or postmodern history (see EXPERIMENTAL HISTORY). The fact that the methodological rituals of tradi-tional modernist history are imposed in the public sphere is a bad habit we should try to break, if only in private (see the ENLIGHT-ENMENT; MODERNISM). Forcing our views on others through the public sphere would be, after all, an unwelcome form of intellectual coercion ill-befitting an ironic and laid-back Rortyan historian. So it's live and let live among historians of every stripe – reconstructionist, construction-ist (see CONSTRUCTIONIST HISTORY) and deconstructionist (see DECONSTRUC-

TIONIST HISTORY). If some historians wish to claim that their own particular method delivers truth through their arrangement of **form and content** then so be it – but let others do it differently if they so wish. While Rorty's position has been variously (and usually unfairly) described as linguistic reductionism, or as being out of touch with reality, or profligate in its incapacity to tell right from wrong, doing history differently does not necessarily equate with social irresponsibility. Indeed, might it not be more irresponsible to beat the past to death with the blunt instrument of a doubtful empiricism in the belief that eventually it will be forced to yield 'the truth'?

Further reading

Ankersmit, F.R., 2005b; Bhaskar, R., 1991; Davidson, D., 1984; Norris, C., 1992; Quine, W.V., 1990, 1969; Rorty, R., 1998, 1992 [1967], 1992, 1991, 1989, 1982, 1979; Sellars, W., 1997 [1956]; White, H., 1973b.

S

SOURCES

The role and functioning of the sources in history depends on the historian's **epistemological** position (see RECONSTRUCTIONIST HISTORY; CONSTRUCTIONIST HISTORY; DECONSTRUCTIONIST HISTORY). For reconstructionist historians the documentary sources are the foundation of the empirical-analytical method and as such they are the raw materials from which the **facts** are generated (see EMPIRICISM). Reconstructionist Arthur Marwick has offered his clarion call to all like-minded historians: 'forget facts, foreground sources' (Marwick 2001: 152–94). As he correctly says, historians do not discover the facts, they engage with **event**s and the connections between them. He is telling us that historians generate knowledge from the primary sources as gained by **inference**. Marwick's historical method can be summarised as a critical analysis of the sources from which **evidence** statements of **justified belief** can be generated. For Marwick the ultimate **truth** in history is that only through the analysis of primary sources (sources from the period under analysis) can we have any knowledge about the past.

Marwick offers a catalogue of the various kinds of such sources the historian is likely to come across, and then he sets out the kinds of question they put to them – his 'catechism'. These are, first, is the source authentic – what is its provenance? When was the source produced? What kind of source is it? How did the source come into existence and for what purpose? How reliable is the author of the source for first-hand information? How was the source understood by contemporaries

– what exactly does it say? Finally, how does the source fit into what we know as derived from other sources both primary and secondary (sources written later than the age it is addressing)? In the end the essential methodology of history according to Marwick is the judicious connection the historian makes between the sources and their meaning. This involves knowledge of the extant range of interpretations (the **historiography**) and an objective reflection whereby early misconceptions are replaced by more convincing interpretations (Marwick 2001: 163).

Clearly the link between primary and secondary sources and what they mean (taken together) is the footnotes. What footnotes are for Marwick (and the vast majority of historians) is that collection of references (referential statements of source) attached (usually using a number system) to what they understand to be statements of justified belief, which are pre-inserted into the main text. Their function is to cement together what reconstructionists and constructionists would view as the three essential features of all histories: the empirical past, the analytical-inferential method and a realist epistemological orientation (see CONCEPTS IN HISTORY). An epistemological sceptic would have a twofold response to this. First, there is nothing 'wrong' in making references to the past. Just because post-structuralists like Roland **Barthes**, for example, stress the indeterminacy of the signifier–signified relationship and many others have stressed that all 'facts' are always events 'under a description' does not mean that we cannot write plausibly about what happened in the past. But, second, there is always the health warning that history is never more than a highly contrived and constructed **narrative** about the past. So while it can be referential it cannot be truthful in the sense of providing the 'true meaning' of the reality of the past. In other words, just because we have trawled the archive for five years does not mean that we have got closer to the meaning of what happened. We can know a lot about *what* happened, but then we have to *write about it*. And that cannot involve any kind of transference of 'given meaning' from the past to present history.

So, it seems, first not only is all our knowledge of the past circumscribed by our current experience but, second, when we write *about* the past following the source catechism as outlined by Marwick all we can hope for is more detailed knowledge of what happened which, in turn, simply provides us with the raw materials which we can then transform into a **representation** of the past. As a deconstructionist historian might say, no written representation can connect the word and the world sufficiently well to provide the reality of the past (see FORM AND CONTENT). In other words, Marwick's precedence of content over form is not the only way to engage with the past. When historians (and the history-consuming public) enquire as to how else we can know the actuality of the past – its truth – if we do not prioritise its content, deconstructionist historians would say sorry, that question begs its own answer. Knowing what happened is not automatically the *only* way to understanding what it means. While knowing what happened will be important to realist kinds of history (which is, of course, what most people are educated to expect and want), history itself can never guarantee any knowledge of what it all means. At the end of the day sources are just those resources from which we make the history that we want and that we as a society think we need.

Further reading

Canary, R. and Kozicki, H., 1978; Carr, E.H., 1987 [1961]; Hexter, J.H., 1998; Hoffer, P.C. and Stueck, W.W., 1994; McCullagh, C.B., 1998; Marius, R., 1999;

Marwick, A., 2001; Munslow, A., 2003b, 1997a, 1997b, 1997c; Stanford, M., 1986; Tosh, J., 2001.

STRUCTURALISM

The modern (see MODERNISM) or post-**Enlightenment** historian engages with the past by demonstrating its possible meanings, by re-animating its inhabitants as they live out their lives over time. The nature of this engagement is determined by the inescapable fact that we cannot experience the lives of people in the past as they did. The past is only alive in the eye and **historical imagination** of the historian as he/she looks at the **evidence** and scours the archive (see FACTS). But, rather than simply accept the harsh epistemological (see EPISTEMOLOGY) limitations of this situation, a peculiar double consciousness has developed in the modernist historian's thinking. The modernist post-Cartesian, post-Enlightenment, liberal humanist (see LIBERAL HUMANISM) historical mind requires the imposition of a methodology and a structure on the past that permits and quickly demands to know its **truth**. The double consciousness that characterises the modernist historian's mind necessarily regards history on the one hand as a privileged, truth-conditional and truth-transmitting discourse, while at the same time acknowledging that the nineteenth-century legacies of **empiricism** and **positivism** are actually inappropriate methodologies through which to (scientifically?) grasp the truth of the past. The emergence of another way of thinking about the past, shorn of those crudities – structuralism – has promoted a highly successful third road to historical understanding.

The historian's double consciousness – he/she knows he/she can only construct the past while longing to reconstruct it – has been the site of much postmodern, deconstructionist and post-empiricist critique (see CONSTRUCTIONIST HISTORY; RECONSTRUCTIONIST HISTORY;

DECONSTRUCTIONIST HISTORY; POSTMODERNISM; GENRE; NEW HIS- TORICISM; POST-STRUCTURALISM). That critique has proven useful insofar as it placed the double consciousness in a context of scepticism about our ability to know things and offer that knowledge within the form of narrative (see FORM AND CONTENT). Such sceptical post-realist perspectives have assisted in puncturing the historian's modern- ist dogma about the absolute need, as well as his/her ability to know the truth of the past. However, the practical realist part of the historian's double consciousness prompts the response that such puncturing has gone beyond the salutary, and has reached the level of absurdity. It is one thing to recog- nise the limitations of history's empiricist, indirect, inferential (see INFERENCE) and over-ambitious positivist methodology, but it is another to argue that historians are, as a result, intellectually incapable of telling fact from fiction, reality from invention or truth from lies, or that meaning is always arbitrary. How did this war over the truthfulness of the discourse of history arise? In one sense it started with Western philosophy itself and its in-built scepticism about how we can know and then represent reality. If our present post- modern condition is indeed marked by a loss of belief in the power of language to accu- rately reflect human experience (the death of REPRESENTATION), its most recent mani- festation began with an anti-foundationalism that rejected the basic tenets of what was the early twentieth-century high-tide of modern- ist thought, structuralism.

A movement called structuralism first emerged with the argument of the Swiss lin- guist Ferdinand de Saussure (1857–1913) that language is based on a knowable (if highly complex) set of rules (Saussure 1959 [1916]). The key idea of structuralism is that language works according to its own internal regulations, and is not directly connected to external reality. Saussure explains how this works through the dominant *langue* (lan- guage's foundational or deep structure) and

its subordinate, the *parole* (examples of the deep structure in operation as a statement). To know how language operates we must first know the system that undergirds any word or statement. According to Saussure, words do not gain their meaning as reflections of their objects in the real world. The word and the world exist in a (strong and) conventional relationship, not a naturalistic referential one. By making the point of analysis the system itself – a synchronic examination that assumes structures are timeless – struc- turalism effectively cancels out history – the diachronic mode of knowing. This insight has been variously applied to other text-based epistemologies, but most notably within the field of literary criticism.

The logic of Saussure's structuralism sug- gests that words are signs defined by their difference from other words and signs. Lan- guage is, therefore, constructed as a series of signs produced by the culturally deter- mined signifier (word)–signified (concept) connection. Although the sign–signifier– signified link is arbitrary, and although, as Saussure suggested, language does not reflect nature (because it is a culturally constituted medium), the modernist historian insists that there is, in practice, a relatively stable connection between word and world (when the historian uses the word 'nationalism' he/ she has enough data to confidently evidence its existence to be secure in the belief that it means what he/she thinks it means). The modernist historian chooses to believe that this union allows for the writing of truthful narrative interpretations based on his/her depth of both contemporary cultural know- ledge and historical context. However, from a structuralist perspective, language is about the structure of the arbitrary connections between signifiers, and does not look beyond the language system at the historically deter- mined signified – the empirical. Structuralists do not search for changes in language or word meanings as being constituted by external change over time; instead they seek out mean- ing in structural relationships. Because the meaning of the sign results from the arbitrary link between signifier and signified, language is a poor conductor for historical truth (or any other kind of truth). Language is always going to be polluted with social meaning and, as Michel **Foucault** suggests, homologous to the power and ideological relationships that exist within the social structure. The historian's language is, therefore, unavoidably presentist and ideological.

Structuralism, as originally formulated by Saussure, though having pretensions to scientificism, did not prove to be the model for the study of the past – it was sweepingly anti-empirical, anti-evolutionary and anti-representational. Other, yet more amenable, social science constructionist history approaches to historical understanding, themselves occasionally and confusingly also called structuralist, were derived from, or were clear rejections of, the nineteenth-century empiricist and/or positivist scientific model. According to the nomenclature devised by Christopher Lloyd there are at least five distinguishable structural or structuralist history approaches – empiricist, systemic-functionalist, interpretist, relational-structurist and structuralist/post-structuralist, with only the last being derived from Saussure's model (Lloyd 1993).

Each approach is an orientation that regularly encompasses several different methodologies. Under empiricism, for example, Lloyd includes a range that covers **biography**, empiricist historical sociology, empirical social history, **cliometrics** and behaviourist individualism. The dominant methodology here is inductivist and inferential. Rather more positivist in inspiration, the systemic-functionalist approaches adopt a deductivist methodology. Interpretist approaches reject all pretensions to scientific explanation of human action and encompass traditional historical interpretationism (what I have called **reconstructionist history**) as well as a variety of sociological and anthropological interpretisms (to include the *Annalistes*). Relational-structurist approaches include those formulated by the sociologist Anthony

Giddens among others. The fifth group noted by Lloyd are structuralist/post-structuralist approaches (Lloyd 1993: 66–88). In the twentieth century, therefore, several structural history approaches to the study of the past have opened up, including the Saussurean structuralist approach. However, because this latter approach emerged in a French historical culture, it was regarded with suspicion by the Francophobic Anglo-American hermeneutic tradition (see HERMENEUTICS).

As Lloyd points out, with the work of Lévi-Strauss, Roland **Barthes**, Michel Foucault, Louis Althusser and Immanuel Wallerstein we had an (often Marxist-orientated) attempt within history-writing to designate the structures of dominance and subordinance in evolving Western industrial and post-industrial society. With Lucien Febvre structuralism was transmuted into an interest in *mentalités*, and with Marc Bloch and Fernand Braudel into the *longue durée* (with **event**s serving only to evidence the enduring power of structures). Inevitably the French *Annalistes* came to terms with empiricism and positivism, claiming to successfully account for historical change and representation in their history. Where they did achieve some plausibility (like Febvre and Le Roy Ladurie) their work seeped into the Anglo-American bedrock, but where they did not, as with Foucault's eruptive epistemes (see EPISTEME), they were far less successful.

Today social science structuralist history continues to flourish in a number of manifestations – demography, economic history, health, migration studies, quantitative studies, technology, social inequality, social mobility studies and political studies, and in theory and **historiography** – though only in rare instances has it prolonged the shelf-life of the covering law (see COVERING LAWS). By the same token, there are few historians today who are attracted by any constructionist or Saussurean structuralist mind-set that views the past as a fantastically complex series of transhistorical language, behaviour and thought codes that can be cracked given enough hard work in the archive. By the 1960s, when the high tide of social science history had been reached, the post-structuralist reaction had set in, rejecting structuralism's aspirations to timeless scientific explanation. The nature of the signifier–signified relationship – with its disruptive nature and endless intertextual deferral of signifier meanings as Roland Barthes and Jacques **Derrida** pointed out – placed bigger question marks over truth, reality, meaning and representation than ever before. The history text could no longer be regarded as providing *the* meaning of the past through the study of textualised evidence.

The importance of both Saussurean and social science structuralism, and their post-structuralist rejection, lies in the way in which it is forcing the modern liberal-humanist historian to ask basic epistemological questions about what they do as historians (see LIBERAL HUMANISM). Is there a past real world that we can grasp rationally, empirically, and can we adequately track institutional and structural changes over time? Can language (more or less) accurately reflect that reality? Is language the servant of the knowing subject? Does our language create history, thus pushing the historian, the historical agent and the evidence to the margins of the process (see AGENCY/STRUCTURE)? How readily do we confuse **concepts in history** with events and **facts**?

Further reading

Caws, P., 1997; Dant, T., 1991; Dosse, F., 1997; Hawkes, T., 1977; Lechte, J., 1994; Lloyd, C., 1993; Saussure, F. de, 1959 [1916]; Snooks, G., 1998; Sturrock, J., 1979; Tallis, R., 1998; Williams, R., 1983.

T

TELEOLOGY

In philosophy teleology refers to the doctrine that all agents that act with **intentionality** are goal-directed. Such thinking is characteristic of Aristotle. In history it means the belief that there is in the past a manifest destiny: history possesses a discernible end-directedness. Although it is usually claimed that the only way to determine whether this is so is by a careful examination of the **evidence**; those who endorse teleological explanations always seem to find them in the evidence. However, for the reconstructionist historian (see RECONSTRUCTIONIST HISTORY) such totalising explanations are of doubtful value, being largely speculative rather than analytic. First of all, if there is actually a direction and, therefore, an end in history how can we yet know it as we have not, presumably, any evidence that we have reached the end of history? But rather more important is the consideration that large-scale teleological explanations are fundamentally anti-historical in that they assume that the past *as a whole* can be accounted for by reference to the consequences of **events**, actions and processes, rather than their immediate (and often largely random) **causation**. Such criticism has been regularly levelled at those historians whose histories appear to be directed by an inner design as, for example, in the work of Giambattista **Vico**, Friedrich **Hegel** and Karl Marx.

One of the most famous of recent teleological explanations is that of the American Francis Fukuyama in his book *The End of History and the Last Man*, in which he claims that the end of history had been reached by 1991 with the victory of liberalism over communism. For Fukuyama the collapse of Soviet communism evidenced the progression of history toward this final cause. Teleology, as used by Fukuyama, suggests that there was a governing and universal power in history that drove it to its unavoidable conclusion. This grand-**narrative** philosophising is usually regarded as a form of doctrinal conviction that has rather lost touch with reality. This criticism is, of course, usually made by those empiricists who claim that their methodology has pushed them to an alternative (and more truthful rather than grandiose) explanation (see TRUTH). The place for teleology in history is, therefore, strictly limited: to helping to explain empirically verified and individual purposive human activity directed toward a known 'end' (see EMPIRICISM).

Such a definition of teleological explanation is founded on the assumption that only individual biological creatures are actually capable of directed action determined by subjective choices and wishes, intentions and designs, desires and wants. By this definition neither Fukuyama's all-conquering liberalism nor Marx's triumphant proletariat can be said to possess purposive intention. An ultimate purpose can be ascribed only to people. Hence, while individuals may indeed have acted according to some inner intentional drive, the question of whether this applies to social institutions, or mass movements, or ideologies is impossible to demonstrate beyond the level of stating what might be possible.

The mechanism historians use to constrain the dangerous impulse toward large-scale teleological explanation is the surgical application of the **colligation** process whereby the connections between events, actions and processes are established and contextualised. However, when colligating, historians quickly become aware that events, actions and processes that occur later in the cause and effect chain were most likely anticipated by earlier purposive action and intentionality. This means that, because the thinking of people in the past was anticipatory of desired outcomes, the past and historical explanation are unavoidably teleological – teleology is already embedded in the past itself. It means that the historian, in interrogating the past, has to understand the end to which the object, text or action was directed by its **author**. As to whether this can be legitimately inflated by the historian sufficiently to sustain a philosophical belief in a manifest destiny depends on several factors: the prejudices of the reader to accept such a claim, the manner in which the sources are disposed of and the plausibility of the composed historical narrative that is built on individual action (see CONSTRUCTIONIST HISTORY).

The philosopher of history Clayton Roberts tries to sustain an anti-teleological position by suggesting that large-scale teleological problems arise only if we confuse colligation with **emplotment**. Roberts defines emplotment as the configuring of events according to their known ultimate goal. Colligation on the other hand means tracing the causation of an event – via a suitable theory – in order to explain it. The former tactic reveals what may be illegitimate patterns in history, while the latter discovers true causes. Emplotted (i.e. teleological) explanations imply a desire on the part of the historian to imagine or prefigure an explanatory outcome and this is not proper **historical explanation** (C. Roberts 1996).

But is this strictly accurate? To emplot the past is to compose a narrative the aim of which is to explain **event**s either by discovering *the* real story in the past or by imposing a meaning believed to be derived from the evidence – colligation is not, as Roberts implies, solely the preserve of non-narrative historians.

Emplotment, in fact, almost always includes recourse to some kind of colligatory causal explanation. The fact that aesthetic choices are not regarded as necessarily secondary to the empiricist research enterprise does not mean that emplotment is teleological and colligation is not (see TROPE/FIGURATION; AESTHETIC TURN). The important point is the subtlety and plausibility with which teleological explanations are made about the purposive action of individual agents and how convincing is their extension to the philosophical level.

Teleological explanations have, therefore, had a bad press among reconstructionist historians because of their assumption that history is almost exclusively a process of discovering individual agent intentionality. From this perspective the historian who believes that he or she *knows* the outcome of history exists in a pernicious and confused state of ideological wish-fulfilment. The objective and distanced analysis of the evidence has clearly been sacrificed to a totalising explanation (an extrapolation too far). While this charge is probably unfair as few, if any, historians ignore individual human actions, such claims actually serve to disguise the fundamental significance of teleological explanations.

Both Western **metaphysics** and its offspring history are teleological in character. Modernist (see MODERNISM) historians view history and explanation as linear and, therefore, temporally directional. We seek to answer the question of what we are and what we may become. To do this we must heed the warnings and lessons of history. We try to find out why something happened in the past in the way it did because we think we have alternatives in the future. It follows that history is full of options. There is no givenness about it. As people in the past had choices so do historians in interpreting those choices. This relationship between cause and explanation, as Friedrich **Nietzsche** argued, is often one of the effects directing the search for cause. It is this that makes history unavoidably teleological both at the level of the philosophy of history and in the pursuit of agent intentionality. It means that teleology confounds the wish to construe history as objective at all but the most basic level of the truth-conditional sentence (see OBJECTIVITY). Once the historian moves to interpretation he/she is making choices about preferred ends, and teleology cannot be avoided.

Further reading

Barnard, F.M., 1981; Carr, E.H., 1987 [1961]; Collingwood, R.G., 1994 [1946]; Donagan, A., 1959; Dummett, M., 1978; Fukuyama, F., 1993 [1991]; Gardiner, P., 1961 [1951], 1959; Hassing, R.F., 1997; Nagel, E., 1979; Roberts, C., 1996.

TROPE/FIGURATION

Tropes are figures of speech, primarily metaphor, metonymy, synecdoche and irony, but we could also include the variants simile, litotes, periphrasis and hyperbole. Figures of speech deploy words in such a way as to change, turn or translate meaning. Operating at the deep level of human thought, the early twentieth-century Swiss linguist Ferdinand de Saussure argued that meaning emerges in language through binary opposition and, as employed by Michel **Foucault**, the sense of otherness or difference thus generated can, in any historical period, surface as a dominant cultural trope (see EPISTEME; STRUCTURALISM). Hence, in his book *Metahistory* (1973), the American philosopher of history Hayden **White** examines the theory of tropes and troping as the means to distinguish the dominant modes of **historical imagination** in nineteenth-century Europe and thus identify their deep and surface structures. The troping process may be extended to include the creation of large-scale metaphors like the base–superstructure metaphor of Karl Marx as the basis of a total explanation of historical change, or to create other models of historical change that rely upon the basic relationships of part–whole/whole–part. The

tropes may thus reside, as the eighteenth-century Neapolitan philosopher of history Giambattista **Vico** suggested, at the heart of every historical period (defined by Foucault as the episteme) *and* in its description.

Because written history is a literary artefact White claims that historians share the same formal **narrative** structures used by writers of realist literature that are based on the tropes as the main categories of figurative language. White uses something like a base–superstructure metaphor himself to explain how this works. Historians construct narratives (stories) to produce explanations employing three superstructural strategies of explanation, namely explanation by **emplotment**, explanation by formal argument and explanation by ideological implication. These strategies of explanation are the surface features of the narrative, with White suggesting a deep or infrastructure of consciousness operating at the level of the tropes that ultimately determines how historians elect to explain the facts explored in their narratives. This is, in effect, a reversal of the conventional priority of content over form as the proper way to approach the discovery of historical knowledge (see FORM AND CONTENT).

Hayden White, as the leading theoretician of the narrativist revival in historical writing, is insistent that recognition of troping as the cognitive process of transition or transfer does not mean accepting textual determinism. Language and its figurative element do not determine what we can say, but they are constraints on how we create meaning (see AUTHOR; DISCOURSE). It is important to understand that language is the medium, not the model of perception.

Further reading

Ankersmit, F.R., 1994; Ankersmit, F.R. and Kellner, H., 1995; Chartier, R., 1997; Domanska, E., 1998b; Jenkins, K., 1995; Kansteiner, W., 1993; Kellner, H., 1980; Lemon, M.C., 1995; McLennan, G., 1984; Munslow, A., 2003b, 1992; Roth, P.A., 1992; White, H., 1998, 1987, 1978, 1973b.

TRUTH

Conventionally, in philosophy, truth is taken as a property of sentences, statements and propositions or beliefs. The sentence is a particular arrangement of words, the statement is the use put by a writer/speaker to the sentence, and the proposition or belief is the content of the statement. In a sentence, then, we state as a proposition or a belief that something 'is true'. This can lead to at least two views about truth, either that it is primarily the property of a linguistic **representation** in that our propositions or beliefs are the result of language, or the other way around, that truth resides *propositionally* whereby propositional truth is expressed in our sentences and statements. This latter view assumes and requires a match between proposition and reality. **Historical explanation** is beset by the tension between these two perceptions of truth. Today most historians would probably accept that because the past is organised through the exercise of their **historical imagination** this means rejecting any absolutist notion of historical truth (see E.H. CARR; R.G. COLLINGWOOD; Benedetto CROCE; Frank R. ANKERSMIT; Giambattista VICO; HERMENEUTICS). Historical interpretations may be better regarded as likely to be true, corresponding to the verified **evidence** and the coherence of the statement as judged by other historians, and the demands of their own culture.

The two theories of truth that most affect the work of the historian are the correspondence and coherence/consensus theories. Historians conventionally prioritise the correspondence theory, which holds that historical truth exists in the correspondence of historical descriptions to the facts – we discover facts by drawing inferences (see INFERENCE) from the evidence that leads to a correspondence between, as Michael Stanford says, 'fact and mind' (Stanford 1998: 66). The argument runs that the more thoughtful and careful our inferences, the closer we are likely to get to the truth. To the extent that such descriptions mirror past reality and are mind-independent they may be regarded as more or less possessing **objectivity** (see MIMESIS). The debate about truth in history hinges, therefore, on the extent to which historical descriptions can be regarded as truthful (see Carl BECKER; Keith JENKINS). Now, although historical descriptions are never or very rarely couched baldly in terms of 'it is a fact that . . .', the implication is often exactly that. To illustrate this, take the statement 'the cotton industry was the key feature of the Industrial Revolution'. It intentionally comes across as a statement of a past reality because the historian believes it to be so. What it is actually is a propositional statement, or a series of **event**s under a description based on the evidence.

Now, the sceptical or practical realist historian accepts that historical practice means having to live with an absence of proof. As Appleby, Hunt and Jacob argue, at best 'the past only dimly corresponds to what the historians say about it [and] practical realists accept the tentativeness and imperfections of the historians' accounts' (Appleby *et al.* 1994: 248). Such historians willingly admit the problems of squeezing the truth out of the past and translating it as history. They know that there are no trans-cultural or trans-historical iron laws of human behaviour to assist explanation, and that **empiricism** is a poor vehicle for studying the past because they cannot stand apart from their object of study and their **evidence** is indirect (see SOURCES). This is compounded because they can only understand and explain the past through **concepts in history** that are mediated by language (did **'class'** exist in the past or is it a concept they have imposed on it?). But this does not mean, as Appleby, Hunt and Jacob maintain, denying the existence of a past reality, or if the past did actually exist that it is unknowable, and it certainly does not mean swallowing the whole postmodern (see POSTMODERNISM) and relativist argument of unfixed and constantly deferred meanings, ending up with no anchors for objective knowledge (see RELATIVISM; NEW HISTORICISM).

The reason for maintaining a belief in the truth of historical descriptions lies in the continuing power of the principle of correspondence between the word and the world. Historians who believe in the truth conditions of historical descriptions do so because language is never so vague as to be wholly unreferential (plus the fact that historical method ensures truth through exhaustive study in the archive and solid inference). Consequently, historical descriptions can still be reasonably defended as being referential and representational even though our eventual written construction of the past is a linguistic creative act of the historian – and here I appropriate Aristotle's term, **mimesis**. Historians, I suggest, work by endorsing a weak version of the correspondence theory – call it a mimetic version – that allows for the existence of reality, knowledge of it and its adequate representation. This is usually summarised by the claim that historical descriptions are true if they are well supported by the evidence. The problem with a representational or mimetic version of truth is, how do we define the fact upon which we base our later interpretational descriptions? Do all our facts have to, at some point, fulfil an absolutist version of the correspondence test?

This unavoidable tension has led historians to seek collateral support in the coherence/consensus theory of truth (see INTELLECTUAL HISTORY). I define this as the accord that exists among well-informed and skilled historians. Such harmony is expressed through the range of other justified descriptions and propositions they make – in my example it means contextualising and verificatory statements being made and agreed about the growing numbers of cotton-spinning mills or cotton operatives employed between certain periods, or the swelling volume of profits from cotton manufacture as compared to, say, wool worsted (see JUSTIFIED BELIEF). So a descriptive historical statement may be regarded as very likely to be true if it coheres with other descriptive statements about the past world and a descriptive consensus is reached. It is probably false if it does not. That 'the cotton industry was the key feature of the Industrial Revolution' is a true statement according to a coherence/consensus theory of truth, so long as the bulk of historians agree with that description based on their knowledge of the evidence. Our prior belief in the correspondence theory allows us to assume, therefore, that the statement must be founded on an earlier correspondence to the facts. Hence if the evidence changes so do the facts and their interpretation, and a new phase of revisionism is launched and a new consensus may emerge – a continuous process of evolving arguments to the best explanation. But, as we know, it does not always work that way – the same evidence is often used to infer quite different meanings.

As is well known, the eighteenth-century German philosopher Immanuel **Kant**, inspired by the **Enlightenment** and the rationalist ideas of **modernism**, argued in favour of truth but admitted in doing so that our knowledge is only of the appearance of things rather than knowledge of things-in-themselves (see EMPIRICISM; EPISTEMOLOGY; G.W.F. HEGEL). His nineteenth-century critic Friedrich **Nietzsche** took up this point, maintaining that if knowledge of things-in-themselves is impossible then truth must be equally unrealisable in respect of correspondence. Nietzsche also rejected Kant's universal a priori (see A PRIORI/A POSTERIORI) cognitive principles in favour of individual perspective, and emphasised the role of language, specifically noting its metaphoric character, in shaping our beliefs and concepts (see TROPE/FIGURATION). It follows that if language is metaphorical, so is truth. In effect what is agreed in society to be truthful *is* truthful or, as Nietzsche puts it, the 'sum of human relations which have been poetically and rhetorically intensified, transferred and embellished, and which, after long usage, seem to a people to be fixed, canonical, and binding' concluding that truths are 'illusions which we have forgotten are illusions; they are metaphors that have become worn out and have been drained of sensuous force, coins which have lost their embossing and are now considered as metal and no longer as coins' (Nietzsche quoted in Cooper 1999: 186). Nietzsche is thus effectively endorsing the coherence/consensus theory of truth as a poor substitute for correspondence.

While having accepted, along with such as Appleby, Hunt and Jacob, the ultimate epistemological inadequacy of history's mimetic methodology (that makes correspondence between description and reality impossible), the deep desire for matching the word with the world, as pragmatic philosophers such as Richard **Rorty** have noted, nevertheless still remains potent (Rorty 1991: 32–3). Moreover, the mimetic or weak process of representational correspondence demands a number of associated beliefs that, paradoxically, tend to be cast as absolutes. Flowing from its realist inspiration and its particular belief in the status of facts, professional mimetic history tends to manifest its truth-claiming status in the deliberate avoidance of trope/figuration in favour of an ethnographic or referential style of **narrative**. Ironically, empiricists incline to a neo-Nietzschean position here, not that truth is metaphor, but that too many metaphors must be injurious to truth, hence the necessity for referential transparency in language. Another disciplinary consequence is the denial of the anarchic, unfixed and unfixable nature of reality – the sublime – in favour of the 'common-sense' need to control the past, which is achievable by the accurate representation of *the* reality of the event. This realist inclination is summarised in the profession's insistence on the priority of content over form (see FORM AND CONTENT). Various other separations like those of fact and fiction, history and the present, and observer and observed, are also strenuously asserted. The **linguistic turn** is denied because it challenges all these

principles, as the postmodern historian might say, recognising its metal as conventional history's unembossed coinage.

In summary, the acknowledged failings of history as a truth-establishing discipline are balanced by invoking the falsifiability principle, whereby historical interpretations are asserted as provisional propositions (hypotheses) to be falsified in the light of the evidence. When we judge that we have reached a point of maximum falsifiability, we are left with a residue that is a description that we believe comes closest to the historical truth. The gap between fact and mind is then at its narrowest. The doubts concerning the possibility of historical truth derive ultimately, of course, from the pervasive condition of Nietzschean-inspired postmodern epistemological scepticism. Doubts exist not only concerning history's mimetic method, but also regarding the adequacy of representational language. The mediatory role of the historical imagination through which the historian chooses to emplot the past as history is also claimed to be a major obstacle to objective knowing and truth (see EMPLOTMENT; Hayden WHITE). This is compounded by cultural relativism because historians cannot escape their epistemic or cultural preferences. At present there seems little likelihood of a *rapprochement* between the sceptics (and relativists) and the supporters of weak correspondence.

Further reading

Alcoff, L.M., 1998; Allen, B., 1998, 1993; Ankersmit, F.R., 2005a, 2005b; Appleby, J. *et al.*, 1994; Audi, R., 1998; Carr, D., 1986a; Carr, E.H., 1987 [1961]; Cooper, D.E., 1999; Davidson, D., 1984; Dummett, M., 1978; Evans, R.J., 1997a, 1997b; Horwich, P., 1990; Jenkins, K., 2003 [1991]; Kirkham, R., 1995; Luntley, M., 1995; McCullagh, C.B., 1998, 1984; Munslow, A., 2003b; Putnam, H., 1981; Quine, W.V., 1990; Rabinow, P., 1999; Rorty, R., 1998, 1991; Stanford, M., 1998; White, H., 1998, 1992.

V

VICO, GIAMBATTISTA (1668–1744)

Giambattista Vico, now widely regarded as the first of the truly self-reflexive modernist (see MODERNISM) philosophers of history, was for much of his career employed as a teacher of rhetoric at the University of Naples. His principal work was *The New Science*, first published in 1725 and then, after a 1730 edition, emerging in its final form in 1744. Vico is a significant historical thinker primarily because of two key ideas: his anti-Cartesian, anti-Enlightenment and, as it turned out, anti-positivist (see EMPIRICISM) principle of *verum ipsum factum* – that which is true is that which is made (as opposed to discovered in nature), and his translation of this metahistorical principle that, when modelled on the life-cycle of human beings, was turned into a stage theory of history (see CONSTRUCTIONIST HISTORY; BIOGRAPHY AND LIFE WRITING). His core notion that confidence in what we know can ultimately be derived only from what we ourselves create means that historians are also a part of history when we write the-past-as-history (see R.G. COLLINGWOOD; Benedetto CROCE; EPISTEMOLOGY; G.W.F. HEGEL; Friedrich NIETZSCHE; Hayden WHITE). As the first modernist philosopher of history, Vico anticipated at least one strand of **historicism**, that to understand the past the historian has to get inside the minds and linguistic customs of people in the past. The Vichian paradox in this is, in order to empathise with the past how can we escape from the concepts (see CONCEPTS IN HISTORY) of the present? Whatever answer we have for that conundrum, empathy for Vico is at least as important in creating historical knowledge as either Enlightenment rational deduction or inductive **inference**.

With his new philosophical method (his empathic new science) Vico tried to answer a basic question that still preoccupies historians: how can we be certain about **truth**? For Vico the closest we get to certainty about the truth of our lives is through the interpretation of our decisions and what we do as human beings (see HERMENEUTICS). Vico claimed that such interpretation was possible only through the (empathic historical) study of social customs, **event**s and, above all, language. This method would allow historians to locate examples of the universal law that governed particular instances or, as he said in his autobiography, to give certainty to the history of languages by reference to the history of things. This Vichian theory of knowledge obliges the historian to understand past cultures in their own terms, and his examination of the history of nations 'proved', at least to Vico's satisfaction, what became his universally applicable stage theory of history.

He reached the conclusion that all nations follow three recurring stages of development, the foundation for which lies in the shared human capacity for the metaphoric construction of reality. This was the universal that Vico found and which could lead to the certain understanding by humans of their activities: the power of the human imagination. Hayden White described this special metaphoric apprehension of the world as containing within itself the potential for generating the tropes – metaphor, metonymy and synecdoche – and in Vico's model of history this is the case (White 1973b: 86) (see TROPE/

FIGURATION). In the first or metaphoric stage all humans create fantastic myths and gods (*fantasia*). In the second stage human beings exercise our metonymically inspired poetic imaginations creating social institutions based on the concept of the heroic individual. After the age of gods and heroes comes the final epoch of what Vico dismissively calls the barbarity of reflection (rational conceptualisation) by humans as we imagine the world synecdochically. It is this poetically inspired rhythm of gods, heroes and humanity that creates nations and distinctive historical periods (see EPISTEME; Michel FOUCAULT). In the Vichian philosophy of history there is, therefore, no gap between the word (language) and the world (the real). The text and the context are indissoluble and the a priori (see A PRIORI/A POSTERIORI) of the metaphor and the a posteriori of its effects in the real world create the feedback loop that is the-past-as-history.

The universal truth Vico discovered – that of the primitive human aesthetic – is reflected in the storytelling power of **narrative**. A mythic or Homeric wisdom precedes all thought and it is this that constitutes our only avenue to truth. In respect of historical explanation this means a convergence with literary interpretation. This is demanded by what is the historicist idea of examining societies through their own linguistic and cultural expressions, rather than any imposed by the historian. This procedure – viewed as either a historical necessity or an impossibility, depending on your point of view – has since been addressed by a variety of thinkers including Johann Herder, Jules Michelet, G.W.F. Hegel, Samuel Taylor Coleridge, Karl Marx, Friedrich Nietzsche, Wilhelm Dilthey, James Joyce, Benedetto Croce, R.G. Collingwood, Michel Foucault and Hayden White. The **historical imagination** itself is the most obvious agency of this human aesthetic power, inasmuch as the factually empirical can be accessed only by the imaginatively inferential (see AESTHETIC TURN; EMPIRICISM). Re-creating the-past-as-history necessitates

imagining the potential connections that are available when writing the historical narrative (see CAUSATION). To see how the historical imagination works requires dissecting the historian's narrative organisation in order to determine how he/she musters his/her metaphors and tropes so as to assign meaning. In so doing we should note Vico's and later Nietzsche's strong insistence that all our concepts are metaphoric (or the other forms of poetic figures) because they are echoes of our primordial imagination.

The influence of Vico has thus been substantial in the thinking of both modern(ist) and postmodern (see POSTMODERNISM) historians. Michel Foucault, for example, assumed in Vichian fashion that historical knowledge issues not just from the philological study and criticism of the **evidence**, but also from our own imaginative creations/social constructions (see SOURCES). Foucault's own construction of the epistemic/figurative basis of historical experience is clearly derived from Vico. Foucault took Vico's belief that narrative and trope represent both the sources and the connections we imagine between them. The legacy of the Enlightenment, Foucault claims, has been to obscure this reality of the power of the imagination and the cognitive ascendancy of language. The result, as Hayden White said, was to make unclear 'to science itself an awareness of its own poetic nature' (White 1978: 254).

In his search for the correspondence between truth and certainty Vico deserted the Enlightenment in favour of the socially designed nature of knowledge. The unreflexive and quite un-Vichian modernist (see MODERNISM) judgement, that history can be secure because its truths derive from a knowable real world through inductive inference based on the evidence, fails, as Vico and later Nietzsche and Foucault argued, to grasp both the frailty of the written form of the-past-as-history-as-text and the power of the aboriginal imagination. For historians of a relativist inclination the legacy of Vico is a break with the belief in distanced empiricism (see RELATIVISM). Writing the-past-as-history they take as an opportunity, therefore, to explore the tropic foundation to our understanding of the-past-as-history-as-text. Along with Foucault, Hayden White took up this idea, suggesting that the mechanism of writing history operates at the subterranean level of language and human consciousness – the prefigurative act being divined in and through 'the dominant tropological mode in which it is cast' (White 1978: 197). Even if the stated aim for conventional reconstructionist (see RECONSTRUCTIONIST HISTORY) and constructionist (see CONSTRUCTIONIST HISTORY) historians remains the discovery of what actually happened in the past, even then they must first 'prefigure as a possible object of knowledge the whole series of events reported in the documents' (ibid.: 30).

Although followed by such as Wilhelm Dilthey, R.G. Collingwood, Michel Foucault and Hayden White, Vico was the first philosopher of history to accept the sway of the human imagination and its translation into figurative language: the-past-as-history-as-text(ual) product. No amount of hypothesis-testing and being fair and just to the evidence can avoid the fact that our primary tool to negotiate the past is language. The historical narrative is not pure **representation**; it is not even poor representation. It is instead a whole series of personal deals struck by the historian between his/her powers of expression and imagination and the evidence. Although Vico sought truth in history – a knowable past because we created it – he also understood that historians are not distanced observers (no matter how much they may desire such Olympian objectivity). Although for Vico the aim is still to approach as closely as possible the truth of the past, he reminds us that the historical imagination cannot re-make the past with each new imaginative insight. But, as the first of the self-reflexive modernist philosophers of history, the legacy of Vico lies, at least in part, in his understanding that historical analysis should be focused as much on the fabulous, the poetic, the imaginative and the cultural, as it is on the sensible, the referential, the empirical and the factual (see CULTURAL HISTORY). While history may not be the same as poetry it is always the historian's imagination that has primacy in its command and composition of the empirical.

Further reading

Auxier, R.E., 1997; Berlin, I., 1976; Collingwood, R.G., 1994 [1946]; Croce, B., 1964 [1913]; Haddock, B.A., 1980; Mazzotta, G., 1998; Mooney, M., 1985; Munslow, A., 1992; Pompa, L., 1975; Tagliacozzo, G. and Verene, D.P., 1976; Tagliacozzo, G. and White, H., 1969; Vico, G., 1968, 1963; White, H., 1978, 1973b.

W

WHITE, HAYDEN (1928–)

Hayden White's major contributions to the study of history are to be found in *Metahistory* (1973), and two early collections, *Tropics of Discourse* (1978) and *The Content of the Form* (1987). In these texts White addresses the relationship between the **historical imagination**, the historical **narrative** and past-lived experience (see EPISTEMOLOGY; ONTOLOGY; NEW HISTORICISM). White maintains that history is the product as much of the historical imagination as of discovery in the archive, and it follows that history does not correspond to a pre-existing, or given, narrative/story. There is no intrinsic meaning to the past; this is provided by the historian who is him/herself the subject of a variety of cultural, professional and ideological discourses (see DISCOURSE). White is not anti-referentialist, but he does argue that we impose our stories on the past teleologically for a variety of reasons. Among these reasons are, of course, the reconstructionist historian's (see RECONSTRUCTIONIST HISTORY) claim to explain or to understand agent **intentionality** through **inference** from the **evidence**, and the constructionist historian's belief that all history is deeply conceptual and/or theoretical (see CONCEPTS IN HISTORY; COVERING LAWS; CULTURAL HISTORY; POSITIVISM; STRUCTURALISM). But for White there is nothing in the nature of historical study or its empirical (see EMPIRICISM) methodological underpinnings that permits historical narratives to relay the past realities of human intentions and beliefs.

For White history is the act of imposing a narrative or **emplotment** of a particular kind on the past. In effect this means that our knowledge of the past is derived through an essentially poetic act. Reliant variously on Giambattista **Vico**, Kenneth Burke, Michel **Foucault**, Northrop Frye and Roman Jakobson, as well as a vast body of work on metaphor and **trope/figuration**, White characterises the deep structures of the historical imagination as conforming to the operation of the four major figures of speech: metaphor, metonymy, synecdoche and irony (all different ways whereby our minds make the connections we 'see' between parts and wholes). It is through this capacity, rather than the evidence (for this capacity determines our selection of evidence), that history is ultimately made. So the history we end up with, in all its varieties and revisions (strictly speaking we should talk of its re-visions), is the result of the aesthetic choices and prefigurations of the historian as well as his/her readership (see AESTHETIC TURN). In White's vision of history the four tropic orientations both determine and emerge in a complex superstructure of strategies of explanation that take the form of four emplotment types (Tragedy, Comedy, Romance and Satire), four modes of argument (Formist, Mechanist, Organicist and Contextualist), and their four respective ideological implications (Anarchist, Radical, Conservative and Liberal).

Given this model and the logic behind it, White insists that history can never provide *the* story, rather it is *a* narrative designed by the historian as he/she organises the contents in the form of a narrative of what he/she believes the past was about (see FORM AND CONTENT). As White says,

Historical situations are not *inherently* tragic, comic, or romantic. ... All the historian needs to do to transform a tragic into a comic situation is to shift his point of view or change the scope of his perceptions. Anyway, we only think of situations as tragic or comic because these concepts are part of our generally cultural and specifically literary heritage. *How* a given historical situation is to be configured depends on the historian's subtlety in matching up a specific plot structure with the set of historical events that he wishes to endow with a meaning of a particular kind.

(White 1978: 85)

This vision of how the historical mind works rethinks many of history's traditional dualities. White is effectively reversing the relationships of content and form, ideology and trope, and empiricism and figurative style, while problematising the connections between the world and the word, the knower and the known, fact (see FACTS) and fiction, past and present, **truth** and interpretation, and history and narrative. The upshot is that White is concerned less with the reality of the past characterised and accessed primarily as an empirical undertaking, than with the composed narrative of the historian – creating what French cultural critic Roland **Barthes** calls the effect of reality (see REALITY/ REALISTIC EFFECT). Although White's model does not, of course, disavow the study of the content of the past, it does require us not only to think about history for what it most patently is, a pre-configured narrative, but also to consider the broader epistemological and ontological implications this has for our definition of what history is, and what it is that historians do.

Further reading
1980 'Metahistory: Six critiques', *History and Theory* themed issue 19; Ankersmit, F.R., 2005b, 1998a, 1994; Carroll, D., 1976; Chartier, R., 1997; Domanska, E., 1998b;

Fay, B. *et al.*, 1998; Jameson, F., 1976; Jenkins, K., 1998a, 1995; Kansteiner, W., 1993; Munslow, A., 2003b, 1997a, 1992; Partner, N., 1998; Roth, M.S., 1995; Roth, P.A., 1992; Vann, R.T., 1998; White, Hayden 2000, 1998, 1996, 1995, 1992, 1987, 1984, 1978, 1974, 1973a, 1973b.

WOMEN'S HISTORY

According to the postmodern women's history historian Joan Wallach Scott, writing in the late 1980s, women's history was then on the brink of producing a thoroughgoing reconceptualisation of historical practice (Scott 1988: 4) (see POSTMODERNISM; STRUCTURALISM). Scott's **post-structuralist** position is that language is the medium for the establishment of **gender** relationships and knowledge about women in the past and the present. For her at that time the direction of women's history was going to make it the vanguard (although she does not use the description) of a new kind of postmodernist history. Almost a decade later Scott had quite clearly shifted her emphasis to the problematic nature of women's history, which had become ever more sophisticated, theoreticised and complex (Scott 1996b). In 1991 she published a brief analysis of how women's history had developed up to then and, as an 'interim report', it reveals her moving away from her earlier claims for a new historical **epistemology** (in the wake of the work of Judith Butler) toward a toned-down and rather more restrained emphasis on the socially constituted nature of gender. This shift back in the direction of knowledge from knowable experience may also be taken as something of a commentary on the failure of **postmodern** (specifically **post-structuralist**) developments to penetrate historical criticism more generally.

In her 1991 interim survey Scott described what she took to be the conventional narrative of women's history. This held that the political dissent of the 1960s (initially in the United

States) generated a desire for the recovery of women from history (creating 'herstory'). Feminism needed to provide role models or heroines for the purposes of post-1968 politics. Then, sometime in the 1970s, the link between academic 'herstory' and political radicalism was almost severed as a new field emerged within the academy – women's history and **post-feminism**. In the 1980s women's history transmuted again with a turn toward gender. At this point the academic and political worlds finally broke contact. The term gender seemed to suggest a new horizon of neutral and non-political history dealing with broad issues of the history of sexuality. So we have an evolution in three decades from political feminism, to women's history, to gender and, regrettably in Scott's opinion, a congruent de-politicisation of the academic study of the feminine (Scott 1991: 42–3).

However, Scott argues that this narrative of women's history is too simplistic. The real history of women's history can only be understood as a much more complex series of parallel developments involving feminist political radicalism and women's history as a historical field, but most importantly in the growing epistemological challenges over those three decades to the discipline of history itself. Scott claimed that many who were researching and writing gender history in 1991 overtly acknowledged an intellectual (theoretical) as well as an ideological (political) allegiance to feminism of some sort or another. The type of feminism endorsed carried with it theoretical and political baggage. This meant that history, more broadly construed, did so too. For her, Scott's feminism required a postmodernist theoretical orientation derived from Jacques **Derrida**'s deconstructionist notion of the disruptive sign. There are some words/ concepts that defy signification because they carry culturally contradictory meanings. The idea of women as a 'supplement' to history falls into this category of contradictory signifiers – the idea of a supplement means both an addition to and, as Scott pointed out, a substitute for what pre-exists. Scott maintained that this led to an irresolvable tension in women's history and might suggest a devastating effect on the nature of history itself.

No doubt including women in history not only forced historians to confront what has hitherto been missing in history by adding women and women's experience, but this move must also entail the second meaning of supplement, a substitution for what at present exists. The question has become, therefore, what is there in women's history and the rethinking behind it that carries with it the power to replace 'proper' history? Proper history is at one level, obviously, history without women, but what does women's history bring to the discipline in epistemological terms? Does it entail a new way of historical knowing? Is there something in conventional Western reasoning that makes it a male sort of thinking? If there is, how can we reconfigure it? What are those special structuring principles in women's history that are at present missing from history ('his-story')? It was (is?) clear to Scott that you cannot have the first kind of supplement without the second. Bringing women (defined implicitly as the other) into history involves rethinking a discipline founded on a binarism that implicitly defines itself as a male **discourse** – the historian's Self as Male defined as such because it is in opposition to the other, which is Female (or a whole string of possible others: nonwhite, proletarian, non-Western, etc.).

The exclusion of women was an essential move because they clearly represented the other – the absence of which confirmed Man's own peculiar sense of himself (defined in his difference to the other). If women were to be embraced(!) in these male-dominant discourses the price would be a literal assimilation. Women would be necessarily and henceforth judged in male terms. They might become equal but they would be surrogate men. The **modernism** that ushered in the **Enlightenment** had at its centre a white, Western European, bourgeois, educated, property-owning, heterosexual male knowing subject (see LIBERAL HUMANISM). The double bind that emerged subsequently in the nineteenth century was that if women were to be incorporated they must become white, Western European, bourgeois, educated, property-owning, heterosexual females. The sense of gender difference (like that of **class**) would disappear only through the process of assimilation.

While eventually rejecting much in his theory of language, the basis of post-structuralist history is Ferdinand de Saussure's structuralist notion that all meaning carried by language is derived instrumentally through arbitrary binary opposition. Exploring this logic Michel **Foucault** and Jacques Derrida argued that knowledge is created and constituted through our human understanding of difference and similarity within a power-laden cultural context. Central to their position is the way in which meanings are derived through the human sense of differentiation and contrast as translated culturally into institutions, theories, epistemologies and practices of opposition, dominance, subordinance and hierarchy. If traditional history was male-dominant (translated as a form of history that demanded polarities built on the master binary of subject–object, like truth–falsity, subjectivity–objectivity, imagination–reality and fiction–truth-conditional **representation**) then, presumably, through the introduction of woman as both the historian and subject matter (the content of the past), we might reasonably expect that history would confront its traditional empiricist-based construction (see EMPIRICISM; FORM AND CONTENT; ORAL HISTORY). Furthermore, ought we not expect this to be achieved by post-structuralist feminists/women's history historians not only as they addressed the language of male dominance, but more significantly as they problematised the very notion of a knowable women's historical experience?

The heart of the epistemological challenge to proper history posed by women's history converges, therefore, on the conceptualisation of difference construed and constituted through the cultural construction of meaning and knowledge, and the power of language (see CULTURAL HISTORY; ONTOLOGY). Can knowledge and its creation be distinguished by means of a male/female duality? Exploring this difference has become the focal point of women's history. It follows that we must ask if there is a sexualised epistemology. So-called post-structuralist feminism argues that the pursuit of equality is a modernist dead-end unless women want to be like men. If not, women should establish a peculiarly feminine way of looking at, and dealing with, the world in linguistic and epistemological terms.

In claiming equality, by dint of being a rational Enlightenment animal, liberal feminists since Mary Wollstonecraft have, in effect, argued in favour of the proposition that men and women are intellectually undifferentiated – for historians this translates (axiomatically?) into the foundational and working principle that there is only one way to create historical knowledge and that means a non-gendered way of thinking about history. But is this not just a cover for a male way of doing history? Recent adherents of a radical feminism, like Toril Moi, have argued against this universalising tendency of Western philosophy, arguing specifically against its dualistic mode of thought, specifically of binary oppositions that formed the basis not only of structuralism but of all Western philosophy. The argument is put that women are marginalised precisely because of the binary form of such philosophy that requires one term to be always dominant (male, bourgeois, white, metropolitan, colonial) and the other subordinate (female, non-white, parochial, colonised). Reversing the hierarchy is necessary (in ideological, political and ethical terms) but is usually far from sufficient to correct the situation (see ETHICAL TURN). So a feminist epistemology or, what has become increasingly popular, a deconstructionist (feminist) history (see DECONSTRUCTIONIST HISTORY) was conjured. This was an intellectual act that politics demanded of the academy.

Unavoidably, so the post-structuralist feminist argument runs, through convention the sexual hierarchy has become associated with male dominance. In philosophical terms this becomes the dominance and superiority of **objectivity** (male) over subjectivity (female), and reason (male) over emotion (female). This is important because maleness associated with reason is reified by social and cultural institutions, and becomes dominant, as Luce Irigaray claims, by a language that is masculinised. So it is that traditional (i.e. male) epistemology conspires to sustain a gendered framework of inequality by its dualistic nature. The debate over a feminist epistemology is thus an integral part of the debate over the nature of epistemology and, it follows, of history as an epistemology.

Women's history (along with **race** and **class** histories) has posed the epistemological question of for whom, from what perspective, and for what purposes do we write and constitute the practices and methods of history? Our answer to that question quite evidently generates particular epistemological expectations. If I assume that the thinking historian normally occupies a disinterested position outside history, an epistemologist seeking the truth about people in the past as they made rational decisions as free agents, I end up with an idealised objectivist and empiricist epistemology (see INTENTIONALITY; FACTS). Feminist epistemologists of a practical realist or **constructionist history** persuasion, however, do not accept that picture. They assume that the historian is not value-neutral and cannot produce an objective history. Rather, it is awash with unstated masculine bias. But, through a better-informed feminist empiricist perspective (empiricism is, for them, still the only game in town), historians can yield ever more truthful (through a necessarily feminised) knowledge. Their informed empiricism will correct history's patriarchal squint.

The British feminist empiricist historian Catherine Hall exemplifies this position. As a sophisticated constructionist history realist she acknowledges that historians construct stories (feminist historians by their personal inclination will create feminist stories), but such story-writing does not take her into agreement with the post-structuralist position that all history must be essentially fictive (Hall 1992: 1). Hall argues that the dynamic of her feminist history consists of constructed stories, but her stories are grounded in the **evidence** as found through laborious archival work, and which appropriate conceptual frameworks guide. Writing at the same time as Scott wrote her interim report, Hall offered her own narrative of the development of women's history. She described British feminist history as profoundly empiricist in methodology and crosshatched theoretically by Marxism. Hall accepts that postmodern (specifically post-structuralist) approaches have tested this gender–class theoretical framework, not least through the argument that the meaning of gender is socially constructed. This, Hall claims, required exploring the different class (and, in post-colonial Britain, race) experiences of women. The upshot has been her recognition that the 'differences between men and women' are established by 'discursively constructing "the other"' (Hall 1992: 13) – but still ultimately grounded in women's experience of the real world, which is then translated faithfully by the historian (Burkitt 1998).

Feminist empiricists, like sophisticated empiricists everywhere, believe in access to knowable truths. Post-empiricist feminists such as Scott, Judith Butler and Elizabeth Deeds Ermarth argue that empiricism – even feminist empiricism – is no guarantor of truthful interpretations. Scott's position seems to be that past experience must be understood primarily through (and thereby defined by) language, and has a very limited compass because women are determined by social situation and male dominance, and such residual agency that exists is derived through discourse. Hence experience is discursively constructed (see AGENCY/STRUCTURE). Postmodern women's history historians, especially those inspired by Derrida like Scott, can apparently find no anchor in knowable realism that permits circumvention of our categories, theories or discourses. Equally, there cannot be any while the gold standard for historical knowledge is founded on the Western philosophical male/female binary. But the problem for feminist historians like Scott is how to generate a feminist epistemology that is not grounded or fixed in women's historical and material circumstances or, if like Hall their preference takes them in the opposite direction, one that is. While Scott is keen to argue that the very concept of experience has been rendered problematic, she nevertheless (by the mid-1990s) has fallen back to the (untenable?) idea that a sophisticated postmodern theorising can make the reality of social structures accessible. While she makes room for non-essentialised meanings and tries to incorporate the feminine unconscious and welcomes recognition of the partiality of the subject–subject relationship, she draws back from the abyss that history cannot know reality, and all we have is that surrogate for the past we call history.

What the practitioners of women's history have done in the past thirty years, however, is to raise within the mainstream of historical thinking the 'problem of history', namely is historical knowing of one kind or one piece? Can we view historians as disembodied and disinterested people who simply convert information into truthful interpretations through the discovery of facts? Women's history has confronted (and replaced?) the historian-as-observer with the historian-as-player, the historian as an **author** caught in a variety of competing discourses. Is it now always a matter of 'whose history' are we writing? Presumably, once knowledge production is situated within a gendered framework, objectivity also has to be acknowledged as being socially constructed?

The enhanced constructionist sophistication that women's history has brought to the profession has not changed the fact that the majority of feminists and women's history practitioners have, as I have already suggested, stayed loyal to their materialist or other culturalist ideological preferences. They were (and remain) unconvinced either that any kind of deconstructionist history offers a better way to study women and gender, or that there is a need to fundamentally alter the conventional reconstructionist, or (their preferred) constructionist, variety of history. For many leftist feminists postmodernism is a non-empirical distraction from the harsh realities of women's changing historical experience, the evidence of which provides the bedrock of facts upon which presentist political manifestos can be built and action taken.

What this indicates to me is that neither feminist empiricists nor some post-structuralists have come to terms with the fact that history is not a truth-acquiring discipline. Both groups accept that it is important to recognise that categories like women and gender are socially constituted and are not reliable transcriptions of past reality. This undoubtedly empowers women's history historians to offer a feminist critique of much social science theory that fails to recognise the polyvalent nature of the meanings of their categories. This allows both groups to reflect upon the gendered representation of women in historical evidence and the situated knowledge that derives therefrom. To explore whether there is a different feminist epistemology is also important, but it often resolves itself into a debate over which kinds of historian have the truest experiential insight. In spite of these insights, to fall back on the foundationalism of an ultimately knowable experience is, I suggest, to make the assumption that gender is a social construction that must and will ultimately be decoded through **inference** from the evidence of experience. The aim of much women's history, even from Scott's post-structuralist perspective, still seems to be to control and domesticate the sublime.

Scott does not pursue anti-foundational post-empiricism, cast as a feminist epistemology, and feminist historians of a more conventional historiographical and epistemological orientation do not accept it. Some hardened empiricists writing in the late 1990s like Jean Curthoys rejected the very notion that the problem inheres in the binarism of Western philosophy, while others like Penelope J. Corfield who, like Hall, continues to acknowledge the richness of the gender history produced by the postmodern discussion of difference, deny that the intellectual landscape of the discipline has been transformed or, indeed, rethought (Corfield 1997: 244–5). For Corfield postmodernism is unlikely to effect a radical change in historical methodology because, as she puts it, not everyone accepts the postmodern neo-idealist notion that reality cannot exist outside the text, and just as importantly debates over the existence of a genuine feminist epistemology remain inconclusive (Corfield 1997: 253).

Further reading

Alcoff, L.M., 1998; Alcoff, L.M. and Potter, E., 1993; Antony, L.M. and Witt, C., 1993; Baker, M., 1998; Bock, G., 1991, 1989; Bordo, S., 1987; Burkitt, I., 1998; Butler, J., 1990; Carroll, B.A., 1976; Code, L., 2000, 1991; Corfield, P.J., 1997; Curthoys, J., 1997; Davis, N.Z., 1995, 1976; Degler, C.N., 1975; Duran, J., 1997; Ermarth, E.D., 1992; Garry, A. and Pearsall, M., 1996; Hall, C., 1992; Haraway, D., 1991, 1988; Hoff-Wilson, J. and Farnham, C., 1990; Irigaray, L., 1992; Kelly, J., 1984; Kerber, L.K., 1988; Laslett, B. *et al.*, 1997; Le Doeuff, M., 1989; Lloyd, G., 1984; Longino, H.E., 1990; Melosh, B., 1993; Mohanty, C., Russo, A. and Torres, L., 1991; Moi, T., 1988; Nelson, L.H., 1990; NeSmith, G., n.d.; Offen, K. *et al.*, 1991; Perrot, M., 1992; Poovey, M., 1988; Rendall, J., 1991; Riley, D., 1989; Rothenburg, P.S., 1998; Rowbotham, S., 1974; Ruiz, V.L. and DuBois, E.C., 2000; Schmitt, F., 1994; Scott, J.W., 1996a, 1996b, 1991, 1989, 1988, 1986, 1983; Shoemaker, R. and Vincent, M., 1998; Smith-Rosenberg, C., 1985; Williams, C.D., 1997.

BIBLIOGRAPHY

(2004) 'Historians and ethics', *History and Theory* (themed issue) 43.

(2004) Dominick LaCapra, *Rethinking History: The Journal of Theory and Practice* (themed issue) 8.

(2004) 'Interchange: genres of history', *Journal of American History*, 91:2.

(2002) 'Unconventional history', *History and Theory* (themed issue) 41.

(2001) 'Agency after postmodernism', *History and Theory* (themed issue) 40.

(2000) 'History and film', *Rethinking History: The Journal of Theory and Practice* (themed issue) 4.

(1998) 'The good of history', *Rethinking History: The Journal of Theory and Practice* (themed issue) 2.

(1980) 'Metahistory: six critiques', *History and Theory* (themed issue) 19.

Achinstein, P. (1983) *The Nature of Explanation*, New York: Oxford University Press.

Adorno, T. (1983 [1966]) *Negative Dialectics*, New York: Continuum.

Adorno, T. and Horkheimer, M. (1972) *The Dialectic of Enlightenment*, trans. J. Cumming, New York: Continuum.

Alcoff, Linda Martin (ed.) (1998) *Epistemology: The Big Questions*, Oxford: Basil Blackwell.

Alcoff, Linda and Potter, Elizabeth (eds) (1993) *Feminist Epistemologies*, New York: Routledge.

Aldrich, Robert and Wotherspoon, Garry (eds) (2001) *Who's Who in Contemporary Gay and Lesbian History*, London and New York: Routledge.

Alexander, Sally (1984) 'Women, class and sexual differences in the 1830s and 1840s: some reflections on the writing of a feminist history', *History Workshop*, 17: 125–49.

Allen, Barry (1998) 'Truthfulness', *Common Knowledge* 7: 19–26.

—— (1993) *Truth in Philosophy*, Cambridge, MA: Harvard University Press.

Allen, Richard (1995) *Projecting Illusion: Film Spectatorship and the Impression of Reality*, Cambridge: Cambridge University Press.

Althusser, Louis (1971) *Lenin and Philosophy and Other Essays*, trans. Ben Brewster, London: New Left Books.

American Historical Association (1995) *Guide to Historical Literature*, New York: Oxford University Press.

Ankersmit, Frank R. (2005a) 'Reply to Professor Saari', *Rethinking History: The Journal of Theory and Practice* 9: 23–33.

—— (2005b) *Sublime Historical Experience*, Stanford, CA: Stanford University Press.

—— (2003a) 'Invitation to historians', *Rethinking History: The Journal of Theory and Practice* 7: 413–39.

—— (2003b) 'Pygmalion. Rousseau and Diderot on theatrical representation', *Rethinking History: The Journal of Theory and Practice* 7: 315–41.

—— (2002) *Political Representation*, Stanford, CA: Stanford University Press.

—— (2001) *Historical Representation*, Stanford, CA: Stanford University Press.

249

—— (2000) 'Exchanging ideas' (with Mark Bevir), *Rethinking History: The Journal of Theory and Practice* 4: 351–72.

—— (1998a) 'Hayden White's appeal to the historians', *History and Theory* 37: 182–93.

—— (1998b) 'Danto on representation, identity, and indiscernibles', theme issue: *History and Theory* 37: 44–70.

—— (1994) *History and Tropology: The Rise and Fall of Metaphor*, Berkeley, CA: University of California Press.

—— (1989) 'Historiography and postmodernism', *History and Theory* 28: 137–53.

—— (1983) *Narrative Logic: A Semantic Analysis of the Historian's Language*, The Hague: Martinus Nijhoff.

Ankersmit, F.R. and Kellner, Hans (eds) (1995) *A New Philosophy of History*, Chicago: University of Chicago Press.

Ansell-Pearson, Keith (1994a) *Nietzsche and Modern German Thought*, London: Routledge.

—— (ed.) (1994b) *Nietzsche: On the Genealogy of Morality*, Cambridge: Cambridge University Press.

Anthias, F. and Yuval Davis, M. (1992) *Racialised Boundaries: Race, Nation, Gender, Colour and Class in the Anti-Racist Struggle*, London and New York: Routledge.

Antony, Louise M. and Witt, Charlotte (eds) (1993) *A Mind of One's Own: Feminist Essays on Reason and Objectivity*, Boulder, CO: Westview Press.

Appleby, Joyce, Covington, Elizabeth, Hoyt, David, Latham, Michael and Sneider, Alison (eds) (1996) *Knowledge and Postmodernism in Historical Perspective*, London: Routledge.

Appleby, Joyce, Hunt, Lynn and Jacob, Margaret (1994) *Telling the Truth About History*, New York: Norton.

Arato, A. and Gebhardt, E. (1982) *The Essential Frankfurt School Reader*, New York: Continuum.

Arditi, B. and Valentine, J. (1999) *Polemicization: The Contingency of the Commonplace*, Edinburgh: Edinburgh University Press.

Ashcroft, B., Griffiths, G. and Tiffin, H. (1994) *The Post-Colonial Studies Reader*, London and New York: Routledge.

—— (1989*)* *The Empire Writes Back: Theory and Practice in Post-Colonial Literatures*, London and New York: Routledge.

Ashley, David (1997) *History Without a Subject: The Postmodern Condition*, Boulder, CO: Westview Press.

Ashton, Owen. R. (1991) *W.E. Adams: Chartist, Radical and Journalist: An Honour to the Fourth Estate*, Whitley Bay: Bewick Press.

Atkinson, R.F. (1978) *Knowledge and Explanation in History*, London: Macmillan.

Attridge, Derek, Bennington, Geoffrey and Young, Robert (eds) (1987) *Post-Structuralism and the Question of History*, Cambridge: Cambridge University Press.

Audi, Robert (1998) *Epistemology: A Contemporary Introduction to the Theory of Knowledge*, New York: Routledge.

Auerbach, Erich (1953) *Mimesis: The Representation of Reality in Western Literature*, trans. Willard Trask, Princeton, NJ: Princeton University Press.

Auxier, Randall E. (1997) 'Imagination and historical knowledge in Vico: a critique of Leon Pompa's recent work', *Humanitas* X: 26–49.

Aydelotte, W.O. (1971) *Quantification in History*, Reading, MA: Addison Wesley.

Aydelotte, W.O., Bogue, A.G. and Fogel, R.W. (1972) *The Dimensions of Quantitative Research in History*, Princeton, NJ: Princeton University Press.

Back, Les and Solomos, John (eds) (2000) *Theories of Race and Racism: A Reader*, London: Routledge.

Baker, Mary (1998) 'Feminist post-structuralist engagements with history', *Rethinking History: The Journal of Theory and Practice* 2: 371–8.

Balibar, Etienne and Wallerstein, Immanuel (1991) *Race, Nation, Class: Ambiguous Identities*, London: Verso.

Bann, Stephen (1984) *The Clothing of Clio: A Study of the Representation of History in Nineteenth-Century Britain and France*, Cambridge: Cambridge University Press.

—— (1983) 'Analysing the discourse of history', *Renaissance and Modern Studies* 27: 61–84.

—— (1981) *Comparative Criticism – A Yearbook*, vol. 3, University Park, PA: Pennsylvania State University Press.

Barnard, F.M. (1981) 'Accounting for actions: causality and teleology', *History and Theory* 20: 291–312.

Barta, T. (ed.) (1998) *Screening the Past: Film and the Representation of History*, Westport CT and London: Praeger.

Barthes, Roland (1988) *The Semiotic Challenge*, New York: Hill and Wang.

—— (1986) *The Rustle of Language*, Oxford: Basil Blackwell.

—— (1984 [1967]) *Elements of Semiology*, London: Jonathan Cape.

—— (1983) *Empire of Signs*, trans. Richard Howard, London: Jonathan Cape.

—— (1981 [1967]) 'Le Discours de l'histoire', *Information sur les sciences sociales* 6: 65–75; trans. with an introduction by Stephen Bann (1981) *Comparative Criticism – A Yearbook*: Cambridge: Cambridge University Press.

—— (1977) *Image–Music–Text*, trans. Stephen Heath, London: Fontana.

—— (1975) *The Pleasure of the Text*, trans. Richard Miller, London: Jonathan Cape.

—— (1974) *S/Z*, trans. Richard Miller, New York: Hill and Wang.

—— (1972) *Critical Essays*, trans. Richard Howard, Evanston, IL: Northwestern University Press.

—— (1967) *Writing Degree Zero*, trans. Annette Lavers and Colin Smith, London: Jonathan Cape.

—— (1957) *Mythologies*, London: Pan Books.

Baudrillard, Jean (1998) *Paroxysm*, interviewed by P. Pettit, London: Verso.

—— (1995) *The Perfect Crime*, London: Verso.

—— (1994) *The Illusion of the End*, trans. Chris Turner, Cambridge: Polity Press.

—— (1983) *Simulations*, trans. Paul Fosse, Paul Patton and Philip Beitchman, New York: Semiotext(e).

—— (1976) *Symbolic Exchange and Death*, Paris: Gallimard.

—— (1975) *The Mirror of Production*, trans. Mark Poster, St Louis, MO: Telos Press.

—— (1973) *Toward a Critique of the Political Economy of the Sign*, St Louis, MO: Telos Press.

—— (1970) *La Société de consommation*, Paris; Gallimard.

—— (1968) *Le Système des objets*, Paris: Denoel.

Bauman, Zygmunt (1998) *Globalisation: The Human Consequences*, New York: New York University Press.

—— (1997) *Postmodernity and its Discontents*, New York: New York University Press.

—— (1989) *Modernity and the Holocaust*, London: Polity Press.

Baynes, K., Bohman, J. and McCarthy, T. (eds) (1987) *After Philosophy: End or Transformation*, Cambridge, MA: MIT Press.

Beard, Charles (1935) 'That noble dream', *American Historical Review* 41: 74–87.

—— (1933) 'Written history as an act of faith', *American Historical Review* 39: 219–31.

Beardsworth, R. (1996) *Derrida and the Political*, London and New York: Routledge.

Beauvoir, Simone de (1952 [1949]) *The Second Sex*, trans. H.M. Parshley, New York: Knopf.

Beck, Lewis White (ed.) (1963) *Immanuel Kant: On History*, Indianapolis, IN: Bobbs-Merrill Co.

Becker, Carl (1945) 'What are historical facts?', *The Western Political Quarterly* 8:3, 330.

—— (1931) 'Everyman his own historian', *American Historical Review* 37: 221–36.

Becker, Lawrence (ed.) (1992) *A History of Western Ethics*, New York: Garland.

Becker, Marjorie (2004) '"When I was a child, I danced as a child, but now that I am old, I think about salvation": Concepción Gonzalez and a past that would not stay put', in Alun Munslow and Robert A. Rosenstone (eds) *Experiments in Rethinking History*, London and New York: Routledge, pp. 17–29.

Beiser, Frederick C. (ed.) (1993) *The Cambridge Companion to Hegel*, Cambridge: Cambridge University Press.

Belchem, John and Kirk, Neville (eds) (1997) *Languages of Labour*, Aldershot: Ashgate Publishing.

Bell, Bernard W., Grosholz, Emily R. and Stewart, James B. (eds) (1996) *W.E.B. Du Bois: On Race and Culture*, New York and London: Routledge.

Benjamin, Andrew (ed.) (1989) *The Lyotard Reader*, Oxford: Basil Blackwell.

Benjamin, Walter (1999) *The Arcades Project*, trans. Howard Eiland and Kevin McLaughlin, Cambridge MA: The Belknap Press of Harvard University Press.

—— (1973) *Illuminations*, ed. Hannah Arendt, trans. H. Zohn, Glasgow: Fontana.

Bennett, Tony (1990) *Outside Literature*, London: Routledge.

Bennington, G. (1994) *Legislations: The Politics of Deconstruction*, London: Verso.

—— (1993) *Jacques Derrida*, Chicago: University of Chicago Press.

—— (1988) *Lyotard: Writing the Event*, Manchester: Manchester University Press.

Benson, Lee (1961) *The Concept of Jacksonian Democracy: New York as a Test Case*, Princeton, NJ: Princeton University Press.

Bentley, Michael (ed.) (1997) *Companion to Historiography*, London: Routledge.

Benveniste, Emile (1971) *Problems in General Linguistics*, Miami, FL: Miami University Press.

Berkhofer, Robert F. (1995) *Beyond the Great Story: History as Text and Discourse*, Princeton, NJ: Princeton University Press.

Berlin, Isaiah (1997) *The Sense of Reality*, New York: Farrar, Strauss and Giroux.

—— (1976) *Vico and Herder: Two Studies in the History of Ideas*, London: Hogarth Press.

Bernauer, James and Keenan, Thomas (1988) 'The works of Michel Foucault, 1954–1984', in James Bernauer and David Rasmussen (eds) *The Final Foucault*, Cambridge, MA: MIT Press.

Bernstein, R. (1983) *Beyond Objectivism and Relativism*, Philadelphia, PA: University of Pennsylvania Press.

Bertens, Hans (1995) *The Idea of the Postmodern: A History*, London: Routledge.

Bevir, Mark (1999) *The Logic of the History of Ideas*, Cambridge: Cambridge University Press.

—— (1994) 'Objectivity in history', *History and Theory* 33: 328–44.

Bhabha, Homi K. (1994) *The Location of Culture*, New York and London: Routledge.

—— (ed.) (1990) *Nation and Narration*, New York and London: Routledge.

Bhaskar, R. (1991) *Philosophy and the Idea of Freedom*, Oxford: Basil Blackwell.

Biography (quarterly journal) (1978–)

Black, E. and M. (1973) 'The Wallace vote in Alabama: a multiple regression analysis', *Journal of Politics*, 35: 730–6.

Black, J. and MacRaild, D. (1997) *Studying History*, Basingstoke: Macmillan.

Blanning, T.C.W. and Cannadine, D. (eds) (1996) *History and Biography: Essays in Honour of Derek Beales*, Cambridge and New York: Cambridge University Press.

Bloch, Marc (1963 [1954]) *The Historian's Craft*, Manchester: Manchester University Press.

Bloom, Ida, Hagemann, Karen and Hall, Catherine (2000) *Gendered Nations: Nationalisms and Gender Order in the Long Nineteenth Century*, London: Berg.

Bloomfield, M.W. (ed.) (1972) *In Search of Literary Theory*, Ithaca, NY: Cornell University Press.

Boas, George (1969) *The History of Ideas: An Introduction*, New York: Scribner's.

Bock, Gisela (1991) 'Challenging dichotomies: perspectives on women's history', in Karin Offen, Ruth Roach Pierson and Jane Rendall (eds) *Writing Women's History: International Perspectives*, Bloomington, IN: Indiana University Press, pp. 45–58.

—— (1989) 'Women's history and gender history: aspects of an international debate', *Gender and History* 1: 7–30.

Bogue, Allan G. (1968) 'United States: the "new political" history', *Journal of Contemporary History*, 111: 5–28.

Bonjour, L. (1985) *The Structure of Empirical Knowledge*, Cambridge, MA: Harvard University Press.

Bordo, Susan (1987) *The Flight to Objectivity: The Cartesian Masculinization of Culture*, Albany, NY: State University of New York Press.

Bouchard, Donald F. (ed.) (1977) *Language, Counter-Memory, Practice: Selected Essays and Interviews*, trans. Donald F. Bouchard and Sherry Simon, Ithaca, NY: Cornell University Press.

Bourdieu, Pierre (1972) *An Outline of a Theory of Practice*, trans. Richard Nice, Cambridge: Cambridge University Press.

Bowman, Paul (2005) *Post-Marxism Versus Cultural Studies: Politics, Theory and Intervention*, Edinburgh: Edinburgh University Press.

—— (2002) 'Ernesto Laclau, Chantal Mouffe, and post-Marxism', in Julian Wolfreys (ed.) *The Edinburgh Encyclopaedia of Modern Criticism and Theory*, Edinburgh: Edinburgh University Press, pp. 799–808.

Bradbury, M. and McFarlane, J. (eds) (1976) *Modernism: 1890–1930*, London: Penguin.

Branstead, E.K. and Meluish, K.J. (eds) (1978) *Western Liberalism: A History in Documents: From Locke to Croce*, London: Longman.

Braudel, Fernand (1980) *On History*, London: Weidenfeld and Nicolson.

—— (1972–3) *The Mediterranean and the Mediterranean World in the Age of Philip II*, 2 vols, trans. S. Reynolds, Glasgow: William Collins.

Breisach, Ernst (2003) *On the Future of History: The Postmodernist Challenge and Its Aftermath*, Chicago and London: University of Chicago Press.

—— (1993) *American Progressive History: An Experiment in Modernization*, Chicago: University of Chicago Press.

—— (1983) *Historiography: Ancient, Medieval and Modern*, Chicago: University of Chicago Press.

Brennan, Teresa (1993) *History After Lacan*, London and New York: Routledge.

—— (1992) *The Interpretation of the Flesh: Freud and Femininity*, London and New York: Routledge.

Brett, Annabel (2002) 'What is intellectual history now?', in David Cannadine (ed.) *What is History Now?*, Basingstoke: Palgrave Macmillan, pp. 113–31.

Brody, David (1979) 'The old labor history and the new: in search of an American working class', *Labor History* 20: 111–26.

Brown, Callum G. (2005) *Postmodernism for Historians*, Harlow: Pearson Longman.

Brown, Merle Elliott (1966) *Neo-Idealistic Aesthetics: Croce, Gentile, Collingwood*, Detroit: Wayne State University Press.

Bruner, Jerome (1992) *Actual Minds, Possible Worlds*, Cambridge MA: Harvard University Press.

—— (1990) *Acts of Meaning*, Cambridge, MA: Harvard University Press.

Bullock, Alan (1985) *The Humanist Tradition in the West*, London: Thames and Hudson.

Bulmer, Martin and Solomos, John (eds) (1999) *Racism*, Oxford: Oxford University Press.

Bunzl, Martin (1997) *Real History*, London: Routledge.

Burckhardt, Jacob (1990 [1860]) *The Civilization of the Renaissance in Italy*, ed. Peter Burke, London: Penguin.

Burke, Peter (2005) 'Performing history: the importance of occasions', *Rethinking History: The Journal of Theory and Practice* 9: 35–52.

—— (1997) *Varieties of Cultural History*, Oxford: Polity Press.

—— (1993) *History and Social Theory*, Ithaca, NY: Cornell University Press.

—— (ed.) (1991) *New Perspectives on Historical Writing*, University Park, PA: Pennsylvania State University Press.

—— (1990) *The French Historical Revolution: The Annales School*, Cambridge: Cambridge University Press.

—— (1989) 'History as social memory', in Thomas Butler (ed.) *Memory, History, Culture and the Mind*, Oxford: Basil Blackwell, pp. 97–113.

Burke, Sean (1992) *The Death and Return of the Author: Criticism and Subjectivity in Barthes, Foucault and Derrida*, Edinburgh: Edinburgh University Press.

Burkitt, Ian (1998) 'Sexuality and gender identity: from a discursive to a relational analysis', *The Sociological Review* 46: 483–504.

Burnette, Joyce (2004) 'The wages and employment of female day-labourers in English agriculture, 1740–1850', *The Economic History Review*, LVII: 664–90.

Burnham, Walter Dean (1965) 'The changing shape of the American political universe' *American Political Science Review*, LIX: 7–28.

Butler, Judith (1991) 'Imitation and gender insurbordination', in Diane Fuss (ed.), *Inside/Out: Lesbian Theories/Gay Theories*, New York and London: Routledge, pp. 13–31.

—— (1990) *Gender Trouble: Feminism and the Subversion of Identity*, London: Routledge.

Butler, Thomas (ed.) (1989) *Memory, History, Culture and the Mind*, Oxford: Basil Blackwell.

Cabrera, Miguel A. (2004) *Postsocial History: An Introduction*, Lanham, MD: Lexington Books.

Callinicos, Alex (1995) *Theories and Narratives: Reflections on the Philosophy of History*, Cambridge: Polity Press.

—— (1989) *Against Postmodernism: A Marxist Perspective*, Cambridge: Polity Press.

Calvet, Louis-Jean (1994) *Roland Barthes: A Biography*, trans. Sarah Wykes, Cambridge: Polity Press.

Cameron, Averil (1989) *History as Text: The Writing of Ancient History*, London: Duckworth.

Canary, R. and Kozicki, H. (eds) (1978) *The Writing of History: Literary Form and Historical Understanding*, Madison, WI: University of Wisconsin Press.

Cannadine, David (ed.) (2002) *What is History Now?*, Basingstoke: Palgrave Macmillan.

Cannon, John, Davies, R.H.C., Doyle, William and Greene, Jack P. (eds) (1988) *The Blackwell Dictionary of Historians*, Oxford: Basil Blackwell.

Caputo, John D. (1997) *Deconstruction in a Nutshell*, New York: Fordham University Press.

Carnes, Mark C. (ed.) (1995) *Past Imperfect: History According to the Movies*, New York: Holt.

Carr, David (1986a) 'Narrative and the real world: an argument for continuity', *History and Theory* 25: 117–31.

—— (1986b) *Time, Narrative, and History*, Bloomington, IN: Indiana University Press.

Carr, D., Flynn, Thomas R. and Makkreel, Rudolph A. (eds) (2004) *The Ethics of History*, Evanston, IL: Northwestern University Press.

Carr, E.H. (1987 [1961]) *What is History?* London: Penguin.

—— (1958–64) *Socialism in One Country, 1924–1926*, 5 vols, Harmondsworth: Penguin.

—— (1950–3) *The Bolshevik Revolution, 1917–1923*, 3 vols, London: Macmillan.

Carrard, Philippe (1992) *Poetics of the New History: French Historical Discourse from Braudel to Chartier*, Baltimore, MD: Johns Hopkins University Press.

Carrier, M. and Machamer, P. (eds) (1997) *Mindscapes: Philosophy, Science, and the Mind*, Pittsburgh, PA: Pittsburgh University Press.

Carroll, Berenice A. (ed.) (1976) *Liberating Women's History: Theoretical and Critical Essays*, Urbana, IL: University of Illinois Press.

Carroll, David (1976) 'On tropology: the forms of history', *Diacritics* 6: 58–64.

Carroll, John (1993) *Humanism*, London: Fontana.

Cassirer, E. (1981) *Kant's Life and Thought*, New Haven, CT: Yale University Press.

Caws, Peter (1997) *Structuralism: A Philosophy for the Human Sciences*, Contemporary Studies in Philosophy and the Human Sciences, Atlantic Highlands, NJ: Humanities Press.

Centre for Contemporary Cultural Studies (1982) *The Empire Strikes Back: Race and Racism in 70s Britain*, London: Routledge.

Chakrabarty, Dipesh (1992) 'The death of history: historical consciousness and the culture of late capitalism', *Public Culture*, 4: 56–65.

Chamberlain, Mary and Thompson, Paul (1998) *Narrative and Genre*, London and New York: Routledge.

Chambers, Iain (2000) *Culture After Humanism*, London: Routledge.

Chandler, D. (2002) *Semiotics: The Basics*, London and New York: Routledge.

Chartier, Roger (1997) *On the Edge of the Cliff: History, Language, and Practices*, Baltimore, MD: Johns Hopkins University Press.

—— (1988) *Cultural History: Between Practices and Representations*, Cambridge: Cambridge University Press.

—— (1987) *The Cultural Uses of Print in Early Modern France*, trans. Lydia G. Cochrane, Princeton, NJ: Princeton University Press.

Chatman, Seymour (1978) *Story and Discourse: Narrative Structure in Fiction and Film*, Ithaca NY: Cornell University Press.

Cixous, Hélène and Clément, C. (1986 [1975]) *The Newly Born Woman*, trans. Betsy Wing, Minneapolis, MI: University of Minnesota Press.

Cockburn, David (1997) *Other Times: Philosophical Perspectives on Past, Present and Future*, Cambridge: Cambridge University Press.

Code, Lorraine (2000) *Encyclopedia of Feminist Theories*, London and New York: Routledge.

—— (1991) *What Can She Know? Feminist Theory and the Construction of Knowledge*, Ithaca, NY: Cornell University Press.

Collingwood, R.G. (1994 [1946]) *The Idea of History*, rev. edn ed. Jan van der Dussen, Oxford: Oxford University Press.

—— (1940) *An Essay on Metaphysics*, Oxford: Clarendon Press.

Connor, Steven (1989) *Postmodernist Culture: An Introduction to Theories of the Postmodern*, Oxford: Basil Blackwell.

Conrad, A.H. and Meyer, J.R. (1958) 'The economics of slavery in the antebellum south', *Journal of Political Economy* 66: 95–130.

Cooper, David. E. (ed.) (1999) *Epistemology: The Classic Readings*, Oxford: Basil Blackwell.

Corfield, Penelope J. (1997) 'History and the challenge of gender history', *Rethinking History: The Journal of Theory and Practice* 1: 241–58.

Cox, C.B. (1963) *The Free Spirit: A Study of Liberal Humanism in the Novels of George Eliot, Henry James, E.M. Forster, Virginia Woolf, Angus Wilson*, Oxford: Oxford University Press.

Cox, Michael (ed.) (2000) *E.H. Carr: A Critical Appraisal*, Basingstoke: Palgrave Publishers.

255

Critchley, Simon (1996) 'Deconstruction and pragmatism – Is Derrida a private ironist or a public liberal?', in C. Mouffe (ed.) *Deconstruction and Pragmatism*, London: Routledge, pp. 19–40.

Croce, Benedetto (1970 [1927]) *An Autobiography*, Freeport, NY: Books for Libraries Press.

—— (1968 [1917]) *The Theory and History of Historiography*, Geneva: Droz.

—— (1964 [1913]) *The Philosophy of Giambattista Vico*, trans. R.G. Collingwood, New York: Russell and Russell.

—— (1923) *History: Its Theory and Practice*, trans. Douglas Ainslie, New York: Harcourt and Brace.

Culler, Jonathan (1983) *Barthes*, London: Fontana.

—— (1982) *On Deconstruction: Theory and Criticism after Structuralism*, Ithaca, NY: Cornell University Press.

Curthoys, Ann (1996) 'Is history fiction?', *The UTS Review* 2: 12–37.

Curthoys, Ann and Docker, John (1997) 'The two histories: metaphor in English historiographical writing', *Rethinking History: The Journal of Theory and Practice* 1: 259–74.

Curthoys, Jean (1997) *Feminist Amnesia: The Wake of Women's Liberation*, London: Routledge.

Daddow, Oliver (2005) 'No philosophy please, we're historians', *Rethinking History: The Journal of Theory and Practice* 9: 105–9.

—— (2004) 'The ideology of apathy: historians and postmodernism', *Rethinking History: The Journal of Theory and Practice* 8: 417–38.

Dant, Tim (1991) *Knowledge, Ideology and Discourse*, London: Routledge.

Danto, Arthur (1998) 'Danto and his critics: art history, historiography and *After the End of Art*', *History and Theory* (themed issue) 37: 1–143.

—— (1997) *After the End of Art: Contemporary Art and the Pale of History*, Princeton, NJ: Princeton University Press.

—— (1985) *Narration and Knowledge*, New York: Columbia University Press.

—— (1981) *The Transfiguration of the Commonplace*, Cambridge, MA: Harvard University Press.

—— (1968a) *Analytical Philosophy of Knowledge*, Cambridge: Cambridge University Press.

—— (1968b) *Analytical Philosophy of History*, Cambridge: Cambridge University Press.

—— (1965) *Nietzsche as Philosopher*, New York: Macmillan.

Darnton, Robert (1986) *Mesmerism and the End of the Enlightenment in France*, Cambridge, MA: Harvard University Press.

—— (1980) 'Intellectual and cultural history', in Michael Kammen (ed.) *The Past Before Us: Contemporary Historical Writing in the United States*, Ithaca, NY: Cornell University Press, pp. 327–54.

David, Paul A. (1967) 'New light on a statistical dark age: US real product growth before 1840', *American Economic Review* 57: 294–306.

David, Paul A., Gutman, Herbert G., Sutch, Richard, Temin, Peter and Wright, Gavin (1976) *Reckoning with Slavery: A Critical Study in the Quantitative History of American Negro Slavery*, New York: Oxford University Press.

Davidson, Donald (1984) *Inquiries into Truth and Interpretation*, Oxford: Oxford University Press.

—— (1980) *Essays on Actions and Events*, Oxford: Oxford University Press.

Davidson, John (2004) 'History, identity and ethnicity', in Peter Lambert and Phillipp Schofield (eds) *Making History: An Introduction to the History and Practices of a Discipline*, New York and London: Routledge, pp. 204–16.

Davies, Stephen (2003) *Empiricism and History*, Basingstoke: Palgrave Macmillan.

Davies, Tony (1997) *Humanism*, London: Routledge.

Davis, Natalie Zemon (1995) *Women on the Margins: Three Seventeenth-Century Lives*, Cambridge, MA: Harvard University Press.

—— (1987a) *Fiction in the Archives: Pardon Tales and Their Tellers in Sixteenth-Century France*, Stanford, CA: University of California Press.

—— (1987b) '"Any resemblance to persons living or dead": film and the challenge of authenticity', *Yale Review* 76: 457–82.

—— (1976) '"Women's history", in transition: the European case', *Feminist Studies* 3: 83–103.

Dayton, Cornelia Hughes (2004) 'Rethinking agency, recovering voices', *American Historical Review* 109: 827–43

Dean, Mitchell (1994) *Critical and Effective Histories: Foucault's Methods and Historical Sociology*, London: Routledge.

de Certeau, Michel (1988 [1975]) *The Writing of History*, trans. Tom Conley, New York: Columbia University Press.

Degler, Carl N. (1975) *Is There a History of Women?*, Oxford: Clarendon Press.

Deleuze, Gilles and Guattari, Félix (1984 [1972]) *Capitalism and Schizophrenia: Anti-Oedipus*, trans. Robert Hurley, Mark Seem and Helen Lane, London: Athlone Press.

de Man, Paul (1983) *Blindness and Insight*, Minneapolis, MN: University of Minnesota Press.

—— (1978) 'The epistemology of metaphor', in S. Sacks (ed.) *On Metaphor*, Chicago and London: University of Chicago Press.

Dening, Greg (2004) 'Writing, rewriting the beach: an essay', *Rethinking History: The Journal of Theory and Practice* 2:143–72, reprinted in Alun Munslow and Robert A. Rosenstone (eds) *Experiments in Rethinking History*, London and New York: Routledge, pp. 30–55.

—— (2002) 'Performing on the beaches of the mind: an essay', *History and Theory* 41: 1–22.

—— (1992) *Mr Bligh's Bad Language*, Cambridge: Cambridge University Press.

—— (1966) *Performances*, Chicago: Chicago University Press.

Derrida, Jacques (1994) *Specters of Marx*, London: Routledge.

—— (1992) *Acts of Literature*, ed. Derek Attridge, New York and London: Routledge.

—— (1982) *Margins of Philosophy*, trans. Alan Bass, Chicago: University of Chicago Press.

—— (1979) *Nietzsche's Styles*, trans. Barbara Harlow, Chicago: University of Chicago Press.

—— (1978) *Writing and Difference*, trans. Alan Bass, Chicago: University of Chicago Press.

—— (1977) *Limited Inc.*, Evanston, IL: Northwestern University Press.

—— (1976) *Of Grammatology*, trans. G.C. Spivak, Baltimore, MD: Johns Hopkins University Press.

Dews, Peter (1987) *Logics of Disintegration: Post-Structuralist Thought and the Claims of Critical Theory*, London: Verso.

Dictionary of Philosophy of Mind, http://www.artsci.wustl.edu/~philos/MindDict/index.html.

Dilthey, Wilhelm (1976) *Selected Writings*, ed. and trans. H.P. Rickman with a foreword by Isaiah Berlin, Cambridge: Cambridge University Press.

Dirlik, Arif (2000) *Postmodernity's Histories: The Past as Legacy and Project*, Lanham, MD: Rowman and Littlefield.

Domanska, Ewa (1998a) *Encounters: Philosophy of History after Postmodernism*, Charlottesville, VA: University Press of Virginia.

—— (1998b) 'Hayden White: beyond irony', *History and Theory* 37: 173–82.

Donagan, Alan (1962) *The Later Philosophy of R.G. Collingwood*, Oxford: Clarendon Press.

—— (1959) 'Explanation in history', in Patrick Gardiner (ed.) *Theories of History*, Glencoe, IL: The Free Press, pp. 427–43.

Dosse, François (1997) *History of Structuralism*, 2 vols, trans. Deborah Glassman, Minneapolis, MN: University of Minnesota Press.

—— (1994 [1987]) *New History in France: The Triumph of the Annales*, trans. Peter V. Conroy Jr., Urbana, IL: University of Illinois Press.

Dowe, P. (1992) 'An empiricist defence of the causal account of explanation', *International Studies in the Philosophy of Science* 6: 123–8.

Downs, Laura Lee (2004) *Writing Gender History*, London: Hodder Arnold.

Dray, W.H. (1995) *History as Re-Enactment: R.G. Collingwood's Idea of History*, Oxford: Oxford University Press.

—— (1989) *On History and Philosophers of History*, New York: Brill.

—— (1986) Review of *Justifying Historical Descriptions* (1984) by C. Behan McCullagh, in *History and Theory* 25: 331–6.

—— (1980) *Perspectives on History*, Cambridge: Routledge.

—— (1970) 'On the nature and role of narrative in historiography', *History and Theory* 10: 153–71.

—— (ed.) (1966) *Philosophical Analysis and History*, New York: Harper and Row.

—— (1957) *Laws and Explanation in History*, Oxford: Oxford University Press.

Dreyfus, Hubert L. and Rabinow, Paul (1983) *Michel Foucault: Beyond Structuralism and Hermeneutics*, second edn, Brighton: Harvester Press.

Drolet, Michael (ed.) (2004) *The Postmodernism Reader: Foundational Texts*, London and New York: Routledge.

Dubow, Saul (1994) 'Ethnic euphemisms and racial echoes', *Journal of Southern African Studies* 20: 355–70.

Duby, Georges (1993) *The Knight, the Lady, and the Priest*, Chicago: University of Chicago Press.

Dummett, Michael (1978) *Truth and Other Enigmas*, Cambridge, MA: Harvard University Press.

Dunaway, David K. and Blum, Willa K. (eds) *Oral History: An Interdisciplinary Anthology*, Walnut Creek, CA: Altamira Press.

Duran, J. (1997) *Toward A Feminist Epistemology*, Savage, MD: Rowman and Littlefield.

Dworkin, Dennis L. (1997) *Cultural Marxism in Postwar Britain*, Durham, NC: Duke University Press.

Eagleton, Terry (1983) *Literary Theory*, Oxford: Basil Blackwell.

Edel, Leon (1957) *Literary Biography*, London: Hart-Davis.

Elam, Diane (1994) *Feminism and Deconstruction: Mis en Abyme*, London: Routledge.

Ellis, John M. (1989) *Against Deconstruction*, Princeton, NJ: Princeton University Press.

Elton, Geoffrey (1991 Routledge edn [1955]) *England under the Tudors*, London: Methuen.

—— (1991) *Return to Essentials: Some Reflections on the Present State of Historical Study*, Cambridge: Cambridge University Press.

—— (ed.) (1990 [1958]) *The New Cambridge Modern History II: The Reformation, 1520–1559*, Cambridge: Cambridge University Press.

—— (1986) *The Parliament of England, 1559–1581*, Cambridge: Cambridge University Press.

—— (1983) *Which Road to the Past?*, New Haven, CT: Yale University Press.

—— (1973) *Reform and Renewal*, Cambridge: Cambridge University Press.

—— (1972) *Policy and Police*, Cambridge: Cambridge University Press.

—— (1970) *Modern Historians on British History, 1485–1945*, London: Methuen.

—— (1968) *The Future of the Past*, Cambridge: Cambridge University Press.

—— (1967) *The Practice of History*, London: Methuen.

—— (1966) *Reformation Europe, 1517–1559*, New York: Harper and Row.

—— (1960) *The Tudor Constitution: Documents and Commentary*, Cambridge: Cambridge University Press.

—— (1953) *The Tudor Revolution*, Cambridge: Cambridge University Press.

Engerman, Stanley L. (1967) 'The effects of slavery upon the southern economy: a review of the recent debate', *Explorations in Entrepreneurial History* 4: 71–97.

Epstein, Julia and Straub, Kristina (eds) (1991) *Body Guards: The Cultural Politics of Gender Ambiguity*, New York and London: Routledge.

Ermarth, Elizabeth Deeds (2001) 'Beyond history', *Rethinking History: The Journal of Theory and Practice* 5: 195–216.

—— (1992) *Sequel to History: Postmodernism and the Crisis of Historical Time*, Princeton, NJ: Princeton University Press.

Evans, Richard J. (1997a) *In Defence of History*, London: Granta.

—— (1997b) 'Truth lost in vain views', *Times Higher Education Supplement*, 12 September, p. 18.

Eysteinsson, A. (1990) *The Concept of Modernism*, Ithaca, NY and London: Cornell University Press.

Fackenheim, Emil (1956/57) 'Kant's concept of history', *Kant Studien* XLVIII: 381–98.

Fairburn, Miles (1999) *Social History: Problems, Strategies and Methods*, Basingstoke: Macmillan.

Fanon, Franz (1968 [1952]) *Black Skin, White Masks*, trans. Charles Lam Markmann, London: MacGibbon and Kee.

—— (1961) *The Wretched of the Earth*, trans. Constance Farrington, New York: Grove.

Fay, Brian, Pomper, Philip and Vann, Richard T. (eds) (1998) *History and Theory: Contemporary Readings*, Oxford: Basil Blackwell.

Feagin, Joe R. (2001) *Racist America: Roots, Current Realities, and Future Reparations*, New York and London: Routledge.

Ferguson, Adam (1998 [1780]) 'History', *Encyclopaedia Britannica*, MultiMedia CD 1999 edn.

Ferro, Marc (1988) *Cinema and History*, Detroit, MI: Wayne State University Press.

Finney, Patrick (1998) 'Ethics, historical relativism and Holocaust denial', *Rethinking History: The Journal of Theory and Practice* 2: 359–70.

Firestone, Shulamith (1971) *The Dialectic of Sex: The Case for a Feminist Revolution*, London: Cape.

Fiumara, Gemma C. (1995) *The Metaphoric Process: Connections between Language and Life*, London: Routledge.

Floud, Roderick (1973) *An Introduction to Quantitative Methods for Historians*, London: Methuen.

Fogel, Robert W. (1989) *Without Consent or Contract: The Rise and Fall of American Slavery*, New York: W.W. Norton.

—— (1975a) 'Past developments and future prospects for ethnic minority groups: three phases of cliometric research of slavery and its aftermath', *American Economic Review* 65: pp. 37–46.

—— (1975b) 'The limits of quantitative methods in history', *American Historical Review* 80: 406–20.

—— (1966) 'The new economic history: its findings and methods', *Economic History Review*, 2nd ser., XIX: 642–56.

Fogel, Robert W. and Elton, Geoffrey R. (1984) *Which Road to the Past? Two Views of History*, New Haven, CT: Yale University Press.

Fogel, Robert W. and Engerman, Stanley L. (1974) *Time on the Cross: The Economics of American Negro Slavery*, 2 vols, Boston, MA: Little Brown.

—— (1971) *The Reinterpretation of American Economic History*, New York: Harper and Row.

Forum (1993) *American Historical Review* 98: 338–81.

—— (1991) 'The objectivity question and the future of the historical profession', *American Historical Review* 96: 675–708.

—— (1989) 'Intellectual history and the return of literature', *American Historical Review* 94: 581–69.

Foucault, Michel (1985, 1986) *History of Sexuality*, vols 2 and 3, New York: Pantheon.

—— (1980) *Power/Knowledge: Selected Interviews and Other Writings*, Brighton: Harvester Press.

—— (1979 [1976]) *History of Sexuality*, vol. 1, London: Allen Lane.

—— (1977 [1975]) *Discipline and Punish*, New York: Pantheon.

—— (1977) 'Nietzsche, genealogy, history', in Donald F. Bouchard (ed.), *Language, Counter-Memory, Practice: Selected Essays and Interviews*, trans. Donald F. Bouchard and Sherry Simon, Ithaca, NY: Cornell University Press, pp. 139–64.

—— (1975) *The Birth of the Clinic*, New York: Vintage Books.

—— (1973a) *Madness and Civilization: A History of Insanity in the Age of Reason*, London: Tavistock.

—— (1973b) *The Order of Things: An Archaeology of the Human Sciences*, New York: Random House.

—— (1972) *The Archaeology of Knowledge*, New York: Harper and Row.

—— (1970) 'The order of discourse', inaugural lecture at the Collège de France, 2 December.

Frederickson, George M. (2003) *Racism: A Short History*, Princeton NJ: Princeton University Press.

Friedlander, Saul (ed.) (1992) *Probing the Limits of Representation: Nazism and the 'Final Solution'*, Cambridge, MA: Harvard University Press.

Frye, Northrop (1957) *Anatomy of Criticism*, Princeton, NJ: Princeton University Press.

Fukuyama, Francis (1993 [1991]) *The End of History and the Last Man*, New York: Avon Books.

Fulbrook, Mary (2002) *Historical Theory*, London: Routledge.

Fuss, Diana (ed.) (1991) *Inside/Out: Lesbian Theories, Gay Theories*, New York and London: Routledge.

Gadamer, Hans-Georg (1998) *Praise of Theory: Speeches and Essays*, trans. Chris Dawson, New Haven, CT: Yale University Press.

Gallagher, C. and Greenblatt, S. (2000) *Practicing New Historicism*, Chicago: University of Chicago Press.

Gallie, William B. (1964) *Philosophy and the Historical Understanding*, London: Chatto and Windus.

Gane, Mike (1991a) *Baudrillard: Critical and Fatal Theory*, London and New York: Routledge.

—— (1991b) *Baudrillard's Bestiary*, London and New York: Routledge.

Gardenfors, P. (1997) 'Meanings as conceptual structures', in M. Carrier and P. Machamer (eds) *Mindscapes: Philosophy, Science, and the Mind*, Pittsburgh, PA: Pittsburgh University Press.

Gardiner, Jane (ed.) (1988) *What is History Today?*, London: Humanities Press International.

Gardiner, Judith K. (ed.) (1995) *Provoking Agents: Gender and Agency in Theory and Practice*, Urbana, IL: University of Illinois Press.

Gardiner, Patrick (ed.) (1961 [1951]) *The Nature of Historical Explanation*, Oxford: Oxford University Press.

—— (ed.) (1959) *Theories of History*, Glencoe, IL: The Free Press.

Garry, Ann and Pearsall, Marilyn (eds) (1996) *Women, Knowledge and Reality*, New York and London: Routledge.

Gasché, Rodolphe (1986) *The Tain of the Mirror: Derrida and the Philosophy of Reflection*, Cambridge, MA: Harvard University Press.

Gay, Peter (1988 [1974]) *Style in History: Gibbon, Ranke, Macaulay, Burckhardt*, New York: Basic Books.

—— (1966–9) *The Enlightenment*, New York: Knopf.

Geertz, Clifford (1983) *Local Knowledge: Further Essays in Interpretative Anthropology*, New York: Basic Books.

—— (1973) 'Thick description: toward an interpretive theory of culture' and 'Deep play: notes on the Balinese cockfight', in *The Interpretation of Cultures*, New York: Basic Books, pp. 3–31, 412–54.

Genette, Gérard (1990 [1983]) *Narrative Discourse Revisited*, trans. Jane E. Lewin, Ithaca, NY: Cornell University Press.

—— (1986 [1972]) *Narrative Discourse*, trans. Jane E. Lewin, Oxford: Basil Blackwell.

Geuss, R. (1981) *The Idea of a Critical Theory*, Cambridge: Cambridge University Press.

Giddens, Antony (1976) *New Rules of Sociological Method: A Positive Critique of Interpretative Sociologies*, New York: Basic Books.

Gilbert, Felix (1972) 'Intellectual history: its aims and methods', in Felix Gilbert and Stephen R. Graubard (eds), *Historical Studies Today*, New York and London: W.W. Norton, pp. 141–58.

Gilroy, Paul (1987) *There Ain't No Black in the Union Jack: The Cultural Politics of Race and Nation*, London: Routledge.

Ginzburg, Carlo (1982) *The Cheese and the Worms: The Cosmos of a Sixteenth-Century Miller*, Harmondsworth: Penguin.

Girard, René (1978) *To Double Business Bound: Essays on Literature, Mimesis, and Anthropology*, Baltimore, MD: Johns Hopkins University Press.

Goldberg, David Theo (2002) *The Racial State*, Oxford: Blackwell.

—— (1990) *Anatomy of Racism*, Minneapolis, MN: University of Minnesota Press.

Goldstein, Jan (1994) *Foucault and the Writing of History*, Oxford: Basil Blackwell.

Goldstein, Leon (1976) *Historical Knowing*, Austin, TX: University of Texas Press.

Goldstein, Philip (2005) *Post-Marxist Theory: An Introduction*, Albany, NY: State University of New York Press.

Goodman, James (2004) 'Blackout', in Alun Munslow and Robert A. Rosenstone (eds) *Experiments in Rethinking History*, London and New York: Routledge, pp. 209–21.

Goodman, Jordan (1997) 'History and anthropology', in Michael Bentley (ed.) *Companion to Historiography*, London: Routledge, pp. 783–804.

Goodman, Nelson (1968) *Language of Art*, Indianapolis, IN: Bobbs-Merrill.

Gossett, Thomas F. (1997 [1963]) *Race: The History of an Idea in America*, Oxford: Oxford University Press.

Graham, G. (1983) *Historical Explanation Reconsidered*, Aberdeen: Aberdeen University Press.

Gramsci, Antonio (1972) *Selections from the Prison Notebooks*, ed. and trans. Quentin Hoare and Geoffrey Nowell Smith, New York: Lawrence and Wishart.

Green, A. and Troup, K. (eds) (1999) *The Houses of History: A Critical Reader in Twentieth-Century History and Theory*, Manchester: Manchester University Press.

Green, William A. (1993) *History, Historians, and the Dynamics of Change*, Westport, CT: Praeger.

Grele, Ronald J. (1999) 'Oral history', in Kelly Boyd (ed.) *Historians and Historical Writing*, London and Chicago: Fitzroy Dearborn Publishers, pp. 881–3.

—— (1991) *Envelopes of Sound: The Art of Oral History*, New York: Praeger.

Grossmann, Reinhardt (1992) *The Existence of the World: An Introduction to Ontology*, London: Routledge.

Gumbrecht, Hans Ulrich (1997) *In 1926: Living at the Edge of Time*, Cambridge, MA: Harvard University Press.

Gutman, Herbert (1975) *Slavery and the Numbers Game: A Critique of Time on the Cross*, Urbana, IL: University of Illinois Press.

Gutting, Gary (1994) *The Cambridge Companion to Foucault*, Cambridge: Cambridge University Press.

Guyer, P. (ed.) (1992) *The Cambridge Companion to Kant*, Cambridge, Cambridge University Press.

Habermas, Jürgen (1987) *The Philosophical Discourse of Modernity*, trans. Frederick Lawrence, Cambridge: Cambridge University Press.

Hackett Fischer, David (1970) *Historian's Fallacies*, New York: Harper and Row.

Haddock, B.A. (1980) *An Introduction to Historical Thought*, London: Edward Arnold.

Hall, Catherine (1992) *White, Male and Middle Class: Explorations in Feminism and History*, Cambridge: Polity Press.

Hamilton, Paul (1996) *Historicism*, London: Routledge.

Hammermeister, Kai (2002) *The German Aesthetic Tradition*, Cambridge: Cambridge University Press.

Hansen, Peter H. (1996) 'The dancing lamas of Everest: cinema, orientalism, and Anglo-Tibetan relations in the 1920s', *American Historical Review* 101: 712–47.

Hanson, N.R. (1958) *Patterns of Discovery*, Cambridge: Cambridge University Press.

Haraway, Donna (1991) *Simians, Cyborgs and Women*, London: Free Association Books.

—— (1988) 'Situated knowledges: the science question in feminism and the privilege of partial perspective', *Feminist Studies* 14: 575–99.

Harlan, David (1997) *The Degradation of American History*, Chicago: Chicago University Press.

—— (1989) 'Intellectual history and the return of literature', *American Historical Review* 94: 581–609.

Harris, James F. (1992) *Against Relativism: A Philosophical Defence of Method*, La Salle, IL: Open Court.

Harvey, Charles and Press, Jon (1996) *Databases in Historical Research: Theory, Methods and Applications*, London: Macmillan.

Harvey, David (1989) *The Condition of Postmodernity: An Enquiry into the Origins of Cultural Change*, Oxford: Basil Blackwell.

Hassing, Richard F. (1997) *Final Causality in Nature and Human Affairs*, Washington, DC: Catholic University of America Press.

Hawkes, Terence (1977) *Structuralism and Semiotics*, London: Fontana.

Hegel, G.W.F. (1975 [1821]) *Lectures on the Philosophy of World History*, Cambridge: Cambridge University Press.

Heidegger, Martin (1962) *Being and Time*, trans. J. Macquarrie and E. Robinson, Oxford: Basil Blackwell.

Heise, U.K. (1997) *Chronoschisms: Time, Narrative and Postmodernism*, Cambridge: Cambridge University Press.

Hekman, Susan (1995) 'Subjects and agents: the question for feminism', in Judith K. Gardiner (ed.) *Provoking Agents: Gender and Agency in Theory and Practice*, Urbana, IL: University of Illinois Press, pp. 194–207.

Hempel, Carl G. (1965) *Aspects of Scientific Explanation*, New York: The Free Press.

—— (1942) 'The function of general laws in history', *The Journal of Philosophy* 34: reprinted in Patrick Gardiner (ed.) (1959) *Theories of History*, Glencoe, IL: The Free Press, pp. 344–55.

Hesse, Carla (2004) 'The new empiricism', *Cultural and Social History* I:2: 201–8.

Hesse, Mary (1983) 'The cognitive claims of metaphor', in J.P. van Noppen (ed.) *Metaphor and Religion*, Brussels: The Free Press, pp. 27–45.

Hexter, J.H. (1998) 'The rhetoric of history', in Brian Fay, Philip Pomper and Richard T. Vann (eds) *History and Theory: Contemporary Readings*, Oxford: Basil Blackwell, pp. 59–68.

—— (1991) 'Carl Becker, Professor Novick, and me: or, Cheer up, Professor N.!' *American Historical Review* 96: 675–82.

—— (1972) *The History Primer*, London: Allen Lane.

—— (1961) *Re-Appraisals in History*, Evanston, IL: Northwestern University Press.

Himmelfarb, Gertrude (1994) *On Looking into the Abyss: Untimely Thoughts on Culture and Society*, New York: Knopf.

—— (1989) 'Some reflections on the new history', *American Historical Review* 94: 661–70.

Hirsch, Eric D. (1976) *The Aims of Interpretation*, Chicago: University of Chicago Press.

Hobsbawm, E. (1980) 'Some comments', *Past and Present* 86: 3–8.

Hoff-Wilson, Joan and Farnham, Christine (1990) 'Theories about the end of everything (editors' note)', *Journal of Women's History* 1: 6–11.

Hoffer, Peter Charles and Stueck, William W. (1994) *Reading and Writing American History: An Introduction to the Historian's Craft*, 2 vols, Lexington, MA: D.C. Heath.

Hollinger, David A. (1991) 'Postmodernist theory and *wissenschaftliche* practice', *American Historical Review* 96: 688–92.

—— (1989) 'The return of the prodigal: the persistence of historical knowing', *American Historical Review* 94: 610–21.

Hook, Sidney (1943) *The Hero in History: A Study in Imitation and Possibility*, New York: John Day.

Horkheimer, Max (1982) 'Traditional and critical theory', in *Critical Theory*, New York: Seabury, pp. 240–4.

Horwich, Paul (1990) *Truth*, Oxford: Oxford University Press.

Hughes-Warrington, Marnie (ed.) (2000) *Fifty Key Thinkers on History*, London: Routledge.

Hunt, Lynn (1998) 'Does history need defending?', *History Workshop Journal* 46: 241–9.

—— (1989) *The New Cultural History*, Berkeley, CA: University of California Press.

—— (1986) 'French history in the last twenty years: the rise and fall of the *Annales* paradigm', *Journal of Contemporary History* 21, pp. 209–24.

Huppert, George (1997) 'The *Annales* experiment', in Michael Bentley (ed.) *Companion to Historiography*, London: Routledge, pp. 873–88.

Hutcheon, Linda (1988) *A Poetics of Postmodernism: History, Theory, Fiction*, New York: Routledge.

Hyland, Paul (2003) *The Enlightenment: A Sourcebook and Reader*, London and New York: Routledge.

Iggers, George (1997) *Historiography in the Twentieth Century*, Middletown, CT: Wesleyan University Press.

Irigaray, Luce (1992) *Culture of Difference*, New York: Routledge.

—— (1985) *Speculum of the Other Woman*, trans. G.C. Gill, Ithaca, NY: Cornell University Press.

Jacob, M.C. (ed.) (2001) *The Enlightenment: A Brief History with Documents*, Boston: Bedford/St Martins.

Jameson, Fredric (1984) *Sartre: The Origins of a Style*, New York: Columbia University Press.

—— (1976) 'Figural relativism, or the poetics of historiography', *Diacritics* 6: 2–9.

Jenkins, Keith (2004) 'Ethical responsibility and the historian: on the possible end of history "of a certain kind"', *History and Theory* 43:4: 43–60.

—— (2003) *Refiguring History: New Thoughts on an Old Discipline*, London: Routledge.

—— (2003 [1991]) *Rethinking History*, London: Routledge.

—— (1999a) 'Invitation to historians: after history', *Rethinking History: The Journal of Theory and Practice* 3: 7–20.

—— (1999b) *Why History? Reflections on the Possible End of History and Ethics under the Impact of the Postmodern*, London: Routledge.

—— (1998a) 'A conversation with Hayden White', *Literature and History* 7: 68–82.

—— (1998b) Review of *The Degradation of American History* by David Harlan (1997), *Rethinking History: The Journal of Theory and Practice* 2: 409–12.

—— (1997) *Postmodern History Reader*, London: Routledge.

—— (1995) *On 'What is History?'*, London: Routledge.

Jenkins, Keith and Munslow, Alun (eds) (2004) *The Nature of History Reader*, London and New York: Routledge.

Jenkins, Keith, Morgan, Sue and Munslow, Alun (eds) (forthcoming, 2007) *Manifestos for History*, London and New York: Routledge.

Johnson, Marc (ed.) (1981) *Philosophical Perspectives on Metaphor*, Minneapolis, MN: University of Minnesota Press.

Jolly, Margaretta (ed.) (2001) *Encyclopedia of Life Writing: Autobiographical and Biographical Forms*, London and Chicago: Fitzroy Dearborn Publishers.

Jones, Charles (1998) *E.H. Carr and International Relations*, Cambridge, Cambridge University Press.

Jones, E.T. (1974) 'Using ecological regression', *Journal of Interdisciplinary History* 4: 593–596.

Jones, Gareth Stedman (1983) *Languages of Class: Studies in English Working Class History, 1832–1982*, Cambridge: Cambridge University Press.

Jordanova, Ludmilla (2000) *History in Practice*, London: Arnold.

Josephson, John R. and Susan G. (1994) *Abductive Inference*, Cambridge: Cambridge University Press.

Joyce, Patrick (2002) *The Social in Question: New Bearings in History and the Social Sciences*, London: Routledge.

—— (2001) 'More secondary modern than postmodern', *Rethinking History: The Journal of Theory and Practice* 5: 367–82.

—— (1998) 'The return of history: postmodernism and the politics of academic history in Britain', *Past and Present*, 158: 207–35.

—— (1995) *Class*, Oxford: Oxford University Press.

—— (1994) *Democratic Subjects: The Self and the Social in Nineteenth-Century England*, New York: Cambridge University Press.

—— (1991a) 'History and post-modernism', *Past and Present* 133: 204–9.

—— (1991b) *Visions of the People: Industrial England and the Question of Class, 1848–1914*, Cambridge: Cambridge University Press.

Kammen, Michael (ed.) (1980) *The Past Before Us: Contemporary Historical Writing in the United States*, Ithaca, NY: Cornell University Press.

—— (1973) *'What is the Good of History?' Selected Letters of Carl Becker, 1900–1945*, Ithaca, NY: Cornell University Press.

Kansteiner, Wulf (1993) 'Hayden White's critique of the writing of history', *History and Theory* 32: 273–95.

Kant, Immanuel (1993 [1786]) 'Conjectures on the beginning of human history', in Hans Reiss (ed.) *Kant: Political Writings*,Cambridge: Cambridge University Press, pp. 221–34.

—— (1933 [1781]) *Critique of Pure Reason*, trans. N. Kemp Smith, London: Macmillan.

Kaye, Harvey J. (1996) *Why do Ruling Classes Fear History?*, New York: St Martin's Press.

—— (1995) *The British Marxist Historians*, New York: St Martin's Press.

Kearney, Richard and Rainwater, Mara (eds) (1996) *The Continental Philosophy Reader*, London: Routledge.

Kellner, Douglas (1989a) *Critical Theory, Marxism and Modernity: Development and Contemporary Relevance of the Frankfurt School*, Cambridge: Polity Press.

—— (1989b) *Critical Theory and Society: A Reader*, New York and London: Routledge.

—— (1989c) *Jean Baudrillard*, Stanford CA: Stanford University Press.

—— (1980) 'White's linguistic humanism', *History and Theory* (themed issue) 19: 1–29.

Kellner, Hans (1989) *Language and Historical Representation: Getting the Story Crooked*, Madison, WI: University of Wisconsin Press.

Kelly, Joan (1984) *Women, History, and Theory: The Essays of Joan Kelly*, Chicago: University of Chicago Press.

Kemp, Sandra and Squires, Judith (eds) (1997) *Feminisms*, Oxford: Oxford University Press.

Kenyon, J. (1983) *The History Men*, London: Weidenfeld and Nicolson.

Kerber, Linda K. (1988) 'Separate spheres, female worlds, woman's place: the rhetoric of women's history', *Journal of American History* 75: 9–39.

Kessler-Harris, Alice (2002) 'What is gender history now?', in David Cannadine (ed) *What is History Now?*, Basingstoke: Palgrave Macmillan, pp. 95–112.

Kiernan, V.G. (1988) *History, Classes, and Nation-States*, Cambridge: Polity Press.

Kirk, Neville (1995) 'The continuing relevance and engagement of class', *Labour History Review* 60: 2–15.

—— (1987) 'In defence of class', *International Review of Social History* 32: 2–47.

Kirkham, R. (1995) *Theories of Truth*, Cambridge: Bradford Books.

Klein, K. (1995) 'In search of narrative mastery: postmodernism and the people without history', *History and Theory* 34: 275–98.

Kloppenberg, James T. (1989) 'Objectivity and historicism: a century of American historical writing', *American Historical Review* 94: 1011–30.

Knight, Alan (1997) 'Latin America', in M. Bentley (ed.) *Companion to Historiography*, London: Routledge, pp. 728–58.

Knox, T.M. (1975) *Hegel's Aesthetics*, Oxford: Clarendon Press.

Kolakowski, L. (1972) *Positivist Philosophy*, London: Harmondsworth.

Kors, A.C. (ed.) (2002) *Encyclopedia of the Enlightenment*, 4 vols, Oxford: Oxford University Press.

Koselleck, Reinhart (1985) *Futures Past: On the Semantics of Historical Time*, trans. Keith Tribe, Boston, MA: MIT Press.

Kousser, J. Morgan (1980) 'Quantitative social-scientific history', in Michael Kammen (ed.) *The Past Before Us: Contemporary Historical Writing in the United States*, Ithaca, NY: Cornell University Press, pp. 433–56.

—— (1973) 'Ecological regression and the analysis of past politics' *Journal of Interdisciplinary History* 4: pp. 237–62.

Kozicki, H. (ed.) (1993) *Developments in Modern Historiography*, New York: St Martin's Press.

Kramnick, Isaac (ed.) (1995) *The Portable Enlightenment Reader*, New York: Penguin.

Krausz, Michael (ed.) (1989) *Relativism: Interpretation and Confrontation*, Notre Dame, IN: Notre Dame University Press.

Lacan, Jacques (1977) *Écrits*, New York: W.W. Norton.

LaCapra, Dominick (2004a) 'Tropisms of intellectual history', *Rethinking History: The Journal of Theory and Practice* 8: 493–570.

—— (2004b) *History in Transit: Experience, Identity, Critical Theory*, Ithaca, NY: Cornell University Press.

—— (2001) *Writing History, Writing Trauma*, Baltimore, MD: Johns Hopkins University Press.

—— (1995) 'History, language and reading: waiting for Crillon', *American Historical Review* 100: 799–828.

—— (1989) *Soundings in Critical Theory*, Ithaca, NY: Cornell University Press.

—— (1987) *History and Criticism*, Ithaca, NY: Cornell University Press.

—— (1983) *Rethinking Intellectual History*, Ithaca, NY: Cornell University Press.

LaCapra, Dominick and Kaplan, Steven L. (eds) (1982) *Modern European Intellectual History: Reappraisals and New Perspectives*, Ithaca, NY: Cornell University Press.

Laclau, Ernesto (1996) *Emancipation(s)*, London: Verso.

—— (1993), 'Politics and the limits of modernity', in T. Docherty (ed.), *Postmodernism: A Reader*, London: Harvester Wheatsheaf, pp. 329–43.

—— (1990) *New Reflections on the Revolution of Our Time*, London: Verso.

Laclau, E. and Mouffe, C. (1985) *Hegemony and Socialist Strategy: Towards a Radical Democratic Politics*, London: Verso.

Ladurie, E. Le Roy (1981) *The Mind and Method of the Historian*, Chicago: University of Chicago Press.

—— (1978) *Montaillou*, Harmondsworth: Penguin.

—— (1974 [1966]) *Peasants of the Languedoc*, trans. J. Day, Urbana, IL: University of Illinois Press.

Lamont, William (1998) *Historical Controversies and Historians*, London: UCL Press.

Landsberg, Alison (2004) *Prosthetic Memory: The Transformation of American Remembrance in the Age of Mass Culture*, New York: Columbia University Press.

Laplanche, J. and Pontalis, J.-B. (1988), *The Language of Psychoanalysis*, London: Karnac.

Laslett, Barbara, Joeres, Ruth-Ellen, Maynes, Mary Jo, Higginbotham, Evelyn and Barker-Nunn, Jeanne (1997) *History and Theory: Feminist Research, Debates, Contestations*, Chicago: University of Chicago Press.

Laslett, Peter (1972) *Household and Family in Past Time*, Cambridge: Cambridge University Press.

Lechte, John (1994) *Fifty Key Contemporary Thinkers: From Structuralism to Postmodernity*, London: Routledge.

Le Doeuff, Michèle (1989) *Hipparchia's Choice: An Essay Concerning Women, Philosophy, etc.*, trans. Trista Selous, Oxford: Oxford University Press.

Le Goff, J. and Nora, P. (1985) *Constructing the Past*, Cambridge: Cambridge University Press.

Lemon, Michael C. (2003) *Philosophy of History: A Guide for Students*, London and New York: Routledge.

—— (1995) *The Discipline of History and the History of Thought*, London: Routledge.

Lentin, A. (2004) *Racism and Anti-Racism in Europe*, London: Pluto Press.

Lévinas, Emmanuel (1984) 'Ethics as first philosophy', in Sean Hand (ed.) *The Lévinas Reader*, Oxford: Blackwell.

—— (1961 [1969]) *Totality and Infinity: An Essay on Exteriority*, trans. Alphonso Lingis, The Hague: Nijhoff.

—— (1947 [1978]) *Existence and Existents*, trans. Alphonso Lingis, The Hague: Nijhoff.

Lewis, Myrdin John and Lloyd-Jones, Roger (1996) *Using Computers in History: A Practical Guide*, London: Routledge.

Lichtman, A.J. (1974) 'Correlation, regression and the ecological fallacy: a critique', *Journal of Interdisciplinary History* 4: 417–33.

Lindquist, Sven (2004) 'A history of bombing', in Keith Jenkins and Alun Munslow (eds) *The Nature of History Reader*, London and New York: Routledge, pp. 182–90.

Linebaugh, Peter (2003) *The London Hanged: Crime and Civil Society in the Eighteenth Century*, London: Verso.

Lipton, Peter (1993) *Inference to the Best Explanation*, London, Routledge.

Lloyd, Christopher (1993) *The Structures of History*, Oxford: Basil Blackwell.

Lloyd, Genevieve (1984) *The Man of Reason: 'Male' and 'Female' in Western Philosophy*, Minneapolis, MN: University of Minnesota Press.

Loades, David (1991 [1979]) *The Reign of Mary Tudor*, London and New York: Longman.

Longino, Helen E. (1990) *Science as Social Knowledge*, Princeton, NJ: Princeton University Press.

Lorenz, Chris (1998) 'Can histories be true? Narrativism, positivism, and the "metaphorical turn"', *History and Theory* 37: 309–29.

—— (1994) 'Historical knowledge and historical reality: a plea for "historical realism"', *History and Theory* 33: 297–327.

Loux, Michael J. (1998) *Metaphysics: A Contemporary Introduction*, London: Routledge.

Lovejoy, Arthur O. (1936) *The Great Chain of Being: A Study of the History of an Idea*, Baltimore, MD: Johns Hopkins University Press.

Luntley, Michael (1995) *Reason, Truth and Self: The Postmodern Reconditioned*, London: Routledge.

Lyotard, Jean-François (2004) 'The Confession of Augustine', in David Carr, Thomas R. Flynn, and Rudolph A. Makkreel (eds) *The Ethics of History*, Evanston, IL: Northwestern University Press, pp. 155–71.

—— (1997) *Postmodern Fables*, trans. George Van den Abeele, Minneapolis, MN: University of Minnesota Press.

—— (1988) *The Differend: Phrases in Dispute*, trans. George Van den Abeele, Minneapolis, MN: University of Minnesota Press.

—— (1979) *The Postmodern Condition: A Report on Knowledge*, Paris: Minuit.

McClintock, Anne, Mufti, Aamir Rashid and Shahat, Ella (eds) (1997) *Dangerous Liaisons: Gender, Nations, and Postcolonial Perspectives*, Minneapolis, MN: University of Minnesota Press.

McCloskey, Donald N. (1987) *Econometric History*, London: Macmillan.

McCullagh, C. Behan (2004) *The Logic of History: Putting Postmodernism in Perspective*, London and New York: Routledge.

—— (1998) *The Truth of History*, London: Routledge.

—— (1991) 'Can our understanding of old texts be objective?', *History and Theory* 30: 302–23.

—— (1984) *Justifying Historical Descriptions*, Cambridge: Cambridge University Press.

McLennan, Gregor (1984) 'History and theory: contemporary debates and directions', *Literature and History* 10: 139–64.

Macey, David (2001) *Penguin Dictionary of Critical Theory*, London: Penguin.

MacKenzie, John M. (1995) *Orientalism: History, Theory and the Arts*, Manchester: Manchester University Press.

MacRaild, Donald M. and Taylor, Avram (2004) *Social Theory and Social History*, Basingstoke: Palgrave Macmillan.

Magnus, Bernd (1993) *Nietzsche's Case*, New York: Routledge.

Magnus, Bernd and Higgins, Kathleen M. (eds) (1996) *The Cambridge Companion to Nietzsche*, Cambridge: Cambridge University Press.

Malik, Kenan (1996) *The Meaning of Race: Race, History and Culture in Western Society*, Basingstoke: Macmillan.

Mandelbaum, Maurice (1977) *The Anatomy of Historical Knowledge*, Baltimore, MD: Johns Hopkins University Press.

Mandler, Peter (2004) 'The problem with cultural history', *Cultural and Social History* 1: 94–17.

Marable, Manning (1995) *Beyond Black and White*, London: Verso.

Marchitello, Howard (2001) *What Happens to History: The Renewal of Ethics in Contemporary*

Thought, New York and London: Routledge.

Marcus, Laura (1994) *Auto/biographical Discourses: Theory, Criticism, Practice*, Manchester and New York: Manchester University Press.

Margolin, Jean Claude (1989) *Humanism in Europe at the Time of the Renaissance*, Durham, NC: Labyrinth Press.

Marius, Richard (1999) *A Short Guide to Writing About History*, New York: Longman.

Marshall, Brenda K. (1992) *Teaching the Postmodern: Fiction and Theory*, New York: Routledge.

Marwick, Arthur (2001) *The New Nature of History: Knowledge, Evidence, Language,* Basingstoke: Palgrave.

—— (1995) 'Two approaches to historical study: the metaphysical (including postmodernism) and the historical', *Journal of Contemporary History* 30: 5–36.

—— (1989 [1970]) *The Nature of History*, London: Macmillan.

Maynard, Steven (1989) 'Rough work and rugged men: the social construction of masculinity in working class history', *Labour/Travail* 23: 159–69.

Maza, Sarah (1996) 'Stories in history: cultural narratives in recent works in European history', *American Historical Review* 101: 1493–515.

Mazierska, Ewa (2000) 'Non-Jewish Jews, good Poles and historical truth in the films of Andrzej Wajda', *Historical Journal of Film, Radio and Television* 20: 213–26.

Mazzotta, Giuseppe (1998) *The New Map of the World: Giambattista Vico's Poetic Philosophy*, Princeton, NJ: Princeton University Press.

Megill, Allan (1985) *Prophets of Extremity: Nietzsche, Heidegger, Foucault, Derrida*, Berkeley, CA: University of California Press.

Meinecke, Friedrich (1972) *Historism: The Rise of a New Historical Outlook*, trans. J.E. Anderson, London: Routledge and Kegan Paul.

Melosh, Barbara (1993) *Gender and American History Since 1890*, London and New York: Routledge.

Mensch, James Richard (1997) *Knowing and Being: A Postmodern Reversal*, University Park, PA: Pennsylvania State University Press.

Merquior, J.M. (1985) *Foucault*, London: Fontana.

Mills, Sarah, (1997) *Discourse*, London and New York: Routledge.

Mink, Louis (1978) 'Narrative form as a cognitive instrument', in R.R. Canary and H. Kozicki (eds) *The Writing of History: Literary Form and Historical Understanding*, Madison, WI: University of Wisconsin Press, pp. 129–49.

—— (1970) 'History and fiction as modes of comprehension', *New Literary History* 1: 541–58.

—— (1969) *The Philosophy of R.G. Collingwood*, Bloomington, IN: University of Indiana Press.

Miskell, Peter (2004) 'Historians and film', in Peter Lambert and Phillipp Schofield (eds) *Making History: An Introduction to the History and Practices of a Discipline*, London and New York: Routledge, pp. 245–56.

Mitchell, B.R. and Deane, P. (1962) *Abstract of British Historical Statistics*, Cambridge: Cambridge University Press.

Mitchell, Juliet (1974) *Psychoanalysis and Feminism*, New York: Pantheon.

Mitchell, Juliet and Rose, Jacqueline (eds) (1982) *Feminine Sexuality: Jacques Lacan and the école freudienne*, London: Macmillan.

Mohanty, C., Russo, A. and Torres, L. (eds) (1991) *Third World Women and the Politics of Feminism*, Bloomington, IN: Indiana University Press.

Moi, Toril (ed.) (1988) *French Feminist Thought: A Reader*, Oxford: Oxford University Press.

—— (1986) *The Kristeva Reader*, Oxford: Basil Blackwell.

Momigliano, Arnaldo (1990) *The Classical Foundations of Modern Historiography*, Berkeley, CA:

University of California Press.

—— (1985 [1966]) *Studies in Historiography*, New York: Garland.

—— (1977) *Essays in Ancient and Modern Historiography*, Oxford: Basil Blackwell.

Mooney, Michael (1985) *Vico in the Tradition of Rhetoric*, Princeton, NJ: Princeton University Press.

Morris, Edmund (1999) *Dutch: A Memoir of Ronald Reagan*, New York: Random House.

Moser, P.K. (ed.) (1987) *A Priori Knowledge*, Oxford: Oxford University Press.

Moss, M.E. (1987) *Benedetto Croce Reconsidered*, Hanover, NH: University Press of New England.

Mosse, George L. (1985) *Nationalism and Sexuality: Middle-Class Morality and Sexual Norms in Modern Europe*, Madison, WI: University of Wisconsin Press.

Mouffe, Chantal (ed.) (1996) *Deconstruction and Pragmatism*, London: Routledge.

Mowitt, J. (1992) *Text: The Genealogy of an Antidisciplinary Object*, Durham, NC, and London: Duke University Press.

Müller-Vollmer, Kurt (ed.) (1986) *The Hermeneutics Reader*, Oxford: Oxford University Press.

Munslow, Alun (2003a) 'History and biography: an editorial comment', *Rethinking History: The Journal of Theory and Practice* 7: 1–12,

—— (2003b) *The New History*, London: Pearson Longman.

—— (2002) 'Objectivity and the writing of history', *History of European Ideas* 28: 43–50.

—— (2001) 'Biography and history', in Margaretta Jolly (ed.) *Encyclopaedia of Life Writing: Autobiographical and Biographical Forms*, 2 vols, London and Chicago: Fitzroy Dearborn Publishers, pp. 114–16.

—— (1997a) *Deconstructing History*, London: Routledge.

—— (1997b) Editorial, *Rethinking History: The Journal of Theory and Practice* 1(1): 1–20.

—— (1997c) Editorial, *Rethinking History: The Journal of Theory and Practice* 1(2): 111–23.

—— (1992) *Discourse and Culture: The Creation of America, 1870–1920*, London: Routledge.

—— (1986) 'Narrative, myth and the Turner thesis', *Journal of American Culture*, 9(2): 9–17 (with R.J. Ellis).

Munslow, Alun and Rosenstone, Robert A. (eds) (2004) *Experiments in Rethinking History*, London and New York: Routledge.

Munz, Peter (1997) 'The historical narrative', in M. Bentley (ed.) *Companion to Historiography*, London: Routledge, pp. 857–72.

Murphey, Murray G. (1986) 'Explanation, causes, and covering laws', *History and Theory* (themed issue) 25: 43–57.

Nagel, Ernest (1979) *Teleology Revisited*, New York: Columbia University Press.

—— (1961) *The Structure of Science: Problems in the Logic of Scientific Explanation*, New York: Harcourt Brace.

Nealon, Jeffrey T. and Giroux, Susan Searls (2003) *The Theory Toolbox: Critical Concepts for the Humanities, Arts, and Social Sciences*, Savage, MD: Rowman and Littlefield.

Nehamas, Alexander (1985) *Nietzsche: Life as Literature*, Cambridge, MA: Harvard University Press.

Neisser, U. (ed.) (1981) *Concepts and Conceptual Development*, Cambridge: Cambridge University Press.

Nelson, L.H. (1990) *Who Knows: From Quine to a Feminist Empiricism*, Philadelphia, PA: Temple University Press.

NeSmith, Georgia (n.d.) *Feminist Historiography 1968–1993*, http://www.inform.umd.edu/EdRes/Topic/WomensStudies/Bibliographies/feminist-historiography.

Nietzsche, Friedrich (1966) *Beyond Good and Evil: Prelude to a Philosophy of the Future*, trans.

Walter Kaufmann, New York: Vintage Books.

Noiriel, Gerard (1994) 'Foucault and history: the lessons of a disillusion', *Journal of Modern History* 66: 547–68.

Norman, Andrew P. (1991) 'Telling it like it was: historical narratives on their own terms', *History and Theory* 30: 119–35.

Norris, Christopher (1992) *Uncritical Theory: Postmodernism, Intellectuals and the Gulf War*, London: Lawrence and Wishart.

—— (1990) *What's Wrong with Postmodernism?*, Hemel Hempstead: Harvester-Wheatsheaf.

—— (1987) *Derrida*, London: Fontana.

—— (1982) *Deconstruction: Theory and Practice*, London: Methuen.

Novick, Peter (1988) *That Noble Dream: The 'Objectivity Question' and the American Historical Profession*, Cambridge: Cambridge University Press.

Nye, Andrea (ed.) (1998) *Philosophy of Language: The Big Questions*, Oxford: Basil Blackwell.

Oakeshott, Michael (1983) *On History and Other Essays*, Oxford: Basil Blackwell.

—— (1933) *Experience and Its Modes*, Cambridge: Cambridge University Press.

O'Brien, G.D. (1975) *Hegel on Reason in History: A Contemporary Interpretation*, Chicago: University of Chicago Press.

O'Brien, Karen (1997) *Narratives of Enlightenment: Cosmopolitan History from Voltaire to Gibbon*, Cambridge: Cambridge University Press.

Offen, Karin, Pierson, Ruth Roach and Rendall, Jane (eds) (1991) *Writing Women's History: International Perspectives*, Bloomington, IN: Indiana University Press.

Olafson, Frederick A. (1979) *The Dialectic of Action*, Chicago: University of Chicago Press.

Palmer, Bryan (1990) *Descent into Discourse: The Reification of Language and the Writing of Social History*, Philadelphia, PA: Temple University Press.

Palmer, Richard E. (1969) *Hermeneutics: Interpretation Theory in Schleiermacher, Dilthey, Heidegger and Gadamer*, Evanston, IL: Northwestern University Press.

Parker, A., Russo, M., Sommer, D. and Yaeger, P. (eds) (1992) *Nationalisms and Sexualities*, New York and London: Routledge.

Parker, David (1998) 'The turn to ethics in the 1990s', in Jane Adamson, Richard Freadman and David Parker (eds) *Renegotiating Ethics in Literature, Philosophy, Theory*, Cambridge and New York: Cambridge University Press, pp. 1–20.

Partner, Nancy (1998) 'Hayden White: the form of the content', *History and Theory* 37: 162–72.

Passerini, Luisa (2000) 'Transforming biography: from the claim of objectivity to intersubjective plurality' *Rethinking History: The Journal of Theory and Practice* 4: 413–16

Payne, Michael (1997) *Reading Knowledge: An Introduction to Barthes, Foucault and Althusser*, Oxford: Basil Blackwell.

Peacocke, C. (1992) *A Study of Concepts*, Cambridge, MA: MIT Press.

Pecheux, Michel (1982) *Language, Semantics and Ideology*, Basingstoke: Macmillan.

Peirce, Charles S. (1958) *Collected Papers*, vol. VII, ed. A. Burks, Cambridge, MA: Harvard University Press.

Pencak, William (1997) 'Foucault stoned: reconsidering insanity and history', *Rethinking History: The Journal of Theory and Practice* 1: 34–55.

—— (1995 [1998]) '"All art is against lived experience": Derek Jarman's *Caravaggio*', *The American Journal of Semiotics* 12: 243–60.

Perks, Robert and Thomson, Alistair (eds) (1998) *The Oral History Reader*, London and New York: Routledge.

Perrot, Michelle (ed.) (1992) *Writing Women's History*, Oxford: Basil Blackwell.

Perry, Matt (2002) *Marxism and History*, Basingstoke: Palgrave Macmillan.

Pickering, Michael (1999) 'History as horizon: Gadamer, tradition and critique', *Rethinking History: The Journal of Theory and Practice* 3: 177–95.

Pieterse, J.P.N. (1990) *Empire and Emancipation: Power and Liberation on a World Scale*, London: Pluto Press.

Pihlainen, K. (2002) 'Of closure and convention: surpassing representation through performance and the referential', *Rethinking History: The Journal of Theory and Practice* 6: 179–200.

—— (1998) 'Narrative objectivity versus fiction: on the ontology of historical narratives', *Rethinking History: The Journal of Theory and Practice* 2: 7–22.

Pittock, Jean H. and Wear, Andrew (eds) (1991) *Interpretation and Cultural History*, Basingstoke: Macmillan.

Pompa, Leon (1975) *Vico: A Study of the New Science*, Cambridge: Cambridge University Press.

Poovey, Mary (1988) *Uneven Developments: The Ideological Work of Gender in Mid-Victorian England*, Chicago: University of Chicago Press.

Popper, Karl (1979) *Objective Knowledge: An Evolutionary Approach*, rev. edn, Oxford: Clarendon Press.

—— (1962 [1945]) *The Open Society and Its Enemies*, London: Routledge.

—— (1959) *The Logic of Scientific Discovery*, New York: Basic Books.

—— (1957) *The Poverty of Historicism*, London: Routledge.

Porter, Roy (ed.) (1997) *Rewriting the Self: Histories from the Renaissance to the Present*, London: Routledge.

—— (1990) *The Enlightenment*, London: Macmillan.

Poster, Mark (1997) *Cultural History and Postmodernity: Disciplinary Readings and Challenges*, New York: Columbia University Press.

—— (1989) *Critical Theory and Poststructuralism*, Ithaca, NY: Cornell University Press.

—— (1987) 'The reception of Foucault by historians', *Journal of the History of Ideas* 48: 117–41.

—— (1984) *Foucault, Marxism and History*, London: Polity Press.

Price, Richard (2001) 'Practices of historical narrative', *Rethinking History: The Journal of Theory and Practice* 5: 357–65.

Priest, Stephen (1990) *The British Empiricists*, London: Penguin.

Prins, Gwyn (1991) 'Oral history', in Peter Burke, *New Perspectives on Historical Writing*, University Park, PA: Pennsylvania State University Press, pp. 114–39.

Putnam, Hilary (1992) *Renewing Philosophy*, Cambridge, MA: Harvard University Press.

—— (1988) *Reality and Representation*, Cambridge, MA: MIT Press.

—— (1987) *The Many Faces of Realism*, La Salle, IL: Open Court Publishers.

—— (1983) *Realism and Reason*, vol. 3, Cambridge: Cambridge University Press.

—— (1981) *Reason, Truth and History*, Cambridge: Cambridge University Press.

Quine, W.V. (1990) *Pursuit of Truth*, Cambridge, MA: Harvard University Press.

—— (1969) *Ontological Relativity and Other Essays*, New York: Columbia University Press.

—— (1963) *From a Logical Point of View*, New York: Harper and Row.

—— (1960) *Word and Object*, Cambridge, MA: Harvard University Press.

Rabb, Theodore K. (1983) 'The development of quantification in historical research', *Journal of Interdisciplinary History* 13: 591–601.

Rabinow, Paul (1999) *Ethics, Subjectivity and Truth: The Essential Works of Michel Foucault, 1954–84*, London: Penguin.

Ranke, Leopold von (1867–90) *Sämmtliche Werke* (Collected Works), vols 33 and 34, Leipzig:

Dunker and Humblot.

Ransom, R.L. and Sutch, R. (1977) *One Kind of Freedom: The Economic Consequences of Emancipation*, Cambridge: Cambridge University Press.

Readings, Bill (1991) *Art and Politics: Introducing Lyotard*, London: Routledge.

Reedy, W.J. (1994) 'The historical imaginary of social science in post-revolutionary France: Bonald, Saint-Simon, Comte', *History of the Human Sciences* 7: 1–26.

Reiss, Hans (ed.) (1993) *Kant: Political Writings*, Cambridge: Cambridge University Press.

—— (1991 [1970]) *Kant: Political Writings*, Cambridge: Cambridge University Press.

Rendall, Jane (1991) 'Uneven developments: women's history, feminist history, and gender history in Great Britain', in Karin Offen, Ruth Roach Pierson and Jane Rendall (eds) *Writing Women's History: International Perspectives*, Bloomington, IN: Indiana University Press, pp. 1–24.

Rethinking History: The Journal of Theory and Practice (1998), Special Issue, 2(3).

Ricoeur, Paul (1994 [1978]) *The Rule of Metaphor: Multi-disciplinary Studies of the Creation of Meaning in Language*, trans. Robert Czerny, London: Routledge.

—— (1984) *The Reality of the Historical Past*, Marquette University: Wisconsin-Alpha Chapter of Phi Sigma Tau.

—— (1984, 1985) *Time and Narrative*, 3 vols, Chicago: University of Chicago Press.

—— (1981) *Hermeneutics and the Human Sciences*, Cambridge: Cambridge University Press.

Rigney, Ann (2001) *Imperfect Histories*, Ithaca, NY: Cornell University Press.

—— (1990) *The Rhetoric of Historical Representation*, Cambridge: Cambridge University Press.

Riley, Denise (1989) *Am I that Name? Feminism and the Category of 'Women' in History*, Basingstoke: Macmillan.

Rinehart, Sue Tolleson (1992) *Gender Consciousness and Politics*, New York and London: Routledge.

Roberts, Clayton (1996) *The Logic of Historical Explanation*, University Park, PA: Pennsylvania State University Press.

Roberts, David D. (1995) *Nothing But History: Reconstruction and Extremity after Metaphysics*, Berkeley, CA: University of California Press.

—— (1987) *Benedetto Croce and the Uses of Historicism*, Berkeley, CA: University of California Press.

Roberts, Geoffrey (ed.) (2001) *The History and Narrative Reader*, London: Routledge.

—— (1998) 'Geoffrey Elton and the philosophy of history', *The Historian* 57: 29–31.

—— (1997) 'Postmodernism versus the standpoint of action', review of *On 'What is History?'* by Keith Jenkins, *History and Theory* 36: 249–60.

—— (1996) 'Narrative history as a way of life', *Journal of Contemporary History* 31: 221–8.

Roberts, Michael (2004) 'Postmodernism and the linguistic turn', in Peter Lambert and Phillipp Schofield (eds) *Making History: An Introduction to the History and Practices of a Discipline*, London and New York: Routledge, pp. 227–40.

Rockmore, Tom (1995) *Heidegger and French Philosophy: Humanism, Antihumanism and Being*, London: Routledge.

Rorty, Richard (1998) *Truth and Progress: Philosophical Papers Vol. 3*, Cambridge: Cambridge University Press.

—— (ed.) (1992 [1967]) *The Linguistic Turn: Recent Essays in Philosophical Method*, Chicago: University of Chicago Press.

—— (1992) 'Trotsky and the wild orchids', *Common Knowledge*, winter: 140–53.

—— (1991) *Objectivity, Relativism and Truth: Philosophical Papers Vol. 1*, Cambridge: Cambridge University Press.

—— (1989) *Contingency, Irony and Solidarity*, Cambridge: Cambridge University Press.

—— (1982) *Consequences of Pragmatism*, Minneapolis, MN: University of Minnesota Press.

—— (1979) *Philosophy and the Mirror of Nature*, Princeton, NJ: Princeton University Press.

Rorty, Richard, Schneewind, J.B. and Skinner, Quentin (1991 [1984]) *Philosophy in History*, Cambridge: Cambridge University Press.

Rosenstone, Robert A. (2003) *The King of Odessa*, Evanston, IL: Northwestern University Press.

—— (2002a) *The Man Who Swam into History*, Bloomington, IN: 1st Books.

—— (2002b) 'Does a filmic writing of history exist?' *History and Theory* 41: 134–44.

—— (1996) 'The future of the past: film and the beginnings of postmodern history', in Vivian Sobchack (ed.) *The Persistence of History: Cinema, Television and the Modern Event*, London: Routledge, pp. 201–18.

—— (1995a) *Visions of the Past: The Challenge of Film to Our Idea of History*, Cambridge, MA: Harvard University Press.

—— (1995b) *Revisioning History: Film and the Construction of a New Past*, Princeton, NJ: Princeton University Press.

—— (1988) *Mirror in the Shrine: American Encounters with Meiji Japan*, Cambridge, MA: Harvard University Press.

—— (1975) *Romantic Revolutionary: A Biography of John Reed*, New York: Alfred A. Knopf.

Ross, Dorothy (1995) 'Grand narrative in American historical writing: from romance to uncertainty', *American Historical Review* 100: 651–77.

Roth, Michael S. (1995) *The Ironist's Cage: Memory, Trauma, and the Construction of History*, New York: Columbia University Press.

Roth, Paul A. (1992) 'Hayden White and the aesthetics of historiography', *History of the Human Sciences* 5: 17–35.

Rothenburg, Paula S. (ed.) (1998) *Race, Class, and Gender in the United States: An Integrated Study*, fourth edn, New York: St Martin's Press.

Rowbotham, Sheila (1974) *Hidden from History: Rediscovering Women in History from the Seventeenth Century to the Present*, New York: Pantheon Books.

Ruben, David-Hillel (ed.) (1993) *Explanation*, Oxford: Oxford University Press.

—— (1990) *Explaining Explanation*, London: Routledge.

Ruiz, Vicki L. and DuBois, Ellen Carol (2000) *Unequal Sisters: A Multicultural Reader in US Women's History*, third edn, New York and London: Routledge.

Rush, Fred (ed.) (2004) *The Cambridge Companion to Critical Theory*, Cambridge: Cambridge University Press.

Saari, Haikki (2005) 'On Frank Ankersmit's postmodernist theory of historical narrativity', *Rethinking History: The Journal of Theory and Practice* 9: 5–21.

Sacks, Sheldon (ed.) (1979) *On Metaphor*, Chicago: University of Chicago Press.

Said, Edward W. (1993) *Culture and Imperialism*, New York: Knopf.

—— (1989) 'Representing the colonized: anthropology's interlocutors' *Critical Inquiry*, 15: 205–25.

—— (1978) *Orientalism*, New York, Pantheon.

Sallis, John (ed.) (1987) *Deconstruction and Philosophy: The Texts of Jacques Derrida*, Chicago: University of Chicago Press.

Samuel, Raphael (1994) *Theatres of Memory*, London and New York: Verso.

Sartre, Jean-Paul (1989) *Existentialism and Humanism*, trans. Philip Mairet, London: Eyre Methuen.

Saussure, Ferdinand de (1959) [1916] *Cours de linguistique générale*, trans. Wade Baskin, London: Fontana.

Schama, Simon (1991) *Dead Certainties (Unwarranted Speculations)*, New York: Knopf.

Schmitt, Frederick (ed.) (1994) *Socialising Epistemology: The Social Dimensions of Knowledge*, Boston, MA: Rowman and Littlefield.

Schorske, Carl E. (1998) *Thinking with History: Explorations in the Passage to Modernism*, Princeton, NJ: Princeton University Press.

Scott, Joan W. (1996a) 'After history', *Common Knowledge* 5: 9–26.

—— (1996b) *Feminism and History*, Oxford: Oxford University Press.

—— (1991) 'Women's history', in P. Burke (ed.) *New Perspectives on Historical Writing*, University Park, PA: Pennsylvania State University Press, pp. 42–66.

—— (1989) 'History in crisis? The others' side of the story', *American Historical Review* 94: 680–92.

—— (1988) *Gender and the Politics of History*, New York: Columbia University Press.

—— (1986) 'Gender: a useful category of analysis', *American Historical Review* 91: 1053–75.

—— (1983) 'Women in history: the modern period', *Past and Present* 191: 125–57.

Searle, John R. (1995) *The Construction of Social Reality*, London: Allen Lane.

—— (1983) *Intentionality*, Cambridge: Cambridge University Press.

Sellars, Wilfred (1997 [1956]) *Empiricism and the Philosophy of the Mind*, Cambridge, MA: Harvard University Press.

Sheridan, Alan (1994) *Michel Foucault: The Will to Truth*, London: Routledge.

Shoemaker, Robert and Vincent, Mary (1998) *Gender and History in Western Europe*, London: Arnold.

Shortland, M. and Yeo, R. (eds) (1996) *Telling Lives in Science: Essays on Scientific Biography*, New York and Cambridge: Cambridge University Press.

Silbey, Joel (1985) *The Partisan Imperative: The Dynamics of American Politics before the Civil War*, New York: Oxford University Press.

Sim, Stuart (2001) *Post-Marxism: An Intellectual Biography*, London: Routledge.

—— (1998) *Post-Marxism: A Reader*, New York: Columbia University Press.

Simon, Bryant (2004) 'Narrating a southern tragedy: historical facts and historical fictions', in Alun Munslow and Robert A. Rosenstone (eds) *Experiments in Rethinking History*, London and New York: Routledge, pp. 156–82.

Singer, P. (ed.) (1991) *A Companion to Ethics*, Oxford: Blackwell.

Skinner, Quentin (1969) 'Meaning and understanding in the history of ideas', *History and Theory*, 8: 3–53.

—— (1986) 'What is intellectual history today?', in Jane Gardiner (ed.) *What Is History Today?*, Basingstoke: Macmillan, pp. 109–12.

Slater, Wendy (2005) 'Relics, remains, and revisionism: narratives of Nicholas II in contemporary Russia', *Rethinking History: The Journal of Theory and Practice* 9: 53–70.

Smedley, Audrey (1999) *Race in North America: Origin and Evolution of a Worldview*, Boulder, CO: Westview Press.

Smith, A.M. (1998), *Laclau and Mouffe: The Radical Democratic Imaginary*, London: Routledge.

Smith, E.E. and Medin, D.L. (1981) *Categories and Concepts*, Cambridge, MA: Harvard University Press.

Smith, Paul (1988) *Discerning the Subject*, Minneapolis, MN: University of Minnesota Press.

Smith-Rosenberg, Carroll (1985) *Disorderly Conduct: Visions of Gender in Victorian America*, New York: Oxford University Press.

Snooks, Graham D. (1998) *The Laws of History*, London: Routledge.

Snyder, P.L. (ed.) (1958) *Detachment and the Writing of History*, Ithaca, NY: Cornell University

Press.

Sobchack, Vivian (ed.) (1996) *The Persistence of History: Cinema, Television and the Modern Event*, London: Routledge.

Solomos, John (1993) *Race and Racism in Britain*, second edn, London: Macmillan.

Sontag, Susan (ed.) (1982) *A Barthes Reader*, London: Fontana/Collins.

Sorlin, Pierre (1991) *European Cinemas, European Societies, 1939–1990*, London and New York: Routledge.

Sosa, E. (1988) 'Beyond scepticism, to the best of our knowledge', *Mind* 97: 153–88.

Southgate, Beverley (2003) *Postmodernism in History: Fear or Freedom?*, New York and London: Routledge.

—— (2000) *Why Bother with History?*, Harlow: Pearson.

—— (1996) *History: What and Why*, New York and London: Routledge.

Spiegel, Gabrielle M. (2005) *Practicing History: New Directions in Historical Writing*, New York and London: Routledge.

—— (1992) 'History and post-modernism', *Past and Present* 135: 197–8.

Spivak, Gayatri Chakravorty (1990) *The Post-Colonial Critic: Interviews, Strategies, Dialogues*, ed. S. Harasym, London and New York: Routledge.

—— (1988) 'Can the subaltern speak?', in C. Nelson and L. Grossberg (eds) *Marxism and the Interpretation of Culture*, Urbana, IL: University of Illinois Press, pp. 271–313.

—— (1987) *In Other Worlds*, New York and London: Methuen.

Stanford, Michael (1998) *An Introduction to the Philosophy of History*, Oxford: Basil Blackwell.

—— (1994) *A Companion to the Study of History*, Oxford: Basil Blackwell.

—— (1986) *The Nature of Historical Knowledge*, Oxford: Basil Blackwell.

Stanley, Liz (1992) *The Auto/Biographical I: The Theory and Practice of Feminist Auto/Biography*, Manchester and New York: Manchester University Press.

Stearns, Peter N. (2000) *Gender in World History*, London and New York: Routledge.

Steedman, Carolyn (2001) *Dust*, Manchester: Manchester University Press.

—— (1986) *Landscape for a Good Woman: A Story of Two Lives*, New Brunswick, NJ: Rutgers University Press.

Stein, Stuart (1999) *Learning, Teaching and Researching on the Internet*, New York: Addison Wesley Longman.

Stevenson, C.L. (1963) *Facts and Values*, New Haven, CT: Yale University Press.

Stoianovich, Traian (1976) *French Historical Method: The Annales Paradigm*, Ithaca, NY: Cornell University Press.

Stone, Lawrence (1992) 'History and post-modernism', *Past and Present* 135: 187–94.

—— (1991) 'History and post-modernism', *Past and Present* 131: 217–18.

—— (1979) 'The revival of narrative', *Past and Present* 85: 3–24.

Strawson, Peter F. (1974) *Freedom and Resentment and Other Essays*, London: Methuen.

Stromberg, Roland N. (1994) *European Intellectual History since 1789*, Englewood Cliffs, NJ: Prentice Hall.

Struckmeyer, Otto Keith (1978) *Croce and Literary Criticism*, Norwood, PA: Norwood Editions.

Sturrock, John (ed.) (1979) *Structuralism and Since: From Levi-Strauss to Derrida*, Oxford: Oxford University Press.

Swierenga, Robert P. (1968) *Pioneers and Profits: Land Speculation on the Iowa Frontier*, Ames, IA: Iowa State University Press.

Tagliacozzo, Giorgio and Verene, Donald Phillip (eds) (1976) *Giambattista Vico's Science of Humanity*, Baltimore, MD: Johns Hopkins University Press.

Tagliacozzo, Giorgio and White, Hayden (eds) (1969) *Giambattista Vico: An International Sym-*

posium, Baltimore, MD: Johns Hopkins University Press.

Takaki, Ronald (ed.) (1994) *From Different Shores: Perspectives on Race and Ethnicity in America*, Oxford: Oxford University Press.

Tallis, Raymond (1998) *In Defence of Realism*, Lincoln, NE: University of Nebraska Press.

Taylor, B. (2004) 'Introduction: how far, how near: distance and proximity in the historical imagination', *History Workshop Journal* 57: 117–22.

—— (1985) *Modes of Occurrence*, Oxford: Oxford University Press.

Taylor, Charles (1985) 'Agency and the self', Part 1 of *Human Agency and Language*, Cambridge and New York: Cambridge University Press.

Temin, Peter (ed.) (1973) *New Economic History*, Harmondsworth: Penguin.

Thernstrom, Stephen (1973) *The Other Bostonians: Poverty and Progress in the American Metropolis, 1880–1970*, Cambridge, MA: Harvard University Press.

Thomas, Keith (1978) *Religion and the Decline of Magic: Studies in Popular Beliefs in Sixteenth- and Seventeenth-Century England*, Harmondsworth: Penguin.

Thompson, E.P. (1978) *The Poverty of Theory and Other Essays*, London: Merlin Press.

—— (1963) *The Making of the English Working Class*, Harmondsworth: Penguin.

Thompson, John B. (1981) *Critical Hermeneutics*, Cambridge: Cambridge University Press.

Thompson, Paul (1978) *The Voice of the Past*, Oxford: Oxford University Press.

Thompson, Willie (2004) *Postmodernism and History*, Basingstoke: Palgrave Macmillan.

Todorov, Tzvetan (1995) *The Morals of History*, Minneapolis MN: University of Minnesota Press.

Toews, John E. (1987) 'Intellectual history after the linguistic turn: the autonomy of meaning and the irreducibility of experience', *American Historical Review* 92: 879–907.

Toplin, Robert Brent (1996) *History by Hollywood: The Use and Abuse of the American Past*, Chicago: University of Illinois Press.

Topolski, Jerzy (1999) 'The role of logic and aesthetics in constructing narrative wholes in historiography', *History and Theory* 38: 200–10.

—— (1991) 'Towards an integrated model of historical explanation', *History and Theory* 30: 324–38.

Torfing, J. (1999), *New Theories of Discourse: Laclau, Mouffe and Žižek*, London: Blackwell.

Tosh, John (2004) 'What should historians do with masculinity? Reflections on nineteenth-century Britain', in Keith Jenkins and Alun Munslow (eds) *The Nature of History Reader*, London and New York: Routledge, pp. 102–4.

—— (2001) *The Pursuit of History*, third edn, London: Longman.

Townshend, Jules and Tormey, Simon (2005) *Introducing Post-Marxism*, London: Sage.

Tridgell, Susan (2004) *Understanding Our Selves: The Dangerous Art of Biography*, Bern: Peter Lang.

Turner, F.J. (1961 [1893]) *The Frontier in American History*, reprinted in R.A. Billington (ed.) *Frontier and Section*, Englewood Cliffs, NJ: Prentice Hall, pp. 38–60.

Van Noppen, J.P. (ed.) (1983) *Metaphor and Religion*, Brussels: The Free Press.

Vann, Richard T. (1998) 'The reception of Hayden White', *History and Theory* 37: 143–61.

—— (1987) 'Louis Mink's linguistic turn', *History and Theory* 26: 1–14.

Vansina, Jan (1985) *Oral Tradition as History*, Madison, WI: University of Wisconsin Press.

Veeser, A. Aram (ed.) (1989) *The New Historicism*, New York: Routledge.

Veyne, Paul (1984) *Writing History: Essays on Epistemology*, Middletown, CT: Wesleyan University Press.

Vico, Giambattista (1968) *The New Science of Giambattista Vico*, trans. Thomas G. Bergin and Max H. Fisch, Ithaca, NY: Cornell University Press.

—— (1963) *The Autobiography of Giambattista Vico*, trans. Thomas G. Bergin and Max H. Fisch,

Ithaca, NY: Cornell University Press.

Vincent, J.R. (1967) *Pollbooks: How Victorians Voted*, Cambridge: Cambridge University Press.

von Wright, Georg Henrik (1971) *Explanation and Understanding*, London: Routledge.

Walker, J. (2004) 'Antonio Foscarini in the city of crossed destinies', in Alun Munslow and Robert A. Rosenstone (eds) *Experiments in Rethinking History*, London and NY: Routledge, pp. 124–55.

Walkowitz, Judith (1992) *City of Dreadful Delights: Narratives of Sexual Danger in Late Victorian London*, Chicago: University of Chicago Press.

Walsh, W.H. (1984 [1967]) *An Introduction to Philosophy of History*, Westport, CT: Greenwood Press.

—— (1981) *Substance and Form in History*, Edinburgh: Edinburgh University Press.

—— (1966) *Metaphysics*, New York: Harcourt Brace.

Ward, Chris (2004a) 'Impressions of the Somme: an experiment', in Alun Munslow and Robert A. Rosenstone (eds) *Experiments in Rethinking History*, London and New York: Routledge, pp. 89–123.

—— (2004b) 'What is history? The case of late Stalinism', *Rethinking History: The Journal of Theory and Practice* 8: 439–58.

Warner, Marina (1996) *From the Beast to the Blonde: On Fairy Tales and Their Tellers*, New York: Farrar, Strauss and Giroux, The Noonday Press.

Warren, John (1998) *The Past and its Presenters: An Introduction to Issues in Historiography*, London: Hodder and Stoughton.

Weber, Max (1957 [1947]) *The Theory of Social and Economic Organisation*, trans. A.M. Henderson and Talcott Parsons, ed. and introduction by Talcott Parsons, Glencoe, IL: The Free Press.

Weber, S. (1987) *Institution and Interpretation*, Minneapolis, MN: University of Minnesota Press.

Weitz, M. (1988) *Theories of Concepts: A History of the Major Philosophical Traditions*, London: Routledge.

Wellek, René (1981) *Four Critics*, Seattle, WA: University of Washington Press.

Whewell, William (1967a [3 vols 1837]) *History of the Inductive Sciences*, London: Cass.

—— (1967b [2 vols 1840]) *The Philosophy of the Inductive Sciences*, London: Cass.

White, Hayden (2000) 'An old question raised again: is historiography art or science?' (Response to Iggers), *Rethinking History: The Journal of Theory and Practice* 4: 391–406.

—— (1998) *Figural Realism: Studies in the Mimesis Effect*, Baltimore, MD: Johns Hopkins University Press.

—— (1996) 'The modernist event', in Vivian Sobchack (ed.) *The Persistence of History: Cinema, Television and the Modern Event*, London: Routledge, pp. 17–38.

—— (1995) 'Response to Arthur Marwick', *Journal of Contemporary History* 30: 233–46.

—— (1992) 'Historical emplotment and the problem of truth', in Saul Friedlander (ed.) *Probing the Limits of Representation*, Cambridge, MA: Harvard University Press, pp. 37–53.

—— (1987) *The Content of the Form: Narrative Discourse and Historical Representation*, Baltimore, MD: Johns Hopkins University Press.

—— (1984) 'The question of narrative in contemporary historical theory', *History and Theory* 23: 1–33.

—— (1978) *Tropics of Discourse: Essays in Cultural Criticism*, Baltimore, MD: Johns Hopkins University Press.

—— (1974) 'Structuralism and popular culture', *Journal of Popular Culture* 7: 759–75.

—— (1973a) 'Foucault decoded: notes from underground', *History and Theory* 12: 23–54.

—— (1973b) *Metahistory: The Historical Imagination in Nineteenth-Century Europe*, Baltimore,

MD: Johns Hopkins University Press.

Wickberg, Daniel (2001) 'Intellectual history vs. the social history of intellectuals' *Rethinking History: The Journal of Theory and Practice* 5: 383–95.

Williams, Carolyn D. (1997) '"Another self in the case": Gender, marriage and the individual in Augustan literature', in Roy Porter (ed.) *Rewriting the Self: Histories from the Renaissance to the Present*, London: Routledge, pp. 97–118.

Williams, D. (ed.) (1999) *The Enlightenment*, Cambridge: Cambridge University Press.

Williams, Raymond (1983) *Keywords*, Oxford: Oxford University Press.

—— (1977) *Marxism and Literature*, Oxford: Oxford University Press.

Williams, Robert C. (2003) *The Historian's Toolbox: A Student's Guide to the Theory and Craft of History*, Armonk, NY, and London: M.E. Sharpe.

Wilson, George M. (1989) *The Intentionality of Human Action*, Stanford, CA: Stanford University Press.

Windschuttle, Keith (1995) *The Killing of History: How Literary Critics and Social Theorists are Murdering Our Past*, New York: The Free Press.

Wiseman, Mary B. (1989) *The Ecstasies of Roland Barthes*, London: Routledge.

Wittgenstein, Ludwig (1995 [1921]) *Tractatus Logico-Philosophicus*, London: Routledge.

Woolf, Virginia (1958) *Granite and Rainbow: Essays*, London: Hogarth Press.

Worton, Michael and Still, Judith (eds) (1990) *Intertextuality: Theories and Practices*, New York: Manchester University Press.

Wrigley, E.A. (ed.) (1966) *An Introduction to English Historical Demography*, London: Weidenfeld and Nicolson.

Wyschograd, Edith (2004) 'Representation, narrative, and the historian's promise', in D. Carr, Thomas R. Flynn and Rudolph A. Makkreel (eds) The Ethics of History, Evanston, IL: Northwestern University Press, pp. 28–44.

Young, Robert (1990) *White Mythologies*, London: Routledge.

—— (ed.) (1981) *Untying the Text: A Poststructuralist Reader*, London: Routledge.

Yovel, Yirmiahiu (1980) *Kant and the Philosophy of History*, Princeton, NJ: Princeton University Press.

Zagorin, Perez (1999) 'History, the referent, and narrative: reflections on postmodernism now', *History and Theory* 38: 1–24.

—— (1990) 'Historiography and postmodernism: reconsiderations', *History and Theory* 29: 263–74.

Zammito, John H. (1998) 'Ankersmit's postmodernist historiography: the hyperbole of "opacity"', *History and Theory* 37: 330–46.

Zinsser, Judith P. (2004) 'A prologue for *La Dame d'Esprit*: the biography of the Marquise du Châtelet', in Alun Munslow and Robert A. Rosenstone (eds) *Experiments in Rethinking History*, London and New York: Routledge, pp. 195–208.

Žižek, S. (1989) *The Sublime Object of Ideology*, London: Verso.

INDEX

Main entries in **bold**

ROUTLEDGE HISTORY

Practicing History
Gabrielle M. Spiegel

This essential new collection of key articles offers a re-evaluation of the practice of history in light of current debates. Critical thinkers and practicing historians present their writings, along with clear and thorough editorial material, to examine the complex ideas at the forefront of historical practice.

The volume gives a synoptic overview of the last twenty-five years' theoretical analysis of historical writing, with a critical examination of the central concepts and positions that have been in debate. The collection delineates the emergence of "practice theory" as a possible paradigm for future historical interpretation concerned with questions of agency, experience, and the subject.

These complex ideas are introduced to students in this accessible reader, and for teachers and historians, this new survey is an indispensable and timely read.

Hb: 0–415–34107–8
Pb: 0–415–34108–6

Available at all good bookshops
For ordering and further information please visit:
www.routledge.com

ROUTLEDGE HISTORY

Historics

Martin L. Davies

From a published author at the forefront of research in this area comes this provocative and seminal work that takes a unique and fresh new look at history and theory.

Challenging basic assumptions made by historians, Davies focuses on historical ideas and thought about the past. The value of history in and for contemporary culture is explained not only in terms of cultural and institutional practices but in forms of writing and representation of historical issues too.

Historics stimulates thinking about the behaviours and practice that constitute history, and introduces complex ideas in a clear and approachable style. This important text is recommended not only for a wide student audience, but for the more discerning general reader as well.

Hb: 0–415–26165–1
Pb: 0–415–26166–X

Available at all good bookshops
For ordering and further information please visit:
www.routledge.com

ROUTLEDGE HISTORY

Making History

Peter Lambert

Making History offers a fresh perspective on the study of the past. It is an exhaustive exploration of the practice of history, historical traditions and the theories that surround them. Discussing the development and growth of history as a discipline and of the profession of the historian, the book encompasses a huge diversity of influences.

Some of the themes covered include:

- the professionalisation of the discipline
- the most significant movements in historical scholarship in the last century
- the increasing interdisciplinary trends in scholarship
- historical practice outside the academy.

The volume offers a coherent set of chapters to support undergraduates, post-graduates and others interested in the historical processes that have shaped the discipline of history.

Hb: 0–415–24254–1
Pb: 0–415–24255–X

Available at all good bookshops
For ordering and further information please visit:
www.routledge.com

ROUTLEDGE HISTORY

What is History For?
Beverley Southgate

An experienced author of history and theory presents this examination of the purpose of history at a time when recent debates have rendered the question 'What is history for?' of utmost importance.

Charting the development of historical studies and examining how history has been used, this study is exceptional in its focus on the future of the subject as well as its past. It is argued that history in the twenty-first century must adopt a radical and morally therapeutic role instead of studying it for 'its own sake'.

This makes compulsive reading for all students of history, cultural studies and the general reader, as notions of historical truth and the reality of the past are questioned and it becomes vital to rethink history's function and renegotiate its uses for the postmodern age.

Hb: 0–415–35098–0
Pb: 0–415–35099–9

Available at all good bookshops
For ordering and further information please visit:
www.routledge.com

ROUTLEDGE HISTORY

Experiments in Rethinking History
Edited by Alun Munslow and Robert Rosenstone

From two of the world's leading postmodern historians, this thoroughly original collection of articles allows students and researchers to understand and learn important new ways of thinking and writing about the past.

This book includes a thorough two-part introduction on theory and practice as well as introductory material in each section that allows the reader to fully engage with the theoretical aspects of the book. It provides a deeper understanding of how to engage with the past today.

This text works as a reader companion alongside the Routledge best-seller *Rethinking History* and provides students with an innovative, engaging and easy-to-read research tool to enhance all history-related course studies.

Hb: 0–415–30145–9
Pb: 0–415–30146–7

Available at all good bookshops
For ordering and further information please visit:
www.routledge.com

ROUTLEDGE HISTORY

The Nature of History Reader
Keith Jenkins and Alun Munslow

In this timely collection, key pieces of writing by leading historians are reproduced and evaluated, with an explanation and critique of their character and assumptions, and how they reflect upon the nature of the history project. The authors respond to the view that the nature of history has become so disparate in assumption, approach and practice as to require an informed guide that is both self-reflexive, engaged, critical and innovative. This work seeks to aid a positive re-thinking of history today, and will be of use both to students and to their teachers.

Hb: 0–415–24053–0
Pb: 0–415–24054–9

Available at all good bookshops
For ordering and further information please visit:
www.routledge.com

ROUTLEDGE HISTORY

History: What and Why?

Second edition

Beverley Southgate

History: What and Why? is a highly accessible introductory survey of historians' views about the nature and purpose of their subject. It offers a historical perspective and clear guide to contemporary debates about the nature and purpose of history and a discussion of the traditional model of history as an account of the past 'as it was'. It assesses the challenges to orthodox views and examines the impact of Marxism, feminism and post-colonialism on the study of history. This second edition has been updated to reflect the continuing, and still increasing, debate surrounding these issues. In particular it discusses:

- historians' fear of postmodernism
- holocaust denial and the Irving/Lipstadt libel trial
- the future of the past in the light of the postmodern challenge.

Hb: 0-415-25657-7
Pb: 0-415-25658-5

Available at all good bookshops
For ordering and further information please visit:
www.routledge.com

'Cavanaugh begins with an engrossing analysis of the dynamics of torture and disappearance as a mode of disciplining the body politic. He judiciously uses psychological and social scientific sources without letting them override the theological focus of the book. He then gives an equally engrossing account of the Church in Chile under Pinochet. His analyses both of Maritain and the "New Christendom" ecclesiology provide an interesting critique of the failures of the Church to respond to Pinochet's repression, while his concluding chapter on eucharistic theology points towards the source of the successful responses made by the Church. Particularly useful and interesting is the way in which eucharistic theology is tied to concrete eucharistic practice. The book is extremely well written and engaging.' **Frederick C. Bauerschmidt, Assistant Professor of Theology, Loyola College in Maryland**

'This is very important book. It should be mandatory reading for anybody concerned with the issue of torture, and will be of vital interest to all those of us involved in Amnesty International and human rights organisations. It has an appeal and a significance far beyond the classroom. Though it is much more theological than Helen Prejean, in its narrative power it has some affinities with *Dead Man Walking*, and will likewise speak to those outside the Church.' **T. J. Gorringe, Professor of Systematic Theology, University of Exeter**

'*Torture and Eucharist* not only has superb qualities as a textbook, but is an outstanding piece of creative ecclesiology. Drawing on the work of scholars such as Milbank, Hauerwas, MacIntyre and Lindbeck, Cavanaugh moves ecclesiology out of the realm of the abstract and ideal into the real world where the Christian Church must struggle to witness to the gospel. In so doing, he shifts the ecclesiological problematic away from now largely barren questions as to the "right" model of the Church into a new and much more exciting area of inquiry.' **Nicholas Healy, Associate Professor of Theology, St John's University, New York**

'The strengths of this book are manifold: sound theology coupled with actual interviews and close social analysis, stimulating argument, and a tight yet imaginative writing style. Its reputation will surely grow steadily over time.' **L. Gregory Jones, Dean, The Divinity School, Duke University**

Challenges in Contemporary Theology

Series Editors: Gareth Jones and Lewis Ayres
University of Birmingham and Trinity College, Dublin.

The series will consist of carefully coordinated books which will engage traditional theological concerns with the main challengers to those concerns. Each book will be accessible to graduate students and good undergraduates as well as scholars. The intention of the series is to promote prospective, critical and contentious positions as well as synthetic summaries of the major positions. Volumes will cover fields that have not yet received sufficient theological discussion and will loosely group around the areas of philosophy; culture and media; ethics; and Christian self-definition.

Already published

These Three Are One: The Practice of Trinitarian Theology
David S. Cunningham

After Writing: On the Liturgical Consummation of Philosophy
Catherine Pickstock

Engaging Scripture: A Model for Theological Interpretation
Stephen E. Fowl

Mystical Theology: The Integrity of Spirituality and Theology
Mark A. McIntosh

Torture and Eucharist: Theology, Politics, and the Body of Christ
William T. Cavanaugh

Forthcoming

The Practice of Christian Doctrine
Lewis Ayres

Theology and Mass Communion
Robert Dodara and John Paul Szura

Alien Sex: The Body and Desire in Cinema and Theology
Gerard Loughlin

Critical Ecclesiology
Philip D. Kenneson

Sex and the Christian Body
Eugene F. Rogers